Ronald J. Manheimer is executive director of the North Carolina Center for Creative Retirement (NCCCR), a program of the University of North Carolina at Asheville, where he also holds an appointment as research associate professor of philosophy. Before becoming the NCCCR's first full-time director in 1988, Manheimer was director of older adult education at The National Council on the Aging (NCOA). He directed NCOA's national arts and humanities programs and its special collection in social gerontology, the Ollie A. Randall Library. Between 1984 and 1989, Manheimer was a member of the American Library Association's Library Services to an Aging Population Committee.

Trained in philosophy with a Ph.D. from the Board of Studies in History of Consciousness, University of California, Santa Cruz, Manheimer has combined theoretical and applied interests in aging by conducting research and developing educational programs for seniors in colleges, universities, libraries, senior centers, nursing homes, and retirement communities. His entry to the field of aging came in 1977 when he volunteered to teach a humanities course at the Thurston County Senior Center in Olympia, Washington. Since then he has served as project director for seven public humanities programs for older adults, funded by the National Endowment for the Humanities. A conductor of workshops and lectures on creativity, the humanities, and aging, Manheimer is the 1993–96 chairman of the American Society on Aging's Older Adult Education Network.

Betty Freidan is the author of *The Fountain of Age*, a book intended to change the way men and women think about growing older and the way society thinks about aging. Her bestseller *The Feminine Mystique* is recognized as a catalyst for the modern women's movement. Friedan is a founder of the National Organization for Women, the National Women's Political Caucus, and the National Abortion Rights Action League. She has received numerous honorary doctorates of humane letters and law and is a visiting professor at New York University and the University of Southern California. Her research for *The Fountain of Age,* conducted at the Center for Social Sciences at Columbia University, the Center for Population Research at Harvard University, and the Andrus Gerontology Center at the University of Southern California, was funded by grants from the Ford Foundation and the National Endowment for the Humanities.

THE SECOND MIDDLE AGE

LOOKING
DIFFERENTLY
AT LIFE
BEYOND 50

To Marion Manheimer, mother, grandmother, great grandmother.

With appreciation.

"A mother's happiness is a son's good fortune.

A son's good future is a mother's happiness."

(Ancient Hebrew saying)

THE SECOND MIDDLE AGE

LOOKING DIFFERENTLY AT LIFE BEYOND 50

RONALD J. MANHEIMER, Ph.D., Editor

with Carolyn Williams
and North Carolina Center for Creative Retirement,
University of North Carolina at Asheville

Foreword by BETTY FRIEDAN

Detroit • Washington, D.C.

The Second Middle Age: Looking Differently at Life Beyond 50

In addition to credits noted on pages, photographs were received from the following sources. UPI/Bettman: pp. 38, 157, 364; © 1988 Helen Marcus: p. 62; AP/Wide World Photos: pp. 115, 131, 194, 248, 457; Archive Photos/Nancy Nugent: p. 174; UPI/Bettmann Newsphotos: p. 323; Archive Photos: p. 446.

Published by Visible Ink Press™
a division of Gale Research Inc.

835 Penobscot Building
Detroit, MI 48226-4094
Visible Ink Press™ is a trademark of Gale Research Inc.

Most Visible Ink Press books are available at special quantity discounts when purchased in bulk by corporations, organizations, or groups. Customized printings, special imprints, messages, and excerpts can be produced to meet your needs. For more information, contact Special Markets Manager, Gale Research Inc., 835 Penobscot Bldg., Detroit, MI 48226. Or call 1-800-877-4253.

Cover and Page Design: Tracey Rowens

Library of Congress Cataloging-in-Publication Data
The second middle age : looking differently at life beyond fifty /
   Ronald J. Manheimer, editor.
     p.   cm.
   Includes index.
   ISBN 0-7876-0481-X
   1. Middle age—United States—Psychological aspects. 2. Middle aged persons—United States—Psychology. 3. Life change events-United States.   I. Manheimer, Ronald J.
   HQ1059.5.U5S43   1995
   305.24′4—dc20   95-7303
                                           CIP

CONTENTS

A Turning Point 1

Old Age Across the Centuries • The Boundaries of Old Age in
America • Aging in the Settlement, Colonial, and Revolutionary
Periods • Old Age in the New Land, 1790 to 1900 • The New
Urban-Industrial Order, 1870 to 1930 • The Great Depression as
a Turning Point in the History of U.S. Aging • The Older Adult
in an Age of Affluence

Recognizing Ourselves 31

The Role of Demographics and Research • How Populations Age
• Population Aging in the United States • U.S. Population
Trends: Past and Future • Diversity Among the Aging Population

Changing 67

The Three Processes of Aging • The Nature of Physical Aging •
The Mental Process of Aging • Aging and Adult Development •
The Social Process of Aging

Working and Retiring 121

Labor Force Participation • Myths and Realities About Older
Workers • Policies and Programs for Older Workers • Alternative
Work Arrangements • Older Women Workers • Retirement •

Retirement as a Social Institution • Planning for Retirement • Adjusting to Retirement • Retirement as a Process • Future Trends

Protecting Health 183

Physical Wellness in the Older Adult • Changing Attitudes Toward Wellness • Healthy Behavior • Aging and Sexuality • Emotional Health • Prevention and Wellness • Mental Wellness • The Meaning of Psychological Wellness • Loss and Mental Wellness • Adaptation and Transformation • Developmental Models of Transformation • The Transformation Process and Aging • The Grief Process • Facilitating Mental Wellness

Finding Community 237

Family Relationships in Later Life • Family Roles in an Aging Society • Marriage, Social Support, and Adult Children in Later Life • Grandparents and Grandchildren • Sibling Relationships • Extended Kin Relationships • Never-Married Midlife Adults • Gay and Lesbian Relationships in Later Life • Divorce and Widowhood • Friendship and Aging • Aging and Friendship Patterns • How Active Are Midlife Adults as Friends? • Values in Friendships • Older People's Friends • Benefits of Friend-ships • Strain in Older Adult Friendship • Improving Older Adult Friendships

Living Smarter 299

Housing for Older Persons • Living Arrangements and Location of Older Americans • Older Homeowners • Home Modifica-tions to Extend Independence • Reverse Mortgages • Neigh-borhood Environment and Alternative Housing Options • Inde-pendent Retirement Housing, Congregate Housing, and Assisted Living Facilities • Manufactured Housing • Continuing Care Retirement Communities • Older Renters and the Production of Rental Housing • Transportation Issues • The Mobility Continuum • Transportation Mandate • Trends • How Aging Impacts Transportation Choices • Accidents • Driver Education • Driver Licensing • Transit

A Bit of History • Emergence of Older Adult Education • National Policies and Older Adult Education • Intellectual Functioning of Older Adults • The Purpose of Education for Older Adults • Program Types and Learners' Motives • Institutions and Exemplary Programs • Support of Older Learners • Lifelong Learning and Links to Other Generations

How Many Volunteers? • Types of Volunteer Work • Service Exchange Programs • Who Volunteers: A Demographic Profile • Who Volunteers: The Personality Factor • Religion and Volunteering • Does Volunteering Make Older People Healthier and Happier? • Why Volunteer? • The Good That Volunteers Do • Special Issues of Older Volunteers • An Untapped Potential? • Where to Begin

Changing Attitudes Toward Leisure • The Meaning of Leisure • Retirement Planning • Limits On Leisure • Time and Older Americans • Continuing to Work •Hobbies • Social and Religious Participation • Minorities and Leisure • Housing and Activities • Sports and Fitness for Older Adults • Entertainment: The Performing Arts and the Media • Travel

Betty Friedan

I knew the minute I heard about it that I wanted to go. Not necessarily for the reason that I gave myself or my friends, though I was too embarrassed to talk about it much. What was a sophisticated urban woman of my age doing, setting off on an Outward Bound wilderness-survival expedition in the North Carolina mountains with nine strangers? Of course, I had always had a secret yen for wilderness exploration, adventure; loved to read books about men sailing across the Pacific in a raft, or climbing Annapurna or Mount Everest, even though I personally was afraid of heights, and never could quite get the hang of sailing.

The traveling I had been doing too much, for too many years now, involved lectures, conferences, TV studios, fancy hotels, dreary motels, and banquets somehow all alike: Chicago, Los Angeles, Washington, London, Pairs, Rome, Detroit. I had made a decade resolution, on my sixtieth birthday, that I was going to give myself some travel just for adventure, trekking in the Himalayas, or a boat ride down the Amazon, before it was too late. But that sort of thing didn't seem to appeal to my friends, and I hated traveling alone. Besides, I was always too busy: deadlines, social calendar, the women's movement, and this endless research on age.

Suffering, still, myself that denial and dread of age that made it so hard truly to celebrate my milestone sixtieth birthday, I had started seeking out individuals, environments, experiences that seemed to promise the different kind of breakthrough that I was calling the fountain of age. In a health spa in Mexico, I had come across a zesty woman whom I had thought to be around thirty-three until she came in to Christmas dinner with her children, grandchildren, and the "younger man" she was living with, a gray-haired architect. She mentioned that she had just signed up for an experiment in wilderness survival that Outward Bound was trying out in September, for the first time, for people over fifty-five. Would you send me their literature, I heard myself asking...

Going Beyond

Sunday: I wake up suddenly, in the black night. My psychological alarm clock works—it's 5:00 A.M. Jerry, who has volunteered to do breakfast, is lighting the stove. I'm glad of the chance to go the john, "wash," and get "dressed" before the others wake up. Does one get more or less inhibited, prize the dignity of privacy more as one gets older? Or does one lose the vanity, modesty, or sexual inhibition of youth? Each one of us here seems to map out her/his own space in this open place. At first, I go quite far away to change, behind a screen of trees or brush. After a day or so, I don't stray so far; I "change" inside my sleeping bag, and like the others, merely avert my eyes, washing my teeth in the same water that will also clean my cup after breakfast.

The Chatooga River, where we head now for two days of shooting rapids, is where they made the movie *Deliverance*. We are handed out life jackets and hard-hat helmets. We pick up three guides, who show us how to paddle the rubber rafts, "drawing" right or left, and "ferrying" across the current by heading beyond where you really have to go, then letting the current swing you back. After lunch (sardines, bread, and cheese eaten sitting on a rock), all the guides and instructors get in one raft and our "crew" is on its own, in the other two. The rapids begin to get scary. We take turns in different positions. I do not volunteer to be captain. I'm glad that no one here knows that I am supposed to be a leader of women. Sitting up in the bow, paired with that big guy, Earl, I begin to get the hang of it: The rhythmic swing of the paddle, the flick of the wrist, and when and how to set the blade against the current, or "draw" or "sweep" in longer circles. They have put

Earl on the left and me on the right, because "draw left" is the crucial stroke to get into, then out of, most of these rapids. After we miss a few, it become clear that Earl, despite his brawn, does not have the upper body strength for a left draw. But if I sweep out to the right, and, Cece behind me backpaddles, Earl's left draw works okay. "Have you done this before?" asks Judy, surprised at my sudden competence. "In summer camp," I remember. "In college. And on my honeymoon. The Songo River." About fifty, forty years ago.

We head into Stage III of the river—not the most dangerous, but getting there. To prepare for tomorrow, when we'll be shooting rapids with drops of twelve feet and more—Corkscrew Rapid, Sock 'Em Dog, Screaming Left Turn, Five Falls, Jawbone—we are given a drill on what to do if you fall overboard. I lie on my back, stiff, with my feet up so they don't get stuck under a rock, and let myself be carried by the rushing current down the rapids like a log. At the bottom the entire waterfall roars over my head and up my nose. For a minute, I panic—I can't get my breath. But it's not asthma, just water. I finally catch the rope, get pulled into shore.

It was liberating revelation, "going beyond" on the Chatooga River, that we ancients, pooling our energies and the skills of our life experience, were able to surmount those dangerous rapids with fewer casualties and less need of outside care or rescue than any younger group. Evidently even in a task that demands the muscular strength easier to come by in youth, qualities that may emerge with age—wisdom born of experience, freedom from youthful competitive compulsion, cooperation, empathy—can more than compensate for whatever losses of muscle power or memory also come with age. I stopped worrying that I could no longer count on total recall of an interview if I didn't take notes; the significance was clearer, deeper, and not forgotten, months later—and I do take notes. To discover that even unathletic I, with some new training, could manipulate a boat around those rapids and bring back skills unused for forty years, convinced me more than any of my research that I might try new, completely different ways of working—in my writing, lecturing, teaching—or even, for a change, something I had never tired before, that I might not be very good at (the cello?). Of course, that is the real liberation of age; the amazing lightness and solidity of no longer feeling the need to prove oneself, to be the best, to outdo the others, to compete—and of being able to fail. What does it really matter?

Generativity

When Jonas Salk stepped down from the presidency of the institute he established at La Jolla after discovering the live polio vaccine, his efforts to examine larger mysteries of the evolution of the human mind and to make a scientific study of spiritual vision, were derided. His subsequent books, *Man Unfolding* and *Survival of the Wisest*, were virtually ignored by the popular press as well as the scientific community. But he continued his work, in his own laboratory at La Jolla, even though he no longer involved himself in institute or scientific politics, carrying out his own sense of professional commitment to the larger, evolving community. In the face of the AIDS crisis, he defied scientific opinion by undertaking research, again using live virus, despite the scientific dismissal of his work when his live polio vaccine was replaced by Sabin's laboratory vaccine.

Generativity is expressed in more mundane terms whenever "senior citizens'" talents are truly used as a community resource, or where they are allowed or encouraged to use their wisdom in work with younger people. In Fort Ord, California, "foster grandparents" go into Army homes where there are problems of child abuse as the mainstay of the Army Community Services Child Abuse Program. They follow formal procedures, including written and verbal reports, and are valued by the Army agency because they go in as "respected, non-threatening presences and help the mothers learn to care for their children without violence."

At age seventy-one, George Kreidler, a former linebacker for the Green Bay Packers who retired at sixty-five after thirty-one years supervising the construction of oil refineries and chemical and nuclear power plants for Bechetel Corporation, was supervising house construction for the homeless for Habitat for Humanity. Retiring to Asheville, North Carolina, he was described as part of "a new breed of active, independent retirees, for whom a need to

help society at large is as important as personal enrichment."
Through the North Carolina Center for Creative Retirement, he
also served as the mentor to a young college athlete, not to win
more games, but for his "academic performance and future direction." Others tutored grade and high school students. Asked his
qualifications for tutoring grade school students, a retired locomo-
tive engineer wrote: "I have my act together."

The Second Middle Age

The Second Middle Age is a valuable resource for guiding you to the
kinds of experiences and challenges I found in my research for *The
Fountain of Age.* The people who put this book together are part of
my friend George Kreidler's enterprise, the North Carolina Center
for Creative Retirement. The advisory team that read all the chapters in advance and suggested improvements are themselves second middle-agers involved with the Center. Their qualification,
besides expertise in numerous professions, is life experience. They
"have their life together." They have also been smart enough to
find leading experts from across the country to contribute to this
volume; I personally know many of these outstanding researchers
and leaders. Along with a new generation of fifty-plusers, these
informed experts have delivered a well-balanced and useful guide
that can help you navigate through the exciting life journey.

Whether you want to raft down a river, volunteer to mentor a young person, or widen your knowledge of new housing
options, this handy book will show you the way. Given the lengthened life course and prospects for continued vitality, even with the
usual aches and pains, life after fifty or fifty-five or sixty can be a
time of new initiatives, a "second middle age" that may even be
more fun than the first one.

Do you have a map to the new highways and byways of life after fifty? You're probably going to need one. The topography has changed, the landscape's been greatly expanded. Never before have so many midlife Americans confronted such an enormous variety of options and choices. This book is designed to be your guide.

The Second Middle Age can help you choose well and wisely as you take a fresh look at life beyond fifty. The national experts who have contributed to its pages describe the best routes to destinations such as good health, second careers, lifelong learning opportunities, appropriate and secure housing, leisure ventures, meaningful relationships, and many other vista points. At times the view can be breathtaking, even a little dizzying. But this book will help you stay focused on how to reach your goals.

The information in this book can function in two ways: one, as a window for looking into the future—yours, your family and friends', your community's; two, as a mirror in which to view yourself from different angles as you change during the post-fifty decades. Planning for the future is one of the best ways to take charge of the changes that will come. By defining your own future you can stave off all the would-be experts waiting to give you their opinion.

Many people will tell you what they think you should look like and how you should act. There are still plenty of stereotypes about "being over the hill" that are founded on outdated information and life-denying myths. But as elder sage Betty Friedan writes in her foreword to this book, we can each experience the "breakthrough" to renewing our zest for life by discovering how the gift of added years can be a "fountain" to nourish continued development. Ms. Friedan chose a wilderness adventure to test her mettle. That's one way to push out the envelope of self-imposed limits. You will have your own expeditions to chart.

Few of us make the journey in isolation. Ms. Friedan wisely states that to experience "the true power of age" we need also to direct ourselves to the well-being of other generations, "to solve the new problems facing our whole society." An important part of having your act together is caring about others. That is why we have included information on how you can stay involved and exercise your leadership as a "second middle-ager." But, you may be asking, what exactly is the second middle age, how did it come about, and am I a part of it?

The Second Middle Age

Lydia Brontë, in her book *The Longevity Factor*, reports that researchers who study how our roles, tasks, and affiliations change over time came up with the term "second middle age" to characterize the continuation of activities and interests in the middle years of life and the later onset of limiting illness.

The term life course refers not to the maximum length of years a human being could possibly live (that's life span, which scientists put at about 115 years), but to our personal and societal expectations for how we should act during different time segments from birth to old age. Included are the activities of play, education, raising a family, work, leisure, retirement, and so on.

Until recently, we have been locked into the "three boxes of life"—education (youth), work (adulthood), retirement (later life)—described in Richard Bolles's now-classic guide to rethinking career options, *What Color Is Your Parachute?* But the lengthening of life expectancy, changes in the workplace and in the nature of work, and even birth control have altered all that. In other words, the life course is not fixed forever, it changes with the times. So does the way we time our life decisions.

The new life course pattern is more flexible than ever before. For example, while some choose to marry at eighteen, others prefer twenty-eight or thirty-eight, and few of us think anything about it. Only a few years ago, couples were expected to marry just after high school or college. Today, many couples plan to start families after having established careers—in their thirties or even forties. While it doesn't strike us as particularly strange now, twenty years ago it would have been out of the ordinary.

Now more people than ever are going back to school to explore career changes or to retool for new ways of doing their same job—using computers, adapting to new organizational approaches, discovering alternative leadership and communication styles. Some people take time away from their jobs for travel and adventure. They aren't waiting for retirement. Some retire early from one career, take a few years off for travel, study, and creative projects, move to a new locale, and then return to work, either full- or part-time. We've broken out the three boxes.

The life course is, thus, a product of health, economics, technology, social policy, and the values and attitudes that are part of our historical legacy. Our ethnic and gender identities also play an important role. Take a recent example of how the life course has been reshaped: adolescence.

Everyone who survived childhood could experience the years thirteen to twenty. But to be a "teenager" is a recent invention. Shopping malls, clothing styles for the youth subculture, rock and roll (or rap and heavy metal), and all the other things we associate with being an adolescent are really the products of post–World War II affluence, enforcement of antichild labor laws that kept kids in school longer, the growing importance of education that meant the majority would go to college, and so on. Being an adolescent, a teenager, is a fairly recent invention.

What is true of adolescence is true of life after fifty. It's a newly constructed stage or age of life, one that's just been discovered by everyone from automobile designers to sign makers, travel agents to coffee roasters, manufacturers of exercise equipment to hospital volunteer coordinators. Take one tiny example: clothes shopping. Not only do you find four choices in that favorite make of jeans (to accommodate your changing physiognomy), but notice the large-print stickers on pant legs with easy-to-read sizes. You won't have to remove your bifocals or fall into the rack trying to squint at the tiny numbers on those hard-to-remove cardboard tags sewn between belt loops. Merchandising experts are getting older too.

So, what about the second middle age? Well, there are four important facts that will help you grasp the concept. Here are the first three.

- Life expectancy in the U.S. (the average number of years people will live, depending on the year they were born) will have risen from forty-seven in 1900 to seventy-six (about seventy-two for men and seventy-eight for women) by the year 2000.

- In 1900 the 4 percent of the population sixty-five-plus could expect to live another twelve years. By 2000, the 13 percent sixty-five-plus U.S. population can count on eighteen or nineteen years.

- The median age in 1900 was twenty-three (half the population was older, half younger). In 2000 the median age will be thirty-six and in 2010 it will be thirty-nine.

What has happened is that, thanks to breakthroughs in preventive and acute care medicine, sanitation, and public safety, more people now survive once life-threatening diseases of childhood (and childbirth), while a longer and healthier life is also now possible for a larger part of the midlife and adult population. In addition, new techniques and technologies help people compensate for losses that would have meant major restrictions for employment and normal functioning. These include corrective surgeries, joint and organ replacements, aides to vision and hearing, restorative and rehabilitation therapies, mental health counseling, and drug therapies to modify chemical imbalances. The list goes on.

A second middle age means that life does not have to be much different when you are fifty, fifty-five, or sixty-plus than it was when you were thirty-five, forty, or forty-five. In fact, for some, the stretching of middle age leads to a better life. It's not just that people today are living longer—meaning a whole lot more older people. The whole life course has been stretched, rubber-band-fashion, so that all stages of life have been extended. Of course, much depends on the cards you've been dealt in the way of health and wealth, and how you have played those cards. People will still have chronic ailments. But, for many, the activities enjoyed at thirty-six can be the same or similar at forty-six or fifty-six. Who is to say otherwise?

And how could middle age be better "the second time around"? Having reached a stage when the children are out on their own (yes, it does happen—to some extent, anyway), and having weathered many of the ups and downs of career, marriage, hopes, and expectations, you bring a new perspective to what you can realistically expect from life and, maybe, a little more savvy about how to identify and reach your goals. And, take comfort in this, you're not alone.

This brings us to the fourth piece of information alluded to previously. It's called the squaring of the population pyramid—those graphs showing how many males and females are alive in five-year age decrements from zero to ninety-plus. As recently as 1955, a population pyramid would be broader at the base (childhood through the forties) and narrower toward the top (almost a point at eighty-five-plus). But the population pyramids for 2000 to 2030 show the effects of healthy agers and baby boomers swelling out the middle years of life, turning the shape into more of a square.

The changes in population composition have already made the U.S., western Europe, and Japan "aging societies" where the average age and the population trend point to predominantly middle-aged populations. That trend is not likely to reverse until the second half of the twenty-first century, if then.

The population revolution means a total rethinking of how we view the life course as a whole, ensure fairness and well-being to all generations, and understand the obligations and responsibilities between generations currently alive and those to come. The new attitude is typified in the new Third Agers.

The Third Age

Another way to look at life differently beyond age fifty is to learn a little French, particularly the phrase "Troisieme Age," the Third Age. In the 1970s a professor at the University of Toulouse started "L'Universite du Troisieme Age," the University of the Third Age, or U3A, for short. Not only did the lifelong learning program for folks over sixty catch on and spread across Europe, England, Australia, Canada, and into the United States, the term Third Age entered our vocabulary to capture the spirit of vitality and adventure characteristic of the young at heart among the sixty-plus generation.

The Third Age is part of a concept that divides life into four ages. The First Age, youth, is a time of dependency when education helps prepare us for future work and family. With the Second Age comes independence and responsibility for earning a living and supporting a family. The Third Age is one of personal achievement and learning for self-development, and the Fourth Age is the period of frailty and decline. Until the second half of this century, only a fortunate few, the wealthy and healthy, had a Third Age. For the rest, the Fourth Age came before they had a chance to enjoy the Third.

As a time of leisure and good health became more equitably distributed throughout the population, people began looking for better ways to appreciate life through learning, travel, gaining new skills, recreation, hobbies, or helping others. British sociologist Peter Laslett, who helped to found a U3A at Cambridge, clarified the importance of the Third Age in his book, *A Fresh Map of Life.*

Laslett gave a social meaning as well as a personal one to the term. His research into health, wealth, and happiness for the sixty-plus generation in England and elsewhere showed him that not only were the majority of people living longer and better, but people were beginning to count on the retirement period to be a time of special opportunities. Now they could actually make plans for the retirement years. Earlier generations did not have these expectations. Retirement signified a kind of early warning system for the end of life. Laslett saw the Third Age as a new social phenomenon.

If you look at any number of new books on marketing to the fifty-plus age group, or attend any one of the numerous conferences on products for those over fifty, you will see Laslett's observation in action. New banking, travel, insurance, investment, health care, exercise, and other products are being developed for a huge part of the population in possession of the greatest portion of the nation's wealth, especially in the form of discretionary income. The majority of Third Agers can determine not only what they *need*, but what they *want* and the form in which they prefer to get it (by mail, by fax, by phone, by computer, via the drive through, through TV advertising or infomercials, or in person).

Laslett's other idea of the Third Age involves the individual's personal experience of time. Third Agers begin to experience a different kind of inner clock. Here's how it works. Suppose you're hiking up a mountain trail. How fast and long you walk determines the distance traversed. You look at your watch and the map and march through objective time. But when you reach the summit, look back at the trail and out toward the horizon, time seems to stand still.

That's the way it is for Third Agers. Subjectively, they have intimations of timelessness. Laslett says this subjective time state is the experience of "completion and arrival." When individuals fulfill their family, career, and social aspirations and obligations, they sense completeness; they've arrived. For some, this happens durting their thirties or forties—during the Second Age. For most, it happens closer to retirement, in the Third Age. The two could overlap. Laslett says it's more a matter of how you feel, not how old you are.

A Third Ager can recall the landmark events of life and fit them together as a meaningful whole, a pattern. The events co-exist in the mind the way episodes in a dream seem to happen in a single time space, an enduring moment. Philosopher Arthur Schopenhauer claimed that one of the benefits for entering the "second half of life" was that we could get a "clearer view of the whole." Part of that holistic view includes the prospects for retirement.

The Changing Meaning of Retirement

Only a generation ago, retirement, symbolized by the rocking chair, meant a short respite from years of hard work, time to visit the grandchildren, and a little travel. What to expect from retirement seemed pretty much given. But that's no longer true. Today you're exhorted, as one ad campaign puts it, to "get off your rocker," and tour the country, launch a second or third career, go back to school, learn to use a computer, join a social cause.

As people exit the work force healthier, more active, and often younger than any previous generation, they're hit with a challenge: be a pathfinder in a new life phase that's still uncharted. As intrepid explorers, many new retirees are traveling unfamiliar roads, pursuing an unprecedented diversity of interests and lifestyles. The results? Retirees are creating a subculture that may prove to be as big and important as the youth generation of the 1950s and 1960s.

Creating new meanings of retirement can be as daunting as it is exciting. Entering a new and strange terrain brings the realization that there are no guarantees about where each path will lead. Couples may have to negotiate differences in expectations and goals. Leisure time and recreation are great but will they lead to boredom? If self-worth and relationship are bound up with a work role or career, how will that void be filled? There's comfort in knowing that others are along for the journey.

AKNOWLEDGMENTS

The Second Middle Age is based on *Older Americans Almanac,* a comprehensive reference work published by Gale Research Inc. Several people helped shape the organization and layout of this edition, including Julie Winklepleck, Dean D. Dauphinais, and especially Gina Misiroglu. We are grateful to Margaret Chamberlain for securing photo permissions. We thank Lawrence Baker for his groundwork and availability.

A cadre of retirees from the North Carolina Center for Creative Retirement (NCCCR) critiqued early drafts of the chapters to help the authors refine their messages. These "second middle-agers" used themselves as a sounding board to assess whether the information in each chapter was clear, concise, useful, and comprehensive. They drew on their own stage-of-life perspectives and their expertise from careers in medicine, gerontology, librarianship, recreation, journalism, and other fields. We thank Martin J. Ambrose, Eone Harger, Leah R. Karpen, Charles William Parton, and Bettina H. Wolff for their valuable contributions.

Editorial work on the publication was based in the offices of the NCCCR, an integral part of the University of North Carolina at Asheville (UNCA) campus. The NCCCR, established in 1987 by an act of the North Carolina General Assembly, is widely recognized for its innovative work promoting lifelong learning, leadership, and community service on the part of retirement-age citizens. UNCA's progressive belief that education knows no age limit, and the university's support of a center where retirees can pursue intellectual and artistic interests while benefiting the campus and community, dramatically exemplifies *The Second Middle Age*'s approach to life after fifty.

Finally, nationally renowned experts from the field of aging contributed their research-based knowledge. We thank the following contributors of chapters to *The Second Middle Age:*

William A. Achenbaum is professor of history at the University of Michigan, Ann Arbor, and deputy director of its Institute of Gerontology. His writings include *Old Age in the New Land* and *Shades of Gray*. Achenbaum is currently a board member of The National Council on the Aging, Inc.

Rebecca G. Adams is associate professor of sociology at the University of North Carolina at Greensboro. She is co-editor of *Older Adult Friendship: Structure and Process,* and co-author of *Adult Friendship*.

Richard F. Afable is assistant professor at the Bowman Gray School of Medicine, Wake Forest University, Winston-Salem, North Carolina. He has spent twelve years in the practice of internal medicine with emphasis on care of the elderly. His scholarly interests include the use of exercise as a therapeutic measure in the treatment and prevention of chronic disability in older people.

Robert C. Atchley is director of the Scripps Gerontology Center and distinguished professor of gerontology at Miami University of Ohio. His *Social Forces and Aging*, the first widely used textbook in social gerontology, has introduced more than 400,000 college students to this new field. Atchley has published more than a dozen other books, including *The Sociology of Retirement, Families in Later Life*, and *Aging: Continuity and Change*.

Lydia Brontë is director of The Long Careers Study, an exploration of longevity's effects on work and life. From 1982 to 1987 Brontë was director of The Aging Society Project, a study sponsored by Carnegie Corporation of New York. Her most recent publication is *The Longevity Factor*.

Lucy Rose Fischer is research scientist at Group Health Foundation in Minneapolis, Minnesota. She previously directed the older volunteers project for the Wilder Research Center. Her most recent book is *Older Volunteers: A Guide to Research and Practice*. She is a fellow of the Gerontological Society of America.

George Gaberlavage is a senior analyst with the Public Policy Institute of the American Association of Retired Persons (AARP), where he specializes in housing and community planning issues.

Deborah T. Gold is assistant professor of medical sociology in the departments of psychiatry and sociology at the Duke University Medical Center, and a senior fellow in the Duke University Center for the Study of Aging. Siblings in late life and coping with chronic disease in late life are among her research interests.

Connie Goldman is a public radio producer, writer, and speaker. For the past decade, all of her work has focused on issues and images of aging. Her nationally broadcast public radio programs include the award-winning series "Late Bloomer." She is co-author of *The Ageless Spirit* and *Secrets of How to Be a Late Bloomer.*

William H. Haas III is associate professor of sociology at the University of North Carolina at Asheville. Haas's publications have focused on health care issues and aging, particularly the impact of retirement migrants on their host local community.

Richard E. Johnson, a pychologist and psychotherapist, is in private practice at the Center for Change in Hendersonville, North Carolina. Johnson uses mythic stories in conducting workshops with adolescents and adults.

Alice Lee and Fred Lee have co-authored *A Field Guide to Retirement* and are currently writing *The 50 Best Retirement Communities in America and 20 that Should Make Future Lists.* Since 1977 they have worked in partnership as consultants running retirement seminars.

Steve Lee is a transportation program specialist with the American Association of Retired Persons (AARP) and is a nationally recognized expert on issues of public transit, older drivers, and transportation safety.

Charles F. Longino, Jr., is Wake Forest University's distinguished professor of sociology and public health sciences. He is associate director of the J. Paul Sticht Center on Aging at the Bowman Gray School of Medicine and the director of the Reynolda Gerontology Program. Longino's essays on aging and demography are found in numerous handbooks and encyclopedias, as well as in such publications as *American Demographics.*

Kyriakos S. Markides is professor of preventive medicine and community health and is the director of the Division of Sociomedical Sciences at the University of Texas Medical Branch in Galveston. Markides is founding editor of the *Journal of Aging and Health* and has authored more than 100 journal articles, chapters, and books, dealing mostly with aging, ethnicity, health, and family relations.

Diane Moskow-McKenzie is a research associate with the North Carolina Center for Creative Retirement at the University of North Carolina at Asheville. She recently conducted a national study of the planning stages of 260 older adult educational programs in senior centers, Shepherd's Centers, OASIS (Older Adult Service and Information Systems), community colleges, four-year colleges, and universities. Her publications include *Older Adults Education: A Guide to Research, Program, and Policies.*

Donald L. Redfoot is a legislative representative on housing and transportation issues with the American Association of Retired Persons (AARP). Previously he served as a congressional staff member to the

House Aging Committee's Subcommittee on Housing and Consumer Interests where he wrote a committee report on the Congregate Housing Services Program.

Harold L. Sheppard is professor of gerontology at the University of South Florida in Tampa. Sheppard was the first research director, and later staff director, for the Senate Special Committee on Aging. He has written and edited several works on the older worker issue and the challenges of population aging.

Gordon F. Streib, graduate research professor emeritus of the University of Florida, has conducted extensive research in the field of aging. In 1989, he received the highest research award of the Gerontological Society of America—the Robert Kleemeier Award. Among his major works are *Retirement in American Society* and *Old Homes—New Families: Shared Living for the Elderly.*

Lyn E. Teven is a freelance writer and retired editor living in Asheville, North Carolina. She has written for newspapers, magazines, and public relations clients, and done freelance editing and writing for U.S. government agencies.

David R. Thomas is associate professor of internal medicine in the Division of Gerontology/Geriatric Medicine at the University of Alabama at Birmingham (UAB), and a scientist at the UAB Center for Aging. He is medical director of the hospital-based Home Care Program in Birmingham, and attending physician in the Kirklin Geriatric Assessment Clinic. Thomas has been active in advocacy for older adults at the state level in North Carolina and Alabama.

During the past two decades there have been clear indications that prevailing ideas about aging and the older American are once again in flux, and it is now regarded as outdated to characterize old age as a "problem." If the experiences of late life are as diverse as experts document and everyday people perceive, then it makes no sense any longer to align with the historical viewpoint of the older population as a monolithic group with the same perceptions, needs, and challenges.

The members of the older population are simply not all alike, and gender differences have become critically important, especially in this century. Prior to 1940 the U.S. Bureau of the Census reported that there were more older men than women. Many women died in early adulthood from complications of pregnancy or childbirth. Due mainly to improvements in obstetrics and gynecology, this pattern reversed. Today, approximately 60 percent of all people over sixty-five in the United States are female. The predominance of women is even more noticeable among those over seventy-five: women constituted 51 percent of this group in 1890, 53 percent in 1940, and 65 percent in 1987. Race also affects the composition of the older adult population. Life expectancy at birth for whites is considerably greater than for African Americans. The incidence of disability occurs earlier and more frequently in later life among African Americans than among whites. Cultural as well as biological forces interact to create diversity and inequity in later years. More than 50 percent of all elderly African-American women subsist on incomes below the official U.S. poverty line, attesting to the effects of racism, sexism, and ageism throughout their lives.

While there is no question that growing older in the 1990s is very different from growing older in previous centuries, surprisingly the older American's *current circumstances* bear remarkable similarities to appearances and experiences in years past. Thus, in addition to describing changes over time, society as a whole must also take note of things that have *not* changed—ranging from moral issues like the work ethic to government benefits such as social security—as well as things that have: senior-citizen discounts, special tax credits, and a strong voice of advocacy. History shows that the dissimilarity that characterizes the lives of older Americans today is hardly the hallmark of the modern era. Older adults had no less dazzling an array of feelings, assets and liabilities, and attributes in earlier times as now. Accordingly, basic continuities in the human dimensions of aging figure in the unique experiences and meanings of old age that have emerged in twentieth century America.

As the United States enters the twenty-first century, it faces a tremendous challenge regarding how to treat its older population, an issue that will require great maturity. Hopefully, it will integrate its history of respect for its elders without repeating its mistakes. And this, indeed, will be this country's real turning point.

Old Age Across the Centuries

Although there have been many social and political advances since the 1700s, one fundamental truth is that people are simply living longer. Historical demographers report that three-quarters of all gains in life expectancy at birth throughout world history have been registered since 1900. A child born ninety years ago could be expected to live about forty-seven years. Today, life expectancy at birth in the United States exceeds seventy-five years. Baby girls on average can expect to live about five years longer than baby boys. Most of the increases in life expectancy result from improvements in prenatal and postnatal care and from the medical profession's success in conquering childhood diseases and epidemics.

Scientists believe that the maximum life span of humans is roughly 120 years, the same amount of time cited in the Old Testament (Genesis 6:3) and by observers in ancient times and the Middle Ages. Modern-day experts validate the number's accuracy. This means that most of us will never attain our full potential longevity—despite enormous gains during this century in life expectancy at birth and modest gains in adult life expectancy. Nature has programmed a demographic gap. The causes of death for most Americans in the late twentieth century (various forms of cancer, cardiopulmonary diseases, accidents) differ from what killed earlier generations (influenza, pneumonia, epidemics, unsanitary conditions). But even if researchers were to find a cure for AIDS, heart attacks, and cancer, most Americans alive today would not become centenarians.

The demographic revolution affects all sorts of interpersonal relationships. More than ever before, most Americans can reasonably expect to live to see their grandchildren. For the first time in U.S. history, there are more people over age sixty-five than teenagers in the population. With increasing numbers of older men and women has come a growing awareness of the diversity of late-life experiences.

No single factor triggers the human aging process. Scientists suspect that the human body has built into it several systems designed to bring on death. Part of the aging process (possibly as much as 50 percent) is governed by genetics. Long-lived people tend to have long-lived parents and grandparents. Many theories for what causes aging have been proposed, but none are widely accepted; auto-immune, error, and wear-and-tear theories, which are further explored in chapter 3, have recently gained popularity. Some scientists contend that cells self-destruct, or inadvertently create glitches in their message systems, or become frayed over the life cycle. Investigators suggest that older people may be vulnerable to diseases simply because they have been at risk longer than younger people. Alcoholism and drug abuse also play a role in life expectancy rates.

Since ancient times people have been fascinated with extending the human life span, but it seems highly unlikely that lifetimes can be lengthened beyond 120 years. A question intriguing scientists in the late twentieth century is whether the gap between average life expectancy at birth and the maximum length of life can be narrowed. Some believe that this can happen: biologists Lawrence Crapo and James Fries have developed the concept of a compression of morbidity—that death occurs after a brief period of frailty or decline, before which the person has enjoyed a long and vigorous life—is a popular, recent version of this long-sought ideal.

Yet, as the number of people reaching old age increases, there is disturbing evidence that much remains to be done before such a compression of morbidity can be engineered. The fastest growing segment of the U.S. population is that over the age of seventy-five. Recent studies of octogenarians and nonagenarians revealed hitherto unreported wide variations in this group's cognitive functioning, physical well-being, economic support, and household status. The incidence of disease clearly rises with advancing years. Chronic disabilities multiply over time. Americans presently sixty-five can expect to live another 16.9 years, but only part of this remaining life expectancy will be active. Members of this age group on average are forecast to be functionally disabled for 6.9 years. Living longer does not invariably enhance life quality.

The Boundaries of Old Age in America

In terms of U.S. experience, Americans have always recognized old age as a distinctive stage of life, beginning around age sixty-five, though there is considerable (and, over time, consistent) variations around this mean. The American Association of Retired Persons (AARP) now accepts as members anyone over the age of fifty who can pay eight dollars for dues. In the early 1800s, the distinguished revolutionary physician, Benjamin Rush, began to keep a detailed diary on the health of his surviving patients, including only those who were at least eighty. In his book *Medical Inquiries on Disease*, Rush wrote:

> The moral faculties, when properly regulated and
> directed, never partake of the decay of intellectual

faculties in old age, even in persons of uncultivated minds. It would seem as if they were placed beyond the influence, not only of time, but often of diseases, and accidents, from their exercises being so indispensably necessary to our happiness, more especially in the evening of our life.

While certain chronological ages have long been used to designate the beginning of old age, the age spread is actually rather wide, especially when compared to the narrow parameters surrounding eligibility for kindergarten or the onset of puberty. The boundaries of old age in America can be bent fifteen years either way, because biological processes warrant such latitude. People begin to manifest the marks of age at varying rates. Some diseases appear age specific in incidence, but most do not. Their duration varies from person to person. Nonetheless, growing older is not simply a biological phenomenon.

Popular opinion holds that President Franklin D. Roosevelt made sixty-five the benchmark for receiving Social Security benefits because German chancellor Bismarck established that age for the German social insurance system in 1881 (the latter actually picked age seventy, to keep costs down). Rather, New Deal policymakers chose sixty-five as a compromise: limiting eligibility to age seventy was too restrictive; providing benefits to people at age sixty was estimated to be too costly.

Culture clearly shapes old age. Many of the popular images held about the elderly result from older people's representations of themselves, ways they interact with different age groups, as well as the contributions they make and the demands they place on society. Across socioeconomic and biological dimensions, older adults have always been very diverse. While others of his generation have died or gone into retirement homes, actor/comedian Bob Hope continues to perform on television specials and with the United Service Organizations. Maggie Kuhn launched the Gray Panthers organization two years after being forced into retirement at age sixty-five. Some people are more physically active at eighty than others at sixty. And so it goes.

The portion of the life span designated as old age is the longest stage of the human life cycle, and wide variations in wealth, power, kin ties, mobility, and personality traits have great impact on the aged.

Certain attitudes toward aging recur throughout world history since ancient times. Fear, respect, despair, and defiance are all key elements characterizing younger people's images of older adults. But there have been shifts over time, despite biological and sociocultural continuities. The social, economic, political, and cultural dimensions of old age have altered at different rates, depending on the political economy and prevailing norms. Variations by race, class, gender, ethnicity, and sometimes even differences in age become significant. In the American experience there have not been any sudden changes in attitudes. Instead subtle modifications in work, sources of support, family relationships, and political options, among other things, have had a cumulative effect on meanings and experiences in the last stages of life.

Aging in the Settlement, Colonial, and Revolutionary Periods

U.S. historians probably know less about continuities and changes in the meanings and experiences of being old during the first decades of New World settlement than about any other era, and within that time frame, more is known about eighteenth- than sixteenth-century developments. (If U.S. history were to predate 1492, beginning with the arrival of the Asiatic migrants, then the historical record is extremely deficient. No ethnographic study of any tribe of Native American elders yet exists.) Little is known about conditions during the seventeenth and eighteenth centuries in the South or in the middle colonies. As more historical information becomes available, some of the current observations will need modifying.

As in most Caribbean and Pacific outposts prior to 1800, youth dominated the Spanish, French, and British settlements dotting the Atlantic and Gulf coasts.

There *were* older people in the New World. Two elderly couples came over on the *Mayflower* but it seems unlikely that seniors were among the founding patriarchs and matriarchs of Jamestown. If they were, they probably did not survive the first years, given the staggering mortality rates in the region. But many of the young and middle-aged people who figured that they would be better off if they crossed the Atlantic passage chose to stay in the New World. That is, they aged in place. In most seventeenth-century Massachusetts towns, twenty-year-olds had roughly a 70 percent chance of surviving past their sixtieth birthday. So, once an area in New England had been occupied by Europeans persistently for about five decades, typically only 1 percent to 3 percent of its population was over sixty-five.

According to the first U.S. census (1790), the median age of Americans was sixteen. Claims that the United States was a "young Republic" thus have a genuine demographic basis.

The situation for older men in seventeenth and eighteenth century New England was sociologically advantageous but psychologically disadvantageous, and very little is known about older women during this period. Ownership of land gave the older adult power and control over their children and status in the local society. The old and the rich (with a high degree of correlation between the two) sat in the front of the meetinghouse and were elected wardens, selectmen, officers of the militia, members of the town council, and representatives to the provincial assembly. Those who arrived first in the community typically acquired large tracts of land, which eventually would be divided among the children of each successive generation. Certain inequities, of course, arose from this arrangement. Those who held title early on to the choicest lots managed to gain wealth with minimal effort. Late-comers, even the shrewdest members of each successive generation, had to hustle if they hoped to do as well. Widows were only entitled to a third of their husbands' estates, which introduced a disparity in women's relative wealth and social standing compared to men.

Roles of Older Persons

Older people contributed to the well-being of fledgling communities by sharing their practical experience, which sometimes was painfully acquired. The aged, after all, were the ones most likely to

remember how their own parents had survived Indian attacks, blizzards, and poor crop seasons. Having worked the land for decades, they were full of clever ideas for increasing productivity in a given vicinity. Older women often managed the domestic scene at advanced ages. Where else could the young acquire such insight? There were yet no *Farmer's Almanac*s for sale, nor were there agricultural extension bureaus or colleges. The aged were especially valued for their spiritual wisdom. Puritans honored gray hairs. Piety was expected, and virtue rewarded.

Older people were not always venerated, however. Many young men in colonial New England chafed under their fathers' rule. Without property, they could not marry. Neither could they take a fully adult role in society, nor act like independent agents. Sometimes waiting was costly: the more siblings who had a claim on the land, the smaller each share; the longer the land had been cultivated, the less fecund it was likely to be (especially if tobacco had been grown). Young women were bound by a different sort of patriarchal custom: they either lived with their parents or with their husbands. Living alone simply was not an option.

So many young people left, heading west or north, figuring that their chances for success were better if they started from scratch. This meant leaving their aging parents behind, at a stage

The Life and Age of Man. Stages of a Man's Life from the Cradle to the Grave. *Hand colored lithograph by James Baille, 1848.*

of life in which the old wanted to be able to count on support from their offspring.

Because of such outmigration the percentage of sixty-year-olds in Hampton, New Hampshire, rose from 4 percent to 6.3 percent from 1656 to 1680. There were 206 adults in Newbury, Massachusetts, (population 420) in 1678; 28 were at least sixty, which represented 6.7 percent of the total population and 13.5 percent of the adult population. Thriving seaports like Boston or county seats like Northampton had smaller proportions of seniors in their midst, because of the steady flow of newcomers. In these places, the plight of the old was different. Surrounded by many people, the aged nonetheless were strangers to whom no obligations were due, effectively isolating them.

The vulnerabilities that economically secure, healthy men faced in late life were even more keenly felt by older women and minorities who lacked status. Though wives traditionally received a third of their husbands' estates, the number of husbands who stipulated in their wills just how much firewood their sons were to deliver to their widows suggested that this custom was not always observed. Aging "spinsters" moved from sibling to sibling before turning to their nieces and nephews. If there were no kin or neighbors to help, elderly women sought poor relief from the local community. In the colonial period, arrangements tended to be informal. Usually provisions were given to enable the elderly to stay at home. Occasionally they were boarded out to the person who assured the town that they could care for them for the least amount of money. African Americans were in a somewhat analogous situation; owners exploited their older slaves as long as possible. Most African Americans since 1619 were denied autonomy and power all of their lives; old age brought only additional pain.

Disability and dependence were an older person's chief fears. Morbidity rates for that period do not exist; available evidence suggests, however, that failing health caused superannuation, a term used in colonial times to describe persons past their productive years. Hence, blind, enfeebled Reverend Ebenezer Gay of Hingham reluctantly quit the pulpit after preaching on his eighty-fifth birthday. In the absence of modern medical and social services, older people unable to take care of their daily physical requirements had to count on the compassion of loved ones or those who lived nearby.

Aging and Political Life

After 1763, as British administrators sought to impose more taxes and regulations on the North American provinces, a call for independence increasingly was heard in many cities and villages. In *Growing Old in America,* David Hackett Fischer contends that the liberating, egalitarian, intellectual, and social forces transforming the provinces in revolutionary ways also affected attitudes toward the elderly. He notes changes in terms used to refer to the elderly, shifts in seating patterns in meetinghouses, compositions of family portraits, and alterations in fashions, inheritances, and child-naming patterns. But other scholars disagree. Historian David Troyansky analyzed the French Revolution in *Old Age in the Ancient Regime,* claiming the young radicals of France celebrated the aged's wisdom, loyalty to tradition, and stabilizing influence.

Other students of the American Revolution and the U.S. Constitution periodically note age differences among the various factions, but interpretations are disputed as well. About a third of the colonists sided with the rebels; a third remained Loyalists, some of whom moved to Canada; and the remainder were utterly indifferent, siding with whichever group had forces close by. Scholars of grass roots allegiances report a tendency for people to make "your enemy into my friend," but none of this is age related. Historians Eric McKitrick and Stanley Elkin have maintained that the young men of the Revolution became Federalists, in opposition to an older cohort of Anti-Federalists, yet they based their conclusion on a small sample. Had they examined the biographies of all of the participants, as Fischer did, they would have discovered that the Federalists were on average a year or so older than the Anti-Federalists.

The truly important legacy of older Americans who lived through the Revolutionary period is that many survived long enough to share their experiences and their values with a rising generation. Benjamin Franklin was the Grand Old Man (at the age of eighty-one) at the Constitutional Convention. Many of his contemporaries also lived past their eightieth birthdays. The first five presidents of the United States, George Washington, John Adams, Thomas Jefferson, James Madison, and James Monroe, were old men when they left the White House. The sixth, John Quincy Adams, was sixty-two when he lost the election of 1828, but then he was elected to Congress two years later, where he served for the next seventeen years. Men and women of more modest fame—Revolutionary soldiers and women who had crossed enemy lines to relay information—were honored at July Fourth ceremonies, where their tales of valor and patriotism were admiringly heard.

These Revolutionary patriots tried (with mixed success) to instill what one writer in the *Niles Register* (1817) called "happy mediocrity." Mediocrity conveyed a sense of Jeffersonian balance—a recognition that many things are important for a good life, but moderation in all pleasures is desirable. The aspect of mediocrity that could be regarded as happy connotes a mature outlook on human existence. Older people, it was said, ranked among those most capable of putting life into perspective, to affirm its positive qualities over its negative features. Particularly at a time in which virtue counted as much as representation, freedom, and democracy, the older population's efforts to embody the fundamentals of human dignity was an important contribution. The spirit of 1776

that animated aging Revolutionary survivors was worth passing on to generations who had not witnessed the epoch firsthand.

Old Age in the New Land, 1790 to 1900

In the first monographs that surveyed the history of the elderly in the United States, considerable attention was paid to shifts in attitudes toward old age. D. H. Fischer has suggested that the period between 1770 and 1820 constituted a period of revolutionary change. During the first 150 years of the New England experience, he has claimed, older people were venerated, while a cult of youth, which inspired Henry David Thoreau and others to debunk the supposed wisdom of age, flourished from 1820 to the 1970s. Another historical study, *Old Age in the New Land*, questions whether the shift from "gerontophilia" to "gerontophobia" was as extreme or as sudden as Fischer maintained. Historian W. Andrew Achenbaum has maintained that, prior to the Civil War, attitudes toward the elderly by and large were positive, because Americans perceived that the aged made valuable contributions to the well-being of others. During the latter third of the nineteenth century, however, changes in the political economy, in science, and in cultural norms caused Americans to reevaluate, in increasingly negative terms, the perceived status of the elderly. Historian Carole

Haber, author of *Beyond Sixty-five*, offers evidence for yet a third position. She has stressed that unflattering comments have been made about older people, especially widows and the poor, from the colonial period to the present day. While confirming that new ideas about aging were expressed by physicians and corporate managers after the Civil War, Haber nonetheless has criticized earlier histories for depicting the elderly's conditions in unduly rosy terms.

Historians concur that there never was a golden age in the history of old age.

Currently a consensus seems to have been reached on two counts. The origins of many contemporary negative assumptions about older adults in the United States can be traced to Aristotle, the Bible, Geoffrey Chaucer, medieval iconography, William Shakespeare, and numerous folk tales, while more positive notions sometimes rework ideas from the classics. Recent scholarship underscores the wide range of conflicting, ambivalent, and ambiguous emotions and ideas that are to be found in every period. Events, trends, legislation, and institutions that took shape after 1900 have caused the most noteworthy changes in the perceived and actual status of seniors over the course of U.S. history. Only with the institutionalization of twentieth century policies like Social Security does the modern era of old age history begin.

Effects of Industrialization on Older Adults

One reason for such continuity was that, prior to the closing of the frontier, the United State remained predominantly an agrarian society. More than 50 percent of all American men gainfully employed were engaged in agricultural pursuits before 1870. In absolute numbers, farming remained the single largest occupational category for males during the next fifty years—despite the fact that fewer and fewer farmers were needed to grow food for the country's burgeoning population.

Even as agriculture declined in importance in the U.S. economy, older people found work on the farm. The saga of Johnny Appleseed illustrates the importance of farming to older people and vice versa. Farming pursuits occupied 54 percent of all men over sixty-five who were gainfully employed in 1890; as late as 1960, elderly men who remained in the labor force were more likely to be reported to be farmers than any other occupation. Why? Farming tends to be less age graded than other enterprises: an aging farmer can reduce his schedule and delegate heavy work to younger hands. On the other hand, it seems likely that many aged people could not afford to give up farming. This probably accounts for the high proportion of aged-African-American tenant farmers and widowed farm managers listed in the federal censuses.

During the initial stages of industrialization, which began to transform the American landscape by the 1830s if not earlier, older men also found jobs in the nonagrarian sectors of the economy. Many worked as skilled craftsmen, taking on apprentices well into their eighth decade. The percentage of men over sixty-five working as carpenters and masons, boot and shoemen, and coopers and blacksmiths exceeded the average of younger men in these same positions. Compared to the population as a whole, elderly men were disproportionately employed as peddlers, merchants, agents, and collectors. A similar pattern obtains for older women of the time. While few were employed outside the home, women over sixty-five were more likely than middle-aged women to be seamstresses, tailors, milliners, and dressmakers; and it was socially acceptable for older widows to run saloons, manage hotels, or take in boarders.

Prior to the Civil War there were few instances of mandatory retirement. (Based on estimates from state and federal census data, it appears that physical debility caused at least 20 percent of men over sixty-five to become superannuated.) Mandatory age ceilings were rare. Appointments to selected judicial offices were restricted by age only in New York (1777), New Hampshire (1792), Connecticut (1819), Alabama (1819), Missouri (1820), Maine (1820), and Maryland (1851). Embarrassed by the bad press surrounding its most distinguished jurist, James Kent, who revealed in his *Commentaries* that he was forced at age sixty off that state's highest bench, New York dropped the old-age restriction for justices in 1846. No other profession, trade, or industry made old age a criterion for employment—but the federal and state constitutions did argue whether *young* people were mature

enough to vote and to hold public office. If there is a bias to be found, it operated against youth.

Older adults often assumed leadership positions in government and in local affairs. Consider their role in developing new religious orders. In their heyday (roughly between 1820 and 1880), Shaker communities from New England to the Midwest developed profitable seed and furniture businesses, attracted many visitors, and adopted thousands of children. The elders and eldresses, all

In the antebellum period Americans built special facilities for orphans, the deaf, the blind, the insane, and the criminal, but old-age homes were rare.

over age sixty, filled all central and local offices. And young men were founders of the Church of Jesus Christ of Latter-Day Saints, but once the Mormons reached Utah, older men generally took charge of matters. Reliance on the old was not unique to these sects. In mainstream Protestant denominations, bishops and other senior officials tended to be drawn from the ranks of the elderly clergy.

Yet few aged African Americans on the plantation possessed health, wealth, prestige, or power. Owners usually required aging slaves to help around the house, oversee younger field hands, and care for their children. Owners sometimes freed their slaves once they were well past their prime and incapable of doing much, thereby cutting their costs and avoiding the responsibility of caring for these slaves during their final illnesses. Members of the slave community saw things differently, however. To them, the aged were respected repositors of family histories and wisdom; some elders, said to possess magical powers and spiritual insights, were held in a mixture of fear and awe. Freed elderly African Americans routinely returned to the slave quarters every night, where they shared bread with their kin, biological or otherwise. Ethnographic evidence suggests that, at least within some tribes, older Native Americans also were accorded ceremonial honors and assured security very late in life.

Prior to 1900, most of the elderly lived, for better and for worse, in what might be characterized as an age-integrated society. People were keenly aware of differences between young and old, but there was much less age grading in the United States than exists in institutions and within social networks today. Particularly in the early days of the Republic, older people, like all others, were to contribute to the well-being of all. The wisdom of age was no less essential than the resources of youth and middle age.

Yet when the aged needed assistance, there really was no safety net in place. Widows and the sick, as in colonial times, had to rely on family members and neighbors. Some states had enacted laws governing family relations, but none stipulated special provisions for the old. Enforcing poor laws, maintaining an almshouse, or erecting private institutions for aged indigents were local matters. Resources varied considerably from community to community. Noisy and filthy, most almshouses provided disagreeable shelter for the older adult.

By the end of the nineteenth century, magazine contributors, social critics, academics, scientists, and other observers of the American scene expressed worries about the status of the elderly. New social and cultural forces created circumstances more threatening than the traditional problems that affected individuals as they grew older. Old age, they felt, was beginning to be considered a *social problem*.

Earlier in the nineteenth century doctors considered old age a natural stage of the human life course, but in the latter years of the century a less positive interpretation of older people's maladies took shape. Translations of J. M. Charcot's *Clinical Lectures on the Diseases of the Aged and Their Chronic Illnesses* (1881) influenced scientific thinking at the research-oriented medical schools of Harvard, Johns Hopkins, Michigan, Pennsylvania, and elsewhere. Taking cues from Charcot's conviction that the pathological manifestations found in elderly patients merited attention, physicians probed elderly people's bodies for the cause of disease in late life. Senility, once a benign synonym for old age, became a technical term referring to the "weakness and decrepitude characteristic of old age." Case studies of senile gangrene, senile chorea, senile pneumonia, and senile bronchitis were published in medical journals. That no cures were found for old age heightened people's sense of dread. Pohl's Spermine Preparations, a potion to restore sexual vigor, did not prove rejuvenating. Eating yogurt three times a day, as Nobel laureate Elie Metchnikoff recommended, did not prolong life. Decay seemed inevitable, a loathsome consequence of living (too) long.

While medical investigators cataloged the hazards of growing older, steel producers, railroad managers, and other captains of industry were independently concluding that older workers grew obsolete. Entrepreneurs and capitalists calculated that it

By 1929, 140 companies, potentially covering nearly a million workers, paid out $6.7 million to 10,644 retiree beneficiaries. Even so, less than 20 percent of the labor force was protected by pension programs.

made more sense to invest in youth. Older workers were reassigned jobs as gatekeepers or watchmen. Supervisors sometimes permitted discharged workers to beg by the factory gates on paydays. In an economic world increasingly governed by the principle of "survival of the fittest," the prevailing view was that only the fittest deserved to survive. Those over forty years old found it harder and harder to make the grade. Those over sixty faced even more barriers.

Early Versions of Retirement

Retirement became a way for large organizations to thrive and for superannuated workers to survive. President Abraham Lincoln established the precedent: in 1862 he pensioned his admirals (all of whom were over sixty) so that he could promote younger men to fight the Civil War at sea. In 1875 the American Express Company permitted selected workers over sixty to receive compensation if they quit their jobs. The Baltimore and Ohio Railroad in 1884 inaugurated a more elaborate plan for workers over sixty-five with at least ten years of service to qualify for pensions. Only seven more companies offered retirement plans by 1900.

Life insurance companies experimented with retirement vehicles. Fraternal orders of workers gave members the option of buying annuities in addition to disability insurance and burial funds. Some union officials expressed slight interest in old-age benefits, but most of the leadership was far more interested in bolstering membership ranks by focusing on the bread-and-roses issues that appealed to younger men and women. Several states permitted savings banks to underwrite tontine insurance, a pooled account declared illegal in 1906. Retirement programs were established for various groups of public employees. By the turn of the century most of the nation's largest cities gave benefits to teachers, police, and fire personnel. County- and state-level bureaucrats gained protection during the Progressive Era. The federal government inaugurated a Civil Service Retirement System in 1920.

Concerted efforts were made in the private sector to relieve the growing number of older people suffering from sickness or poverty. Benefactors left money to build old-age homes for their (upper) middle-class friends and servants. Philanthropists such as Benjamin Rose gave $3 million in 1911 to enable "respectable and deserving" residents in Cleveland to remain in their homes. Andrew Carnegie set aside $10 million to provide annuities for college professors. Religious and ethnic organizations in every metropolitan area erected old-age homes to which older members of their community might turn when necessary.

Decades after states had established school systems and earmarked funds to delinquents, orphans, and other needy youth, legislators reluctantly considered the merits of old-age assistance. Fearing costs and generally seeing no compelling need to act, some states tried to resist appeals by commissioning panels of experts to investigate the situation. The tack occasionally worked. A 1910 Massachusetts survey reported that conditions for the non-institutionalized aged poor were "comparatively good." Besides being expensive, concluded the blue-ribbon panel, providing old-age relief might destroy thriftiness, weaken family ties, lower wages, and prove unconstitutional. Indeed, several of the first state programs—including Arizona (1914) and Pennsylvania (1925)—were declared invalid by their respective state supreme courts; hidden provisions or lack of funds rendered old-age assistance systems in four other states inoperative.

The Pension Debate

Ironically the executive and legislative branches of the federal government were even more adamant than state officials in opposing old-age pensions. President Franklin Pierce's 1854 case against initiating national welfare schemes deterred his successors from committing the federal government to provide welfare. Bills for old-age relief were routinely submitted to every session of Congress after 1909, but none passed. (Most considered Bismarck's 1881 landmark measure and Britain's 1908 old-age assistance policy too undemocratic.) Yet for decades Washington had been exceedingly generous to one segment of the elderly population— veterans. In 1818, Madison approved a plan to relieve indigent

Revolutionary War soldiers, most of whom were then at least fifty-five. Congress so underestimated the number eligible for benefits that it imposed a means test a year later: applicants had to plead poverty to gain benefits. Similarly, veterans of the War of 1812 and the Mexican War were granted huge land bounties when they were old men. Thanks to successful lobbying from the Grand Army of the Republic, Union veterans and their spouses gained more and more financial and health benefits the older they got: Congress declared in 1907 that old age per se was a disability, thus opening the Treasury's coffers to more claimants. A decade later pensions were the costliest item in the federal budget. By 1929, veterans' pensions represented 80 percent of all the financial transfers being made to older Americans. For a select few, Washington was operating a de facto old-age welfare state.

Citing so many innovations in quick succession may give the misleading impression that old-age dependency and the diseases of old age had become major issues by the first years of the twentieth century. This is not the case. There was no massive exodus of older men from the marketplace. According to the census, nearly 70 percent of all men over sixty-five were gainfully employed in 1900. (Some historians argue that, if certain technical adjustments are made to the census data, labor force rates actually remained constant, or possibly even rose slightly, between 1870 and 1930.) In any case, due to deaths, disabilities, layoffs, strikes, and closings, most American workers never became eligible for corporate old-age pensions before 1929. Scientific interest in old age can likewise be exaggerated. Heart disease, epidemics, children's illnesses, and mental disorders attracted far more attention in the medical profession than did late-life maladies. Until his brother-in-law did him a favor and pulled a few strings, I. L. Nascher could not find a publisher for *Geriatrics* (1914). Nascher, a medical doctor and researcher, coined the term "geriatrics"; he and a junior colleague constituted the entire membership of his geriatric society (the nation's first and only such organization) until his death.

As the economic dislocations wrought by the Great Depression attained crisis proportions in the early 1930s, the patchwork quilt of economic and social services for older Americans became unstitched. With unemployment rates reaching 25 percent, thousands of young and middle-aged workers lost their jobs and had difficulty finding work. Grim as it was, younger people still fared better than the aged. Older workers were among the first to be fired; many never earned another dollar. Labor force participation rates dropped more precipitously (nearly 17 percent between 1930 and 1940) for workers over sixty-five than for any other age group.

In addition to being unable to support themselves through gainful employment, few seniors could count on income from other sources. Hopes that former employers or unions would help the elderly in desperate straits were dashed. Under the law, corporate pensions were viewed as gratuities, which could be distributed or withheld as managers chose. Granting pensions seemed a less plausible strategy for keeping a business afloat than reinvesting in the firm or retaining valuable young workers on the payroll. In any case, many companies declared bankruptcy and had nothing to give. Earlier, in more prosperous years, many people tried to save as much as they could for their old age. But those precious funds were lost in the 1930s as banks went under. Most family members wanted to help the old, of course, but their sons and daughters had children of their own to feed. In many instances there simply was not enough of anything to go around.

Private sources of support dried up along with public ones. Charitable organizations anticipated a downturn of only three to four years, since that seemed to be the length of earlier recessions. But the longer the Great Depression dragged on, the less money there was available to distribute. By 1934, moreover, half the states were on the verge of bankruptcy. To maintain operations as long as possible, bureaucrats cut back and then discontinued benefits across the board. Old-age assistance plans were suspended. Experts at the time estimated that as many as two-thirds of all the nation's elderly were potentially dependent. Old age as a social problem was no longer a topic of passing academic interest;

Some people are more physically active at eighty than others are at sixty.

COPYRIGHT MARIANNE GONTARZ

the Great Depression had made the plight of America's elderly a major priority.

The Coming of Social Security

For the first time in history older people began to mobilize politically to demand redress. In the 1930s a California-based physician and failed real estate agent, Francis Townsend, proposed that older Americans be granted two hundred dollars each per month, on the condition that they not work and that they spend the money in thirty days. Novelist and reformer Upton Sinclair inspired a pension scheme based on scrip, the Ham and Eggs movement. Two radicals—Louisiana senator Huey Long and Detroit radio activist Father Charles Coughlin—pledged to eliminate old-age poverty, hoping to rally the aged to their radical causes.

President Franklin Delano Roosevelt, however, waited until the third year of his presidency to take decisive action. Why the delay? It cannot be that he was insensitive to the issue, because in 1929, as governor of New York, he had signed into law the country's most progressive old-age assistance scheme. Nor was he the only national politician under pressure from elderly constituencies: the number of bills before Congress sharply increased; the American Federation of Labor, which had opposed federal old-age intervention, reversed its position in 1933. Apparently FDR felt that other measures aimed at institutional reforms, human relief, and national reconstruction merited higher priority; however, by the time he signed the Social Security Act in 1935, the Supreme Court had already invalidated many of his New Deal programs. Many scholars insist that the Social Security Act was FDR's greatest accomplishment.

The first title of the 1935 Social Security Act dealt with old-age assistance. The federal government promised to match (up to fifteen dollars a month) half the pension awarded to eligible persons in a given state. Those who were denied benefits were given the right to appeal a local officials' decision. Significantly, benefits could not go to the institutionalized aged, a regulation calculated to accelerate the demise of the almshouse. In order to keep the future costs of Title I in bounds, an old-age insurance plan was established under Title II. Employers and employees were to contribute up to one-half percent of the first three thousand dollars of the salary of workers in selected areas of the economy; once the old-age insurance trust fund was large enough, benefits would start being paid out beginning in 1942. Other provisions of the omnibus legislation allocated funds for the blind, for mothers with young children (which eventually became Assistance to Families with Dependent Children), for the unemployed, and for public health services.

Social Security under Fire

Because of its complexity, Social Security was misunderstood from the start. Polls at the time indicate that people trusted that they would get something back for their contributions, but few knew the first thing about how the system worked. Kansas senator Alf Landon derided the measure as socialistic, and his political advisers figured that attacking Social Security might win him the 1936 election. Even Supreme Court justices were ambivalent: *Helvering v. Davis* (1937) upheld the constitutionality—not necessarily the wisdom—of the act. The 1939 amendments, which greatly affected the scope and the philosophy of the original measure, added to the confusion. Before the first Title II benefit was ever paid, Congress increased the beneficiary pool to include the spouses and children of workers who contributed to the program, though it did not raise Social Security taxes so as not to impede economic recovery.

Historians, economists, and social scientists have long debated the original intent and eventual impact of the 1935 Social Security Act and its 1939 amendments. Compared to other New Deal measures, which straightforwardly regulated banking or promoted conservation, Social Security controlled people's options in murky, complicated language. Did Title II endorse the Townsendite strategy of insisting that older people stop working as a condition for receiving benefits? The evidence is very ambiguous. Did Title I reinforce racism? It may have. Southern legislatures claimed that they were too poor to enact old-age assistance plans, a tack that kept African Americans off pension rolls. Title II also worked against the interests of aged minorities: farmers were not covered under Social Security until 1954; older African Americans, most of whom had remained in agrarian pursuits, therefore did not earn Social Security retirement benefits for two decades because their employment was not covered. However Social Security did not then foment intergenerational tensions, even though lawmakers had to decide whether to finance pensions for elders (who voted) with school taxes earmarked for children (who did not vote), but the generational-equity debate became a factor in national politics in the late 1970s. Nonetheless, the enactment of the Social Security Act is a clear turning point in the history of old age.

The Older Adult in an Age of Affluence

Throughout most of U.S. history, major changes in the older population's status occurred after transformations in younger people's conditions. The aged remained in farming longer. They organized politically later. Their values were traditional, at odds with the Roaring Twenties generation characterized by novelist F. Scott Fitzgerald as "the damned and the beautiful." Increasingly after the 1930s, however, dealing with the problems of the elderly required taking bold steps, innovating, making tough choices. By the middle of the twentieth century, older Americans were pioneers—and not just because large numbers were retiring to Sunbelt communities throughout the South. In numbers greater than any previous group, those coming of age after World War II experienced the blessings and banes of longer lives, of enjoying the rights (and rites) of retirement. More likely to live alone or at a distance from their children, they kept contact through phone calls and rapid transport, and while many of these issues are amplified later in this almanac, their historical novelty is significant to mention.

Particularly since World War II, public and private institutions have coordinated efforts to achieve genuine economic security for seniors. Social Security became the single most important source of income; coverage gradually became universal; and benefits also increased, initially whenever Congress adjusted rates, and then, after 1972, through automatic cost-of-living adjustments pegged to inflation. In the late 1940s, the Supreme Court backed the rights of unions to negotiate pensions, which spurred a revival of private pension plans with eligibility and benefit structures typically complementary to those prevailing under Social Security. The Employee Retirement Income Security Act of 1974 offered financial and tax incentives to the self-employed, among others, to shelter money for use in later years.

As a result of this concerted interest in old-age security, the poverty rate among seniors dropped from 33 percent in the early 1960s to 12 percent in 1987. (Without Social Security, as many as two-thirds of all older Americans presently would have incomes below the poverty line.) Such a remarkable achievement demonstrates that social engineering through policymaking sometimes works as intended. Yet success has been uneven. Elderly women and minorities still tend to have less income at their disposal than retired white males. And for the first time in U.S. history, a greater percentage of the nation's children (20 percent) are likely to be poor than are the old.

Emergence of Organizations on Aging

Nor has government limited its concern to the economics of aging. Acquiring basic information about the elderly's needs early on became a high priority. In 1939, with support from the Josiah Macy

Foundation, the Public Health Service established a Gerontological Research Center (GRC) in Baltimore. Under eminent gerontologist Nathan Shock's direction this became one of the country's premier training units for biomedical investigators. Thirty-five years later, a greatly expanded GRC became the internal wing of the National Institute on Aging, the eleventh branch of the National Institutes of Health. On the social science/policy side, the Federal Security Agency in 1950 began to gather data and a year later convened a group of experts in Washington to discuss a host of problems besetting seniors. Their mission was to propose ways of promoting better social adjustment in late life. The success of this approach led to the 1961 White House Conference on Aging, which became a decennial affair.

Often taking cues from those interested in the well-being of children, scholars and advocates established private organizations directed at the mature population. In the 1930s Lillien Martin, a retired Stanford psychologist, opened an Old Age Center in San Francisco to help her peers "sweep out the cobwebs." Educator William McKeever started a School for Maturates in Oklahoma City. Just as the Macy Foundation helped the government establish a unit devoted to aging research, so too it facilitated the first meetings of professionals who chartered the Gerontological Society in 1945 to advance research in aging, training, and policy making. Twelve years later, Ethel Percy Andrus, a retired Los Angeles high school principal, started the National Retired Teachers Association. Her organization really flourished after she met Leonard Davis, who proposed a mutually beneficial insurance program for her members. Andrus's group is now called the American Association of Retired Persons. It now boasts 37 million members. After the Roman Catholic Church, it is the second largest social organization in the United States. The National Council on the Aging (NCOA) owes its origins to a grant from the Ford Foundation after the 1961 White House Conference on Aging. NCOA now depends heavily on federal funding under Title V of the Older Americans Act (OAA), which came out of President Lyndon B. Johnson's concept of a Great Society.

Most of the social policies developed during the 1960s were targeted for special groups—African Americans, youth, infants, people living in Appalachia, in cities or on farms. The needs of older citizens often were reserved—or relegated—for special consideration, because as a group the elderly were considered sicker and poorer than the population at large. The summer of 1965 proved a bonanza for the elderly. Medicare and Medicaid offered them hospital insurance and, if indigent, coverage for long-term care. The preamble to the Older Americans Act, moreover, envisioned seemingly boundless federal support as the nation's aged sought to pursue meaningful, secure, healthful lives. Delegates to the 1971 White House Conference demanded—and received—a wide range of social services for senior citizens. OAA amendments enacted in the mid-1970s mandated that states provide social services for men and women over sixty. State Offices of Aging became increasingly important. Networking became ever more complex.

—*W. A. Achenbaum, Ph.D.*

McGeorge Bundy

Foundation president

SNAPSHOT

I don't believe in retirement per se. It never occurred to me to retire at sixty-five. I was halfway through a job at Ford I intended to finish. I believe retirement age no longer works for most people; most people over sixty-five don't think of themselves as old."

Former Ford Foundation president McGeorge Bundy was born in 1919. His father was a lawyer; his mother had many charitable and educational interests, including family planning and the women's suffrage movement. Bundy attended the Groton School and Yale, where he received a bachelor's degree in mathematics, then served in Latin America during World War II. In 1946, shortly after returning to civilian status, he helped Henry Stimson, secretary of war during World War II, organize his papers and write his memoirs. After two years, he returned to Harvard, became an assistant professor of government, and was appointed dean at the age of thirty-four. Bundy contended that being dean was the most excellent training he'd ever had. "If you like decisions, if you like helping a first-rate outfit stay first rate and get better, if you like the process of dealing with other human beings on a common enterprise or resisting the bad ideas that a few people will have from time to time," Bundy remarks, "Harvard then was a wonderful place."

Bundy left Harvard to become assistant for National Security Affairs in Washington, D.C., under President John F. Kennedy. Working for the Kennedy administration "was very intense," Bundy recalls, "in the sense that you were doing one part of the daily business that mattered to the president of the United States. . . . You learned your job by doing it. And you learned simply from the contrast, that you have to know your man as well as your set of problems. You can only help a president the way he wants to be helped. You can't teach him to do it Ike's way."

Accepting an invitation to be president of the Ford Foundation in New York City in late 1966, Bundy was known for his quick wit and occasionally tart tongue, which won him a reputation as a formidable opponent. He hired a staff as energetic as he was and set out to tackle a whole range of social problems. Bundy achieved many of his objectives during his tenure at Ford, which many consider legendary.

In the 1970s Bundy taught history as a visiting professor at New York University. In 1979, when he reached the Ford Foundation's retirement age, he began teaching full-time at New York University and started several writing projects. Currently on the staff of Carnegie Corporation of New York, Bundy is part of a three-man commission exploring the future of arms control. A student of the nuclear arms problem from a historical point of view for more than a decade, Bundy provides strictly "policy-making, recommendational" input.

—*Lydia Brontë*

A **prevalent** myth about old age in the United States is that being old takes a similar form in all older people—that most seniors think, feel, act, and look basically the same and have similar needs. While no one would speak of a "typical" thirty-year-old or middle-aged person, there is a tendency to lump together all 31 million Americans over sixty-five as "the elderly." This misconception of the homogeneity of older adults is held not only by the younger generation, but even by senior advocacy groups, who at times pursue their interests as if they represent a constituency with one common agenda and set of values.

Older Americans have been portrayed in the popular media in two fundamental ways: as frail, sick, and dependent, or as greedy geezers racing around on golf course cartways. But neither of these stereotypes is accurate, and since the United States as a whole society is growing older, with its average age rising dramatically, it is crucial to understand the diverse experiences and situations of people as they age. In a matter of decades this nation has gone from the youth orientation of the post–World War II baby boom, with its crowded public school classrooms and burgeoning college campuses, to a society concerned with Social Security, long-term care insurance, aging parents, and issues of generational equity. Among the most significant factors contributing to variations in the aging experience are those of race, ethnicity, and gender, with rapid growth and increasing diversity the hallmarks of the older adult population in the United States. One of the tasks of demographers is to help make sense of all these factors, and to identify the key differences between members of the older generation.

The Role of Demographics and Research

Populations are studied by the science of demography. As members of an interdisciplinary field, demographers come from a number of specialties such as sociology, economics, geography, biology, and statistics. Demographers are interested in the *size, distribution, structure,* and *change* in populations.

Size refers simply to the number of people in a population. Distribution of populations refers to geographic spread, along with issues of density or concentration of people (such as rural versus urban). The structure of a population refers to characteristics of the group under study, such as the age mix, ratio of men to women, or marital status. Formal or pure demographers are only interested in those characteristics that would influence change within a population. Change within populations arises from the three demographic processes of *mortality, fertility, and migration.*

But a comprehensive study of aging in America involves more than statistics, theories, models, and polls. Researchers need to look at people earlier in life and follow them up into old age. They need to go beyond studying older people to studying the aging *process,* employing a life course perspective that involves taking into account more than just the passage of time as captured by chronological age. A life course approach involves looking at people as they go through a variety of stages in the life course, an approach that ultimately demands longitudinal data. There is an increasing number of longitudinal studies in aging research but very few in the area of ethnicity and aging.

Research on the general population is revealing a great deal about life course transitions but little about such transitions in the various ethnic populations. For example, is the experience of widowhood or retirement different for minorities and, if so, why? Findings indicate that most older women seem to adjust to widowhood in the long run; however, when widowhood is an unexpected or "unscheduled" event, as in middle-age (or earlier), the consequences are more severe. Is this true in different ethnic populations? What are the factors that might make the impact of widowhood (either early or late) different in different ethnic contexts? The same issues can be raised about retirement, the transition to the "empty nest," or divorce. What about the impact of declining health of elderly parents on their middle-aged children? Are the stresses of caregiving different and, if so, how and why? Who does the caring, and is it shared by more people in certain populations where the number of offspring is larger?

Research must go beyond trying to find out whether people in certain ethnic groups are worse off or better off than people in other groups and examine how they are different. Is the life course experienced differently?

In addition to an absence of a life course perspective, research in the field of ethnicity and aging often lacks a historical perspective. For example, there is evidence of strengthening intergenerational relationships among Italian Americans immigrating to the United States around the turn of the century from what was the case back in Italy. The challenges of the new land apparently led to strengthening family ties instead of weakening them, as modernization theory would predict.

The life course is, apparently, a cultural concept; its experience becomes altered with social and historical changes. What researchers know about the experience of the life course in a given group today may not resemble what is experienced a generation or two into the future. That does not mean that they should not study the life course. What they can do (and are increasingly doing) is to study aging and the life course in a variety of ethnic groups and social classes under different social and historical circumstances. This also means that researchers must engage in cross-cultural or cross-national research. Only through such comparative research can they hope to make significant contributions to knowledge in the form of theory that can guide both research and social policy.

Important special problems in this type of research relate to sampling, sample size, difficulties in collecting data, equivalence of measures in different cultural contexts, and issues of data analysis.

Race, ethnicity, and gender are significant factors influencing the variety of ways people age.

However, appropriate techniques are becoming increasingly available. With regard to more specific and more applied research areas, there are many opportunities for research, including data on caregiving of disabled or demented elderly, bereavement, gender differentials in life expectancy, comorbidity, diet and nutrition, doctor-patient relations, health services access and utilization, and rates of institutionalization. This chapter aims to introduce a number of perspectives in an effort to demystify the myths of aging, and present a balanced approach to looking at demographics and their role in better understanding the aging process.

How Populations Age

One type of population change is a shift in the age structure of a society. To a demographer individuals grow older, but populations age. A population is said to be aging when its median age rises. Conversely a population can become younger if the age structure shifts in the other direction, and the median age declines. All three of the core demographic processes can contribute to the aging of a population.

Mortality Reduction

A population can age when there is a reduction in mortality and, consequently, more people grow older. *Life expectancy* is the average number of years of life remaining at a specified age. Typically it is reported at birth and sixty-five years old. When a society reduces mortality, then life expectancy at birth or at sixty-five moves closer to the *life span,* the theoretical age limit a species can survive under optimal conditions. Demographers often define life span as the age at which one-tenth of 1 percent (0.1 percent) of the original birth cohort survives. According to the U.S. Bureau of the Census, this appears to be approximately 100 among humans, although some experts suggest the life span could be as much as 115.

Among the developed nations the first major stage in mortality reduction came about within the younger age groups. An epidemiological transition occurred at the beginning of the industrial era. Improvements in public health, provision of sufficient and sanitary food supplies, and better housing constrained the spread and deleterious effects of acute infectious diseases, such as cholera, pneumonia, typhus, typhoid, and tuberculosis. Decrease of the acute self-limiting disorders allowed the young to live and grow older, and face the diseases of later life. The second and more difficult stage of mortality reduction comes in later life, when medical science combats the more complex chronic conditions: cardiovascular disease, cancers, and stroke.

Fertility Reduction

Another mechanism that ages a population is a reduction in fertility. When fewer people are being born, the proportion of younger members in the population decreases, and conversely the proportion of the older members increases. As a result, the smaller cohorts of females will in part reduce the future fertility when they become *fecund* (that is, have the capacity to reproduce, from ten to forty-nine years of age). Even if fertility again increases, there will be fewer fecund females, and this will constrain the youthful trend in the society.

So-called replacement rate fertility is the projected number of births per 1,000 fecund women that a society needs to maintain a stable population size. Among the industrialized nations, the replacement rate is 2,100 per 1,000 women, or 2.1 per woman. Of 2,100 per 1,000, the 2,000 serves to replace the women and their mate(s), while 100 compensates for deaths among females before they come to reproductive age. When a nation falls below replacement rate fertility, an increasingly higher proportion of the population is older; hence, the nation ages.

Migration

Finally the aging of a population can be influenced by migration. Just as a reduction in fertility ages a population, so does out-migration of young adults from an area, and the corresponding loss of their fertility leaves behind an older population. In-migration of older adults can also create an aged population, even as normal fertility and mortality processes continue. Of course the converse of these migration processes, such as the immigration of the young, can make the age structure more youthful.

Population Aging in the United States

Numerically, the U.S. elderly population has grown in a dramatic fashion since the turn of the century. The sixty-five-plus population in 1900 totaled just over 3 million, and as of the 1990 census it stood at 31.2 million, a 913 percent increase. An even more overwhelming increase of 2,024 percent is reported for the eighty-five-year-old and older age group, which went from 123,000 in 1900 to 3 million in the last census. Projected increases between 1990 to 2050 are not as large, although the fastest growth is still in the eighty-five-plus age group. Between 1990 and 2050 the group sixty-five years old and over will grow by 155 percent to about 67 million. Yet during the same period the eighty-five and older group will increase by 422 percent to over 16 million.

U.S. Population Trends: Past and Future

The nation's aging throughout this century and into the middle of the next century is charted in Table 1. Median age climbed steadily through the first half of this century from twenty-three in 1900 to thirty in 1950. The baby boom dropped the median age to twenty-nine in 1960, and by 1970 it dipped to twenty-eight years of age. By 1980 the median age had again risen to thirty. By 2020 the median age is projected to rise by ten years. As the baby boom ages out of the population, the median age will reach forty-three in 2050.

Coming to Terms with Demography

Aging refers to the increase in the overall age of a population as measured by the median age. *Younging* refers to a decrease in the median age of a population.

Cohort is a group with a common characteristic. The term is most commonly used in demography to identify a group of people born within a specified time period, as in birth cohort.

Dependency or *support ratios* are measures of the composition of a population supported by or dependent on other members of society.

Fertility refers to the actual birth performance of individuals or groups. *Fecundity* is the physiological capacity to reproduce and is frequently reported as women fifteen to forty-four years old, although the U.S. government reports birth from ten to forty-nine years old. *Natality* refers to the role of births in population change.

Life expectancy is a synthetic measure based on current age- and sex-specific death rates, and it addresses the average number of years of life remaining. Typically it is reported at age sixty-five.

Life span is the theoretical limit or maximum age a species could live under optimum conditions. It is typically defined as the age beyond which less then 0.1 percent of the original cohort survives.

Migration is a form of spatial mobility involving a change of usual residence between clearly defined geographical units. *Immigration* refers to migration into a nation, and *emigration* specifies the movement out of a country. Migration within a country's border is described by the terms *in-migration* and *out-migration*. *Donor* locales refer to the places people leave, and *host* locales refer to places that receive migrants. Items that promote people leaving a location are called *push factors,* and those items that attract people to a locale are called *pull factors.* A *move* is a residence change within the country.

Mortality refers to death as a component of population change.

Senescence is the biological process of aging by which the organism becomes less vital and more vulnerable to changes in the environment.

Sex ratio is a measure of sex composition of a population. It is defined as the number of males per one hundred females. *Old-old* is defined by demographers as those seventy-five years old and older. *Old-oldest* is defined by demographers as those eighty-five years old and older. *Young-old* is defined by demographers as those fifty-five to seventy-four years old.

Kenneth B. Clark

Psychologist

SNAPSHOT

I believe that people should go on with what they are doing as long as they want to. I never thought about retirement; I thought about changing focus."

Educator and psychologist Kenneth Clark was born in Panama in 1914, of Jamaican immigrants. Clark immigrated to the United States to join his mother and sister, and he still remembers coming through Ellis Island with his grandmother.

Clark went to public school in Harlem and then attended Columbia University where he switched from medicine to psychology in his sophomore year. He earned a master's degree at Howard University, then a Ph.D. in social psychology from Columbia in 1940. "I didn't think of my studies in terms of using an understanding of psychology to improve racial understanding," Clark reflects. "I thought at that point that I was using psychology to understand *human beings*."

The first African American to teach at City College in New York, Clark subsequently taught at several other colleges and universities in the New York area before being assigned to the Office of War Information during World War II. His group at OWI studied the morale of civilian African Americans to find out whether racism and prejudice had a persistent negative affect on them. But a year later he left the office because he wasn't getting enough support and was being undermined by the Federal Bureau of Investigation.

Clark returned to City College. He and his wife, Marine, whom he had married in 1938, received a fellowship to research self-image in children. Clark traveled around the country, using dolls to test children's self-image. Their research was published in 1940, generating concern that children were being conditioned into negative self-images by gender and racial prejudices.

Clark's findings of the effects of prejudice and discrimination on children came to the attention of National Association for the Advancement of Colored People (NAACP) attorney Thurgood Marshall, who later served on the U.S. Supreme Court. Marshall recruited Clark to work on *Brown v. the Board of Education*, the school segregation case, to develop a social science brief to be used as expert testimony during the trial. When school segregation was declared unconstitutional, Clark reveals, "I was jumping for joy . . . we certainly didn't anticipate that our research was going to have any revolutionary impact."

Clark wrote a similar report on adolescents in Harlem, participated in the creation of Harlem Youth Opportunities, and wrote his 1965 prize-winning book, *Dark Ghetto*, on youths in Harlem. Later he and his wife co-founded the Northside Center for Child Development in Harlem.

When Clark retired from his teaching position at City College in 1975, he faced the protest of students, faculty, and administration. But he objected: "I never gave retirement a thought. I just wanted something different from teaching," Clark explains.

Since leaving City College, Clark started the Metropolitan Applied Research Center and Kenneth B. Clark & Associates, a consulting business with particular emphasis on race relations and affirmative action programs. The NAACP, the U.S. Department of State, AT&T, Chemical Bank, Con Edison, IBM, and NASA number among his clients. Clark received the Spingarn Medal and the 1986 Presidential Medal of Liberty, and is the author of several books and numerous articles, including *Prejudice and Your Child* (1955), *Dark Ghetto* (1965), and *Pathos of Power* (1975).

—*Lydia Brontë*

With 12.6 percent of the population over sixty-five, the United States is one of the oldest countries in the world. Only Northern Europe (16 percent) and Western Europe (14 percent) have more age-dense populations. Exceptionally low fertility, in part, has aged Northern Europe (1,800 births per 1,000 women) and Western Europe (1,600 births per 1,000 women). Among the less developed nations, the percent of the population sixty-five years and over stands where the United States was in 1900, at 4 percent. As the baby boom generation ages, the elderly will be over one-fifth of the nation's population by 2025, and the oldest old (eighty-five-plus) will account for one in twenty of the population in 2050. Projections of the percent of the elderly and oldest-old found in Table 1 are based on replacement rate fertility, or 2,100 children per 1,000 women. Fertility below replacement rate would increase the proportion of the elderly population.

Table 1: Median Age, Percent Sixty-five Years Old and Older, Percent Eighty-five Years Old and Over, and Dependency Ratios: 1990 to 2050

	Median Age	Percent 65+	Percent 85+	65+	Dependency Ratios 0–17	Overall
1900	23	4.0	.2	7	76	84
1910	24	4.3	.2	–	–	–
1920	25	4.7	.2	8	68	76
1930	26	5.4	.2	–	–	–
1940	29	6.8	.3	11	52	63
1950	30	8.1	.4	–	–	–
1960	29	9.2	.5	17	65	82
1970	28	9.8	.7	–	–	–
1980	30	11.3	1.0	19	46	65
1990	33	12.6	1.2	20	41	62
2000	36	13.0	1.7	21	39	60
2010	39	13.9	2.2	22	35	57
2020	40	17.7	2.3	29	35	64
2030	42	21.8	2.7	38	36	74
2040	43	22.6	4.1	39	35	74
2050	43	22.9	5.1	40	35	75

Source: *Statistical Abstract of the United States, 1985.* U.S. Bureau of the Census. "Projections of the Population of the United States by Age, Sex, and Race: 1988 to 2050." Gregory Spencer. Current Population Report Series P-25, No. 1018 (January 1989).

The Life Expectancy Controversy

James Fries and Lawrence Crapo, using a demographic model called a survival curve, estimate that even in the absence of disease, the average life expectancy at birth will be eighty-five, with a standard deviation of four years. Their calculations are in line with a life span of one hundred years.

Can life expectancy be extended further than Fries and Crapo suggest? Cellular biologist Leonard Hayflick contends that cells only replicate a limited number of times, the so-called Hayflick Limit. This limit illustrates the concept of *senescence,* or the basic biological aging of an organism, by which it becomes less vital and more vulnerable to the environment. Finding the cures to various diseases, no doubt, will extend life expectancy to some degree. Yet such cures cannot extend human life indefinitely. The National Center for Health Statistics estimates a cure for all heart disease would extend life at birth by 5 years; another 3.7 years could be achieved with a cure for cancer, and 0.91 year for strokes. Yet the ultimate biological clock still ticks, even though various disease entities are conquered.

Unless a method is found to reverse the primary aging process, there is a limit to mortality reduction. Researchers argue that the vast efforts and resources that go to cure cancer, stroke, and cardiovascular disease are shortsighted. Cures for the nation's three big killers still leave a biological limit on life. It also leaves an older and frailer population. Researchers suggest more resources are needed for research on how to unlock the basic biological limit on longevity.

Immigration

Recent immigration into the United States rivals in size the great waves at the turn of the century. In part this counterbalances the rapid aging of the population caused by reduction in fertility and mortality. Over a quarter (28.4 percent) of the U.S. population growth arises from immigration. Immigrants are typically young individuals. In addition, Latin-American immigrants, which comprise 35 percent of legal migrants, have a higher than average fertility. Among all women in the United States in 1980 between thirty-five and forty-nine years of age, the lifetime fertility rate was

2.6. In comparison, Latin-American immigrant women in the same age group experience a lifetime fertility rate of 3.1.

Dependency ratios displayed in Table 1 are a source of some debate. Increase in the old age dependency ratio has many concerned for the future of Social Security and Medicare programs, yet others point to the dramatic decrease occurring in the youthful dependency ratio. The overall dependency ratio is less volatile, leading some to suggest that aging of the nation will not be burdensome. Still it is worth noting that youth and older adults tend to obtain economic support from different sources. The young are supported by their families and by local and state taxes that subsidize education, whereas the older adult population is supported through intergenerational transfers (taxing the working-age population to pay benefits to the retired by way of Social Security and Medicare), through pension programs, and by their own savings and investments. Hence the nation overall may carry the same amount of dependency in the past as it will in the future (comparing 1920 with 2030 and beyond), but the sources of support are far different and may not easily be transferred from one generation to another.

Recent Factors in U.S. Population Aging

Complex forces are unfolding that have and will continue to rapidly age the U.S. population. The nation was growing older through much of the early part of this century until after World War II. The post–World War II baby boom, which reached its peak in the late 1950s, turned the aging of the population around and helped make the U.S. population younger. The migrants coming to shore in record numbers during the first decade of this century were growing older and contributed to the aging of the nation after World War I. Fertility dropped during the 1920s, which some attribute to a surge of feminist perspectives in that decade; then, especially low birth rates occurred during the depression years; and with the mobilization of men, there were relatively few births during the war years. The post–World War II demobilization, the economic upswing during the 1950s, and a resurgence of traditional family values spurred the baby boom. At mid-century the aging of the U.S. population stalled for a decade and a half.

The structure of a population refers to characteristics of the group under study such as the age mix, ratio of men to women, or marital status.

COPYRIGHT MARIANNE GONTARZ

The aging of U.S. population has resumed and is being driven forward by a number of variables. The post–War World II baby boomers have aged thirty years and are now moving into middle age. In two more decades (about 2010) the baby boom generation will start to retire. The aging of the baby boom generation is accented by the "birth dearth" that followed; if the 1950s saw a return to traditional family values, the women's movement of the 1960s had an effect on the life and fertility of the baby boom generation's leading edge.

As the nation moved through the 1970s and into the 1980s, baby boom women increasingly enrolled in college. In 1959 only 5.9 percent of women completed four years of college; by 1989, 18.1 percent had obtained a bachelor's degree—an increase by a factor of 2.2. In comparison, according to the U.S. Bureau of the Census, males going to college increased by a factor of 1.5. Median age of marriage among females increased from 20.3 years old in 1960 to 23.7 years old by 1989. According to the National Center for Health Statistics, a clear pattern is emerging of delayed fertility among college-educated women.

Another ten to fifteen years will tell if this deferred fertility will mean reduced fertility, further accentuating the aging of our population. Even women not motivated by career interests are sharing the labor force with their husbands in order to make ends meet and achieve the middle-class dream. Divorce also propels women into the work force, and according the National Center for Health Statistics, divorce has doubled in the last three decades, moving from 9.2 per 1,000 married women fifteen years and older in 1960, to 20.7 in 1988. Hence far more women are working now than in the past, from 34.9 percent in 1960 to 57.4 percent in 1989. Not surprisingly, the fertility of women age thirty-five to forty-four in the work force (2,034 births per 1,000 women) is lower than that of women age thirty-five to forty-four who are not in the labor force (2,417 births per 1,000 women).

Along with decreased fertility, the reduction in mortality is aging the United States. The battle against acute infectious disease is about over, and so life expectancy at birth has not increased as fast in the second part of this century as it did in the first. Nevertheless, it is still growing and helps age the nation. Medical science now turns its attention to the reduction of chronic mortality, and at age sixty-five life expectancy is now being extended.

More Life to Live: Some Differences in Life Expectancy
According to the National Center for Health Statistics, in 1991 the United States had the largest expenditures for health care in the world ($751.8 billion), with 13.2 percent being the greatest percent of the gross national product (GNP) devoted to health care, and at $2,868 the largest per capita expenditures on health care. Yet compared to other industrialized nations the United States has a rather low life expectancy. At birth male life expectancy is twenty-second and female is sixteenth in the world. Life expectancy in the United States at age sixty-five ranks twenty-fifth for males and tenth for females in comparison to other countries. This disparity between the nation's output for health care and the outcome in terms of life expectancy is typically explained by the conjunction of three factors.

First is the issue of lifestyle, which encompasses such well-known factors as smoking, drug abuse, malnutrition, lack of exercise, and the often unrecognized factor of violence. The U.S. homicide rate is ten times that of the Europeans and is the tenth biggest killer in the United States. Among our young, murder is one of the most significant causes of death, ranked third among five- to fourteen-year-olds and second among fifteen- to twenty-four-year-olds. Since these deaths occur so young in life, a reduction in violent deaths along with mortality from motor vehicle accidents would probably make the single largest contribution to life expectancy at birth. In addition, those in poverty typically lack knowledge about health care, often lead deleterious lifestyles, and cannot afford to purchase health care. Finally, most of the nations that have higher life expectancies than the United States have either a national health care system or national insurance plan. Such mechanisms insure universal access to health care. In 1989 some 15.7 percent of those under age sixty-five did not have health care coverage in the United States. And those who cannot gain access to health care are at greater risk of premature death.

Life expectancy is not shared equally by all in the United States. Life expectancy is greater for females than for males. In 1991, on the average, at birth a women could expect to live 6.9 years longer than her male counterpart. The differential in life expectancy is down from 7.7 years in 1970.

The degree to which nature or nurture influences this difference is not clear. The expansion of the difference in male to female mortality in this century (differential mortality in 1900 was two years) has been explained in part by the reduction of maternal mortality (death during childbirth). Researchers detailed the widening of the mortality differential between the sexes as attributable to degenerative lung and cardiovascular diseases. Based on the prevalence of smoking among males and its link to those disorders, researchers consider smoking an important external factor in the difference in life expectancy between the sexes. But this may now be changing based on the increased prevalence of cigarette smoking among females since World War II. Lung cancer recently became the number one cancer killer among females.

African Americans and whites display stark differences in life expectancy of over 7.0 years at birth in 1991. Since the differential mortality in 1900 was 14.6 years, the evidence over the course of this century indicates that the divergence has been reduced as the burden of the racial difference in society has decreased. Still, a report in the *Journal of the American Medical Association* ascribes 38 percent of the differential mortality to the socioeconomic differ-

ence between the races. An additional 31 percent of the mortality difference can be ascribed to six well-known risk factors (smoking, systolic blood pressure, cholesterol level, body-mass index, alcohol intake, and diabetes), some of which are certainly directly tied to lifestyle.

Much attention has been given to the Acquired Immune Deficiency Syndrome (AIDS) epidemic and the inevitable mortality associated with the disease. Since its recognition only a decade ago, AIDS has become the ninth largest cause of mortality in the United States. With a death rate of 11.7 per 100,000, it accounts for 1.4 percent of the mortality in the nation. Yet the overall death rate in the United States is 860.3 per 100,000, with disease of the heart (285.7 per 100,000) contributing 33.2 percent of the mortality. Cardiovascular disease is followed by neoplasms (such as cancers; 204.1 per 100,000) with 23.7 percent of the mortality, and cerebrovascular diseases (such as strokes; 56.9 per 100,000) at 6.6 percent of the nation's mortality. Compared to the big three chronic diseases, AIDS is a relatively small contributor to U.S. mortality, yet it is an infectious disease. Among the reproductive age groups, AIDS is a much more significant component of mortality.

No doubt AIDS will make a significant impact on the lives of millions of Americans, though it is too early to fully assess the impact of the disease on the aging of America. How fast the disease spreads through the population will be influenced by how quickly and to what degree changes in lifestyle occur, not to mention how soon a vaccination or cure for the disease is discovered.

Gender, Mortality, and Health

One of the most established gender differences in modern society is the considerable gap in life expectancy between men and women. In the United States, for example, women are expected to live approximately seven years longer than men. In 1986, the life expectancy at birth of white women was 78.8 years compared to 72.0 for white men. The corresponding figures for non-whites are 75.1 and 67.2 years. The gender gap in life expectancy at birth increased over much of this century and was at its highest around 1980, showing modest declines during the 1980s. Recent declines are the result of relatively larger gains made by men.

For some time, demographers have identified a reversal in the life expectancy of whites and non-whites at advanced ages referred to as the racial mortality crossover. It appears that non-whites have lower life expectancies at every age than whites until about ages seventy-five or eighty when a reversal is observed wherein the life expectancy of non-whites becomes greater. This reversal is thought to be associated with higher early mortality of non-whites that leads to the survival to advanced ages of only the hardiest people.

Why Do Women Live Longer than Men?

This question has occupied the minds of scholars and researchers for some time. There is considerable debate in the literature regarding the relative importance of specific factors, but there is general agreement that both biological (genetic or hormonal) and psychosocial factors are involved. With respect to the latter, it is agreed that men's greater rates of smoking and other negative health behaviors account for some of their excess mortality. However, increases in smoking rates among women after World War II have contributed to the fact that lung cancer mortality among women has become equal to (if not greater than) breast cancer mortality. Nevertheless, lung cancer mortality continues to be considerably higher among men than among women.

Other factors with psychosocial origins explaining men's lower life expectancy include considerably higher mortality rates from accidents, suicide, and other violent causes. A recent and emerging cause of death afflicting men at much higher rates than women is AIDS.

Although there is agreement in the literature that psychosocial factors do not account for the total gender gap in life expectancy, biological factors are also involved, particularly with respect to mortality from heart disease. Recent studies indicate, for example, that an excess male mortality from diseases of the heart is observed among nonsmokers. It appears that the female advantage is related to the protective influences of sex hormones.

While biological factors probably account for much of the female advantage in heart disease mortality, there is not sufficient convincing evidence that they also contribute to women's overall advantage in mortality from cancer, where psychosocial factors are probably more important. Smoking rates appear to be the greatest contributor to gender differences in cancer mortality, and women's higher smoking rates after World War II have contributed to increases in women's lung cancer mortality in recent years.

Differences in mortality rates and life expectancy provide only a partial picture of gender differences in health in middle and old age. Also important is the differential prevalence of chronic conditions, many of which are nonfatal but disabling nevertheless.

Although women's greater longevity can be explained to a large extent by psychosocial factors, genetic and hormonal factors are also important, especially with regard to their advantage in mortality from disease of the heart.

Louis Harris

Pollster

Go all out, flat out. That's the way to lead life. If you're wrong, so be it, but if you're right, at least you've done it. All out, flat out means going at 100 percent of your capacity. I really believe that."

Pollster Louis Harris was born in 1921 to a prosperous family who lost everything during a bank run in 1928, a week after his father died. Harris was seven at the time. The family's only source of income during the depression was the rent on a commercial garage, but the renter rarely paid; Harris resorted to selling magazine subscriptions to support his family and save money for college.

Initially Harris dreamed of becoming a lawyer, but that aspiration evolved into a desire to be a journalist. Harris worked for his high school newspaper, then got a paying job as the Hill House High School correspondent for the *New Haven Register*. He used his earnings to buy himself a second-hand typewriter to teach himself to type; it cost $8.75, a small fortune in 1933. "That was blood money," Harris reflects. He later became editor of the school magazine and associate editor of the newspaper.

Harris studied at the University of North Carolina at Chapel Hill, where he got "a wild but very formative college education." He served in the navy, for which he received a commendation, then worked briefly for the American Veterans Committee as its research and program director. One day he noticed an article in the *New York Herald Tribune* about a poll that had been done on veterans. Harris went to see the pollster, Elmo Roper, who offered Harris a job as his assistant.

Harris started his own polling firm in 1956, Louis Harris & Associates in New York, "on a wing and a prayer." His clients had encouraged him to open his own office, and they supported his business in the early days of the firm. Soon he was doing extremely well, polling for a variety of political candidates and for the American Federation of Labor and Congress of Industrial Organizations. Eventually, as the accuracy of his polls made him famous, he became chief pollster for John F. Kennedy's presidential campaign in 1960.

Polling is his calling, Harris believes, and he works tirelessly at it to keep on top of all national trends and attitudes: "Data is always talking to me. I have a feel for what people are trying to say. I try to glean it out. . . . I always worked hard. I thought nothing of working until three in the morning and going to work in the morning and working hard all day. It's always been work, work, work for me."

Harris has advanced the field of polling dramatically by initiating such changes as using computers to assist the CBS Vote Profile Analysis. He is also the author of six books on contemporary American issues and has written a syndicated weekly column called "The Harris Poll" since 1963.

—*Lydia Brontë*

Women's greater suffering from nonfatal conditions is not easily understood. Perhaps their greater longevity is important. Recent gains in life expectancy appear to have been accompanied by more illness and disability in the older years and not by a compression of morbidity into fewer years just prior to death as some researchers would suggest. In the years to come, it seems likely to predict that increases in life expectancy will be accompanied by a greater concentration of infirmities in old age, particularly among women. Medical professionals, as well as policymakers, need to be less concerned with lengthening life and more concerned with preventing disabilities and with improving or maintaining older people's quality of life.

A discussion of the composition of our aging society often leads to comparing the older age group to other age groups or strata. Focusing on the differences between age strata tends to obscure the variance among older adults. This section reviews some of the major variations within the older adult population in the United States.

Age

A common misconception about older adults is that the one thing they all have in common is being old. Yet the amount of time from the artificially defined beginning of old age at sixty-five to the maximum expectation of the life span encompasses over thirty-five years. Sociologist Bernice Neugarten helped gerontologists think about the diversity among older adults by suggesting there are significant differences between the young-old (fifty-five to seventy-four years old) and the old-old (seventy-five years old and older). Considering the growing percent of the population over eighty-five, sociologists Matilda White Riley and Marvin Suzman added the concept of the oldest-old to gerontological jargon.

The oldest-old are intensive users of medical and social services. Those eighty-five and over have the highest rates of functional disability, physician visits, hospitalizations, length of stay in hospital, nursing home placement, and poverty rates. The compression of mortality into advanced old age has produced the fastest growing age group, whose members are frail and in great need of supportive services. This presents the nation with serious policy implications. High private and public cost of supporting this age group has caused some to suggest controversial solutions, such as altering the basic premise of Social Security and Medicare by requiring financial need rather than age as a criterion for benefits. Ethicist Daniel Callahan, in *Setting Limits*, suggests even more radically that there may come a time in an individual's life when all but simple comforting medical care is withheld, and nature is allowed to run its course.

Race

Conceptual development in the field of ethnicity and aging remains limited. Early efforts have their origins not in an intellectual tradition, but in the efforts of certain advocacy groups to highlight the double disadvantage of being old and being African American. The well-known double-jeopardy hypothesis growing out of these efforts has been applied to a variety of ethnic groups and has been discussed extensively in the literature. The double-jeopardy hypothesis fits under a larger framework often referred to as the multiple hierarchy stratification model, which treats ethnicity as one source of inequality among other social structural variables—namely, social class, gender, and age. The bottom of the social hierarchy is thus occupied by poor, older, ethnic minority women, while the top is occupied by middle- and upper-class middle-aged (or younger) white men.

Another broad theoretical perspective grew out of the modernization theory of aging. This general theory of aging predicts that the status of the elderly declines in the historical transition from traditional agrarian, rural societies to more complex, industrialized modern ones. According to modernization theory, technology increases life expectancy, and consequently the numbers and proportions of older people who have to compete for a shrinking number of jobs. Older people are thrown out of the labor force and thus command less power in relation to younger generations. This kind of perspective can be applied to ethnic groups immigrating to a modern society from a simpler one. Thus, it may be predicted that the status of the elderly in such immigrant groups will decline in the modern society. The theory can also be applied to so-called traditional ethnic groups within a society who may be undergoing a process of assimilation into the larger society. An example would be Mexican Americans in the United States, most of whom are U.S.-born.

Older people today are predominately white, as demonstrated by the data from the 1990 census (see Table 2). However, because migration streams into this country have shifted in this century from Europe to Latin America and Asia, and since minority groups traditionally have had higher fertility rates than white Americans, literally the complexion of the country will change. And over the course of time additional color will be added to the aging of America. While today approximately 14 percent of our older population is from minority groups, that figure will double in fifty years, and by the year 2050, 32 percent of the older adult population will be from minority groups.

Table 2: Older Population by Age, Race, and Sex: 1990

Age	Total Male	Total Female	Total White	White Male	White Female	Total African American	African-American Male	African-American Female
50+	28,061,328	35,678,939	55,536,383	24,537,888	30,998,495	5,681,930	2,368,572	3,313,358
55+	22,546,590	29,843,164	46,031,512	19,880,504	26,151,008	4,502,919	1,836,596	2,666,323
60+	17,512,220	24,345,778	37,063,096	15,549,693	21,513,403	3,470,170	1,379,677	2,090,493
65+	12,565,173	18,676,658	27,851,973	11,214,909	16,637,064	2,508,551	965,432	1,543,119
85+	857,698	2,222,467	2,788,052	764,450	2,023,602	230,183	68,592	161,591

Age	American Indian Eskimo, & Aleut (AIEA)	AIEA Male	AIEA Female	Asian & Pacific Islander (API)	API Male	API Female	Other Race	Other Male	Other Female
50+	304,375	138,523	165,852	1,235,259	564,180	671,079	982,320	452,165	530,155
55+	227,661	101,635	126,026	923,608	412,095	511,513	704,054	315,760	388,294
60+	165,842	72,281	93,561	672,975	298,586	374,389	485,915	211,983	273,932
65+	114,453	48,089	66,364	454,458	204,447	250,011	312,396	132,296	180,100
85+	9,205	3,274	5,931	29,738	12,399	17,339	22,987	8,983	14,004

Age	Hispanic (Any Race)	Hispanic Male	Hispanic Female	Total
50+	3,110,222	1,402,955	1,707,267	63,740,267
55+	2,354,233	1,038,736	1,315,497	52,389,754
60+	1,714,925	736,365	978,560	41,857,998
65+	1,161,283	481,409	679,874	31,241,831
85+	94,564	33,497	61,067	3,080,165

Source: U.S. Bureau of the Census. 1990 Census of the Population.

Sex/Gender

While a person's sex—male or female—is fundamentally a biological factor, gender is a social and cultural factor. Both sex and gender have long been of interest to gerontologists as ways of explaining differences (explanatory variables) in various aging-related phenomena, including social roles, health and mortality, economic status, retirement, and family relationships. In the instance of mortality, it has long been recognized that factors of sex and gender account for differences in life expectancy and result in considerably more older women than older men in the population. The sex ratio (number of men per one hundred women) decreases steadily in old age, reaching only thirty-nine for persons aged eight-five and over. This dramatic imbalance demonstrates that what are typically thought of as universal problems of old age are, in fact, more likely to be women's experience, such as widowhood, social isolation, poverty, and institutionalization.

Despite the fact that there are many recognized differences between men and women in old age and in the aging process, there is surprisingly limited literature documenting and explaining gender diversity in gerontology. This is particularly evident in theoretical development in the field. For example, there is scant reference to gender differences in a recent important volume on theories of aging. Moreover, the subfield of gender studies in aging remains undeveloped. The following section outlines the development of interest in gender issues by gerontologists; it also discusses gender differences in health and longevity, economic factors, and family relationships.

Throughout the entire life cycle, one's sex is an important variable influencing one's social experience. Contemporary older adult women were raised at a time when gender was more of a dividing factor in the social world than it is currently. As people advance into late life, differential mortality makes growing old more and more often women's work. The sex ratio becomes ever more extreme moving from the young-old to the oldest-old. Between sixty-five to sixty-nine years old the sex ratio is eighty-four; for those ten years older it declines to sixty-five males per one hundred females, and at eighty-five and older the ratio plummets to thirty-nine males for every one hundred females.

Marital Status

As the sex ratio increasingly favors females in terms of longevity, it reflects a change in marital status. With advancing age, marriage gives way to widowhood; at all ages men are far more likely to be married. At ages sixty-five to seventy-four, 80.6 percent of men and 53.3 percent of women are married, but by eighty-five-plus only 47.9 percent of men and 8.8 percent of women live with their spouses. Further review of the data reveals that most of the elderly were once married (94 percent to 96 percent). Compared to present standards, few have divorced, an even rarer event among the old-

est-old. Overall the patterns maintain, but clearly there is variation between whites, African Americans, and those of Hispanic origin.

As people advance into late life, differential mortality makes growing old more and more often women's work.

Household Composition and Housing

Living arrangements of older adults reflect marital status. Differential mortality heightens the chances of a woman living alone. A slightly higher percentage of women not living with their spouses tend to live alone rather than with other family members, compared to the men not living with their spouses. Men are slightly more likely than women to live with other family members in later life. It is also much more probable for members of the African-American and Hispanic communities to live with family members other than their spouses than their counterparts in the white community.

According to the book *Aging America: Trends and Projections*, of those older households in the community, 76 percent live in owner-occupied units, and the rest are renters. There is diversity within the age groups. Those seventy-five years of age and older are more typically renters, compared to the sixty-five- to seventy-four-year group (31 percent versus 21 percent). Women were renters more frequently than were men (35 percent versus 17 percent). This, in part, is a reflection of widowhood, since among those living alone, 62 percent are renters, as compared to those living with spouses, where 88 percent are homeowners. Of the owner-occupied households, 83 percent are owned outright. Twenty-nine percent of elderly rental units benefit from some sort of housing subsidy or rent control.

Approximately 5 percent of the population sixty-five and over is in nursing homes at any one moment. However, this seemingly low percentage is misleading and diminishes concern for issues of institutionalization in later life. At any given moment, only 5 percent of the sixty-five-plus age group is institutionalized, but 22 percent of the age eighty-five-plus group lives in nursing homes. It has been estimated that of those sixty-five-plus in 1990, 43 percent will live some portion of their remaining life in a nursing home. This illustration underscores how deceptive statistics about the sixty-five-plus age group can be. Growing old is not static; it is a dynamic process.

Family Structure and Family Relationships

As already noted, the low economic status of many elderly women is the result of their marital status and living arrangements. For many reasons, such as higher economic resources of males, Social Security programs that favor married couples, and savings from joint living arrangements, women who are married fare much better economically than women who are not, a matter that is complex and goes beyond marital status and living arrangements.

Yet the correlation between living arrangements and economic well-being is high. In 1987, 75.1 percent of all American men age sixty-five and over were married and living with their spouses. The comparable figure for older women was only 29.8 percent. A total of 48.7 percent of all older women were widowed, with the comparable figure for men being only 13.9 percent. These differences are associated with women's greater life expectancy, their greater propensity to marry men older than themselves, and men's greater propensity to remarry (typically younger women) after they become widowed.

While disabled and demented men are most likely to be cared for by their wives, disabled women are more likely to be cared for by an adult child or by another relative. Caregiving of elderly people in modern society is almost exclusively a task carried out by women, many of them elderly themselves. Although some elderly disabled women are cared for by their husbands and some by their daughters or other relatives, many become institutionalized, particularly those who are single or without children.

The greater likelihood of women living alone, coupled with their greater longevity, is a major factor behind their much greater rate of nursing home institutionalization: approximately three out of four nursing home residents are women.

The growth of the older population and its greater longevity with more disability concentrated in the older years means that the burden of caregiving is increasingly becoming greater. While institutional care is increasing, approximately 80 percent of long-term care is provided by family members, most of them women. Supporting this care and relieving its burden has not been a policy goal in the United States. Researchers note that health and social benefits are allocated on the basis of the older person's health and economic status and not on the basis of his or her family care situation. Thus, Medicare and Medicaid fund institutional care but not in-home care, day care, and other services that could relieve the burden on caregivers.

That women provide more care is, among other things, a sign of their greater involvement in social networks. It is well established that older women have more people in their support networks, they engage in more frequent contact with others, and they give and receive greater support. Women's more extensive social networks are important in helping them adapt to declines in health and to losses such as widowhood. At the same time, men are more likely to remarry after widowhood.

The advantage of older women in social networks and supports is not without costs. Emerging literature suggests that women's greater embeddedness in social networks may take its toll on their physical and emotional well-being because of the greater reliance on them. This appears to be particularly the case in more family-oriented populations such as Mexican Americans and Italian Americans.

The literature on family relationships of older people has given considerable attention to relationships with their children (and, to a lesser extent, grandchildren). An important concept describing such relationships is *intergenerational solidarity.* One dimension of intergenerational solidarity is *associational solidarity,* which reflects the observable activities or encounters that characterize the interaction between family members. The literature generally shows relatively high associational tendency for elderly parents to live in quarters independent from their children. The literature also shows that women, both older and middle-aged, are more likely than men to be in contact with family members in other generations. Research shows that this holds also for African Americans and Mexican Americans, with the latter exhibiting the highest levels of associational solidarity among major ethnic groups.

Another dimension of intergenerational solidarity is *affectual solidarity,* or the subjective judgments concerning the quality of family interaction—the perception of closeness, warmth, and satisfaction with interaction. The limited evidence available suggests rather high levels of affection between parents and children, particularly between elderly mothers and their daughters.

Educational Attainment

Successive cohorts both among the nation's younger and older adult populations are better educated. The gap in median years of school widens from 1950 to 1970; since 1970 the gap has narrowed. A similar pattern is found for the percent completing high school, although that divergence peaks in 1980.

Women's more extensive social networks are important in helping them adapt to declines in health and to losses such as widowhood.

The initial difference in education between the two age groups is an interesting example of *cohort effect*. The divergence between the young and old arises not only because of biological or social maturation (*age effect*) but also from the influence of socio-historical events on different age cohorts. In this case the widening gap in education between the generations (1950 to 1980) arises from the contrasting experiences of childhood and adolescence for those sixty-five and over and the younger age groups. People born before the turn of this century and in its first two decades grew up in the transitional phase of late industrialization, when child labor laws were first enforced and mass education became compulsory. In comparison to the younger age groups, the earlier cohorts of today's elderly grew up at a time when education was a luxury, not a requirement.

Obtaining a college education continues to demonstrate increased divergence. This also is an artifact of cohort effect. In this case the younger generations benefited from the growth in recent decades of public higher education. The difference between the generations is further accented by the disruption of the life cycle in a whole cohort of young adult caused by the Great Depression. Education and career plans of many young men and some women were radically altered in the 1930s as they and their families were forced to adapt to the economic downturn.

On an individual level, in part, the experiences of later life vary from cohort to cohort as each one is better educated. Each new cohort brings a different perspective to the challenges of later life arising from the abilities and expectations associated with education. Significant change can be expected from the impact of better educated older cohorts on society. Education is associated with increased participation in politics and the electoral process, more aggressive health-seeking behavior, different styles of consumerism, and the desire for lifelong learning.

Labor Force Participation

Active involvement in the labor force decreases quickly after age sixty, yet up to a quarter of males work after the traditional retirement age and 10 percent beyond seventy years old. Generally those who continue to work in later life either tend to have a professional and rewarding position or are in economic need. Women have lower labor force participation rates than men throughout the later portion of the life cycle. This trend may change as middle-aged women (forty-five to sixty-four) become well represented in the labor force. As of 1989, 70.5 percent of all women between the ages of forty-five and fifty-four were in the labor force.

Income Distribution

A conceptual framework that has relevance to the study of both gender and ethnicity is the *multiple hierarchy stratification* perspective, which views gender as a source of inequality along with race/ethnicity, class, and age. Although this formulation is relatively recent, social scientists have long recognized that gender stratifies societies according to such variables as power, prestige, and income. Unlike the case with life expectancy, in modern society women have generally been disadvantaged relative to men in these social and economic variables.

Women's socioeconomic disadvantage in old age represents a continuation of disadvantages experienced throughout the life course. While the economic status of all elderly in the United

States has risen both in absolute terms and in relation to younger persons, a significant gender gap clearly remains. The gender gap is particularly large with respect to women living alone. For example, in 1987 white married elderly couples had a median income of $21,000, while single white elderly women had an income of only $8,000. The situation was much worse for African-American elderly women who had a median income of only $5,000. Approximately 80 percent of elderly women had yearly incomes under $13,000 in 1987.

The sharp differences in income by marital status noted above are usually given as evidence that widowhood causes drastic declines in women's income, since after their husbands' deaths pension income ceases and income from other sources declines. While this is true to a large extent, this hypothesis is based on cross-sectional data taken at a given point in time.

Households headed by persons over age sixty-five have median incomes ($22,806) that are 63 percent of the incomes of households headed by those twenty-five to sixty-four years old ($36,058). Still within the elderly population there is a great diversity of income. Median income is highest among the white, younger elderly, and those who live within intact families. Regardless of the other characteristics such as age, race, or marital status, women always have lower economic resources than men have. Several of these variables do come together in a compounding effect and create extreme economic hardship for the oldest-old widowed women, and this is particularly true for African-American women.

Fewer older adults live in poverty today than in previous times. Most of the decline in poverty took place between 1966 (when 28.5 percent of our population sixty-five-plus was in poverty) to 1978 (when the poverty rate dropped to 14 percent). Thereafter, it drifted upward to 15.7 percent in 1980, and then dropped to a 1989 low of 11 percent. In the same time period, poverty among eighteen- to sixty-five-year-olds was less volatile: 10.5 percent in 1966, reaching a high of 12.4 percent in 1983 and settling at 10.2 percent in 1989. The pattern of poverty in later life mirrors the income distribution: the oldest, the widowed, and minority women are most apt to experience poverty. This leads some to suggest that there is a triple-jeopardy status for being old, a

Elizabeth Janeway

Writer and social commentator

SNAPSHOT

I guess I always thought I'd like to be a writer . . . most of my family had a kind of capacity to write, the way some families can sing or have musical talents."

Elizabeth Janeway was a highly successful novelist for twenty years and then became even more successful writing nonfiction. Born in New York City to a large, slightly eccentric family, Janeway became accustomed to the idea of writing early in her life. Later, winning a short story contest at Barnard College "gave me a sense of assurance that I could get published, which was a valuable thing," Janeway recalls.

Janeway attended Swarthmore for a year before the depression, then wrote advertising copy "for Abraham and Strauss' basement" and earned a degree in history at Barnard. Then she worked part-time at Book-of-the-Month Club, devoting the rest of her time to her first novel, *The Walsh Girls.*

"I wrote it over seven years and I wrote it three times," Janeway recalls. "I didn't know how to write a novel; I had to figure out how to do it, and I am a rewriter by nature. I finally finished it because I was about to have a second child, and I sort of thought, you can have one child and still think of yourself as a writer, but if you have two children, you are a housewife, dear, and you'd better face up to it. And I didn't want to. So I finished it very fast the winter I was pregnant with Bill. I completed it about two weeks before he was born." *The Walsh Girls* was featured on the first page of the *New York Times Book Review,* and Janeway subsequently wrote six more novels and four children's books.

In the 1960s, Janeway began to take stock of the massive upheavals occurring in society. "It came to me that it was going to be hard to write fiction, because so much in the world was changing," she says. "Not just the outer things, but the basic premises fiction takes for granted. So I decided to turn to nonfiction, and wrote *Man's World, Woman's Place*, which presented a view of the changes in those fundamental assumptions—what they had been, how they had affected men and women, and how we looked at the world. Again, I had to write it three times—learning how to write nonfiction is very hard if you have been used to the advantages that fiction gives—characters and dialogue and suspense and narrative that hold people's attention. If you don't have those things and if you have to do it on your own flat feet, it's harder." It wasn't long before Janeway made a lateral career change, from being a fiction writer to being a social commentator. She has written books on the women's movement and on other current issues, including *The Powers of the Weak*, which examines how subordinate groups in any society use their powerlessness.

Janeway and her husband, Eliot Janeway, have recently moved from their five-story house into an apartment. Now that the move is completed, Janeway is getting ready to start another book.

—*Lydia Brontë*

woman (who is more likely to become a widow), and a person of minority status.

Older families are not as liable to be as far below the poverty line as those families headed by a twenty-five- to sixty-four-year-old. The elderly are slightly better off than the general population in terms of living above the poverty line, yet they are far more likely to live within 124 percent of the poverty line (7.7 percent versus 4.1 percent) in what is called near poverty, or between 125 and 149 percent of poverty (8.1 percent versus 4.1 percent).

Fewer older adults live in poverty today than in previous times.

The significance of near poverty is that, for a matter of a few hundred or thousand dollars a year, one is no longer eligible for certain federal government benefits such as Section VIII housing, food stamps, Medicaid, and Supplemental Security Income. Perhaps instead of a cut-off line, benefit levels should taper off between poverty line and the top end of near poverty.

Interconnected Factors

This section has focused on three broad areas where research has shown great gender diversity: longevity and health, economic status, and family relationships, and these conceptual perspectives have emphasized women's disadvantage.

But the extent of disadvantage or advantage in this area is not simple. There is no doubt, for example, that women live longer than men, but at the same time they do so with more disability. In the economic arena, it is clear that older women and women in general are severely disadvantaged. As for the area of family relationships, the picture is mixed: while women have more contact with family members, their greater embeddedness in social and family networks often takes its toll on their physical and psychological well being. Moreover, because of their greater rates of widowhood, many more older women than men spend their later years institutionalized.

Health, economic, and family factors are interconnected. To understand gender differences in one arena, one needs to study gender differences in the other arena. Taken together, the picture that emerges is one in which older women occupy an inferior position in modern society. Social policies in place, at least in the United States, often discriminate against older women and further contribute to their low status in society. Older women and women in general are indeed a minority group in a sociological sense, much like many ethnic groups often are.

—*William H. Haas III, Ph.D; Charles F. Longino, Jr., Ph.D.; Kyriakos S. Markides, Ph.D.*

Ask any person what growing old in America means, and you're sure to hear a number of different responses. Most obviously, aging can be viewed as a biological phenomenon involving maturation, maturity, and the decline of the human body and its various functions. Aging can also be viewed as a process of mental development that involves a great deal of continuity in functioning, some declines in functioning, and some increases in functioning. Aging is also viewed from a developmental perspective, which involves how people adapt to their environment as they grow older, and the various "coping styles" they adopt to do so. Or aging can be viewed as a social phenomenon in which chronological age is used to define people's capabilities and opportunities.

These perspectives come into play in any discussion of what it means to be an older adult today. Although categorizing the concept of aging into three compartmentalized units, if you will, is a convenient and standard approach taken by social scientists and layperson alike, they are limiting in and of themselves. Because attitudes about the very nature of growing old are undergoing tremendous changes, when the four basic physical, mental, developmental, and social aspects are examined together, they provide an enlightened perspective that can be used to better understand what aging in the 1990s really means.

The physical aspects of aging as a process of maturation,

maturity, and decline is useful for guiding the work of physiologists, and it tends to accurately describe what happens to various bodily functions in general over the life span. But for most purposes the maturation-maturity-aging aspect has two serious limitations. First, because there is so much variability among people and between functions even within the same person, this perspective is not very useful for deciding what to expect in specific individuals. Second, because many declines in physical functions can be completely or partially compensated for, a discussion of physical aging greatly overestimates the effects of aging on social functioning. Although many people aren't aware of it, social impairments due to aging do not become widespread until well after age seventy-five.

Mental aging can be viewed either as a process of change in specific mental factors such as memory or motor coordination, or as a more global process of evolution in the mind and its various dimensions. From the perspective of specific traits, aging has a wide range of results. Functions such as vision, reaction time, or memory that have a strong dependence on the body and its level of functioning are much more likely to decline with age than are learned functions such as vocabulary, creativity, or problem solving that depend more on the mind and are more easily maintained by practice. Because some mental functions increase steadily with age, some remain relatively constant, and some decline, we cannot assume the effects of aging on mental capacities to follow any single pattern.

From a developmental perspective, aging can be viewed either as a process of moving through several discrete stages or as a continuous process of unfolding. Aging can solidify identity by providing a large amount of experience about the self. The reduction in job and parenting responsibilities that often accompanies aging can reduce the potential for conflict among the various aspects of identity. More often than not, aging is more a process of identity maintenance than a process of identity formation.

Social aging involves the use of age by society to assign people to roles based on their chronological age or life stage. Age is used to determine eligibility, evaluate appropriateness, and modify expectations with respect to various roles in society. Because roles largely define the participation of people in their society, aging is a socially satisfying process to many people because it increases the duration and therefore the security of their role relationships.

The life course is an ideal sequence of roles a person is expected to play as he or she moves through life. There are many versions of the life course, depending on the gender, ethnicity, or social class of the individual. And then there are our own personal decisions that help shape the course of our lives. As people grow older, their accumulated decisions about various life course options result in increased differentiation among them. It becomes challenging to define "age norms," but as age increases, opportunities for formal socialization decrease. Role anticipation allows people to prepare for and to smooth life transitions. Adaptation and negotiation processes allow people to fit themselves to new roles and vice versa.

Aging can have both positive and negative outcomes; it is mainly positive for most people; and it is unpredictable for any given individual. Variety among people increases with age as a result of biological, psychological, developmental, and social processes that operate differentially. Because no single set of assumptions about the effects of aging can capture the reality of aging, this chapter offers a number of combined perspectives.

It is common to think of our life span as having a period of maturation in which the person develops capabilities, a period of maturity in which the person exercises full capacity, and a period of aging in which the person experiences declining capacity. This view is based on the biological characteristics of life in both animals and plants, but it is too simplistic to apply to the human life. Biological aging is the result of many processes that progress at different rates. For example, the kidneys typically show diminished functioning much sooner than the skin does. In addition, maturity occurs for different physical functions at different ages. For instance, people usually reach sexual maturity several years before they reach full height. To confuse matters further, most physical functions vary quite a bit among individuals at all stages of life.

The Three Processes of Aging

Aging is a socially satisfying process to many people because it increases the duration and therefore the security of their role relationships.

COPYRIGHT MARIANNE GONTARZ

Examining the effects of aging on mental functioning shows that some capabilities diminish with aging, others increase, and some remain relatively constant throughout adulthood. For example, accuracy of visual perception generally declines with age, vocabulary usually increases, and lifestyle habits tend to remain relatively constant throughout adulthood. Variability for mental functions is as great as that for physical functions.

On the other hand, social aging is largely an arbitrary process of defining what is appropriate for or expected of people of various ages, based only very loosely on concrete information about the capabilities of people of various ages. Thus, airline pilots must retire at age sixty even though nearly all are still quite capable of effective performance. The age when young people are considered old enough to marry varies from age thirteen to sixteen in some subcultures, to twenty-five or thirty in others. As a result social aging adds yet another dimension of variability to an already complex issue.

Dual Aspects of Aging

Aging is not one process but many, and it has both positive and negative aspects. On the positive side, aging increases experience and thus brings opportunities to gain wisdom or to become quite skilled at subtle arts and crafts ranging from politics to music. Wisdom and experience can give an older person the kind of long-range perspective that is invaluable in an adviser or mentor. Older people can also be keepers of tradition. They have invaluable information about many unrecorded events that have happened over the years in families, workplaces, communities, and the nation. Aging can also bring personal peace and mellowing. Once the heavy responsibilities of employment and childrearing are set aside, later life can be a time of freedom and opportunity. On the negative side, aging for some people is experienced as a series of losses. They may lose physical or mental capacities, what they perceive as their beauty; they may outlive their spouse and friends; or they may lose their positions in organizations, opportunity for employment, and the income that is associated with their working lifestyle. Aging is not predictable. For some it is a wonderful progression of a full life, for others it is a deteriorating and incapacitating time, and for still others it is somewhere in between.

How aging is viewed by society reflects aging's two-sided nature. In some quarters, such as politics, the advantages of age are stressed and rewarded. In others, such as industrial employment, the disadvantages are emphasized as hindrances. In still others, such as the family, both the positive and negative aspects of aging are experienced.

The double-edged sword of aging is documented in the current literature on aging, the media, and the health care profession. Some researchers emphasize the negative aspects of aging. They focus on sickness, poverty, isolation, and demoralization. The theories they develop seek to explain causes of these unwanted outcomes. They tend to see aging as a social problem. Other researchers emphasize the positive. They look at older people and see that most have good health, frequent contact with family members, modest but adequate incomes, and a high degree of satisfaction with life. They develop theories to explain how aging can have such positive outcomes. They see aging as a social issue

Eileen Ford

*Business owner
and writer*

SNAPSHOT

I work because I like to work, and also because I am driven. . . . If I retired, I wouldn't sit around and wait to die."

Founder of the Ford Model Agency with her husband, Jerry, Eileen Ford was born in 1922 and grew up on Long Island. Ford always knew that she was going to work, because her mother told her that she would be a lawyer. Her own ambitions were more flamboyant. First she wanted to be a movie star with bleached hair, plucked eyebrows, and a white fox fur stole. Then she was going to be a show business agent. She pursued neither.

While attending Barnard College, where she majored in psychology, she took summer jobs as a model. After graduation, she worked as a photographer's assistant, a fashion reporter, an advertising copywriter, and a stylist. Through a friend, she met Jerry Ford and fell instantly in love with him. When he graduated, he was sent to San Francisco for training before he and his unit were shipped out to the Pacific; Eileen borrowed money from everyone she knew for a train ticket, so they could get married.

When she returned to New York, Eileen worked as a stylist at the Constables department store, where she got to know a number of models who worked there. After the war was over and Jerry returned, Eileen became pregnant and realized she would need to find work that could be done at home. Several of the Constables' models needed an appointments secretary, so she took them on. By the time the baby was born, Eileen was managing eight models, and Jerry took over part of the work. The Ford Agency was born and the couple has headed the agency together for over forty years.

Neither Eileen nor Jerry Ford intended to start a modeling agency; it "just happened," and once established it "grew like Topsy," Eileen says. "You have to be in the right place at the right time to do what we did." They started a children's agency because Teri Shields wanted a new agent for her daughter Brooke, who at age eight was getting too tall for the taste of her current agent. Their men's agency was launched when they bought out a rival agency started by Huntington Hartford. The Ford Agency became the largest modeling agency in the world and today represents some of the most famous models.

Ford, who has also written five books on beauty and modeling and raised four children, continues to travel around the country and the world seeking new talent. She describes her work essentially as "helping people," and she is still as passionate about it as she was forty years ago. "I work because I like to work, and also because I am driven. I know that; I'm restless," she acknowledges. "If I retired, I wouldn't sit around and wait to die. I would write a book. I would work as a volunteer for the Humane Society. Even if I were just a surrogate grandparent at the New York Family Hospital, there are so many things you can do to help people."

—*Lydia Brontë*

applying to only a minority of elders. Certainly both kinds of outcomes exist, and understanding both of these perspectives is important. However, it is also important to acknowledge that positive outcomes outnumber the negative by at least two to one.

The dual nature of aging is reflected in the fact that aging is both a social problem and a tremendous social achievement. A significant minority of older Americans do have difficulty securing

A majority of older Americans are in good health and need little in the way of social services.

adequate incomes, employment, social services, adequate health care, and adequate housing and transportation. Yet a large majority of older Americans are in good health, have modest but adequate retirement income, own their own homes, drive their own cars, and need little in the way of social services. And the fact that most older people do not need assistance makes it possible to do something for those who do.

Diverse Experiences of Aging

Variety is a key idea to any discussion on aging. A group of one thousand ten-year-olds followed throughout their lives would become more unlike one another with each passing year. Some of these differences are created by differing physical attributes, such as athletic ability, or mental attributes, such as problem-solving ability or mechanical aptitude. Others are due to emerging personality factors such as dominance-submissiveness or the need for achievement. Still other differences result from the different sex roles of males and females. People also vary widely in terms of their values, beliefs, and aptitudes, often according to the social class, race, ethnic group, size of community, or region of the country in which they grew up. Of course some experiences may be shared—such as language, political orientation, or economic philosophy. In a pluralistic society like America, aging is a highly variable set of processes that makes for a huge variety of possible experiences and outcomes.

The challenge is to identify those dimensions of aging that can best organize the vast chaos represented by the individual experiences of millions of people from all walks of life. Fortunately, although there is no denying the great variety in the older population, certain processes, events, transitions, and outcomes are common to just about everyone. And there are areas of life where we can discover the relative proportions of people who have various kinds of essentially similar situations.

Some generalization is inevitable when developing an overview, but it may gloss over exceptions—sometimes important ones. However, it is not necessary that an individual's experiences match a particular generalization in order for it to be true in general.

Ideas about physical aging are tied to the concept of the *life span*—the length of life that is *biologically possible* for a given species. Among animals there are wide variations in life span, and these variations are thought to be programmed into the genetic makeup of the species. The life span of human beings is about 120 years, the maximum genetically possible length of life. *Life expectancy* is the average length of life that would occur under current mortality rates. For example, under mortality conditions in 1900 in the United States, the average length of life that could be expected was forty-six years. Under conditions prevailing in 1990, life expectancy had risen to seventy-five years. By the year 2000 life expectancy will no doubt be even higher. But even when life expectancy was short, some members of the population survived

The Nature of Physical Aging

to old age. Life span and life expectancy both refer to a biological life cycle. As discussed later, *life course* is a culturally defined program suggesting what people should do and be during various socially defined stages of life.

Physical aging involves processes that reduce the viability of the body and increase its vulnerability to disease. Reduced viability occurs at all physiological levels—cells, molecules, tissues and organs, and control systems. The increase in vulnerability to disease results mainly from a decline in the functioning of the immune system.

Causes of Aging

The search for explanations of aging has produced numerous possibilities. Aging may result from:

- A hereditary genetic program that sets limits on growth, aging, and longevity

- Age-related declines in the functioning of the genetic program that cause newly formed cells to be less effective than their predecessors

- Age-related lowered efficiency of the immune system in identifying and destroying potentially harmful germs, viruses, or mutated cells such as cancer cells

- A decrease with age in the capacity of the endocrine system to control various vital functions such as respiration rate, temperature, or blood pressure

- Age-related decline in the capacity of the nervous system to speedily and efficiently maintain bodily integration and to prevent bodily deterioration

It will be some time before these various potential explanations are fully researched and sorted out. It is likely that they all play some part in aging and that no single key will unlock the mystery of physical aging.

The significance of physical aging is what happens to the human body during the life span. As mentioned, human bodies go through a period of maturation, during which the body grows and develops to its peak level of functioning; a period of maturity, during which physical functioning remains at peak levels; and a period of aging, during which the body gradually loses its capacity for peak performance. Each of the body's systems and organs is on a slightly different schedule for maturation, the duration of maturity, and the point of onset and rate of aging.

This framework is valid and useful for guiding the work of physiologists, but generalists are not as interested in aging's effects on peak physical performance as in its effects on the ability to perform physically in order to support a typical adult lifestyle. They also want to know how to compensate for the effects of aging, or the ability to perform to a socially defined minimum rather than to a physiologically defined maximum.

More useful to the general public is information on compensating mechanisms such as corrective lenses, hearing aids, or medication. To regard many of the age changes as compensable means there is a substantial reduction in the physical decrements due to aging. This is not to say that aging brings no decrements. It does. However, if a minimum level of functioning required of a typical adult is accepted, then social impairments resulting from aging do not become widespread until well after age seventy-five.

What Are the Facts about Physical Aging?

There is a genetically determined maximum life span for the human species, but heredity and environment can substantially alter this species-wide maximum. Thus, as a group of age peers increases in age, so do physical and mental variations among the individuals, so even though physical aging is generally well described, no one can predict when it will occur for a particular function in a particular individual or the rate at which the change will occur.

Physical and mental aging affect human functioning in many ways. Physical aging alters energy levels; affects stature, mobility, and coordination; alters physical appearance; and increases susceptibility to physical and mental illness.

Three basic questions merit consideration:

1. What usually happens?
2. Can decrement be prevented, treated, reversed, or compensated for?
3. What are the social consequences of the typical change?

Physical Energy

The amount of physical energy available to a person is a function of the body's capacity to deliver oxygen and nutrients throughout the body and to remove waste products. This process requires a vast amount of coordination among the various bodily systems. Because aging reduces both the body's capacity to coordinate its systems and the level of functioning of these systems, aging reduces the supply of physical energy that the body can mobilize.

For example, the ability to get oxygen into the blood peaks at about age twenty, remains relatively high through about age forty-five, and then declines steadily. At age eighty, the volume of oxygen that can be absorbed into the blood is only about half as much as at age forty. Glucose (the basic fuel for cell metabolism) utilization is also impaired with age. Accordingly, although muscle strength remains relatively constant through age seventy, maximum work output declines steadily after age forty.

However, the socially important issue is the extent to which this decline interferes with typical social functioning. Physician Nathan Shock, in the *Handbook of the Psychology of Aging,* reports that at low to moderate levels of physical work, age does not affect ability to perform work, but does result in a somewhat longer time required to recover from work. Since most work preferred by American adults is in the low to moderate range, it is thus well within the physical capacities of older adults who do not have disabling chronic conditions (at least 60 percent of the older population).

But availability of physical energy is more than simply the body's ability to perform work. It is also a function of drives. Drives frequently experienced as feelings of tension or restlessness are unlearned bodily states that make people want to act. When a person is hungry, for example, feelings of tension and restlessness do not have to be learned—they just appear. The sex drive is another example.

People who have sex often tend to maintain that pattern into late life. Women sometimes experience physical changes in their sex organs following menopause, and without treatment these changes can lead to painful coition and orgasm. This difficulty in turn can lead to a reluctance to engage in sex. However, this condition is treatable and is not a change in sex drive per se. For men, physical illness rather than a declining sex drive appears to be the most important biological factor influencing sexual behavior. For men who encounter a reduction in sexual behavior in later life, social factors, such as the death of a spouse or institutionalization, and psychological factors, such as fear of failure, play at least as important a part as physical aging.

One common myth about aging is that it causes the sex drive to disappear. Years ago, researchers William Masters and Virginia Johnson concluded that with regard to sex, the old adage "use it or lose it" appears to be largely true.

Stature, Mobility, and Coordination

Physical activity also depends on the structure of the body and the ability to move effectively. As people grow older, they get shorter, partly because bones that have become more porous develop curvature, and partly because some older people carry themselves with a slight bend at the hips and knees. A height loss of three inches is not uncommon. Height loss is currently more common among older women, but this may change in the future as more women take preventive steps to avoid osteoporosis. Older women are especially likely to find themselves too short to reach conveniently in environments where heights and widths are the common "adult standard." For example, standard kitchen cabinets, sinks, and counters tend to be too high and too deep.

Ability to move may also be influenced by aging, for with age the prevalence of arthritis increases and connective tissue in joints stiffens. However, how these changes influence ability to flex and extend arms, legs, or fingers is unknown and is a major area in need of research.

Much more is known about coordination. Physical coordination is a complex process that involves taking in sensory information, attaching meaning to it through perception, selecting appropriate action based on that perception, transmitting instructions to various parts of the body that need to act, and initiating action. Coordination depends on several bodily systems. Sensory systems provide information. Neurological systems transmit that information to the brain. Various parts of the brain handle perception and selection, initiation, and monitoring of action. Various muscle groups perform action under the control of the nervous system and the brain. In most cases, these separate functions occur in such rapid succession that the interval between sensation and responsive action is slight. This rapidity is especially true of practiced skills such as typing, playing a musical instrument, or operating familiar equipment.

Aging can influence coordination by influencing any of the systems that support physical activity. In fact, sensory systems and muscle groups are generally more than able to perform well into old age. According to researchers, coordination and performance are much more likely to be influenced by age changes in brain-based functions.

For example, suppose a seventy-year-old man is just learning to play the piano. His eyesight and sense of touch would probably be quite adequate to the task, as would his muscle tone and strength in his arms and fingers. His progress would be much more likely to be limited by the speed with which he could interpret notes and decide which keys to play and when. Chances are that he would have to go very slowly until the translation process became habitual. On the other hand, a seventy-year-old man who had been playing the piano with skill for sixty years would probably encounter very little difficulty in continuing to play, because his skills would be mainly automatic and would require very little conscious interpretation or decision making. The contrast between performance in practiced skills versus new skills is probably a primary reason why many older people find little pleasure in trying to learn new skills requiring intricate physical coordination. Young people also experience frustrations in trying to learn new skills, but they do not have a large, contrasting backlog of much less frustrating practiced skills.

When older people must learn new skills, particularly those required for employment, they are able to do so. Neverthe-

Age-related changes in appearance do not predictably influence physical attractiveness.

less, there are definite changes in observed physical coordination as individuals age. The most important differences from the point of view of social functioning are in reaction time, speed of response, and ability to make complex physical responses.

Reaction time increases with age. This increase is very slight for simple tasks, such as responding to traffic signals, but becomes greater as the tasks get more complex. The more choices involved in the task, the longer it takes older people to react compared to the young. Overcautiousness among older people compared to the young may play a big part in slowed reaction, because older people are perceptibly slower only when they have time to be cautious.

The slowing of reactions in older people may also result partly from a tendency toward care and accuracy. Older people tend to spend more than an average amount of time checking their results; therefore, part of their slowness may be the difference between the time required for accuracy and the time required for certainty.

Exercise, increased motivation, and practice can reduce the age effects of slowed reaction time. Extended practice may eliminate slowing completely. Finally, individual differences in reaction time are so great that, even with age changes, many older people respond more quickly than many young adults.

Speed of movement also tends to decline with increasing age. In fact, when older people try to hurry, their control capabilities are often so poor that their movements appear jerky in comparison with the more fluid motions of younger people. For simple movements such as sewing, the decline with age is very slight, whereas for complex movements such as typing, in which the same muscles must be more controlled, the slowing with age is generally more marked. However, people are quite variable with respect to this and all other physical functions. For example, in 1922, Mike Bachman, a seventy-eight-year-old printer, gained fame illustrating how fast the then-new Linotype machine for setting type could be operated. While Bachman sat at the Linotype, the foreman was kept busy providing trays fast enough to receive the set type from Bachman's machine.

Although physical coordination generally declines with age, it is much less marked for practiced skills. Older people are apparently more effective in processing and coordinating responses over well-established networks than they are at establishing new ones. It is possible for them to learn new skills, but it is easier to ply established ones. This tendency may be one important reason why older people seem to prefer "tried and true" methods rather than new ones.

Physical Appearance
Wrinkled skin, "age spots," gray hair, and midriff bulge are common examples of age-related changes in appearance. Yet these changes do not predictably influence physical attractiveness. If people are held to a narrow, idealistic view of physical beauty or attractiveness, then few would meet the standard. But in terms of practical attractiveness—the ability to draw positive attention through one's physical appearance—there are plenty of unattractive younger people. Many people find that they become more attractive as they grow older, yet many others fear what aging may do to their appearance, especially if they see it as one of their major assets. Some people in middle age or later resort to surgically alter-

ing the effects of aging on their appearance, citing reasons of job security, marital security, and social attitudes about appearance.

Most people tend to be preoccupied with physical aspects of attractiveness and ignore other aspects. Yet many of the most attractive people entice with their enthusiasm, attention, and personality. And these aspects of attractiveness can also improve with age. Nevertheless some people experience aging as a loss of attractiveness, and this change can be difficult to deal with. Far more grow older with mates and friends who affirm by their actions that changes in physical appearance are not nearly so important.

Susceptibility to Physical and Mental Illness

Health is a central factor in everyone's life, and most people can take good health for granted. However, poor health affects people's life satisfaction, participation in most social roles, and even the way other people respond to them. In later life, declining health cuts across all social, political, and economic lines. However, disabling illness is more common and occurs at earlier ages among people at the lower socioeconomic levels. Health is a major determinant of one's ability to participate in the family, the job, the community, and leisure pursuits. Health needs absorb a larger amount and proportion of older people's incomes.

Health is a continuum, with two extremes: complete wellness on the positive end and death on the negative end. Wellness is not merely an absence of disease but is the positive vitality experienced by those who are optimally healthy. Health promotion programs take wellness as a positive goal to be pursued. Prevention of illness is an important part of wellness, but by no means all of it. The number of wellness programs tailored to the needs of elders has increased sharply in recent years. They focus on the roles that diet, stress reduction, and physical and mental exercise play in promoting wellness. Illnesses are malfunctions or disorders that have a negative effect on the organism's ability to function and can be classified either by their expected duration or by the magnitude of their effect on functioning. Acute illnesses or injuries are expected to be short term or temporary. They include such conditions as the common cold or a sprained ankle. Chronic illnesses or injuries are expected to be long term or permanent. Examples include paralysis, amputation, diabetes, or emphysema.

Acute and chronic illnesses: Both acute and chronic illnesses can cause people to restrict their activities. Minor disabilities cause some restrictions, but not in major activities such as employment, child care, or housework. Minor disabilities interfere with some kinds of activities, but they do not interfere with major life roles. Major disabilities interfere with central life activities such as employment, going to school, or childrearing, and disabilities can be mental as well as physical.

Aging affects both the kinds of illnesses people are likely to have and the degree of limitation that illnesses or injuries cause. Compared to younger people, older people are less likely to have acute conditions such as colds or flu but are more likely to have chronic conditions such as diabetes or allergies. Regardless of the type of condition, older people are more likely to be disabled by them than younger people.

Despite the high prevalence of chronic conditions among older people, only a small proportion are severely handicapped. So although the expected increase in chronic conditions among older people does occur, the proportion who escape serious limitation by these factors is surprisingly large. According to the National Center for Health Statistics, in 1990 over 20 million older Americans reported no serious limitations in activity caused by health problems.

The major chronic physical illnesses that limit the activities of older people are heart conditions, arthritis, and visual impairment, and they affect 22 percent, 20 percent, and 9 percent of the older population respectively. Diabetes, cancer, and allergies are the other main chronic illnesses among older people.

Older people are also much more susceptible to injury from falls compared to younger people, and several experts found that falls were the leading cause of accidental death among people over the age of seventy-five. Older women are especially likely to fall. The most common cause of falls in the elderly is tripping or stumbling over something at home, often related to poor coordination or poor eyesight. However, many falls occur as a result of dizziness, a side effect of chronic illnesses such as high blood pressure (hypertension) and the medications used to treat them.

Many health care professionals assume that a certain amount of limiting illness is normal in an aging person. Physicians sometimes tell older patients that they must accept a certain amount of disability as a normal part of the aging process. This assumption is absolutely untrue. Although limiting chronic conditions are common among older people, many of them are preventable, most are treatable, and all can be compensated for to some extent. And limiting physical illness is not typical of older people until after age ninety.

Although in 1990 nearly 90 percent of the older population had one or more chronic conditions, 62 percent were not limited in any way by them, and only about 22 percent were severely limited by them.

The social consequences of chronic conditions fall into two major categories: functional limits imposed by the illness and social limits imposed by other people's perceptions of the illness. Social limits caused by people's assumptions about the effects of illness are often much more severe than the actual physical limits. Poor health is also by far the greatest limitation on participation in the community and on leisure pursuits, but the proportion of older people affected in nonemployment areas is less than 20 percent.

Mental disorders: The term "mental disorder" is defined as a noticeable dysfunction of behavioral or psychological patterns, and its occurrence is associated with personal distress or impaired ability to function in everyday social roles. The incidence and seriousness of mental disorders is affected by age. Of the nonorganic disorders such as schizophrenia, paranoia, anxiety, and depression, depression is the most likely to have its onset in later life, usually in response to losses either in physical functioning or of social resources through death. Depression can also be a side effect of some medications used to treat diseases common to later life. Symptoms of depression include a depressed mood, loss of interest in almost all usual activities, loss of appetite, sleep disturbance,

The assumption that a certain amount of disability is a normal part of the aging process is absolutely untrue.

COPYRIGHT MARIANNE GONTARZ

psychomotor retardation or agitation, feelings of worthlessness, guilt or self-reproach, or suicidal thoughts or behavior. According to recent statistics, as much as 30 percent of the older population may exhibit mild depression, and 2 percent to 6 percent show signs of major (disabling) depression. Fortunately, depression is the most treatable nonorganic mental disorder.

Organic mental disorders, also called dementias, are typified by mental confusion, loss of memory, incoherent speech, poor orientation to the environment—and sometimes poor motor coordination, agitated behavior, depression, or delirium as well. About 55 percent of dementias in the elderly are caused by Alzheimer's disease, a progressive and irreversible deterioration of brain tissue. The remainder are caused by strokes, brain tumors, nutritional deficiencies, alcoholism, adverse reactions to drugs, and a variety of other factors. The prevalence of all types of dementia increases with age.

Some varieties of dementia can be treated, but because symptoms of all types are similar, diagnosis is problematic and must be inferred from laboratory tests such as computed tomographic scans (often called "cat" scans), electroencephalograms, blood tests, and metabolic screening as well as previous medical history. For example, if a physician sees a patient with symptoms of dementia, before settling on a diagnosis, he or she may check for malnutrition, find out what drugs the patient has been taking, and check for infections or diseases such as diabetes, hyperthyroidism, congestive heart failure, alcoholism, or stroke. If none of the possible causes of reversible dementia is present, then it is usually assumed that the patient has Alzheimer's disease, for which there is currently no effective treatment.

The field of mental aging is concerned with mental processes such as thinking, creativity, and problem solving, as well as the nature and content of consciousness, and the role of consciousness in behavior. Additionally interchanges between the person and the physical or social environment are key to a discussion of the psychological aspects of aging, as well as the person's adaptations to both internal experiences and external experiences of the world. This broad set of issues—which is by no means complete—produces many views about the nature and results of mental aging, with two of the major perspectives of particular interest.

The Mental Process of Aging

Two Aspects of Mental Aging

The first aspect of mental aging involves the study of various separate mental dimensions such as perception or intelligence. This perspective is useful for developing a basic factual description of aging's effects on specific mental processes, such as hearing or problem solving. The second is a more global perspective, called human development, which looks at the mind and its various dimensions as an evolving whole. This second perspective is useful for gaining insights into aging's effects on the interaction between mental processes, subjective experiences, and adaptive strategies on the one hand and the individual's social environment on the other.

Processes such as perception, motor coordination, and reaction time have obvious ties to physical aging. They depend on sensory organs, neurological transmission, and muscular capacities to take in information, process it, and coordinate action based on that information. Research supports the maturation-maturity-aging model, which predicts general declines with age in psychophysiological functioning.

However, with "higher" mental processes, such as intelligence, learning, memory, creativity, thinking, and problem solving, the dependence on biological functioning is not as direct, and the effects of aging are much less clear-cut. For example, scientists used to think that intelligence declined with age, and the scoring formulas for standardized intelligence tests contained an "age credit" that allowed for the fact that older people usually scored lower on such tests. However, in the 1970s research began to appear based on studies of various aspects of intelligence in the same people over time. According to a team of researchers who recorded their findings in the *Journal of Gerontology*, when mental abilities were divided into those that are based on neurological processes in the central nervous system, such as visual flexibility, versus those that are based on learned abilities to evaluate or diagnose or solve problems, an interesting difference appeared. Learned abilities increased over time for adults of all ages, while biologically based abilities declined for all adults over forty. There was no decrement in learned abilities, and the decline in overall ability was due to declines in functioning within the central nervous system. Functions that were closely linked to biological functioning were negatively influenced by age, and those based on learning and experience were not. Thus, the maturation-maturity-aging view of aging is not appropriate for mental abilities that rest on prior learning and experience. In these areas, models based on stability or increment are more accurate.

The Senses and Aging

The senses are the means through which the human mind experiences the world both outside and inside the body. The sensory process is not particularly complex. Sensory organs pick up information about changes in the internal or external environment and pass this information on to the brain. All the input from the sensory organs is collected and organized in the brain. The subjective result is called sensory experience.

The minimum amount of stimulation a sensory organ must experience before sensory information is passed to the brain is called a threshold. All individuals have their own unique thresholds for each sense. The higher the threshold, the stronger the stimulus needed to get information to the brain. For example, some people require very little sound before they begin to hear, while others require a considerable amount. This section looks at the sensory processes as a function of age—both with changes in threshold that occur with increasing age and with the complete failure of a particular sensory process.

Vision is usually affected dramatically by aging. Increasing age decreases the ability of the eye to change shape and therefore to focus on very near objects, which means that many older people find reading glasses necessary, for example. The tendency toward farsightedness increases about tenfold between age ten and age sixty, but does not appear to increase much thereafter. Close work of all kinds becomes more difficult without glasses, but many find adjusting to bifocal or trifocal lenses very aggravating.

Proper focusing of the eye on the image requires the proper quantity of light. The eye of the average sixty-year-old admits only about one-third as much light as the eye of the average twenty-year-old, which means that greater levels of illumination are required by older people. Older people seem to adapt to darkness about as fast as the young, but research has found that their level of adaptation is not nearly as good. This decline makes moving about in a dark house and night driving more dangerous for older people.

Color vision also changes as the individual grows older. The lens of the eye gradually yellows and filters out the violet, blue, and green colors toward the dark end of the spectrum. The threshold for these colors increases significantly as people grow older, and it is much easier for older people to see yellow, orange, and red than to see the darker colors. For older people to get the same satisfaction from looking at colors in their surroundings that young people get, their environment must present more yellow, orange, and red, and less violet, blue, and green.

About 25 percent of people over seventy have cataracts, a condition in which clouding of the eye's lens diffuses light, heightens sensitivity to glare, and impairs vision. To people with cataracts the world looks darker, objects are less distinguishable from one another, and visual acuity is often quite poor. Treatment involves surgically removing the lens and replacing it with a contact lens. This treatment generally improves vision but requires a period of adjustment.

Only a small percentage of older people are blind. For example, according to the National Center for Health Statistics, 2.6 percent of Americans age sixty-five to seventy-four and 8.3 percent of those age seventy-five or over are legally blind. Yet these people constitute a large proportion of the blind population. One California study found that 55 percent of the blindness in that state occurred after age sixty-five and that 85 percent occurred after age forty-five. Thus, although blind people are a relatively small proportion, blindness is definitely related to age.

Hearing, the second major sense, involves detecting the frequency (pitch) of sound, its intensity, and the time interval over which it occurs. As people grow older, their reactions to frequency and intensity change, but there is no evidence to indicate that the ability to distinguish time intervals changes significantly with age. Why these changes occur is not clear.

Hearing loss begins at about age twenty. Very gradually, as people get older, they generally lose their ability to hear high frequencies and to discriminate among adjacent frequencies. Intensity threshold also changes with advancing age. Older people cannot hear some frequencies no matter how loud, but even within the range of pitch that they can hear the intensity level necessary to produce hearing is greater, particularly for higher pitches. As a result, older people enjoy music with more low-pitched sounds and with uniform intensity. Older people must play radios and televisions louder in order to hear them. Background noise is more distracting to older listeners than to the young. Estimates of the proportion of older adults having severe hearing loss range from 13 percent to 33 percent.

Hearing loss can have a major impact on speech communication. Age-related changes in ability to discriminate among sounds make speech more difficult to hear, especially when people talk fast, when there is background noise, and when there is sound distortion or reverberation. Among older people, 30 percent of men and 25 percent of women have difficulty hearing faint speech, and 5 percent of both men and women cannot hear even amplified speech. Hearing aids often can help, but they also can be frustrating in the presence of background noise because they tend to amplify it too.

Taste, as a sense, certainly can have a good deal to do with satisfaction. The evidence indicates that all four qualities—sweet, salt, bitter, and sour—show an increase in threshold after age fifty. Nevertheless, it is unlikely that large changes in taste sensitivity occur before age seventy. People in later life are apt to require more highly seasoned food to receive the same taste satisfactions they received when they were twenty.

The senses of taste and smell are of greater importance than the research on them indicates. These senses are major components in one's capacity to enjoy, and also make important contributions to one's capacity to survive. For example, taste is important in detecting spoiled food, and smell can alert people to the presence of smoke or natural gas.

In short, the senses provide the means for assembling and classifying information, but not for evaluating or remembering it. Perception and memory are our major means of processing information.

Perception

The process of evaluating information gathered by the senses and of giving it meaning is called perception. Most research shows an age decrement in perception. One possible reason for this loss is that aging affects the speed with which the nervous system can process one stimulus and make way for the next. The "trace" of the initial stimulus in the nervous system interferes with ability to perceive subsequent stimuli. Thus, older people can be confused or irritated by visual images that change too rapidly, or by auditory stimuli presented at a rapid pace.

Memory

There are three stages of memory. Registration is the "recording" of learning or perceptions. In concept, registration is analogous to the recording of sound on a tape recorder. Retention is the ability to sustain registration over time. Recall is retrieval of material that has been registered and retained. Obviously, in any type of memory, a failure at any of these stages will result in no measurable memory.

There is an age deficit in memory. However, some older people escape memory loss altogether. People who exercise their memories tend to maintain memory well into old age. As age increases, the retention of things heard becomes increasingly superior to the retention of things seen, and use of both gives better results than the use of either separately.

Mental Functioning

Sensation, perception, and memory are all very important for the functioning of the individual, yet in human beings these processes

take a backseat to mental functioning. The term mental functioning refers to a large group of complex processes, subdivided for
convenience into intelligence, learning, thinking, problem solving,
and creativity.

Intelligence embraces both a potential and an actual ability, but in
practice, researchers consider only measurable ability. As many as
twenty basic abilities go together to make up intelligence. Family
relationships expert Lillian Troll, in her book *Continuations: Adult
Development and Aging,* reports that abilities that require quick
thinking, such as timed matching tasks, decline steadily after
about age forty. This decline is no doubt related to age changes in
response speed. Tests of stored information such as vocabulary or
general information may continue to increase to the end of life.
Tests of logical abilities such as arithmetic reasoning often show a
plateau throughout adulthood.

Other researchers feel that individual differences are so
great that age is of little predictive value. In addition, studies of
intervention suggest that age changes can be altered, even in old
age. Although biological aging undoubtedly influences intellectual functioning, the impact of environment has been underestimated or ignored by the medical community. If environment is not
conducive to "intellectual acquisition and maintenance," functioning may also be impaired.

Learning is the acquisition of information or skills. When someone
improves performance at a given intellectual or physical task, he
or she has learned. All studies of performance indicate a decline in
learning with age.

Clearly, however, factors other than learning ability affect
performance. These factors include motivation, speed, intelligence, ill health, and physiological states. In practice, it is extremely difficult to separate the components of performance in order to
examine the influence of learning ability, although a number of
studies have attempted to do so. Because research to date has not
been able to isolate learning ability from other causes of perfor-

mance and because very little longitudinal research has been done on learning, it is not clear what effect age has on learning ability.

From a practical point of view, learning performance seems to decline as age increases, although the declines are not noticeable until past middle age. All age groups can learn. If given a bit more time, older people can usually learn anything other people can. Extra time is required both to learn information or skills and to demonstrate that learning has occurred. Tasks that involve manipulation of concrete objects or symbols, distinct and unambiguous responses, and low interference from prior learning are particularly conducive to good performance by older people.

Via intelligence, learning, and memory, human beings have at their disposal a great many separate mental images. Thinking, problem solving, and creativity all involve the manipulation of ideas and symbols.

Thinking: Simply put, thinking involves manipulating ideas. It helps bring order to the chaos of data brought into the mind by perception and learning because it differentiates and categorizes data into constructs called concepts.

Older people seem to be particularly poor at forming concepts. Concept formation often involves making logical inferences and generalizations. Older people have been found to resist forming a higher order generalization and to refuse choosing one when given the opportunity. All studies seem to agree that as age increases, a person's ability to form concepts declines.

Concept formation is not completely independent of other skills such as learning and intelligence, but at the same time it is not completely dependent on them either. A substantial part of the decline with age in measured ability to form concepts appears to be genuine.

Problem solving involves the development of decisions out of the processes of reason, logic, and thinking. Whereas thinking involves the differentiation and categorization of mental data,

From a practical point of view, learning performance seems to decline as age increases.

COPYRIGHT PAUL GILMORE

problem solving involves making logical deductions about these categories, their properties, and differences among them. Problem solving differs from learning in that learning is the acquisition of skills and perceptions, whereas problem solving is using these skills and perceptions to make choices.

In solving problems, older people are at a disadvantage if they must deal with many items of information simultaneously. They have more difficulty giving meaning to stimuli presented and have more trouble remembering this information later when it must be used to derive a solution. The number of errors made in solving problems rises steadily with age. This difficulty is why older people are often befuddled by forms they are asked to complete, particularly if the instructions are complex.

Compared to young adults, older people take a longer time to recognize the explicit goal of a particular problem. Their search for information is thus characterized by haphazard questioning rather than by concentration on a single path to the goal. They attain information randomly, have trouble separating the relevant from the irrelevant, and thus tend to be overwhelmed by a multitude of irrelevant facts. They also tend toward repetitive behavior, a tendency that can be disruptive in situations where the nature of problems and their solutions is constantly or rapidly changing.

Creativity is often defined as unique, original, and inventive problem solving. Research based on this definition reveals that age is unrelated to the degree of creativity attributed to a specific contribution. The age at which the volume of creative work is greatest depends on the field. For example, in pure mathematics, theoretical physics, or computer design, creative work tends to peak in early adulthood and drop off sharply in midlife, whereas in novel writing, history, and philosophy, creative work tends to peak in midlife with little or no drop-off thereafter. Those areas where peaks usually occur in early adulthood often involve being able to apply enormous amounts of mental energy to concentrate on abstract problems within a system of abstract symbols. By contrast, areas that peak later are those based on a broad mental perspective and cumulative experience. Certainly individual exceptions are prevalent enough in every field and declines are gradual enough that no one should assume that older people automatically reach an end of their creativity, particularly at any given chronological age.

Mental aging is definitely not a unitary process. Some mental functions decline with age, others remain relatively constant, and others improve steadily. The closer the tie to physical functioning, the more likely a function will decline with age. Getting information is a problem for only a small proportion of older adults. Most can successfully compensate by using glasses or hearing aids. Age changes in the ability to process information can be minimized by continuing to practice skills such as thinking, problem solving, and creativity. Losses can be offset by compensating. For example, declining short-term memory can be offset by note taking. Learning can be improved by slowing down the pace of the material being presented.

Considering the various mental processes separately results in a piecemeal approach. The adult development approach to mental aging provides a more holistic alternative.

Adult development is concerned with the evolution of adaptive capacity over the adult life span. Adaptive capacity resides in the coping styles contained in the personality and in the self-concept. The self-concept contains ideas about the self that form the basis for initiative and self-confidence, or lack of them. The key questions for the developmentalist are how aging influences:

1. What people must adapt to
2. The approaches they take to realize adaptation
3. The way people see and react to themselves

Erikson's Stage Theory

The concept that people go through stages of development has been around a long time. Perhaps the most influential stage theory of adult development was formulated by social psychologist Erik Erikson. Erikson's theory is mainly concerned with how people develop an identity in childhood and adolescence, but he also considered development in old age. Erikson upheld that identity is formed on a foundation of trust, autonomy, initiative, and industry. These qualities develop in childhood and allow individuals to form a view of themselves as capable, worthwhile, and safe. People who do not develop these qualities have difficulty trusting others, have doubts about their abilities and feel guilt about their poor performance, feel inferior to others, and feel no basis for confidence in their ability to face the changes brought on by adulthood. Obviously, these two extremes are end points of a continuum, and individuals can vary considerably along it in terms of bringing a strong sense of positive identity into adulthood and later on into old age.

According to Erikson's theory, in early adulthood the main issue in human growth and development is learning to establish intimacy—close personal relationships such as with a friend or mate. This process involves learning to unite one's own identity with that of another person. People who do not learn to develop intimacy remain isolated, relating to others but never having a sense of unity with them. In middle adulthood, the issue is generativity versus stagnation. Generativity is the ability to support others, particularly one's children and other members of younger generations. It involves caring and concern for younger people and also an interest in making a contribution to the world one lives in. Stagnation results when an individual does not learn to contribute to others. It is typified by a lack of interest in others, especially the young, a feeling of having contributed nothing, and the appearance of just going through the motions. In late adulthood, the issue is what Erikson labeled ego integrity versus despair. Integrity involves being able to look at one's life as having been meaningful and being able to accept one's self as a whole being having both positive and negative dimensions, without being threatened by this acceptance. Integrity provides the basis for approaching the end of life with a feeling of having lived completely. Despair is the result of rejecting one's life and oneself and the realization that there is not enough time left to alter this assessment. Such a person is prone to depression and fear of death.

Erikson's theory contends that life is a process of continuous growth, provided one adequately resolves the issues of life's successive stages. In order to develop intimacy, one must first have developed a positive identity. In order to develop generativity, one must have the capacity for intimacy. And in order to develop integrity, one must have the feelings of connectedness and contribution that come from intimacy and generativity. This progression of human growth is closely tied to chronological age in childhood by the expectations of home and school, but in adulthood the individual is freer to move at his or her own pace. Thus, although generativity may be typically something people are learning in middle adulthood and certainly something they are supposed to be learning, many people are still trying to learn to deal with identity or intimacy, and they may feel irritated or overwhelmed by demands that they exhibit generativity.

Erikson's framework provides a tool for relating to people. By listening to older adults, one may get a sense of where they stand on the issues Erikson raised, which in turn promotes understanding not only of their behavior but also their priorities and their aspirations.

Process Theory

For many psychologists, adult development does not involve discrete stages but instead results from the continuous operation of

Joan Erikson

Therapist and writer

Discovering one's own capacities and power makes it possible to recreate yourself."

Dancer, artist, jewelry designer, and therapist Joan Erikson has managed her enormously varied career around her role as wife and mother. Raising four children, encouraging and helping her husband in his career, and still managing to create an identity of her own was, she emphasizes, a process that took place over time, often difficult, often bumpy. One of the subjects of Mary Catherine Bateson's book, *Composing a Life*, Joan Erikson is a model for both women and men on how to manage and adapt to change.

Born in 1903 in a tiny community in Canada where her father was the local Episcopal minister, Erikson had what she called a "chaotic and disorganized" childhood, which fueled her desire to have a strong and healthy family of her own one day. After two years of college without a clear career objective, Erikson, who loved studying dance, decided instead to become a teacher and enrolled in Columbia Teacher's College. There a wonderful dance teacher who, like Erikson, was tall, convinced her to consider dance again: "She was as big as me and she danced beautifully and I thought, `To hell with it. I'm going to be a dancer,' " Erikson recounts. "So that's what I became. Suddenly I knew who I was, and what I was doing, and why I was doing it. It was grand. Of course, that brings success! You can't help it if you're that enthusiastic."

In 1928 she went to Europe to work on her dissertation

for a year and ended up staying two and marrying a young psychologist she met there, Erik Erikson. The Eriksons returned to the United States and spent time at several universities, Philadelphia to Cambridge to Yale, finally settling at Berkeley where Joan became deeply involved with the schools.

After World War II, when the McCarthy period began, Erik Erikson was so profoundly offended by the university's practices of loyalty oaths and preferential treatment of senior professors that he resigned. Buoyed by the favorable reception of *Childhood and Society*, which had just been published, the couple returned to the East Coast, where Erikson accepted a position in psychiatry at Austen Riggs Hospital in Stockbridge, Massachusetts. Then Joan Erikson came into her own.

She received permission to organize structured activities for the hospital's young patients. For five years, Erikson generated programs and health-giving relationships among the patients and staff at Austin Riggs and encouraged better relations between the hospital and the townspeople. When her husband took a sabbatical to write *Young Man Luther*, Erikson gave up her position to be with him. For many years she had edited her husband's work—his English was still craggy enough that he needed a keen editorial eye. By working as an invisible partner with her husband, she helped reshape and greatly expand psychological theory and practice.

After organizing a half-way house and launching her career as a writer, Joan Erikson began working at the Erikson Center at Harvard, established in 1982 to promote intergenerational integration of lives around the life cycle principles, with the support of all the growth-enhancing and healing arts. "We teach and learn how to live and grow creatively," she explains. "Could anything be more challenging and engrossing?"

—*Lydia Brontë*

various processes of development. Psychologist Klaus Riegel contends that human development arises out of contradictory ideas or actions produced by the constant changes occurring in the person and his or her environment. Riegel saw these contradictions not as deficiencies to be corrected but as invitations to a new level of integration. For example, a person might notice that at times she is cautious, and at other times she is adventuresome. Accepting both views as valid parts of herself is a higher level of integration than putting them in opposition to one another and trying to make herself be only one or the other. Thus, says Riegel, "developmental and historical tasks are never completed. At the very moment when completion seems to be achieved, new questions and doubts arise in the individual and in society."

Psychologists Susan Whitbourne and Camilda Weinstock address more specifically the dynamics of continuous development. They argue that adult identity is an integration based on a person's knowledge about his or her physical and mental assets and liabilities, ideas (motives, goals, and attitudes), and social roles. Identity serves to organize the interpretation of experiences—the assignment of subjective meaning to them. And identity can be modified by experience. The day-to-day contradictions that appear between the identities people bring to experience and the feedback they get from it can be responded to in numerous ways. People who are flexible about the content of their identities realize that identity is a theory of the self that is constantly being tested, modified, and refined through experience. To the extent that people's observations about themselves are honest, the theory gets better as time goes on. That is, the results people's identities lead them to expect are the results they get. A large measure of human growth involves living with doubts and fears while developing the knowledge and skills necessary to perform at a personally satisfying and socially successful level. Once skills are developed, they are maintained by practice.

Sometimes people develop an identity but refuse to test it. They use their identity to decide how to act, but they do not let the results modify their ideas about themselves. Other people never quite develop a firm identity that could be tested. They don't really know what to expect of themselves in various situations, and the result is that they behave in inconsistent and confusing ways.

Identity

Aging affects the stability of identity in several important ways. First, the longer one has an adult identity, the more times one's theory of self can be tested across various situations. This experience usually results in a stable personal identity that stands up well to the demands of day-to-day living. Second, the reduction in social responsibilities associated with later adulthood can reduce the potential for conflict among various aspects of identity. Third, aging for most people means continuing familiar activities in familiar environments. Most have long since developed skill and accumulated accomplishments in these arenas. All they need do now is maintain them.

The identity perspective also provides a basis for predicting when change might reach crisis proportions. When change in either the individual or the environment is so great that it cannot be integrated without a fundamental reorganization of one's theory of self, an identity crisis results. An identity crisis means reassessing the very foundations of one's identity. The changes that precipitate the crisis may occur in the individual or in the social situation.

Consider these examples:

- Mr. F has learned that within six months to a year he will be totally blind.

- Mrs. T's husband died six weeks ago. They had been married forty-seven years.

- Mr. M retired from teaching after forty-one years.

- Mrs. B has become increasingly frail. After sixteen years of living alone as a widow, she must move in with her divorced, middle-aged daughter.

None of these changes need automatically trigger an identity crisis. Whether an identity crisis occurs depends on how central the changed dimension is to the individual and whether the change was anticipated. Profound physical changes usually have less ambiguous outcomes than social changes. Going blind would be a profound adjustment for anyone. But how much Mrs. T is affected by her husband's death depends on how her relationship

As older adults, men may be retired, be great-grandfathers, or act as family historians.

with him has fit into her identity. Whether they were inseparable companions whose selves were completely intertwined, or whether theirs had been a marriage of convenience that had endured mainly by force of habit, could make a substantial difference in whether or not his death brings on an identity crisis in his wife. Mr. M may well be able to give up teaching easily if he feels that he has completed what he set out to do as a teacher and that it is time to move on. He may not be able to leave easily if he is being forced to retire when he feels he still has something to contribute. How Mrs. B resolves her dilemma depends on how she feels about being dependent—what it implies for her identity—particularly in her relationship with her daughter. Identity crises are not produced by events alone—they stem from the interpretation of events in the context of a particular identity.

The Social Process of Aging

Individuals' lives are also structured by their social environments. People interact with one another not only as individuals but as role players. And the roles are organized sequentially into a life course tied to age or life stage. In addition, social processes such as socialization involve the individual with his or her social world. All these aspects of the social environment can be influenced by age.

Aging and Social Roles

Social roles are crucial to a comprehensive discussion on aging because individuals often define themselves in terms of these roles, and their places in society are determined by them. Roles are the expected or typical behavior associated with positions in the organization of a group. A large part of everyday life consists of human relationships that are structured at least partially by the social roles of the various actors. But in everyday life the action is much more like improvisational theater, for the characters and dialogue are made up right on stage, not scripted as with formal theater.

General role definitions serve as the background for initial interactions in new role relationships, but almost immediately role players begin to incorporate personal information into their expectations for their specific relationship. They each gradually modify and refine their expectations to take an increasing amount of personal information into account.

When life is filled with relatively new relationships, as in young adulthood, people are uncertain about what to expect from others and what is expected from them. But when life is filled with long-term relationships, there is a large component of security in knowing what to expect—even if the relationship is not all it could be. In middle age and later life, most role relationships for most people are long-standing relationships that are highly personalized.

In adulthood, advanced age occasionally makes people eligible for valued roles such as retired person, but more often it makes them ineligible for roles they value. Whether one is merely assigned to roles, whether one must have the opportunity to achieve them, or whether one selects them, one does not simply play or take over or retain roles. They are usually available as a result of having met certain criteria. In most societies, particular rights, duties, privileges, and obligations are set aside for children, adolescents, young adults, the middle-aged, and the old. In today's culture, the primary eligibility criteria are health, age, gender, social class, ethnicity, color, experience, and educational achievement. These criteria may be gradually modified and personalized in some cases, but overall these attributes govern role eligibility in predictable ways.

Throughout the life process, the field of roles people are eligible for keeps changing. Young boys can legitimately be members of a neighborhood peer group, pupils, and not employed—all things they cannot be as adults. As young men, they can be auto drivers, soldiers, and voters—all things they cannot be as children. As older adults, they can be retired, be great-grandfathers, or act as family historians—all things they cannot do as young adults. Of course, age also works negatively, as when older people are prevented from holding jobs, even if they want to work.

Age also serves to modify what is expected of people in particular roles. Young people are often dealt with leniently in adult roles because of their inexperience. In old age, the standards may also be different. For example, it is more socially acceptable for an eighty-year-old father to be more dependent in his relationships with his offspring than a fifty-six-year-old father.

Roles that adults play provide various degrees of access to advantages such as prestige, wealth, or influence. Highly rewarded roles can be obtained either through family background or individual initiative or both. But despite the rhetoric that an open class system exists in which one can rise from rags to riches, in reality only a small minority of people ever move out of the social class into which they were born.

Growing older in an advantaged social position generally means being able to accumulate personal wealth and prestige. People do not become wealthy, revered, or influential just by becoming old, but by playing an advantaged role for a number of years. A great many of the richest and most influential Americans are old, but their age is not the reason why they are rich or influential. In fact, their wealth and influence discounts their age in the sense that rich and powerful people are much less likely than others to be disqualified from participation purely on account of age. Age disqualification happens mainly to people who are already relatively disadvantaged.

One can also be advantaged by having exceptional skills. Great writers, musicians, artists, therapists, diplomats, and others can use their skills to offset their age and to avoid being disqualified. Artists Pablo Picasso or Georgia O'Keefe never had to worry

As people grow older, their accumulated decisions about various life course options produce increased differentiation among them.

about age discrimination—their talents remained in demand. Other people find that presumptions about the effects of age often offset ordinary skills and lead to disqualification.

Some of the disqualifying character of age is related to erroneous beliefs about the predictability of age's effects on performance. But some is related to the scarcity of leadership positions, the desire of younger people to acquire them, and the willingness of older people to give up responsibilities.

The Life Course

The life course is an idealized and age-related progression or sequence of roles and group memberships that individuals are expected to follow as they mature and move through life. Thus, there is an age to go to school, an age to marry, an age to "settle down," and so forth. But the life course in reality is neither simple nor rigidly prescribed. For example, various subcultures (whether based on gender, social class, ethnicity, race, or region of the country) tend to develop unique ideas concerning the timing of the life course. This leads male auto workers to favor retirement in the mid-fifties while physicians prefer the late sixties. In addition, even within subcultures, there are often several alternatives. Thus, like a road map, the abstract concept of the life course in reality is composed of a great many alternative routes to alternative destinations.

Although very-late-in-life options may diminish somewhat because of social and physical aging, the older population is considerably more differentiated than the young. Yet even with the increased complexity of the life course with age, certain generally accepted standards serve as a sort of master timetable for the entire population. Even though there are many exceptions and variations, most Americans start school, finish school, get married, have children, experience the "empty nest," and retire—each within a span surrounding a particular chronological age, the age at which these events are supposed to happen for people of their social class, ethnicity, and gender. Most people spend their lives reasonably on schedule, and when they get off schedule they are motivated to get back on again.

Life course stages are related to chronological age, education, and occupational careers. More dimensions could be added, but the important point is that various social institutions tend to prescribe their own development program related to the various life stages.

The various stages of the life course are made real for the individual in three ways. First, they are related to more specific patterns such as the occupational career. Second, specific expectations or age norms accompany various life stages. And finally, particular types of choices are forced during given phases of the life course.

Age Norms

Age norms dictate what people in a given life stage are allowed to do and be, and what they are required to do and be. Age norms sometimes operate very generally to specify dress, personal appearance, or demeanor in a wide variety of social roles. Other age norms govern approach, entry, incumbency, and exit from social roles, groups, or social situations. Many age norms are passed down through tradition. On the other hand, legal age norms are often the result of compromise and negotiation. A series of assumptions underlie age norms. These assumptions, often uninformed, concern what people in a given life stage are capable of—not just what they ought to do, but what they can do. Thus, both children and older people experience limited opportunities because others assume that they are not strong enough, not experienced or educated enough, or not capable of adequately mature adult judgments. For instance, older workers are passed by for training opportunities because of the limiting mind-set many people hold that "you can't teach an old dog new tricks." Older job applicants are passed over on the assumption that people age sixty have too few years left to work to warrant investing in them. By the same token, young adults are passed over because they "don't have enough experience."

Sometimes age norms make useful and valid distinctions. For example, few people would want to share the road if six-year-olds were behind the wheels of the other cars. But, beginning with adolescence, it becomes increasingly difficult to justify the essentially arbitrary nature of many age norms. And the greater the gap between the actual level of individual functioning and the level implied by the age norm, the more likely that age norms will be seen as unjust.

Conformity to age norms is encouraged by several factors. People are taught early in life by their parents, teachers, and peers how to apply age norms to themselves. If they do not conform, friends, neighbors, and associates can be counted on to apply informal pressures. In the formal realm, regulations bring bureaucratic authority to bear. And finally, laws put the full power of the state behind age norms. For example, the idea that airline pilots should retire by age sixty is supported at every level along this continuum.

Decision Demands

The sometimes chaotic nature of the alternatives presented by various life courses has been mentioned earlier. This chaos is minimized to some degree by age, gender, social class, ethnicity, and so forth. But how do people get into specific situations? It is impossible to assign people to each and every niche in complex, rapidly changing societies. Decision demands force the individual to work within the system to find a slot in the social organization.

Decision demands require that selections be made from an age-linked field of possibilities. For example, after completing preparatory education, young adults usually enter a period of job experimentation. The field of possibilities expands dramatically immediately after graduation and continues to expand while the individual gains job experience. But there is an increasing expectation that people will find positions of employment into which they will settle; during this period the field of jobs for which they are eligible may slowly contract. Contraction also occurs as jobs are selected by others of similar age and experience. For many jobs, career tracks are difficult to begin after age thirty-five.

Decision demands tend to be concentrated in the first half of the life course. That is, individuals are required to make choices and select their career tracks in all sorts of areas—education,

Helen S.

A folksinger and clinical social worker who, at age sixty-five, made a move from urban to rural life after years of careful planning. She offers her views on coming to terms with aging:

"When I was fifty I began looking for a place where I might want to settle. I earned my living as a touring folksinger and clinical social worker and didn't want to change my clinical work, maybe just do less of it. I certainly didn't want to give up my music, so I had to find a community that offered me the opportunity to earn a moderate kind of living. I have always loved the woods, and as soon as I became eligible for Social Security, I sold my house and moved from the city.

"I had to supplement my income from Social Security. Having been a single parent raising two children, I had only part-time jobs, leaving me with no pension. Fortunately I found a position as a therapist here in the local health clinic and can work as many hours as I like. That's how I earn enough to support my singing. This way I have the best of both worlds. I can't imagine not singing.

"I think what I have learned and what I would try to get across to anybody counseling on the subject of aging is that first of all, unless you cease to exist, old age is coming, so there's no sense pretending it isn't coming. After you digest that one—and a lot of people don't; they fight it until they are in a mess about it—you need something else that has nothing to do with aging: it has to do with living. That is, you need to have developed the capacity somewhere for making yourself happy. When you know that, then you can face most of what happens to you at any age."

—From Connie Goldman's "Late Bloomer" public radio series

Socialization produces a measure of continuity from one generation to another.

employment, family, community, voluntary associations, and so on. Lifestyles developed before or during middle age tend to persist as long as health and money hold out. Thus, middle-aged people who want to switch tracks or get involved in new areas sometimes confront the fact that the available slots were taken earlier by their age peers.

On the other hand, those middle-aged people who do retrain and switch careers often find that their new careers develop at an accelerated rate compared to those younger people starting at the same time. This acceleration is probably due to their greater maturity and general experience plus the underlying notion that a person's position in an organization should match his or her life stage.

Social Processes

Socialization is a group of processes through which a group encourages and/or coerces its members to learn and conform to its culture. *Acculturation* is the actual learning of a culture. Much of what individuals seek to learn through acculturation is aimed at making them more effective role players. To the individual, socialization and acculturation are important prerequisites for getting whatever society has to offer. If people know and understand the social system, they can potentially put the system to use. If they do not understand the culture, their lives can be confusing and unpredictable.

Socialization produces a measure of continuity from one generation to another. Society needs new participants, and socialization is a major process through which society attracts, facilitates, and maintains participation. The efforts of the group to help individuals learn the system range from formal, structured programs in which the group is responsible for the outcome, to unstructured, informal processes in which the individual is responsible for the outcome. For example, families are expected to teach children to speak, and schools are expected to teach children to read and write. On the other hand, adults must generally find out on their own how to locate a library.

Age affects what the individual is expected to know and what he or she needs to know in order to be an effective participant in society. Early in life, the emphasis in socialization is on learning language and customs; then it shifts to preparing for adult social roles. In adulthood, expectations gradually shift toward self-initiated acculturation; that is, adults often recognize their need for knowledge and skills and seek them without waiting to be told. At the same time, fewer publicly supported, formal opportunities exist for socialization in adulthood compared to the opportunities that exist for young people.

Older people often have few required contacts with the general community. They associate primarily with people they know and who know them. In addition, most older people continue to function mainly in roles they have occupied for many years. The point is that most roles older people play are roles they have been socialized to for a long time. Aging often results primarily in adjusting the nuances of role playing rather than its basic structure.

Most societies pay little attention to their adult members' needs for maintenance or renewal of knowledge or skills. In this age of the computer, for example, where do middle-aged or older adults go to learn how to use this often complex method of dealing with information? This pattern seriously hampers the ability of some older members of society to remain integrated in the society, particularly in terms of the knowledge and skills required for employment. If older people need information and skills that are necessary for participation in society but are not readily available, then the socialization processes in the society are not adequate.

The process of role anticipation involves learning the rights, obligations, resources, and outlook of a position one will occupy in the future. To the extent that the future position is a general one, it need not represent an unknown. Through fantasies, it is possible to anticipate what the future will hold, identify potential problems, and prepare in advance. The role changes common to later life can often be anticipated, thus smoothing the process of transition.

However, many roles taken up in later life have a degree of vagueness that allows some flexibility in playing them but at the same time hinders anticipation. Such roles are not "packaged," as roles that young people play often are. For example, the role of high school student is much more clearly defined than the role of retired person. As a result, older people must often negotiate new role definitions with significant other people in their environment. Thus, in late adulthood, acculturation—learning or relearning how to function in one's social milieu—depends heavily on the characteristics of others with whom the older person must negotiate. The attitudes of others concerning who the older person is becoming are probably crucial to the content of acculturation in later life. As images of aging become less stereotyped in American culture, the outcome of these negotiations can be expected to become more positive and individuated.

Social roles, even the specific ones such as mother or teacher, tend to be defined in terms that allow room for interpretation. Adaptation to roles is a process of fitting role demands to the individual's capabilities and vice versa. Negotiation—the interpersonal aspect of this adaptation—takes place between role players. This process of tailoring the role to fit the individual and the situation means that it is impossible to describe the role of the grandfather, but looking at how grandfathers play their roles reveals similarities and differences applied to the role by different people.

Thus, through socialization society tells its members that retirement is normal and that it should occur around age sixty-five. Through acculturation, an individual comes to believe that retirement is normal and that it should occur around age sixty-five. Through anticipation, the individual identifies potential problems associated with retirement and tries to solve them in advance. Once the individual retires, the process of adaptation involves tailoring the rather vague retirement role to fit the needs of the individual. Part of this process may involve negotiations between couples about what the retirement role will consist of and how it will influence their life together.

Society's Response to Aging People

In addition to the social factors influencing individual aging directly through social roles, the well-being of aging and older people is also affected by society's response to aging and older people as a social category. There are various social responses to aging; how aging interacts with social class, ethnicity, and gender; and how aging people are responded to by the economy, politics, and government, and health care and social service systems.

General social responses to aging exist in the ideas of a culture, in the media and educational materials through which people learn these ideas, and in the attitudes and actions that result. Americans appear to be genuinely ambivalent about aging. While most people seem to want to think well of older people, aging poses both real and imagined threats to important social values. Family security, freedom of choice, and general happiness are all vulnerable to the ups and downs of one's own aging, the aging of family members for whom one may be responsible, and the aging of society in general. In addition, popular notions present aging as a threat to such social values as productivity and efficiency. Yet general beliefs and stereotypes about aging are not predictably negative or inaccurate; sometimes they are and sometimes they are not, though negative and inaccurate beliefs about older people as jobholders do underpin widespread age discrimination in employment.

People seem to dislike both the idea of aging and the people who experience it. This is true throughout the life cycle. And this dislike seems to result from the public's association of aging with unpleasant outcomes such as illness, unattractiveness, and inability. On the other hand, people also seem to like the idea that wisdom, warmth, and goodness increase with age. Such is the nature of ambivalence.

Contemporary children's books and adult novels generally portray aging in a positive and humanistic light. Children are presented with the ideal that older people are to be treated with respect. Older characters are depicted with a full range of human qualities. Even contemporary television drama recognizes multigenerational relationships as a natural and interesting part of life. There are more older characters in continuing series portraying well-developed, successful people in family or job situations. More than 90 percent of the older characters are portrayed positively. Nevertheless, older people in television news programming seem to be held to the inaccurate view of later life as a life stage beset with serious problems, and this reinforces the prevalent view of later life as an undesirable life stage.

Such ambivalent beliefs, attitudes, and perceptions about aging as a threat to important values translate into age prejudice, or ageism, and age discrimination. Age discrimination imposes negative outcomes on older people just because they are older. Some of it is subtle, as when older people are ignored or avoided in interaction or social planning. It is more direct where people are denied participation because of their age. Direct age discrimination is especially prevalent in the occupational sphere, in mandatory retirement policies for instance, but also appears to operate in volunteer work and other areas as well. Age discrimination also occurs when public agencies fail to orient public programs meant for the general population as much toward older people as they do toward younger people.

Societal disengagement is the withdrawal of interest in the contributions or involvement of older people. It is not a mutually satisfying process but one that is imposed on older people by the withdrawal of opportunities to participate and by circumstances such as ill health. Like age discrimination, the more general

Maggie Kuhn
Activist

My feeling is that in late life we are free to transcend our own history and to be progressive. To take a new view of ourselves and the world. And we are concerned about the tribe's survival, not our own. Let's get that across to people."

Philadelphia organizer and activist Maggie Kuhn, founder of the Gray Panthers, was born August 3, 1905, in Buffalo, New York. The family settled in Cleveland, where Kuhn attended the women's college of Western Reserve University. She planned to be a teacher, but when her creativity was not viewed favorably by her teaching supervisor, she accepted a job with the Young Women's Christian Association (YWCA). A natural organizer, she was good at the job and loved it. She also pursued graduate study at Columbia University Teacher's College, taking the equivalent of a master's degree in a joint program with Union Theological Seminary, and then worked for the YWCA in Philadelphia. Kuhn's work was with businesswomen, but quickly developed into supervising Works Progress Administration workers and maintaining liaison with forty other agencies in the Greater Philadelphia area, including the Federal Job Corps and the Youth Conservation Corps.

During World War II Kuhn worked for the YWCA national staff in New York in the United Service Organizations Division and helped reorganize the Unitarian general alliance. Kuhn's father, a Presbyterian, humorously described this as "doing missionary work among the Unitarians." Several years later Kuhn returned to Philadelphia to help care for her mother and work with a Presbyterian organization, editing the organization's journal and working on their program unit. She kept this job for twenty-two years, until she retired at the age of sixty-five. During the last several years of her tenure, she was posted to the Interchurch Center in New York, near Riverside Church.

"They told me [retirement] . . . was mandatory on my sixty-fifth birthday," Kuhn recalls. "If I had been a man, I could have been negotiating for a year at a time; but this was not the case. There were six of us in the New York area, an interesting group of women who were confronted with the same difficulty." Kuhn remembers: "We got together and discussed it and we said: 'The question is, what do we do with the rest of our lives?' And we said, 'We can't answer that alone. We've got to deliberate it, and get some kind of a collective answer.' So we wrote that in a very simple manifesto, and called a meeting at the International House of Columbia. A hundred people showed! It was in June, 1970; a historical moment."

Kuhn and her friends had chosen Vietnam as their topic, and they decided to "stand with the kids" and demonstrate, calling themselves the "Consultation of Older and Younger Adults for Social Change." They were invited to appear on a talk show at WBAI in New York, but the producer winced to hear their name and said: "That name will get you nowhere. You're the Gray Panthers!" The semantic link to the black civil rights movement delighted them, and they adopted the name.

process of societal disengagement rests not so much on the functional needs of society as on its prejudices.

The general social treatment of aging and older people reflects ambivalence. On the one hand, age prejudice institutionalized the removal of older adults from the labor force; on the other hand, retirement income systems transformed retirement into a reward. Society's treatment of the older age categories is softened by centuries-old family values of respect and caring for elders.

In May 1972, Kuhn attended the General Assembly of the Presbyterian Church at its annual meeting in Denver, Colorado. When the featured VIP failed to appear at the press conference in the hotel, the press officer begged Kuhn to fill in and talk about her Gray Panthers. There was a huge media turnout for the conference—all the wire services as well as the *Denver Post*, the *Washington Post*, and the *New York Times*. "A month later I was on the Johnny Carson show," Kuhn recalls. "It was unbelievable."

Kuhn had a goal in mind, but she did not expect her path to develop as it has. "I didn't set out to start a movement," she says. "In many ways it was to answer this very odd question: What do you *do* with the rest of your life, when you've been so involved with your work? You see, people who have work they love have a certain amount of privilege. And their personal and their professional lives are blended." But it isn't just those who are privileged to have work that they love who must worry about what to do after "retirement." Kuhn sees it is a universal problem: "Those who do not have work they love, hate what they do, and aren't affirmed by their jobs are glad to leave them. But *then* what do they do? They're miserable, too."

—*Lydia Brontë*

Aging and Social Inequality

Social class affects aging by influencing the attitudes, beliefs, and values people use to make life course choices and by influencing life course opportunities, particularly in terms of education and jobs. People whose social-class backgrounds lead to middle-class jobs or higher approach aging with much greater resources— knowledge, good health, adequate retirement income—compared to the working class and the poor. The positive picture of individual aging presented earlier is primarily middle class because most older Americans are middle class. On the other hand, many of the problematic aspects of aging are concentrated among the working class and the poor.

Racial discrimination has concentrated African Americans disproportionately in low-paying jobs and in substandard housing; this fact applies more to older African Americans than to African Americans in general. Compared to older whites, older African Americans have lower Social Security benefits, fewer private pensions, and greater incidence of illness and disability.

Older Native Americans face an even worse situation than older African Americans. Excluded from participation in American society and heavily concentrated in rural areas and on Indian reservations, older American Indians are much less likely than other older people to have access to services. Compared to older whites, older Native Americans are much less likely to have had middle-class jobs and much more likely to have inadequate incomes and poor health.

The picture for older Asian Americans is mixed, although all groups show some negative effects of racism. Japanese-American elders have had jobs that closely parallel those of whites and as a result have retirement incomes closer to those of whites than any other racial category. There is great diversity among older Chinese Americans in terms of jobs and retirement income. Filipino-American older people are more likely to have had low paying jobs and thus low retirement incomes. Despite their lower incomes, older Asian Americans tend to be in better health than older whites.

The Hispanic population is quite diverse also. Older Hispanic Americans tend to be better off than older African Americans but not as well off as older non-Hispanic whites or older Asian Americans in terms of health and retirement income.

Of the categories of people who experience discrimination in American society, women experience the greatest inequality. Women who opt to be homemakers are quite vulnerable economically to the breakup of their marriages through divorce or widowhood. Those who are employed are concentrated in "women's work," which tends to be low paying and not covered by private pensions. As a result, retirement incomes of women are only about 55 percent as high as those for men.

Multiple jeopardy increases the probability of having poor health and inadequate income. Being a woman is the greatest disadvantage, followed by having less than high school education (being working class) and by being African American. Social inequality has a great influence on aging through its effect on jobs and lifetime earnings and their consequent impact on health and retirement income in later life.

Aging, Health Care, and Social Services

Health care and social services to older people have increased dramatically in scope and amount since the early 1960s, but the size of the older population has increased even faster. As a result, there are substantial gaps in national programs to finance health care and social services, and continued inflation, especially in health care costs, has prevented these gaps from closing.

When individuals have difficulty in getting adequate services, they may think theirs is an isolated case and ask, "Why me?" But in the case of health care and social services to elders, the problems are greatly influenced by the haphazard nature of the social structures that provide these services. In health care, although all models of care delivery have their appropriate applications, the medical model has tended to dominate definitions of who could get services, what services they could get, and who could provide them. In addition, national programs for financing health care for older people have emphasized funding for institutionally provided medical services and discouraged less expensive institutional services such as personal care and noninstitutional services such as home care. The dominance of the medical model is in large part due to an imbalance of resources and credibility between physician-directed advocates and advocates for the social and holistic models of care, which call for a greater variety of care alternatives and involvement of a wider variety of types of caregivers.

Medicare, a major financier of hospital care for older people, is much less effective in its coverage of physicians' fees, home health care, and long-term care. It completely ignores the needs for eyeglasses, hearing aids, dental care, and immunizations.

Medicaid is a major source of funding for long-term care, but to qualify for it, older people must deplete their resources until they become eligible for welfare. Medicaid is not available to most middle-class older Americans.

Because inflation in health care costs has been substantially higher than in other areas of the economy over the past several years, severe problems have developed in financing Medicare and Medicaid and private health insurance as well. A large portion of the federally supported effort originally intended to address enforcement of care quality and accomplish planning has instead gone into trying to contain increasing costs. There has been a resulting reduction in the number of people being served and an increase in the financial burden borne by older people and their families, but there has been little effect on the rate of inflation in health care costs.

Social services are provided to elders through a network of federal, state, and local agencies created by the Older Americans Act and funded through the Older Americans Act, Social Services Block Grants, local United Way agencies, local foundations, and a variety of other minor sources. The Older Americans Act has encouraged the development of an array of services that is similar in most communities, including information and referral, transportation, outreach, both congregate and home-delivered meals, homemaker and home health services, telephone reassurance, and legal services. However, funding levels for these services have been at spartan levels, especially when compared with the sums spent on health care.

As a result of the increased number of older people and the increasing costs of health and social services, a debate has emerged over whether age or need is the more appropriate criterion to use in establishing eligibility for services. This debate is likely to remain spirited.

—*Robert C. Atchley, Ph.D.*

In mid-1992, two separate front-page articles appeared in the *New York Times* related to aging and work. The first reported revised estimates of the older population in the next century, with some researchers predicting three times the conventional population projections of more conservative demographers at the Census Bureau. The second article detailed the unexpectedly high costs incurred by some state governments due to their policies of encouraging early retirement.

These headlines about the future of the older population and the public cost (in dollars and experience) of early retirement dramatize the importance of work and retirement for public policy and private decision makers. The burgeoning over-fifty population that will grow ever larger as we move through the first half of the twenty-first century presents new challenges to government, business, education, social services, and individuals alike.

What are the best policies for either encouraging retirement in order to create new openings in the work force or to entice people to remain working, whether full- or part-time? How will our country take advantage of its human capital in the form of accumulated knowledge, expertise, and judgment possessed by mature workers? And how will each man and woman in the middle years of life confront the issues of enjoying work, feeling productive, drawing enough income, or making important changes when goals remain unmet? Certain trends and events must be considered when trying to answer these questions.

- The average age of a U.S. worker will reach forty by the year 2000.

- The passage of the Age Discrimination in Employment Act of 1967, and amended in 1978 and 1986, has prohibited hiring or firing based on age and eliminated mandatory retirement.

- The public has been more aware about aging due to dissemination of gerontological knowledge beyond the research and academic community.

- The ratio of retirees to workers, the "dependency ratio," has changed significantly during the past thirty years.

Attitudes toward work and retirement continue to change. With the growing popularity of the idea of "productive aging," the over-fifty work force is seen as a tremendous national asset. Many companies are experimenting with retraining programs, phased retirement, and even inducements to stay on after retirement as part of an expert pool for special projects and troubleshooting. Global competition and corporate downsizing are taking their toll. But with a smaller, less well-prepared younger work force coming along, many mature workers may find new and unexpected opportunities. As this chapter shows, midlife and older employees have qualities that make them an excellent investment.

Labor Force Participation

Earlier in the twentieth century, the prevailing view was that people, usually men, would remain in the labor force as long as possible. Older workers would retire only because they were forced to. Greater economic security and changing attitudes have led to the current average age of withdrawal from the work force at sixty-three.

A simple comparison of age groups in the work force in 1972 and 1992 vividly illustrates the effects of aging on the work force. Table 1 reveals the following:

1. For men, the percentage in the work force has declined between 1972 and 1992 in all age categories.

2. The older the age group in any one of the two years indicated, the lower its rate of participation in the labor force.

3. After the age group fifty-five to fifty-nine there is a marked drop in participation rates.

4. There is a dramatic contrast between men and women in changes in labor force participation rates.

The first item is quite well known: Participation in the labor force declines in accordance with age. But the pronounced drop in the rate after ages fifty-five to fifty-nine (for both years, but especially in 1992) is explainable primarily by the availability of "early" retirement at age sixty-two, under the Social Security system. This helps to account for the drop from the 1972 rate for men sixty to sixty-four (71 percent) to that of 1992 (56 percent), a decrease of 15 percent.

The number of persons age sixty-five and older has increased tenfold since 1900, and the number potentially available for work has correspondingly grown, but since 1950 the number of older people in the work force has remained almost steadily at around 3 million.

While the twenty-year period saw declining rates for men of all ages, the very opposite applied to women under the age of sixty-five. Even for women sixty-five to sixty-nine, the difference between 1972 and 1992 shows only a tiny decline—from 17 to 16 percent. While older men are taking advantage of early retirement opportunities, older women working outside the home are remaining in the work force longer. There are many reasons for this, the primary one of which is financial need. Working women may be waiting for their husbands to retire. They also may be seeking to add years toward higher pension coverage—especially if they have taken time out for childrearing.

The overall participation rate of women forty-five to sixty-four has climbed dramatically since the 1940s when, due to the wartime effort, many women entered the labor force. Until recently, women were not expected to work outside the home, particularly

Contrary to what was believed around the turn of the 20th century, the work capacity of older persons is of such quality to warrant continued employment in a variety of occupations.

middle-aged and older women. But that trend has changed as gender roles have undergone a transformation. Middle-aged women, in contrast to men, have been streaming into the labor force. As of 1989, 70.5 percent of all women forty-five to fifty-four were in the labor force, nearly double the percentage of 1950.

One consequence of large numbers of women entering the work force is the now-common phenomenon of the dual-career couple. As these couples enter their fifties or sixties, the men move toward retirement, but their wives may choose to stay employed since many are just hitting their career stride, having delayed entry or reentry into the work force while taking time out for childrearing. Current research indicates that the majority of couples cope quite well with this separate timing of retirement.

Statistics on employment and retirement rates of men and women can be misleading. The figures mentioned above do not differentiate between full-time and part-time participants in the work force. Furthermore, rates of "labor force participation" are essentially average annual percentages of persons working or looking for work, as a proportion of the total working-age population (or of specific age groups). But such averages referring to "participation rates" are not the same as figures that show how many persons in any given year have had any degree of "work experience." This is especially important when dealing with older workers because the U.S. Department of Labor's statistics on persons of any given age who have worked in any past year show that there are many more older workers who have had such work experience than statistics on their participation rates would indicate. For example, among men sixty to sixty-four, the participation rate in 1991 was 56 percent, but in fact the U.S. Bureau of Labor Statistics shows, for that same year, more than 3.1 million men sixty to sixty-four (64 percent) actually had some degree of work experience. In other words, participation rate statistics tend to underestimate the numbers of people with actual work experience—and such discrepancies are greatest in the case of older people, starting at about age fifty-five.

Table 1: Labor Force Participation Rates by Age and Gender, 1972 to 1992

	1972	1992
Men		
All Ages	79	76
20–24	85	83
25–54	95	93
55–59	87	80
60–64	71	56
65–69	35	27
70 & over	16	11
Women		
All Ages	44	58
20–24	60	70
25–54	48	56
60–64	35	36
65–69	17	16
70 & over	5	1

Source: U.S. Department of Labor, Employment and Earnings, for December 1972 and May 1992. Figures are rounded percentages.

Employment

Older employed workers can be found in nearly every industry and occupation, a fact that contradicts a widespread image or stereotype. However, their proportions in selected industries and occupations may differ from those of younger people. Furthermore, gender makes a difference. One should not talk about "older workers" as members of one homogeneous population. For example, older women are disproportionately employed in service and clerical jobs, compared to men. And among men, the older ones have the highest self-employed percentage—higher than younger men and older women. Men age sixty to sixty-four and sixty-five-plus also are relatively well represented in executive and managerial occupations (see Table 2). This type of contrast also applies to the occupation designated as "operators, fabricators, and laborers" (such as semi- and unskilled laborers); older men have the highest percentage, compared to younger men and older women.

Unemployment

Many of the problems of older workers (defined by some legislation as persons over forty or forty-five) surface during times of widespread, general unemployment when such workers seek reemployment; when companies go out of business (or relocate); and also in situations involving opportunities for retention, promotion, and/or training in an enterprise.

Looking only at unemployment rates among different age groups reveals that older workers tend to have lower jobless rates when compared to younger workers. This is true especially when unemployment rates of teenagers (15 percent in 1989) are compared to those of the older workers (3 percent in 1989 for those over sixty-five). Indeed, workers age sixty-two and older typically have the lowest unemployment rates.

A more comprehensive picture of unemployment and age, however, reveals some interesting points:

1. When older workers do become unemployed, they tend to stay unemployed much longer than do younger unemployed workers.

2. Once they become unemployed, many workers sixty-two and older leave the labor force completely because at that age they became eligible for retired worker benefits under

the Social Security system, and possibly for private pensions. In fact, many private pension plans make it possible for workers under sixty-two to leave the paid work force.

3. The government does not count as unemployed any worker who is not looking for employment. But when workers lose their jobs, a large proportion of them eventually become discouraged in their job search and stop looking completely. These workers—typically in the older age groups—are classified as "discouraged" workers, and the official jobless measures do not include them.

4. Contrary to popular belief, most older job-losing workers (until they reach age sixty-five) are looking for full-time jobs, not part-time ones. Unemployed people in their late fifties and early sixties (or older, in some instances) have a high degree of commitment to being in the labor force.

5. Among older unemployed workers, very few voluntarily leave their previous jobs. That is, the vast majority (except for those sixty-five and older) have lost their previous jobs. Even among those sixty-five and older, as of 1987, 45 percent of the men and 39 percent of the women were "job losers." Actually, among older unemployed persons, very large percentages of those sixty-five-plus tend to be reentering the labor force, or entering for the first time (for example, homemakers), to look for employment. In 1987, the percentage for men was 48 percent; for women of the same age group, it was 55 percent.

While it is true that most people sixty-five and older are retired and remain retired, large numbers nevertheless are looking for employment. Their job search is motivated by both psychological and financial reasons.

The reasons for the unemployment of older workers have to do not only with the ups and downs of the economy but also with such factors as "structural changes"—for example, increased foreign competition, the movement of companies to other countries and regions of the United States, changes in the population structure, and changes in the industrial/occupational makeup of the total U.S. employment. Factory and office closings, reduced need for products and services, downsizing, and the abolition of occupations are among the factors that produce "displaced workers."

A 1986 report by the Department of Labor, based on U.S. Bureau of the Census surveys, found that older workers (fifty-five and older) had the highest percentages of displaced workers because companies had closed or moved. Many people believe that older workers tend to be protected by "seniority" rules, but in fact companies going out of business or relocating are more likely to be in declining industries, industries from which workers have a higher chance of being displaced. Such industries, including manufacturing, tend to have an older age profile than growing new industries.

The problems of older workers are highlighted or dramatized by data about what happens to them once they become unemployed. Among workers with at least three years in the labor force who then lost their jobs in a previous five-year period, the Department of Labor reported in 1990 that only 53 percent of the group fifty-five to sixty-four years old and 28 percent of those sixty-five and older found new jobs—percentages far below those for the younger age groups. Table 3 shows the rates by age for (1) reemployment, (2) continued joblessness, and (3) exit from the labor force.

While many in the youngest age group, once unemployed, enter or reenter the education system, older workers in the same situation—especially those sixty-five and older—are more likely to take advantage of retirement benefits under Social Security and/or private pensions. Leaving the labor force is one explanation for the sixty-five-plus group having a lower "still-unemployed" percentage than nearly all the other, younger age groups. If the job losers who have left the labor force were excluded from the category, then the rates of job losers still jobless would rise to 23 percent of the fifty-five- to sixty-four-year-olds and 26 percent of the sixty-five-plus group. In other words, even after eliminating job losers who left the work force, older workers still had the highest rate of unemployment, compared to those job losers under the age of fifty-five. Some of this difference may be due to differences in job skills, but earlier research analyses show that even when "non-age" factors are accounted for, age by itself still is a factor in the job-finding success rates of older workers.

While most people sixty-five and older are retired, large numbers nevertheless are looking for employment.

COPYRIGHT ALICE A. HARDIN

Furthermore, in 1991, a year characterized by high general unemployment, the labor force participation rates of men fifty-five to sixty-four and sixty-five-plus declined from previous years. In addition, the discouraged worker numbers—those who gave up the job search—rose by 33 percent from 1990 to 1991, which was a higher rate of increase than for younger workers seeking employment. Finally, According to the American Association of Retired Persons Public Policy Institute, the same period witnessed an increase in older workers employed only on part-time basis, even though they were seeking full-time employment.

In short, older workers tend to have lower jobless rates than younger ones, but once they do become unemployed, they stay unemployed longer and/or become discouraged and give up altogether (and therefore are no longer counted as unemployed). Furthermore, if they do find new employment, most if not all research indicates that older men reemployed on a full-time basis tend to find jobs that pay less than did their previous full-time jobs.

Table 2: Employed Persons by Occupation, Sex, and Age, 1988 Annual Averages (in Percentages)

Occupation	All Ages 16+	45–54	55–59	60–64	65+
Men					
Executive, administrative, managerial	13.6	18.6	17.6	17.4	16.4
Professional specialty	11.9	14.0	13.3	13.1	13.1
Technicians	2.9	2.5	1.8	1.4	0.9
Sales	11.1	11.2	11.6	12.4	16.1
Admin. support, including clerical	5.7	4.7	5.3	5.2	5.8
Service	9.6	7.0	7.8	9.9	11.8
Precision production, craft, repair	19.7	20.0	19.6	17.4	10.7
Operators, fabricators, laborers	20.9	18.2	17.8	16.8	10.9
Farm operators and managers	1.7	1.9	3.1	4.1	10.1
Farm workers, forestry, fishing	2.8	1.8	2.1	2.4	4.2
Total percentage	100.0	100.0	100.0	100.0	100.0
Total number (in thousands)	63,273	10,201	3,954	2,638	1,911
Women					
Executive, administrative, managerial	10.8	12.5	10.7	10.3	8.6
Professional specialty	14.4	15.6	13.8	10.2	10.6
Technicians and related	3.3	2.8	2.3	1.5	1.2
Sales	13.0	10.6	11.8	13.2	14.5
Admin. support, including clerical	28.3	28.6	27.5	29.6	24.6
Service	17.9	16.1	19.8	20.6	27.6
Precision production, craft, repair	2.3	2.7	2.4	2.6	2.9
Operators, fabricators, laborers	8.8	9.9	10.1	10.3	7.2
Farm operators and managers	0.4	0.6	0.9	0.8	1.8
Farm workers, forestry, fishing	0.7	0.6	0.7	0.8	1.0
Total percentage	100.0	100.0	100.0	100.0	100.0
Total number (in thousands)	51,696	8,246	2,938	1,904	1,286

Source: U.S. Department of Labor, Bureau of Labor Statistics, unpublished data.

Table 3: Labor Market Experience of Job Losers by Age

Age	Reemployed	Still Unemployed	Left Labor Force
20–24	76%	10%	14%
25–54	78%	14%	8%
55–64	53%	16%	31%
65 & older	28%	10%	62%

Source: U.S. Department of Labor, 1990 data. Percentages rounded.

Studs Terkel

Radio interviewer and author

T he life span is increasing, and we've got the least to lose. Make some trouble. Let's do it."

Studs Terkel is America's foremost oral historian and chronicler of the American working class. He was born in New York City in 1912 to working-class parents; his father was a tailor with poor health. When Terkel was eight, his father became ill, and the family moved to Chicago. His mother ran a rooming house and later a small hotel to support the family. His childhood experiences stimulated his intense interest in people, primarily those of a lower middle class.

Terkel attended the University of Chicago, earned his law degree, and passed the bar exam. But the minutely detailed aspect of legal practice bored him completely. To this day he considers his three years of law school a "waste of time." His next job was to count "baby bonds" with the Treasury Department in Washington, D.C. "It drove me nuts, of course," Terkel gives as his reason for quitting.

Back in Chicago, he joined a Works Progress Administration–sponsored labor theater group performing such controversial plays as Clifford Odets's socialistic *Waiting for Lefty*, then he played the role of a gangster in the radio soap opera "Ma Perkins."

Other radio jobs included disc jockey, sportscaster, and commentator. This latter role proved to be a perfect vehicle for expressing his liberal pro-Roosevelt leanings. Since most of his colleagues were anti-Roosevelt, he "got kicked off the air a lot." Always willing to be outspoken, Terkel built his career on his socially consciousness willingness to stir up debate and controversy.

In the 1950s, he was part of the "Chicago Style TV" group with Dave Garroway and "Kukla, Fran, and Ollie." Terkel's show, "Studs' Place," was taken off the air because of his "big mouth," so to speak.

By the early 1950s he landed a job with WFMT, then a small classical music station. Terkel, who has been with WFMT now for over forty years, developed the author interviews for which he is famous. "I work like an old-time craftsman," he recounts. "In other words, what I do isn't an art, it's a craft. Either I'm a good craftsman or I'm not. I have to do my homework." As for his current motivation, Terkel declares: "The thing I live for now is to make trouble. I like the idea of making trouble. The young seem to have lost that, at least for the moment. So it's got to be some other group . . . the most unexpected group. And the most logical group."

—*Lydia Brontë*

Loss of a job in one's midlife and in older years can have a severely negative effect on a longer-term (or permanent) basis, when comparisons are made with younger job losers. Compared to younger workers, older job losers have few opportunities for second chances.

The term "older workers" does not do justice to these workers' great diversity or to the fact that they can be found in nearly every industry and occupation (see Table 2). But there are important differences. For example, older women are disproportionately employed in service and clerical jobs compared to men. Older men hold the highest percentage of self-employed jobs, and they are well represented in executive and managerial occupations. However, the times are changing and the appearance of larger numbers of older professional women may alter this picture.

In 1905 the declarations of the famous physician William Osler mirrored the common perception of the older adult in the work force, a turn-of-the-century mind-set that has plagued older adults for decades. Said Osler, "I have two fixed ideas. . . . The first is the comparative uselessness of men above forty years of age. . . . My second fixed idea is the uselessness of men above sixty years of age, and the incalculable benefit it would be . . . if, as a matter of course, men stopped work at this age."

Nearly a century later, however, in 1991, Dr. T. Franklin Williams, former director of the National Institute on Aging (NIA), testified to Congress, "Contrary to earlier views that aging is associated with inevitable declines in physical and mental functioning, we now know with great confidence that there are few inevitable declines, and that most people can, and many do, continue to function into their seventies and eighties and even longer at much the same levels as they have functioned in earlier years." Williams relayed the concept of an extended functioning capacity as a response to the common myth that an older person's faculties and capabilities diminish with graying hair.

This simply isn't true. When there was a widespread call for special performance tests to determine the work capacity and qualifications of older workers, experts in the field of industrial gerontology maintained that since testing and evaluation of persons of younger ages are conducted, there is no reason *not* to use the same standards and criteria for all ages. Data already disclose that younger persons in workplaces frequently develop some level of disabling symptoms or conditions, and that—after treatment or rehabilitation—they can return to their previous jobs. In other cases, work modifications accommodate a wide range of disabled employees of all ages.

Regarding the impact of such chronic ailments as coronary disease, studies by the National Institute on Aging have shown that it is possible to predict the capabilities of people not only in their forties and fifties, but in their sixties and seventies, over several years after diagnosis. NIA former director Williams maintains that if individuals pass such tests (with no signs of heart disease), then the risk of having some sort of heart attack over the following

four or five years is only about 3 percent for both the forty to fifty-nine age group and the sixty to sixty-nine age group.

Williams and other experts (going as far back as the famous Ross McFarland of Harvard University, in the 1950s and 1960s) believe there is no scientific, medical reason for determining the eligibility for hiring and for continued employment on the basis of chronological age in any profession or job. Rather eligibility should be determined through the testing and evaluation of individuals, regardless of the year of their birth.

Another concept evoking attention is heterogeneity: individual variability within any age group, and the overlap of work capacity measures between different age groups. One milestone longitudinal study reported that not only were there no changes over several years in cognitive abilities of people in their sixties and early seventies, but there were no differences for those in their forties and fifties. More than half of the oldest groups had very similar scores to adults in their twenties.

It is possible to measure the capacity (both physical and mental) of any specific individual for performing a given job. This kind of analysis is being done all the time for younger workers and, again, there is no reason to construct special measurements or tests for older persons. However, variability in measures is so great within any one age category, and the overlap between age groups on these measures so great, that age by itself is not a useful criterion for determining work capacity.

The passage of the Americans with Disabilities Act in 1992 points to the need for greater information about the range of abilities affecting the employability and reemployability of older persons. In a 1987 study of ten items involving mobility, endurance for confined movement, lower and upper body strength, and fine motor skills (such as grasping with fingers) among workers fifty-five to seventy-four years old, the National Center for Health Statistics found, for example, that:

- Only 5 percent were unable to walk a quarter mile.

- Only 4 percent were unable to walk up ten steps.

- Only 6 percent were unable to stand on their feet for two hours.

- Only 10 percent were unable to stoop, crouch, or kneel.

- Only 5 percent were unable to lift or carry twenty-five pounds.

Among people who had retired for non-health reasons, the percentages were only slightly higher. The 1987 National Center for Health Statistics' full report provides greater details by specific age groups within the general fifty-five- to seventy-four-year-old population. Overall, the study found that 73 percent of those still working had no difficulty with any of the ten work-related activities, compared to 60 percent of those retiring because of non-health reasons and only 14 percent of those retiring because of health reasons. According to the report, "Potentially, many of the people who had retired for reasons other than their health could have remained in the labor force." Workplace adaptations, as well as accommodations by workers themselves who might be labeled "disabled," along with monitoring of possible discrimination on the basis of both age and "disabilities," are necessary requirements for addressing this issue. More than 65 percent of the employers in the study considered workers fifty-five and older to be "more reliable, punctual, or loyal," while less than 5 percent rated them as being less so.

The rate of absenteeism among older workers tends to be lower than that among younger workers, but the evidence indicates that once absent, they may be away from the job longer. Injuries—as a cited cause of absenteeism—may be fewer, but the severity of the older workers' injuries tends to be greater. These kinds of measures need to be viewed with a comprehensive perspective as women become an increasing part of the total labor force. Middle-aged women, for example, may tend to have longer work interruptions than men, largely because they still have to bear the bulk of family caregiving. Any useful analysis of such measures as absenteeism and tardiness needs to take into account gender, marital status, age, and the extent to which middle-aged and older workers have older family members who may constitute a "risk factor" for such workers. As women swell the ranks of the middle-aged and older worker population, it is possible for the statistics on absenteeism and tardiness to increase—even if age per se is not the explanation.

According to a 1991 report for the Small Business Administration, small businesses generally rated the labor market experience and skills accumulations of older workers as superior to those of younger workers.

Policies and Programs for Older Workers

In recent years, policy discussions have included an interest in deferring retirement beyond the typical retirement age. Work continuity, training and retraining, alternative work arrangements, and "second careers" have been among the specific topics explored in such discussions. Emerging challenges are associated with the employment experiences of older women. In terms of history, retirement is a relatively new achievement—a mark of a civilized industrial society. For some time, early retirement has been viewed as an even stronger measure of such a society. But another view accompanies such sentiments: men and women need to feel useful, and one medium of that usefulness is participation in the paid labor force. For some older adults, retirement means a reduced income, so working is a better option. Also, the "unused" or "wasted" contributions that otherwise could be made

Michelle C.

A sixty-eight-year-old talent agent in the world of rock and roll, Michelle tells how she uses her years of experience in the entertainment industry to help young talent:

"I began my career at age fifteen, making radio commercials for women's cosmetics. I became a talk show host and a radio and television writer. When I married, I gave up my on-air career to write advertising copy. Several years ago a young man asked my help in getting a job at a radio station. That was the start of my new career in helping young people get a foothold in the entertainment industry.

"I meet a lot of twenty-year-old disc jockeys who play hard rock, and I think that's funny. Since I was a performer myself, I think I am a pretty good judge of talent, and if the way they present their music amuses me at my age, then it must be good! I think what I understand is the music's rhythmic noise—it makes me want to dance. I also know a good voice when I hear one. When I think a voice is good, I work hard to sell it to radio and television stations all across the country. For years I helped people find jobs. The big difference now is that I get paid for it.

"I don't just get a person a job and take the money and run. I'm interested in careers, and as long as they are with me they get career guidance. The thing they don't know how to do is to handle themselves in political situations in the entertainment business, and I'm an old and practiced warrior at that.

> "I think when I go in to see station managers and owners, they are a little surprised by my age and that I am a woman. I just come in and sit down and talk about the talent I represent and what they have to offer. The only time that I get really rough is when the contract that I have negotiated is violated. I just don't allow that.
>
> "As I grow older, I would like to feel that a number of people young enough to carry on would make me a part of their lives."
>
> —*From Connie Goldman's "Late Bloomer" public radio series*

to the economy, as a result of premature or (in previous years) compulsory retirement, have been bemoaned.

Work Continuity

Despite the many reasons, or incentives, for older workers to retire—or the disincentives to remain in the labor force—there nevertheless are workers who do continue in the paid labor force. How do they differ from those who have retired?

One obvious difference is that "work continuers" need to remain in the work force for financial reasons; their personal and household incomes tend to be lower than those of retirees of the same ages. Continuers are less likely to be eligible for, or to be receiving, an employer's pension, private or public.

While the evidence is not too well established, the fear of eroding real income (purchasing power) may be influencing today's workers to remain longer in the labor force. As a general rule, the greater the years in retirement, the lower one's personal and/or household income; conversely the older one is at the time of his or her retirement, the greater that person's income.

As another confirmation of people's financial reasons to continue working, continuers are more likely to be still paying mortgages for their homes and also more likely to be renters, which is typically an indication of their lower socioeconomic sta-

tus. To be sure, the general rule indicated earlier requires some modification: middle-aged and relatively young older workers who can expect a relatively high retirement income and who have negative attitudes toward their work (or have some attraction toward retirement activities) may be able to and want to leave the labor force. They tend to retire at an early age. But generally speaking, the longer a person waits to leave the labor force, the greater will be his or her income at retirement time.

For some older persons, retirement means a reduced income, and they need to work for that reason.

COPYRIGHT SUSAN GRANADOS

The significance of these relationships is that, to the extent that a worker can time his or her age of retirement and becomes aware of the financial advantage of delayed retirement (depending on type of pensions, etc.), the odds are increased that he or she will continue to stay in the labor force. One qualification to such a statement has to do with the feelings a worker has about the job.

The aforementioned propositions are confirmed by the fact, for example, that people in professional occupations tend to remain in the labor force longer than workers in unskilled jobs—despite their higher retirement-income potentials, compared to the potentials of nonprofessionals. Again, one of the primary reasons is that the job satisfaction levels of professionals are higher than those of lesser-skilled workers. Just as important, if not more so, is that the odds for poor health conditions are lower among professionals, thus removing one of the most important reasons for relatively "young-age" retirement. In addition, a far lower proportion of retired professionals cite income from work as the one factor they missed most about not working any longer, compared to retirees from other occupational levels.

Work continuers in the older ages also retain a level of work commitment (measured by negative preferences for retiring completely) almost the same as younger adults. This applies to those sixty-five and older as well as to those fifty-five to sixty-four years old. Whether for financial or social-psychological reasons, more than 80 percent of the sixty-five-plus continuers claim they do not look forward to leaving the labor force completely—compared to only 45 percent of those fifty-five to sixty-four. But much of this wide difference is due to the fact that the very oldest workers that contributed to these statistics had no private pension coverage.

Training and Retraining

Given the fact that in the 1990s the average age of American workers is about forty, and the further reality that the economy, the industrial/occupational structure, and technology are changing, the need for continuous education and training/retraining may become greater than in the past few decades. One advantage of this "aging of the work force" is that it could mean a more experienced group of middle-aged and older workers whose background makes them prepared to meet changing labor demands and technologies. Employers and their representatives (as well as policymakers) will have to change their images about the capacity and the willingness of middle-aged and older workers to learn new skills, and adapt to social and economic changes. Any reluctance or failure to provide for and encourage training for such workers could contribute negatively to the nation's levels of productivity in a world of global competition.

Organizations need to conduct current and expected skill needs surveys, assess their personnel's age and skill profiles, and plan accordingly. This type of planning involves recognition of, and preparation for, such career events as plateauing, burnout, and skill obsolescence. This perspective and strategy are the subject not only of organizations and government agencies in the United States, but also in most of the industrialized and industrializing countries in the world.

One frequently overlooked feature of training and the older worker is the possibility of using older persons themselves as trainers—an untapped reserve in the workplace or in the community. Many experts claim that the processes of learning among older adults are essentially the same as among younger men and women, but there can still be the problem of persuading middle-aged and older workers to volunteer for training programs. Some may be concerned about their capacities or pace of learning in the midst of younger trainees; some skills might require longer learning time, with more instructor assistance. But for many others, there are no such fears, but rather resentments for having to be the victims of age segregation in the classroom or workplace.

So, although older trainees might need more time to learn certain skills, they tend to perform on the job no differently from younger trainees. In the environment of technological dynamics, frequent and continuous training or retraining can make older workers even more ready and capable of adjusting to changing skill demands.

Private Sector Training Programs

Worker training programs exist in most industries. Some are conducted in-house while others are offered through trade schools, community colleges, four-year colleges, and universities. These adult education courses are often supported by companies through tuition assistance, when employee training is deemed job related. Employers are more likely to provide or pay for men ages forty-five to fifty-four to take adult education courses than other age groups. According to researchers, courses taken by women are less likely to be subsidized by employers, yet they provide or subsidize more than half of such courses taken by middle-aged women.

Public Sector Training Programs

In addition to private sector training programs, the federal government also plays a role in training older workers. Two programs, the Senior Community Service Employment Program (SCSEP) and the Job Training Partnership Act (JTPA), offer training opportunities to those who meet fairly restrictive eligibility requirements.

SCSEP (based on Title V of the Older Americans Act) was established to promote part-time opportunities in community services for low-income adults. SCSEP participants must be at least fifty-five years old and have incomes not exceeding 125 percent of the poverty level.

Under SCSEP, qualifying older workers are placed in part-time (twenty to twenty-five hours per week) public service jobs in such settings as day-care centers, schools, hospitals, and senior centers. Federal funds may be used to compensate participants for up to 1,300 hours of work per year, including orientation and training. SCSEP is designed to help older workers transition to private sector jobs once on-the-job training has been accomplished. The program has been criticized because it reaches so few older workers (65,000 in 1990), offers limited (usually low-tech) retraining, and does not offer preplacement training.

SCSEP gives grants to national nonprofit sponsoring organizations, such as the National Council on the Aging and the National Council of Senior Citizens, and state agencies that receive federal funds to manage employment programs. These agencies, in turn, administer the programs.

The largest government-sponsored training program is JTPA, which was enacted in 1982 as a replacement to CETA, the War on Poverty era's Comprehensive Employment and Training Act. JTPA primarily serves youth, but through its Title II-A it channels funds to adults fifty-five and older. JTPA programs, sponsored

Older workers can get training from both private sector training programs and the federal government.

by local governments and private sector planning agencies, involve classroom training, job-search assistance, and on-the-job training.

Alternative Work Arrangements

The concept "alternative work arrangements" refers to the scheduling of workers of any age to engage in employment on terms that differ from conventional patterns, particularly the typical five-days-a-week, eight-hours-per-day, year-round model. All of these different forms of work-time allocation (including job sharing) can be subsumed for practical purposes under the category of part-time work.

From 1960 to 1982 the percentage of middle-aged and older workers employed on a part-time basis (in a variety of settings for the distribution of their time) had been increasing, but it has apparently leveled off since. According to U.S. Department of Labor data, this was especially the case among both men and women sixty-five and older.

In 1991 Louis Harris and Associates, with support from the Commonwealth Fund, carried out a representative national survey of three thousand adults over the age of fifty-five to investigate their involvement in productive activities. The Commonwealth-Harris survey showed that 38 million older Americans (more than 70 percent of those fifty-five or older) were actively contributing to society through work, volunteerism, or caregiving. The survey further showed that many mature workers want to—and actually do—work on a part-time basis, for financial and/or other reasons. Some of these workers would like to retire, but probably will continue in the labor force on a part-time basis—some as long as they can. The Commonwealth Fund study found that 83 percent of persons fifty to sixty-four years old said that they would prefer part-time work. Even though interest in working part time is higher among older workers, evidence suggests that among unemployed older workers, more than three out of every four (78 percent in 1991) were looking for full-time jobs. Also, while nearly one-half of workers sixty-five or older are working part-time voluntarily, only 14 percent of workers of all ages work on such a basis out of choice.

One barrier to part-time opportunities—with one's previous employer especially—can be an employer's pension rules, which prohibit receipt of their retirees' private pensions if they work for that employer more than a certain number of hours per year (but still less than on a full-time basis). Travelers Insurance, in need of qualified personnel who knew that company's work culture, found that it made more sense to bring back on a part-time basis their recent retirees, instead of recruiting other workers through private employment agencies. But the company had to liberalize its limits on hours worked per year for continued pension eligibility in order to utilize successfully their well-trained, experienced "former" employees.

One of the problems concerning part-time jobs for older workers is that they too often are jobs that pay very little and provide few, if any, fringe benefits. While there are some obstacles that may prevent older adults from seeking and finding full-time employment after having retired from another employer, some advocates feel that efforts should be made to provide opportunities that do include higher wages and nonwage benefits.

Such jobs may be hard to find in the current economy, but Hilda Kahne believes that "new concept" part-time work should be developed in a wider range of occupations that could pay wages and benefits on a pro-rata basis, that is, on less than a full-time basis. "New concept" part-time jobs could expand if and when shortages of workers in the younger age groups are felt, and employers seek alternative solutions. Many older workers—especially those sixty-two and older—have financial reasons for not working on more than a part-time basis. If they were to earn beyond a certain level (about $10,000 in 1992), they would lose one dollar in Social Security retired worker benefits for every three dollars over that limit. But from the public policy point of view, such retired worker benefits are available only to men and women sixty-two and older who—as the benefit implies—are "retired." For administrative convenience, a dollar threshold is used to differentiate fully retired from partially retired and fully employed adults. "Retired worker" benefits are not available to workers at a certain age regardless of their labor force status.

One of the other problems associated with part-time work for older adults is that for many employers, part-time workers tend to be more costly and not as productive as their full-time employees, according to a study for the National Commission for Employment Policy. This partly explains why workers are offered a lower hourly wage if they work on a part-time basis. Another problem is that employers tend to completely lay off their workers during a period of declining product or service demand, instead of reducing hours of work.

In addition to the possibility that employers find it less expensive to hire on a full-time basis, part-time jobs tend to be concentrated in industries that typically pay low wages to begin with. Careful statistical analyses indicate that compensation increases sharply with hours per week. Besides such arrangements, job redesign and other "organic" principles can be used to facilitate the performance of older workers—indeed, all workers, for that matter.

Part-time Work and Job Sharing
Another option that some people work out with employers before retiring is the possibility of working on call. Many people enjoy the freedom to determine their own schedules while choosing assignments from employers as they come along. Members of this

contingency work force may return to a familiar work setting to help with special projects, train new employees, or substitute for a vacationing or ill employee.

Certain businesses, such as banks, insurance companies, aerospace companies, and retail department stores have actively recruited retirees for part-time work. Former workers may have advantages over temporary replacements unacquainted with procedures and practices familiar to the retiree. Many companies find mature workers especially dependable, conscientious, polite, and in possession of excellent interpersonal skills.

Some part-time positions are devised through job sharing. Two part-time workers divide the tasks of one full-time job. Some people find their own partner from within the company or business and propose job sharing to their employer. Of course with job sharing and other forms of part-time work wages are often lower and benefits minimal. The individual needs to carefully evaluate the pros and cons of part-time work as an option to continued full-time employment.

Second Careers

Working in the same occupation after many years is becoming less frequent today than in the past. The candidates for second (or third) careers may be persons whose organizations conventionally have early retirement options, as young as forty-five, fifty, or fifty-five, and who feel they are too young for full-time retirement. They may also include those whose retirement income is felt to be too low for full-time retirement. Also, the candidates are made up of men and women who undergo the loss of employment due to company shutdowns, reductions in force, and/or company relocations. Once in such a position, job hunters move on to occupations other than their previous ones. Finally, research has also found that there are workers who become dissatisfied and unfulfilled in their jobs and seek a marked change in their work lives in the form of new careers in their middle and later years.

Vast Unused Human Resources

According to the most recently completed and comprehensive analysis of the question about just how many older persons not

working now are ready and able to work, and how many have sufficient skills and education, there are approximately 1.1 million men (age fifty-five to sixty-four) and women (fifty to fifty-nine) who meet these criteria. The labor force economists who directed the study for the Commonwealth Fund found that most of these 1.1 million men and women deemed available for employment did not view themselves as "early retirees" and wanted to continue full-time jobs when they did leave the labor force. They were the ones who had lost their jobs and, by and large, had retired involuntarily. Others who had retired for other reasons (because of poor health or having to care for relatives) wanted to return to work when the original circumstances no longer prevailed.

It is a conservative estimate that 1.1 million men and women not in the labor force are available for employment. First, the figures

Many women return to the work force after first having "retired" and are already receiving their retired-worker benefits.

are restricted to men fifty-five to sixty-four years old and women fifty to fifty-nine. Second, and more important, the 1.1 million estimate was arrived at only after a series of screening questions aimed at a sample representing more than 7 million. Answers to those questions eliminated more than 6 million people in the above age groups who were not working at the time of the study.

Just as important is the fact that official government estimates of the size of an available older worker pool are roughly only half the 1.1 million determined by the Commonwealth Fund study. The labor force economists directing the Commonwealth Fund study feel that the questions used by the government are not appropriately worded and/or are incomplete.

If the expected demographic changes do lead to a shortage of younger and qualified labor force entrants and job applicants, it should be clear from these and other research findings that there are at least 1 million people in the fifty to fifty-nine age group (women) and fifty-five to sixty-four group (men) quite adequately prepared, able, and willing to meet any employer demand for labor.

Older Women Workers

Women began their greater participation in the paid labor force in the United States and other Western countries, as a result of factors associated with urbanization and a variety of other reasons and conditions, including:

- World War II opened up jobs that were previously the domain of men.

- The possibility of lower fertility released many women from childrearing, allowing them to seek and obtain jobs.

- Increased education made women more eligible for job openings.

- Families found it more advantageous to work for paid employment once a wide range of goods and services produced outside the household were available, rather than having to produce them within the household.

Possibly the increase in part-time jobs—especially for women still needed at home—also raised the level of their general participation. Over a period of time, young and middle-aged women in such situations eventually grew older, and their attachments to the paid work force was greater than what characterized women of previous generations. Thirty or more years ago, there was very little attention paid to older female workers. One major reason was that few women, certainly compared to the 1990s, were in the labor force on a full-time basis with a long-term commitment to the labor market. Furthermore, in the 1950s, the tendency was for women who lost their jobs to remain out of the labor force. The participation of women in the work force—and on a relatively steady basis—has increased tremendously. Today, women out of the labor force are also more likely to seek new jobs than in past decades.

Many women return to the work force after first having "retired" and already receiving their retired-worker benefits, according to the data from the Social Security Administration. These returning workers tended to be women who did not have a private pension to augment their Social Security benefits, especially if their health permitted the return. In particular, unmarried women were more likely to return to work because of their low unearned incomes. Wives were much more likely to be working if their husbands were working than if their husbands were no longer working. It is also worth noting that retired-worker women were more likely to be at work again if:

- They had been in their longest-held job at least ten years.

- They had been working in a nonprofit organization.

- They were in self-employed jobs.

- They were in service occupations in such longest-held jobs.

Except for women who had worked for state governments, unmarried women were clearly more likely to be working than married ones. Finally, the research results from the Social Security Administration's New Beneficiary Survey indicate that "the factors associated with employment appear to be similar for men and women." These new trends and phenomena mean that there are increased numbers of women in the labor force who continue to be in (or to reenter) the labor force into their middle and upper ages. Furthermore, the increase in the numbers and percentages of

Liz Carpenter

Journalist

SNAPSHOT

I was born at a time when your life expectancy was only sixty-three years. But today, thanks to God, Shirley MacLaine, or medical science, we've been given fifteen to twenty more years."

Liz Carpenter has become the unofficial advocate of the aging American population since her book *Getting Better All the Time* was published in 1986. "No one remains the same person after meeting Liz," raved humorist Erma Bombeck. "She makes Auntie Mame look like a shut-in."

Born in Salado, Texas, in 1920, Liz Carpenter later moved to Austin with her family. She has always expressed herself, arguing politics around the kitchen table with her out-spoken family members. Strongly opposed to the rampant corruption of the big tycoons of the day and the promise offered by Roosevelt's New Deal, Carpenter became a "true Southern liberal."

After graduating from the University of Texas Journalism School, she went to Washington, D.C., with a scrapbook full of clippings and knocked on doors at the National Press Building. Esther Van Wagner Tufty, who represented the Michigan League of Home Dailies, hired the young reporter, giving Carpenter the opportunity to attend several of Franklin and Eleanor Roosevelt's famous press conferences. She married Leslie Carpenter in 1944, then worked for United Press. In 1952 the Carpenters formed their own news bureau in Washington through the *Arkansas Gazette* and the *Tulsa Tribune*, and represented up to twenty newspapers. Carpenter served as the president of the Women's National Press Club in 1954, and in 1960 her career took a major turn.

After attending the Democratic Convention that nominated John F. Kennedy and Lyndon B. Johnson, Carpenter joined the election campaign as Lady Bird Johnson's press liaison. Soon she was flying all over the country with the Johnsons and the Kennedys, concentrating her special efforts on Texas. "Although I loved working in the press building, I found that being a participant was so much more fun that just being a critic," Carpenter reflects. After the election, Johnson appointed her as his executive assistant, the first woman to hold the position. From 1963 to 1969, she served as Lady Bird's press secretary and chief of staff. Carpenter wrote a book about that era, *Ruffles and Flourishes: The Warm and Tender Story of a Simple Girl Who Found Adventure in the White House.*

Then public relations firm Hill & Knowlton sought her out to serve as vice-president, and in 1971 she helped found the National Women's Political Caucus. President Ford appointed Carpenter to the International Women's Year Commission, and President Carter named her assistant secretary of education for public affairs. "I think one of the most aging things is to have no sense of purpose," Carpenter expresses. "When you work, you have a sense of purpose."

—*Lydia Brontë*

never-married, divorced or separated, and widowed women in recent decades makes the issue of older women workers even more urgent than in the past. Many of them, especially in the oldest groups of the old, might have few, no, or the wrong skills, when seeking employment for the first time, or when reentering the labor force after many years of not working in the paid labor force.

Working women's problems are made even more severe (especially for those not married) when it comes to such things as coverage by private pensions and/or the adequacy of such pensions—as well as the amount of retired-worker benefits they can expect from the Social Security system. A good part of these problems stems from such facts as lower wage and occupational levels (compared to men in general), and fewer constant, uninterrupted years in the work force. This nation's public and private retirement income programs require work experience. Since women are out of the labor force for many years—typically for childrearing or care for spouses and elderly parents and relatives—they do not benefit from such programs as much as men do.

It remains to be seen whether future generations of women workers will have more continuous, uninterrupted work experience than today's women. Unlike other countries, such as in Western Europe, American women receive no pension credits for the time they are temporarily out of the labor force.

Retirement   Between now and the year 2000, 5 million Americans will shed their workplace identities and start new lives as retirees, trading familiar ground for the unknown. With few role models to watch, many will enter this life stage asking, "What now?"

Most people do not get married just because they fall in love. They go through a period of dating and an engagement. The same is true of retirement. Most people don't retire just because they turn sixty-two or sixty-five (the Social Security threshold ages). The decision to retire is usually the result of a gradual process that moves in stages. Sometimes the contemplation of retirement occurs because a co-worker, friend, or relative close in age retires. There's the sudden thought: That could be me! The process of retirement starts well before the actual event occurs. Daydreaming about "my retirement," in which people imagine enjoyable ways they might spend their time, is a kind of rehearsal of possible future roles and situations. Sociologists call it "anticipatory socialization." Usually it triggers planning and exploration of how to get from here (work) to there (not working).

However, retirement, as complete disengagement from paid employment, in not for everyone. A January 1995 article in *Worth* magazine exhorts people to forget about retiring, that if retirement is a dream, it's also a nightmare of boredom, unproductivity, financial disaster—in short, a bad idea. Some retirement guides argue that work is the essence of what it means to be a human being. So, if you do retire, you will need to find the moral equivalent of work—such as serious volunteering, finding a second or third career, or even running for political office.

Planning for retirement is, thus, not just calculating how long a person's reserves will last but reviewing a wide range of options that include taking a full- or part-time "bridge" job to ease gradually from a work-centered life to one of increased leisure, discovering a second career in which one becomes passionately involved, diving into a "cause" that helps others, or joining the "snowbirds" who migrate in their RVs back and forth across the country. In other words, many models of life after fifty have emerged in a relatively short span of time. Retirement, as we know it today, is a recent invention.

The experience of retirement has become more common since the turn of the century. As a proportion of the life cycle, retirement has increased dramatically for men (see Table 4). While most Americans do not plan extensively for retirement and relatively few take part in formal retirement planning programs, the majority find retirement a positive and rewarding time of life. On an individual level retirement is not just an event or a static portion of life, rather it can be considered a dynamic and evolving process with stages or phases.

To many people, retirement denotes an older person leaving the work force to enjoy leisure activities while receiving Social Security checks and other pension income. Yet leaving the work force, receiving a retirement income, or following leisure pursuits do not necessarily occur in a fixed order. For example, should a displaced sixty-year-old worker living off his or her savings and seeking continued employment be considered retired? Similarly, what is the status of a fifty-five-year-old receiving monthly pension checks after thirty years service with an employer, but also holding a full-time position with another employer?

Retirement may not always be associated with a single event such as turning sixty-two or sixty-five. Nor is retirement tied

Table 4: Life Cycle Distribution of Education, Labor Force Participation, Retirement, and Work in the Home: 1900 to 1980

Subject	Year					
	1900	1940	1950	1960	1970	1980
	Number of Years Spent in Activity					
Men						
Average life expectancy	46.3	60.8	65.6	66.6	67.1	70.0
Retirement/work at home	1.2	9.1	10.1	10.2	12.1	13.6
Labor force participation	32.1	38.1	41.5	41.1	37.8	38.8
Education	8.0	8.6	9.0	10.3	12.2	12.6
Preschool	5.0	5.0	5.0	5.0	5.0	5.0
Women						
Average life expectancy	48.3	65.2	71.1	73.1	74.7	77.4
Retirement/work at home	29.0	39.4	41.4	37.1	35.3	30.6
Labor force participation	6.3	12.1	15.1	20.1	22.3	29.4
Education	8.0	8.7	9.6	10.9	12.1	12.4
Preschool	5.0	5.0	5.0	5.0	5.0	5.0
	Percent Distribution by Activity Type					
Men						
Average life expectancy	100	100	100	100	100	100
Retirement/work at home	3	15	15	15	18	19
Labor force participation	69	63	63	62	56	55
Education	17	14	14	15	18	18
Preschool	11	8	8	8	7	8
Women						
Average life expectancy	100	100	100	100	100	100
Retirement/work at home	60	60	58	51	47	40
Labor force participation	13	19	21	27	30	38
Education	17	13	14	15	16	16
Preschool	10	8	7	7	7	6

Sources: U.S. Bureau of the Census, "Educational Attainment in the United States: March 1981 and 1980," *Current Population Reports Series* P-20, no. 390 (August 1984) (median years of school for persons twenty-five years or older, 1940–80).

Best, Fred. *Work Sharing: Issues, Policy Options, and Prospects,* Upjohn Institute for Employment Research (1981), page 8 (1900 estimates of median years of school for persons twenty-five years or older).

National Center for Health Statistics. "Life Tables." *Vital Statistics of the United States,* 1987. Vol. 2, Section 6 (February 1990) (life expectancy data).

U.S. Department of Labor, Bureau of Labor Statistics. "Worklife Estimates: Effects of Race and Education." *Bulletin* 2254 (February 1986).

to withdrawal from the labor force, or the pursuit of leisure activities, or obtaining retirement income based on former employment.

Difficulty in coming to terms with the meaning of retirement is reflected in studies conducted by the gerontological community. Researchers Joseph Quinn and Richard Burkhauser note that several different criteria have been used in the study of retirement:

1. Subjective appraisal of one's retirement status

2. The receipt of retirement income or income based on previous work status such as Social Security or employer pension plan

3. Degree of labor force participation such as complete labor force withdrawal, quarter time or less work, a rapid reduction in work hours, or a departure from a primary job

Researchers also note the difficulty of operationally defining retirement, and some stress the importance of two major dimensions: (1) the receipt of pension income, whether from Social Security or from an employer program, based on previous work history; and (2) a reduction in or a cessation of labor force participation. Merging these two concepts together, another criterion for retirement emerges: when the major source of a household's income shifts from wage earnings to pension income. Thus, retirement may be defined as that stage in life marked by a distinct decline in labor force participation, combined with an increase in household income derived from past work history.

A constellation of complex forces has come together with industrialization to create the social institution of retirement. On an economic level the mechanization of production and the shift from human and animal energy to fossil fuels increased the productivity of society, which affects the development of retirement in two ways. First, increased productivity means that the average worker produces more than he or she needs for mere survival. This excess can be channeled into benefits for a later time in life when the worker withdraws from the labor force. An example of how this surplus is transformed monetarily is the 7.05 percent

Retirement as a Social Institution

FICA tax paid to the federal government by both employees and employers, which is transferred to the retired population through Social Security and Medicare.

A second way this productivity influences retirement is through the reduced need for labor in a society. Industrial modes of production require fewer labor force participants. Retirement, like adolescence and young adulthood, is a stage of the life cycle that arose after industrialization. By extending the requirements for time spent in education for youths and young adults, and by encouraging labor force withdrawal in the later years, the size of the labor force is controlled. Retirement and the financial means to support retirees reduce unemployment among younger people and the possibility of social unrest, which may be associated with large-scale unemployment.

On a demographic level, the increase in life expectancy, which coincides with industrialization, further increases the retirement stage of the life cycle. As a society moves through industrialization, there is an increase not only in the standard of living but also in scientific knowledge, in medical applications, and in public health technology. These changes bring about an increase in life expectancy at birth (47.3 years in 1900, versus 75.5 years in 1991), hence allowing more individuals to live to retirement age. In the more advanced industrial societies, medicine is able to make inroads at extending life expectancy at age sixty-five (the extension was 13.9 years in 1950, versus 17.4 years in 1991), further increasing the retirement age population.

Bureaucratic organization is a form of social technology, which is more frequently found in an industrial society, allowing for the handling of a large number of units (such as applications and checks in a standardized way). Such organization enables intergenerational transfers of money, such as Social Security, to support the retired population. According to the U.S. Social Security Administration, during 1992, Social Security collected $307.1 billion from 132 million workers (94 percent of the work force). In turn, approximately $254.8 billion in benefits were paid out to 25.7 million retired workers and 7.6 million survivors during the same year. This transfer was completed at an administrative cost of only .7 percent. The Health Care Financing Administration paid out

Celeste Holm

Actress

B eing an actress is being everything. You can do anything. I teach, I lecture, I write. It's a wonderful springboard for almost anything."

Celeste Holm was born in Brooklyn, New York, and fell in love with the theater after seeing Russian ballerina Anna Pavlova perform. At first she trained to be a dancer, but after attending boarding school in Paris, where the language difference proved unnerving, she concentrated on acting because of its "universal" appeal.

Holm played leads in all her school plays, and recalls that even then people treated her as a "professional." After graduating she found work in New York, where she says at first she "took anything," but it was not long before she got her first role in the successful Broadway play *The Women*. Roles such as Ado Annie in the smash *Oklahoma!* soon followed. Holm recalls her audition for the Rodgers and Hammerstein musical *Green Grow the Lilacs*, where she fell flat on her face while getting on stage: "Because I had fallen on my face I was no longer nervous. I mean after that happens there's nowhere to go but up." Needless to say, Holm got the part.

During World War II Holm worked at the Stage-door Canteen, where she "waited on tables and danced with the soldiers." The atmosphere at the canteen heightened Holm's desire to contribute to the war effort; she embarked on a tour of France and Germany to entertain the American troops abroad. After the war, Holm launched her film career in Hollywood. War-torn Europe made the glittering world of show biz seem overwhelmingly artificial, so throughout her Hollywood career Holm, like many actors, developed a healthy disrespect for the studio system. "There was a whole process arranged to make you feel like two cents worth of dirty ice," she explains.

Holm refused to play the role of the naive young starlet, and while she did her share of "stupid musicals," she also enjoyed worthy material. Over five decades Holm worked in films, plays, and television. Accolades include an Academy Award for her work in *The Gentlemen's Agreement*. She is currently president of the Creative Arts Rehabilitation Center and even finds time to study semiotics at Claremont College. When asked why she never retired, Holm says: "If actors retired there'd never be a John Gielgud or a Katherine Hepburn. Actors never retire."

—Lydia Brontë

$83.9 billion in hospital insurance and $49.2 billion in supplemental medical insurance to 35 million enrollees at an administrative cost of 1.3 percent and 3.2 percent respectively. In addition to the federal government's social insurance programs, there are 729,922 private pension plans, 201 state pension programs, and 2,213 locally administered programs. State and local plans pay benefits to 920,515 and 1.9 million people, respectively. According to 1992 statistics from the U.S. Bureau of Labor Statistics, private plans hold assets of $1.5 billion and pay benefits to 12.5 million Americans. These are all examples of the complex bureaucratic structures that help sustain a large retirement population.

Planning for Retirement

As with other stages of the life cycle, the greatest amount of preparation for retirement is informal. Some individuals start to read pertinent literature and talk with their spouses, other relatives, and friends as early as fifteen years ahead of their planned retirement. The prevalence of this pattern and the intensity of this style of informal planning does increase with age.

Financial planning is one important element for a comfortable retirement. While it is never too late to take steps to secure a retirement income, advance planning may allow for more options. The 1981 President's Commission on Pension Policy concluded that a household would need to receive 75 percent of preretirement income in retirement to maintain its standard of living. However, this high a replacement income in retirement would require a high rate of savings every year.

There are several forms of retirement income to replace income from work in retirement. The most significant is based on Social Security. However, other forms of income, such as pension plans, individuals retirement accounts, and Supplemental Security Income, all play a role in solid financial footing in later years. Other issues—ranging from health and lifestyle to legal concerns—all play a role in planning for retirement and, in some ways, are closely tied to finanical issues.

Women's retirement income is likely to be less adequate than that of retired males. Researchers report women have a more unstable work history and work in lower-paying positions. Both factors adversely influence pension benefits and also Social Security benefits. The disparity between the pension coverage of women and men has decreased overall. Women's pension coverage has increased between 1972 to 1988 from 38 percent to 48 percent of the full-time worker force, while men's coverage decreased from 54 percent to 49 percent. Yet in the age group closest to retirement (fifty-five to fifty-nine years old) the disparity in coverage was far wider, with female coverage at 49 percent and male coverage at 60 percent.

African Americans' retirement incomes reflect discrimination, which has constrained labor force participation and earnings. The white median monthly retired worker Social Security benefit in 1990 was $612.60, versus the African-American benefit of $505.80. According to the U.S. Department of Labor, there is a small disparity in pension coverage between African Americans at 43 percent, and whites at 49 percent. During 1971, 18 percent of whites were receiving benefits, and only 7 percent of African Americans had pension income.

Women's retirement income is likely to be less adequate than that of retired males.

Despite gender and race barriers, retirement is a complex process involving several decisions that are influenced by a constellation of factors. The process begins with preretirement attitudes or specific events that alert a person to consider the option of retirement, and continues as a person grows older and simply obtains more information about the choices available to him or her. This section takes a look at some key areas that contribute to successful retirement planning.

Social Security

The Social Security Act was signed into law in August 1935 and was designed to help those in later life who found it difficult to continue to work. It also served the economic function of reducing the labor force participation of older workers during the Great Depression, thereby opening up jobs for younger workers.

Amendments to the act have been made throughout the years. After Title II retirement and survivors benefits (1939), permanent disability benefits (1957), and Medicare Title XVIII (1965) have been added. The amended act also includes other programs: black lung disease, Supplemental Security Income (SSI), unemployment insurance, Aid to Families with Dependent Children (AFDC), Medicaid, maternal and child benefits, food stamps, worker's compensation, Railroad Retirement, and energy assistance. While technically all of these other programs are part of the Social Security Act, they are funded by general tax revenues, not by Social Security taxes, and are not administered by the Social Security Administration. What most people think of as Social Security is what the federal government calls OASDHI or Old-Age, Survivors, Disability, and Hospital Insurance, which is funded by the Federal Insurance Contributions Act (FICA).

Social Security is the primary source of income in later life. Some 38 percent of all income received by those sixty-five years old and older comes from the retirement and survivors benefit. According to the U.S. Senate Special Committee on Aging, practically all older adult households (94 percent) receive Social Security benefits. A sizable minority of these households depend significantly on Social Security. Some 13 percent receive no income other than Social Security, and 3 percent receive four-fifths of their income from Social Security.

A statement of individual earnings and an estimate of one's benefits can be obtained by submitting form SSA-7004-PC-OPI, "Request for Earning and Benefit Estimate Statement," which is available from any Social Security Administration office. Full retirement benefits can be secured at age sixty-five. As of current legislation, the qualifying age for full retirement benefits slowly rises starting in 2003, ending in the year 2027 with an age of sixty-seven. Early retirement benefits can start as early as age sixty-two, but at a reduced amount. Those who take early benefits collect on the average about the same total amount of benefits, but in smaller installments. For each year benefits are delayed after normal retirement age (sixty-five), benefits are increased until seventy years of age. Additionally, Social Security benefits can be reduced before age seventy if one's earnings rise above a yearly preset limit.

Concerns about social security: Two concerns about Social Security are frequently heard. First, some believe the system will not be able to support the retirement payments to the generation born between 1947 and 1963 (the baby boomers). When the baby boomers reach retirement age, it is often said that only three workers will be paying into the system for each retired beneficiary. Yet between now and their retirement, the baby boom generation is paying large amounts into the system, which is accumulating a sizable reserve. Yearly reports from the Board of Trustees of the Federal Old-Age and Survivors Insurance and Disability Insurance Trust Fund indicate the trust fund is adequately growing in size in order to help subsidize workers' payments during the retirement of the baby boomers.

The 1992 Board of Trustees, Federal Old-Age and Survivors Insurance and Disability Insurance Trust Fund report shows that Old-Age and Survivors Insurance (OASI) is projected to be healthy for the next fifty years; however, assuming a worst-case scenario, the Disability Insurance (DI) portion is projected to be in financial trouble by 1995 and Hospital Insurance (HI) by the year 1998. Changes legislated in 1983, which went unnoticed by most taxpayers, took the bankrupt OASI trust fund to its present level of $306.2 billion in assets and prevented Medicare from bankrupting as projected in the early 1990s.

A second concern is that the system has diverted its assets to other government programs. The trust funds are invested in U.S. Treasury bonds, and in this respect the Social Security system is "investing" in the national debt. Still, it's important to remember that none of the money designated on a pay stub as FICA (Social Security) has ever been directly spent outside of the system. Once, during the early 1980s, Congress permitted a portion of the Social Security taxes designated for Disability Insurance and Medicare to be used to pay the retirement benefits. That inter-trust fund borrowing stopped on June 30, 1983, and the trust fund for the retirement benefits (OASI) has since paid back the money it borrowed to the DI and Medicare (HI) trust funds.

The inter-trust fund borrowing occurred because of unusual economic circumstances, when high inflation was accompanied by high unemployment. In the late 1970s and early 1980s, the soaring cost of oil and other economic factors pushed the yearly inflation rate above 10 percent. Because of automatic cost-of-living adjustment based on the inflation rate, retirees' Social Security benefits increased, and the payout of the system rose quickly. At the same time, unemployment was high, and real wages lagged behind inflation. Therefore, the system's income, or the collection of Social Security taxes, did not keep up with inflationary demands on the system. Changes in the Social Security Act legislated in 1983 put in place a fail-safe mechanism to protect the system. If the financial health of the system is endangered, the cost-of-living increase would be indexed to the lower rise in wages or prices.

In all likelihood, Social Security will be available to all older adults and will be an important aspect of their retirement income well into the twenty-first century. Those in the lowest income groups find Social Security a very important part of their income. Railroad Retirement pension or Social Security makes up 79 percent of the income of those who fall below the poverty level. Social Security or Railroad Retirement income decreases in the percentage it comprises of a household's income as one rises above poverty. For those who live at three to four times the poverty level, Social Security makes up only 37 percent of their income. Conversely, other sources of retirement income become more important with rising income levels. Both pensions, interest, and dividends rise from 3.7 percent of income for those in poverty to 23.8 percent for pensions and 21.7 percent (interest and dividends) of income in the group whose incomes is three to four times the poverty level. While Social Security is an important aspect of financial maintenance in later life, secure financial well-being requires additional sources of retirement income. Most retirees need a three-legged stool: Social Security, pension, and some form of savings and/or investments.

Pensions

Pensions are an important source of retirement income. Employer-based pensions account for about 18 percent of all the income for the sixty-five-years-old and older age group. Those in higher income brackets receive a larger portion of their retirement income from pensions.

The quick rise in pension coverage in part resulted from a Supreme Court decision (*Inland Steel Company v. NLRB*, 1949) over

Pension coverage has grown rapidly: only 17 percent of the full-time workers were covered in 1940, versus 52 percent in 1970.

collective bargaining on issues of deferred compensation like pension programs. Coverage has remained static since the 1970s because of the decline of unionized industry and the growth of the service sector of the economy, which typically does not provide this benefit to employees. Coverage varies widely, with larger employers and particular industries more likely to offer coverage. According to the U.S. Bureau of Labor Statistics, over 39 percent of covered workers are enrolled in an additional supplemental plan.

Approximately two-thirds of covered employees are vested in their plans; that is, they are entitled to a pension benefit even if they leave their employer before retirement. According to recent statistics, one-third of the private sector retirees over fifty-five years old are now receiving pension income. In the inflationary period from 1978 to 1982, postretirement benefit increases were noted in 51 percent of all retirement plans. In the more stable period from 1984 to 1988, however, only 22 percent of plans had such benefit increases. Public employees have the highest level of pension coverage. According to the U.S. Senate Special Committee on Aging, all federal employees are covered as well as 85 percent of state and local public employees. Seventy percent of the state and local employees are vested in their plans. Over one-third of the beneficiaries have received postretirement benefit increases.

Pensions come in two basic varieties: defined benefit plans and defined contribution plans. The former type usually offers benefits as a function of the employee's years of service or based on years of service and rate of pay. According to the U. S. Senate Special Committee on Aging, the large plans tend to be funded by the employer, with only about 3 percent of the contributions to such plans coming from employees. According to the U.S. Bureau of the Census, defined benefit plans make up about 27 percent of the pension plans in 1985.

Defined contribution plans specify the amount of employee contributions. Benefits are determined by the amount of contributions and the accrued interest in the accounts. These types of plans are growing as a proportion of all pension plans. In the ten-year period from 1975 to 1985, these plans increased from 69 percent to 73 percent of all pension plans. Not only has the number of such plans grown, but also the number of participants involved has increased enormously. In 1975 there were 11.5 million participants in defined contribution plans, and by 1985 there were 35 million participants. This represents a growth rate of 204 percent, compared to a growth rate of 20 percent in the defined benefit plans.

Both types of plans receive special tax treatment from the federal government. Employers do not pay a tax on their contributions to the plan, and the earnings of the trust funds are not taxed. Employees do not pay tax on the contributions made by their employers or the earnings until benefits are paid out.

Regulatory pension plans: The Employee Retirement Income Security Act (ERISA) of 1974 established standards for financing and administrating private pension programs; the 2,414 state and local government programs are not regulated by federal laws. ERISA established the employer-funded Pension Benefit Guaranty Corporation, to insure the solvency of pension plans, as it also stipulated vesting, or ownership of pension rights. The 1986 Tax Reform Act enhanced previous vesting rules. Full vesture will occur after five years of employment if no benefits are previously vested, or full vesture will occur at seven years if the employer offers some percent of vesting before five years of service. The Retirement Equity Act of 1984 took an important step in pension coverage when it specified that spouses can obtain survivors benefits and that divorced spouses also have certain rights.

401K plans: A recent innovation in pensions and retirement savings are 401K plans, which can take the form of a defined contribution pension plan or a supplemental pension savings plan. Named after the section of the Internal Revenue Service code that set up their tax deferred status in 1978, such plans have grown rapidly in the 1980s. Approximately 41 percent of employers offer such plans now.

These plans allow for sole employer contributions, employer one-to-one matching contributions, or employee salary reductions. Tax deferments on the plans are limited to yearly ceilings of $30,000

While Social Security is an important aspect of financial maintenance in later life, secure financial well-being requires additional sources of retirement income.

for profit sharing programs and $8,475 for salary reduction programs. Distribution is based on retirement or termination of employment. Early withdrawal of funds can occur under "immediate and heavy financial needs," although there is typically a penalty associated with it. As with all ERISA covered plans, guidelines are in place to keep highly compensated staff (top management or professionals in a practice), from unique or disproportionately extended benefits.

Individual Retirement Accounts (IRAs)

IRAs are a special form of savings put aside during working years to provide income in later life. The money deposited into an IRA is tax deductible, although there are penalties (10 percent) on withdrawal from the accounts before the age of fifty-nine. Heavy penalties are also leveled if withdrawals are not begun by age seventy. According to the U.S. Bureau of the Census, at the end of 1989 an estimated $465 billion were held in IRAs. Mutual funds held the largest percent of these funds (24 percent), followed by commercial banks (21.3 percent), and savings institutions (21 percent).

Supplemental Security Income (SSI)

SSI is a program designed to augment the income of people who are over the age of sixty-five, blind, or disabled. To be eligible for the program, households must fall below federal poverty standards. In 1992 eligibility was based on monthly income below $422 for an individual or $633 for a couple. However the first $20 of existing monthly income is excluded from the above figures, along with the first $65 dollars of earned monthly income and one-half of remaining earned income. The value of social services provide by federal, state, or local programs are not considered for eligibility.

Along with the income test, there is also an asset test: an individual may have $2,000 or less and a couple may have $3,000. The exclusions from these assets are homes, household goods, and personal effects with a limit of $2,000 in equity value; $4,500 in the market value of a car, unless used as transportation for medical treatments or employment; burial plots; $1,500 in burial funds per individual; and $1,500 in cash values of insurance policies.

Benefits are designed to supplement income, but not to lift the household out of poverty. The 1991 maximum benefit for an individual ($407) left the person at 75 percent of the poverty level; couples fare a bit better at 89 percent of the poverty level with a maximum benefit of $610. All but eight states will add to the federal benefits. Three states (Alaska, California, and Connecticut) provide supplements designed to bring benefits up to the poverty level. Those eligible for the program are also eligible for food stamps and Medicaid. According to the U.S. Senate Special Committee on Aging, about one-half of older adults who are eligible for SSI do not participate. More information about SSI can be obtained by writing to the Social Security Administration and asking for their booklet SSI Publication no. 05-11000.

Health Issues

After income, health is probably the most important issue considered in retirement planning. Good health can make retirement a pleasurable experience, while health care costs can be a significant drain on a retirement budget. The first principle of good health, like financial planning, is that one should start early in life to learn about and to adopt a healthy lifestyle.

A second aspect of health in retirement planning is how to pay for health care. These costs continue to rise at a rate faster than inflation, and older adults are the most intensive users of all health care services. According to the U.S. Senate Special Committee on Aging, the older population comprises almost 13 percent of the U.S. population, but utilizes over one-third of the nation's health care dollars. In a ten-year span starting in 1977, the average annual growth rate in health care spending on the elderly was 14 percent. By 1987, the per capita expenditure for the older adult population reached $5,360.

Medicare: Medicare, while almost universal in its coverage of the population sixty-five and older, is not universal in its coverage of health care costs. Medicare covers 45 percent of the health care costs of seniors. Out-of-pocket and private insurance funds cover 37.4 percent of the health care costs of the population sixty-five and older. Medicaid (for the financially impoverished) covers 12 percent of health costs for older adults.

Medicare is divided into two parts. Hospital Insurance (Part A) is financed through the Social Security tax (FICA). This part covers in-patient hospital care, skilled nursing facility care after hospitalization, home health care, and hospice care. If a person is one of the few not eligible for Medicare, then Part A coverage can be purchased. In 1994 this cost was $245.00 a month. Part B of Medicare or supplemental medical insurance is paid for in part (approximately 75 percent) by general tax revenue, and the balance in premiums is paid by beneficiaries; the 1994 monthly premium was $41.40. Part B covers physician services, outpatient hospital care, diagnostic tests, durable medical equipment, and ambulance services.

Both parts A and B have cost-sharing mechanisms. These include deductibles, coinsurance, and allowable charges. Medicare also does not cover routine examinations, most out-patient pharmaceuticals, dentistry, corrective lens, private duty nursing, and much nursing home care.

"Medigap," or supplemental, insurance to cover the cost and services Medicare does not cover, can be a valuable part of any health insurance package. A booklet on how to shop for compatible health insurance for Medicare, entitled *Guide to Health Insurance for*

People with Medicare (518-Y), is available through the Consumer Information Center, Department 59, Pueblo, Colorado 81009.

Medicaid: Medicaid is the federal-state partnership to provide health care for those who are impoverished. Long-term care frequently causes a financial burden in later life and requires many older adults to turn to Medicaid. The National Center for Health Statistics reports that in 1991 older adults comprised 11.9 percent of the program recipients; and 33 percent of the vendor payments were made on behalf of older adults, with most of the payments going to long-term care.

The Consolidated Omnibus Budget Reconciliation Act of 1985 mandates that former employees be able to purchase health insurance for up to eighteen months at the rate the employer pays after leaving a job. Such coverage is extended to retirees. It is especially helpful to those who retire before they are eligible for Medicare at age sixty-five. An extension of this coverage was part of the Omnibus Budget Reconciliation Act of 1986. Employees can purchase continuing coverage, until death, if the previous employer files for bankruptcy. Spouses can only purchase thirty-six months of continuing coverage.

Other health care benefit programs: After the passage of Medicare, employers started to offer retiree health care benefit programs as a form of deferred compensation. Growth has been significant but, as with pensions, this benefit has been instituted only among larger employers. Approximately 84 percent of firms with over 2,500 employees offer such a program, but only 47 percent of firms with 100 to 250 employees offer this form of deferred compensation. According to the U.S. Department of Labor, about 7 million former employees and their spouses were covered in 1983. Typically, the employee must pay some part of the cost of this benefit.

Rising medical costs, longevity, and a growing number of pensioners has led some employers to alter or even attempt to abolish health care benefit programs. In general the courts have ruled the elimination of such plans illegal if they were in place when the retiree became vested, unless the employer explicitly

The AARP is the largest and most visible interest group in the United States serving second middle agers.

reserved the right to do so. Many employers have altered the plans though, by raising co-insurance and premiums.

Legal Issues

Legal issues such as power of attorney, guardianship, wishes for kinds of medical treatment, disposition of estate, and burial wishes become more important with advancing age. While poor health, disability, and death can occur at any stage in life, for obvious reasons the likelihood of these events increases in later life. Thus, putting one's legal house in order provides security that one's wishes will be respected. In addition, family members are supported in difficult decisions by knowing their loved one's decisions.

Wills and estate planning: Wills and estate planning should be reviewed and updated on a regular basis. Less frequently considered by most persons are the steps to be taken in case one becomes incapacitated. Among intact married couples, one's spouse may act for the benefit of the other person in most matters. Difficulty arises for widows and widowers who, when they cannot act on their own, need to have a guardian appointed to act in their place in legal and financial matters, such as the disposition of their homes.

Medical decisions: Finally, consideration needs to be given to the control of medical treatment. Living wills can indicate that individuals do not want life prolonged by extraordinary means if the hope for recovery is small. A second document, an advance medical directive, allows individuals to express their wishes about a number of categories of medical procedures if they become incapacitated and are unable to act on their own behalf. These documents need only be signed in front of a witness and notarized. It is advisable to discuss one's intentions with the attorney handling the estate. It is very important that a person's wishes be made known to family members and to physicians.

Housing

Because housing needs alter as circumstances in later life change, planning an exploring options early on rather than reacting quickly to changed circumstances alleviates stress and helps ease the transition into retirement. Most older adults (76 percent) own their residences. Yet, there are still costs associated with ownership, such as taxes, insurance, utilities, repairs, and maintenance. Excluding repairs and maintenance, housing costs as a percent of income in 1989 were 17.1 percent for homeowners without a mortgage, 26 percent for homeowners with a mortgage, and 36.5 percent for renters sixty-five years old and older.

Changes in family patterns (such as children moving out) and lifestyle (such as a decrease in formal entertaining) may mean that a larger home purchased earlier in life is no longer required. A smaller home, where maintenance costs may be lower, needs to be weighed against the sentimental value of the home.

A house is the most valuable asset owned by most older adults. Some 68 percent of elderly households' net worth is in the form of home ownership. The U.S. Senate Special Committee on

Aging reports some $700 billion to $1 trillion is tied up in the home equity of older adult households. This asset can be tapped by the sale of a home. The sale requires that either a less expensive home is purchased or the household rents property. A one-time exclusion from taxation of $125,000 worth of capital gains from the sale of a home after the age fifty-five allows the owner to invest that capital and use it as a source of income.

Another way a house can be used as an asset is through reverse annuity mortgages. The homeowner obtains what amounts to a home equity loan from a financial institution. The homeowner can receive regular payments while living in the house; a line of credit or a lump sum distribution principle and payment comes due upon the death of homeowner or the sale of the property. Further information can be obtained by writing: AARP Home Equity Information Center, American Association of Retired Persons, 601 E St. NW, Washington, D.C. 20049.

A small number of people move into planned or naturally occurring retirement communities, which brings high levels of morale and life satisfaction to many during a time of life that might otherwise be lonely. This high morale arises, in part, from living in a community that offers a rich social network with interesting activities. And people in such communities tend to be in good health and are financially secure, hence they might be expected to express higher life satisfaction.

Adjusting to Retirement

The traditional work ethic is still held by some people in society, but this emphasis is eroding. Popular beliefs live beyond the reality of social experience. The work ethic and a strong self-identity on the job are identified as the reasons some people have difficulty adjusting to retirement. This is a mistaken generalization for most Americans, for the evidence from a number of national studies presents a different picture. In 1981 the National Council on the Aging reported 90 percent of those participating in a national sample felt they made the right decision about retirement. Only 6 percent of those polled said they retired too early; 1 percent reported they retired too late, and 3 percent were not sure. Longitudinal research finds neither life satisfaction, morale, nor self-esteem is adversely influenced by retirement.

Health

There is neither a decline in physical health nor mental health because of retirement. In fact some (typically unskilled workers) report improvement in their physical health associated with retirement. Men with Type A behavior before retirement often lose these traits in retirement.

There is a potential for the casual observer to fall victim to spurious reasoning. Both retirement and health status are related to advanced age. So while it may appear that retirement is causing poor health, in actuality growing older not only increases the likelihood of retiring but also succumbing to illness. It is not unusual for those in their sixties to have health problems and even die, whether they are retired or still in the work force. Additionally, since health problems may select individuals out of the work force, it is not unusual to find these people reporting health problems in retirement. Yet retirement is not the causal agent; conversely, poor health often causes retirement.

Health is frequently mentioned as deteriorating because of retirement, but evidence indicates this is not the case.

Marital Issues

Marital satisfaction, as in the case of health, often has been suggested to decrease in retirement. Typically the notion is offered that wives are not accustomed to increased contact with their husbands. This perspective was supported by research in the 1950s. Anecdotal stories are sometimes heard of the middle- or upper-middle-class husband redirecting his instrumental role from the office to the domestic aspect of household management—and much to the annoyance of the wife! Retirement has less of an impact on shared domestic activities than had been previously thought. Males tend to stay within their sex roles. However, companionship in leisure activities does increase and is important in the appraisal of marital satisfaction.

Overall, the research on marital satisfaction in retirement indicates that couples adjust well. Research shows no difference in

Hugh Downs

Broadcast journalist

SNAPSHOT

Though I love my work, I have never regard-ed it as anything but a means to an end, my job must enhance my life."

With fifty years in broadcasting, Hugh Downs is one of the most familiar figures in American television. Born in Akron, Ohio, in 1921, he began his broadcasting career as a teenager on a hot summer day in 1939. His family had suffered finan-cially in the depression. Downs was a freshman at nearby Bluffton College, and his father thought that he should quit college and get a job to help the family survive. Downs had won his college scholarship in a public speaking contest, so on a whim he stopped in at the town's 100-watt radio station to see if he could get work as a radio announcer. He auditioned, and even though the program director announced cheerfully that his performance was "really quite bad," the station need-ed someone immediately, and Downs was hired as a staff announcer for $12.50 a week.

But his father was not impressed: he did not consider radio broadcasting a real job. "Keep looking for a job for a week," Downs's father advised, "if you don't find a job, go with the radio station." Downs reported years later that "even after I'd put decades in broadcasting behind me, my father refused to believe I had found a real job."

By the 1950s Downs worked in Detroit, hosting broad-casts for various radio stations. After serving in the infantry dur-ing World War II and several other jobs, Downs helped launch "The Tonight Show"—the first real television talk show—with

Jack Paar. When Paar quit "The Tonight Show" five years later, Downs became host of the fledgling "Today" show, in 1962.

Downs stayed at the "Today" show for nine years, and also reported for and narrated for a number of NBC news documentaries and specials, including the Emmy Award–winning "The Everglades" (1971). Then, on October 11, 1971, Downs took early retirement at age fifty to pursue other interests: writing, consulting, and hobbies, particularly flying gliders and doing aerobatics, and established his retirement home in Carefree, Arizona.

Though he expected "retirement" to be more leisurely than his hectic work life, his energy level was high, and he kept adding to his list of things to do. Downs admits: "I took on such a load that my secretary said at one point, 'I wish you'd go back to work; you'd have more free time!' She was right. When I went back to work I had more free time. I jokingly said more than once that every time I retired I got busier than before."

In 1976 Downs was called by the producers of the pilot show "20/20." The premiere had been a disaster, but the network thought the concept was worthwhile and decided to change the format and the people involved. "I was lucky they called on me for the second show," Downs notes. "Even then, for some months, they felt a need to grab the viewer by the lapels and say, 'Don't go away, because we are going to be interesting.' "

Downs's return to broadcasting was one of the most successful comebacks in media history. The "20/20" program has the reputation for covering issues and providing information its viewers want and need, tackling cultural features, investigative reports, and stories on science, space, medical issues, children's problems, aging, and exploration. Downs holds the Guinness record for the hours on network commercial television; when he celebrated his fiftieth year in broadcasting in May 1989, a commemorative segment on his career was aired on "20/20."

—*Lydia Brontë*

Carl R.

An eighty-three-year-old poet, Carl reflects on the joys of retirement and creativity:

"I couldn't wait to retire. I never looked back. I never gave it a moment's thought. Social work was in the past; it was buried. I had reawakened creatively. I wrote and published poems when I was young, but having family obligations, I gave up writing and developed a career in social work. Several weeks before my retirement, I received a letter from someone who had admired those earlier poems. That letter inspired me and I couldn't wait to begin writing.

"As I grow older I really have not detected any loss of imagination. The only change I've seen in myself is some slowing up and having to stop writing because I feel a little sleepy. I take a nap right after lunch. I don't spend as much time on writing as I did before and the work is slower, but in no other ways are there differences. In fact, there may be some benefits in that slowness—it improves thought.

"People talk about creativity as if it were some kind of a mystery, something to be achieved. Creativity is something that is part of our nature. People just need the time and opportunity to express themselves. . . . It's there."

—*From Connie Goldman's "Late Bloomer" public radio series*

marital satisfaction between retired and nonretired couples of similar ages. Some 70 percent of retired couples reported they were extremely satisfied with their marriage, 27 percent satisfied, and only 3 percent dissatisfied. No change in couples' marital satisfaction was reported over six years, moving from preretirement to retirement. One study did report change in marital satisfaction associated with retirement: 60 percent of couples indicated marital satisfaction increased, and 10 percent said it decreased.

Social Isolation

Social isolation has been suggested to occur because of retirement, as work is frequently an important means for building social ties. Only a small percent of retirees decrease their social participation and feel an increase in isolation and loneliness. Women do report slightly lower activity levels in retirement than their male counterparts. Part of this drop in social life is related to widowhood. Some observers have suggested that isolation in retirement is more prevalent among the working class, with lower social participation in later life the result of both the nature of the work, which did not provide as much social integration, and a lower income, which constrains social activity. Overall, retirement is rarely the cause of lower social involvement.

Retirement as a Process

There is little doubt that retirement involves degrees of disengagement from society, but it may not signal a unilinear decreasing engagement in the social world. In retirement, people develop routines that fill their lives and offer many satisfactions. Some retirees are busier than others. Some people engage and reengage in diverse social pursuits. Over the course of time there are necessary individual adjustments as people encounter the physical and psychological difficulties associated with later life. Some observers suggest middle age is a time to develop the recreation and leisure interests one will pursue in retirement. Whether before or after retirement a range of activities should be considered, such as education, recreation, self-improvement, and volunteer and civic involvement. A range of activities allows continuing involvement, even if health problems force one to give up the more physically demanding interests. Both physically and mentally engaging tasks help to keep one vital and alert, and allow a person to ease into the stage of life known as retirement with a number of rewarding interests and activities in place.

The development of the institution of retirement has been accompanied by a supportive culture milieu involving national pensions and a public health program for the older adult. There is broad acceptance that individuals deserve retirement as a reward for years of effort in the work force and for their contributions to society.

For many people, the traditional work ethic is perhaps more accurately described as the remuneration ethic. These people work until their pension benefits and savings will support their desired lifestyle, and then say, "It's not worth it to work anymore." Furthermore, many people have embraced a "choice ethic"—that the good life is one that permits the individual the greatest amount of choices. Certainly retirement gives people a greater range of choices as to how they will spend their time than if they remained in the work force.

Future Trends

The status of older workers in the short- and long-term future will depend on a number of factors and trends, as well as on retirement and work policies determined by our major institutions—government, employers, and employee organizations. Those factors and trends include the following: an expected shortage of young entrants into the labor force, which could put a premium on the retention and employment of older workers; the legislated increases in age of retirement for full benefits under Social Security over the next several years; the possible leveling off (or even decrease) of private pension coverage and benefit levels; and a more vigorous implementation of the Age Discrimination in Employment Act.

Partly related to the above is the much-discussed issue of an increasing "burden" of nonworking older adults that could be imposed on the working population: that alleged burden could be reduced by increasing the working population side of the ledger through the retention of older workers in the labor force. Incentives and disincentives to remain in the labor force and/or against retiring are already in process.

As for the youth labor shortage, there is no question that the rate of increase in young labor force entrants is extremely low over the next several decades. But some experts doubt that such a shortage will be as great as others have projected, especially if and when increases in productivity occur. In fact, from a historical viewpoint, productivity increases due to automation, for example, have frequently been the result of labor shortages.

But there does remain the issue of the quality of that future work force. Many employers are concerned about the skill and attitudinal competencies of entry-level applicants and employees, especially when compared to those of older adult employees. Besides increasing their own training programs to meet these deficiencies of new employees, some companies plan on keeping their existing workers longer than otherwise. This could have a substantial influence on the "early retirement" trends.

A 1992 survey by the Conference Board found that in comparing their older workers with "average age" workers, the older ones were reported as being better in turnover, absenteeism, and overall job skills. Older workers were evaluated as better in motivation, production, and cost effectiveness—even when some "high-cost" factors such as health care costs were taken into account.

Frances Lear

Magazine editor

SNAPSHOT

I'm the latest bloomer ... I started my career at sixty-two! I think that, although I hate to chart anything by chronology, I've had more growth from fifty-five on than during all the rest of my life put together."

Frances Lear, founder of *Lear's* magazine and the woman who worked to revolutionize the attitude of a nation toward women who "weren't born yesterday," overcame many obstacles before beginning her real career at the age of sixty-two.

An adopted child, she reports being neglected by her mother and abused by her stepfather. She ran away from home at sixteen to work as a sales clerk; between the ages of sixteen and thirty-four, Lear speculated that she must have had "fifteen different careers, because I was forever hating what I was doing, and wanting to be something better, and use my head more." During this time, she also graduated from Sarah Lawrence College.

In 1957 she married Norman Lear, the television writer and producer. The marriage lasted twenty-eight years and produced two children. Though Lear worked closely with her husband, she was dissatisfied with the subordinate role assigned to women in Los Angeles. Interested in the women's movement during the late 1960s, Lear founded The Women's Place Inc., a Los Angeles consulting firm for women, which engaged in government-funded work projects. When the urgent need for qualified women in industry became apparent, Lear established Lear, Purvis, Walker & Co., the first executive search firm in America specializing in the placement of women executives.

> When Lear relocated to New York, she had the idea of starting her own magazine for "women like me." In 1988 she launched *Lear's* magazine to be "an early road map to much of the second half of life." *Lear's* was the first magazine targeted to the interests of educated, affluent women thirty-five and over, for which Lear was named Editor of the Year by *Advertising Age* in 1989.
>
> —*Lydia Brontë*

On the other hand, that very same survey found that despite these overall positive ratings, three-fifths of the employers were using early retirement incentives if they were engaged in downsizing their labor forces. If this is the case, there looms the high risk of losing the actual and potential skills of these experienced workers. According to the survey: "Employers are faced with the ironic possibility that they will be remediating large numbers of unqualified job entrants while simultaneously encouraging the early exit of many highly trained employees."

At the individual, organizational, governmental, and societal levels, the next several years will be characterized by extensive discussions and debates surrounding the issue of early retirement. Any examination of the benefits and costs of early retirement should include evaluations from the standpoint of the potential retiree; the worker who replaces such retirees; the employer; and the government. For example, from the perspective of a person considering retirement, the benefits could include the value of increased leisure, while the costs could include how much is lost in no longer having a salary or wages exceeding the level of the pension. From the viewpoint of the employer, the costs include those factors already cited above, while the benefits include, for example, the value of having to pay lower wages and salaries (and perhaps less costly fringe benefits).

The government benefits from having a reduction in expenditures for unemployment compensation (if the older worker becomes unemployed and does not leave the labor force), and other income transfer costs; and even an increase in income tax revenues, assuming the retiree is replaced by another worker not previously working. On the other hand, on the cost side, the government faces a loss of Social Security contributions and income taxes, assuming the retiree is not replaced by another worker. The social, psychological, and financial implications of a longer-than-expected period of retirement may be a reality now dawning on individual workers and their families, as well as on American communities and the government

—Harold L. Sheppard, Ph.D.; William H. Haas III, Ph.D.; Gordon F. Streib, Ph.D.

Physical wellness, mental wellness, health promotion, and disease prevention have traditionally been neglected in any discussion of the older population and now deserve greater personal and societal attention. The life expectancy of Americans has increased steadily throughout this century, and as the largest portion of our population ages, there is a great need for maintenance of health and function into advanced years. The goal of the medical profession, mental health professionals, and support groups alike is to create a network for the older adult to tap into—so that with increased education, support, self-maintenance exercises and techniques, and the resultant self-esteem and empowerment that comes from being "enlightened," every individual can become a *healthy* American who can live and work in the community with a sense of contribution rather than mere existence. The priority of the health care profession is not merely added years, but an improved quality of life. And unlike years past where a family doctor was responsible for the health of his patients, the 1990s health care field advocates that the responsibility of good health begins with the individual.

Wellness is a term that describes a positive state of being, that is, a condition in which an individual is without illness, feels well both physically and emotionally, is functionally independent, and is generally in good health. Health is defined as a state of com-

Physical Wellness in the Older Adult

plete physical, mental, and social well-being. Physical wellness is a state of bodily well-being in which diseases and physical impairments are absent or their effects kept to a minimum, and where the person has the best possible functional capability, given the variables of normal aging. Physical wellness, however, implies more than the state of one's condition at a specific time. The activities of health promotion, preventive and healthy behaviors, and preservation are all involved. Wellness conveys the understanding that quality of life has top priority and that longevity is desirable as long as it is accompanied by good health and personal satisfaction.

The concepts of physical wellness and good health in the older adult can seem contradictory. People tend to experience bodily losses as they grow older and are commonly afflicted by multiple illnesses and disabilities. The question arises, therefore, can health and wellness be promoted in older people? Recent thinking indicates that this is not only possible, for many if not all older people, but highly desirable. This is the philosophy of the wellness movement.

From a historical perspective, aging has been accepted as a biological process in which physical changes take a predictably downhill course, ultimately resulting in illness and death. A person is perceived as aged when physical features typical of the older person appear (such as gray hair or wrinkled skin) or age-related illness occurs (such as osteoarthritis, dementia, or many cancers). Consistent features of aging are the inevitable losses: physical ability, mental capacity, socialization, and ultimately life. While the process is universal, it varies dramatically from one person to another.

Although aging is a predictable process of losses and change, the rate and expression of these losses are variable and unique to the individual. The health status of older people varies greatly, and age may be best measured by physical and psychological characteristics rather than in years. This variability in aging is determined by disease, hereditary factors, environmental influences, and individual characteristics. For example, an aging person who has few medical problems could be considered healthy with a greater potential for quality life than a younger person who suffers from acute or chronic illness and is frail and dependent.

The health status of older people varies greatly, and age may be best measured by physical and psychological characteristics rather than in years.

COPYRIGHT MARIANNE GONTARZ

Functional markers such as independence in daily activities and socialization are generally better predictors of longevity than age.

Health and health maintenance are important topics in the discussion of wellness and aging. Up until the 1970s, physicians and other caregivers in the United States approached older people in much the same way as they did younger individuals: they defined health as the absence of disease. Health care meant diagnosing disease and recommending cures (surgery and medication). Since older adults were commonly affected by chronic diseases normally not curable (such as osteoarthritis and dementia), caregivers often used to forego treatment in older people, assuming these chronic afflictions to be part of normal aging and that intervening was thus futile. Preventive measures and health promotion were considered inappropriate.

The shift in thinking during the last half century acknowledges the variability of health in older people. Greater value is placed on quality of life and functional capacity. Although disease fighting is still important to health care, current thinking puts greater emphasis on preventive measures and health promotion. For example, billions of dollars have been spent in the treatment of

Changing Attitudes Toward Wellness

hip fractures but until recently very little has been done in the way of prevention. Recent research recommends preventive measures such as exercise and hormone therapy to prevent osteoporosis; the improvement in capability and increased bone strength may ultimately help prevent hip fractures.

The other important component of the shift in philosophy is the belief that quality of life is more valuable than quantity of life. Compression of morbidity is a popular concept that highlights the goal of confining or compressing disability and physical illness into the shortest possible time period. Ideally, these undesirable but expected events would occur just prior to death, as close as possible to the finite maximum life expectancy (estimated at about eighty-five years for most of the population).

Although disease fighting is still important to health care, current thinking puts greater emphasis on preventive measures and health promotion.

The concepts of physical wellness and health must respect the individual goals and wishes of older people. One goal may be to achieve a reasonable life expectancy. For example, a seventy-year-old woman may wish to live an additional decade or more; this is a reasonable goal considering that the average seventy-year-old woman can expect to live an additional eight to twelve years. Another goal of older people is to remain independent and self-sufficient. Currently, a woman who reaches age seventy can expect to live six of the next twelve years with some degree of dependency, often so significant that long-term care in a nursing home or similar facility may be required. An obvious goal is to prevent this from occurring. Therefore, the concept of physical wellness for the elderly must take account of the changes inherent to older people and use individual life goals as a measure of good health and a positive state of being.

That it is sound and practical to advocate health and physical wellness for the older population can now be affirmed, based upon a greater understanding of the aging process, the value placed on quality of life with less emphasis upon longevity alone, and on the individual and collective goals of older people.

The basic goals of physical wellness are as follows:

1. To prevent disease

2. To prevent or limit disability

3. To maintain optimum health and function

4. To minimize the duration and manifestations of disease and disability when they occur

The activities to achieve these goals are carried out by the individual and his or her health care providers, which may include a physician, a nurse, a therapist, a counselor, the family, or friends. These activities include healthy behavior and specific preventive measures.

Healthy Behavior

Healthy behavior is generally considered the most consistent and effective method for promoting good health. While this is true in all age groups, it applies particularly to the older adult considering that late life is usually the time when the negative effects of negligent behavior become most evident. For example, smoking is unhealthy behavior which, started at a younger age, can and often does result in cancer and/or chronic disease in later life. In contrast, favorable behavior such as regular aerobic exercise and maintenance of ideal body weight might be more valuable to older people than younger people in terms of actual benefit and the impact on quality of life.

Healthy behavior as it pertains to the older adult can be categorized as (1) activities in early and middle years to prevent disease and disability later, and (2) activities by older people to maintain health and prevent or lessen the manifestations of disease and disability. Healthful life behavior for the younger person includes a healthy diet, aerobic exercise, tobacco cessation, limited alcohol consumption, good dental hygiene, and limited access to direct sunlight. Healthful life behavior for the older adult includes these same lifestyle components, but also includes accident and fall prevention, the avoidance of multiple drugs, especially over-the-counter medications, and socialization.

Exercise

There is increasing evidence that the benefits of exercise extend into advanced age. Regular aerobic exercise (such as walking, biking, and swimming) can improve bodily functions and prevent or forestall some illnesses. Exercise is a key component of fitness—a notion very popular today that can apply to all ages. Fitness is comprised of five elements: cardiovascular endurance, muscular strength, muscular endurance, flexibility, and body composition. Exercise can also improve self-image and emotional well-being. Graded exercise that is tailored to individual abilities can be advocated as an important part of health promotion and maintenance in the older adult.

But not many older people exercise. Data from 1985 show that fewer than 10 percent of those over the age of sixty-five jog, swim, cycle, or do calisthenics on a regular basis. This contrasts with up to 40 percent of those under age sixty-five who exercise regularly and vigorously. Only one-third of older people do *any* type of regular physical exercise, and most of these do casual walking only.

These data may reflect an age bias toward exercise as healthy behavior; exercise was not considered a social norm in years past and many older people are fearful of injury or potential for disease. Thus, in order to recommend regular exercise for the older adult, a caregiver must consider individual capabilities, weigh the risks of injury, and attempt to qualify and quantify individual benefits.

The physical benefits of exercise in older people range from maintenance of ideal body weight to possible prevention of such conditions as diabetes, heart disease, and osteoporosis. Regular exercise can also improve functional capabilities such as gait, balance, transfer from chair and bed, and many activities of daily living such as toileting and bathing that require physical strength. The benefits of a consistent exercise program are many, but include:

1. Increased flexibility and range of motion in joints resulting in better agility and coordination

2. Increased strength and endurance

3. Greater stamina and less chronic fatigue

4. Prevention of bone deterioration

5. Increased efficiency of cardiovascular and respiratory systems

6. Decreased digestive problems and constipation

7. Decreased chronic stress, tension, and mental fatigue

8. Decreased cholesterol levels

9. Better weight control

10. Improved sense of overall well-being

Recent data have shown that elderly people can exercise effectively. Aerobic ability as measured by oxygen consumption can increase with physical training. Weight lifting is an exercise elderly people rarely perform, but studies have shown that even persons in their nineties can increase strength and muscle mass through weight training. Most exercise data report the result of short-term training programs (four to twelve weeks); whether older people will exercise for longer periods of time and whether the benefits are long lasting remains to be seen.

A study of two hundred men and women from ages fifty-six to eighty-seven at the Andrus Gerontology Center at the University of Southern California produced encouraging findings. The group took part in regular exercise three to five times a week over a five-year period and showed distinct improvement not only in cardiovascular health, flexibility, and muscle tone, but in condition of teeth, gums, and skin tone.

Exercise in the older adult should be prescribed by physicians or therapists in much the same way medications are prescribed. A physical examination and assessment of physical ability must be done to screen for cardiac and respiratory problems before any older person begins an exercise program. The prescription should be individualized, providing maximum benefit while keeping in mind the needs and goals of the older person. For example, a progressive walking program may be best for an older person who is overweight and wishes to lose weight and suppress appetite (such as taking a brisk walk for thirty minutes, three times per week). On the other hand, a very old person having trouble with housework may do well with focused weight training to improve

Table 1: American College of Sports Medicine Guidelines

In order to achieve benefits from exercise, the American College of Sports Medicine (ACSM) issues guidelines based on the latest research. They suggest an individual perform aerobic exercise using large muscle groups fifteen to sixty minutes, three to five days per week. Having strong muscles, tendons, and ligaments may prevent injury and low back pain, and encourage faster recovery from injury, more strength to do everyday chores, and more muscle tone. To get the most from this aerobic exercise, you should exercise at an intensity level called your training heart rate zone, used to gauge how hard you are exercising. Ask your doctor to work with you in determining this level, using the following gauge.

Training Heart Rate Zone

Objective: To determine your personal training heart rate zone.

Note: To determine your resting heart rate, take your pulse while resting for ten seconds and multiply by six. This is your resting heart rate per minute.

Intensity of Exercise

1. Estimate your own maximal heart rate (MHR)
   MHR = 220 minus age (220 – age)
   MHR = 220 – _____ = _____ bpm (beats per minute)

2. Resting Heart Rate (RHR) = _____ bpm

3. Heart Rate Reserve (HRR) – MHR – RHR
   HRR = _____ – _____ = bpm

4. Training Intensities (TI) = HRR x TI + RHR
   50 Percent TI = _____ x .50 + _____ = _____ bpm
   75 Percent TI = _____ x .75 + _____ = _____ bpm

5. Training Heart Rate Zone. The optimum training heart rate zone as determined by the ACSM is between 60 to 90 percent. However, individuals who have been physically inactive or are in the poor or fair cardiovascular fitness categories should use 50 percent training intensity during the first few weeks of the exercise program.

Training Heart Rate Zone: _____ (50 percent TI) to _____ (75 percent TI).

If your heart rate falls below the optimum zone, you are not working hard enough to achieve aerobic benefits. If your heart rate is above this zone, slow down; overworking increases risk of injury and overexertion. Exercise heart rates for individuals on certain types of medications, such as beta blockers and high blood pressure medication, will be much lower.

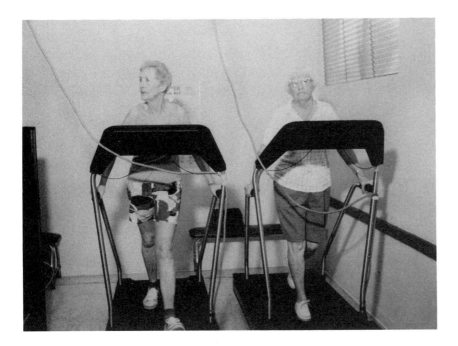

upper body strength and stamina. As with younger people, the older person should be encouraged to exercise regularly.

Excercise in the older adult may be prescribed by physicians or therapists in much the same way medications are prescribed.

Diet and Nutrition

Good nutrition is a key component of wellness. It means a proper intake of foods (type and amount) to provide for normal bodily function. Dietary excesses or deficiencies can lead to disease conditions, especially in older people who lack the nutritional reserves needed to avoid illness during times of physical stress. A proper balance of the major food groups is important: carbohydrates, proteins, fat, and grains and fiber.

Most Americans take in excess fat, many eating 50 percent or more of their diet in the form of fat (30 percent or less is desirable for the average adult person). Also, as energy needs tend to be

Bernice K.

B ernice K., age sixty-five, participates along with her husband, Ralph, in the Senior Olympics, a series of thirty-four sports competitions throughout the United States that emphasizes the social and recreational aspects of sports as much as competition. She relates how taking part in this program has enhanced the couple's quality of life:

"After Ralph retired and our four daughters completed their education, we began to do some things with our lives that we hadn't had an opportunity to do before. We both started to participate in local Senior Olympics. Ralph suffered a heart attack a few years ago, and our life changed. He gained a lot of weight. I dedicated myself to help him to bring it down.

"As a result of our walking exercise and change of diet, I lost forty-two pounds. I became interested in race-walking and qualified for the national competition. My six events are horseshoe, archery, one-mile race walk, discus, shotput, and high jump. Ralph does quite well in horseshoes. We travel to meets and are away from our home for up to three months at a time. The number of people in the games is growing rapidly. In one California meet, there were over three thousand entries.

"The Senior Olympics movement is composed of an inspiring group of people. They are all young at heart. Things happen to everybody; they have all sorts of physical handicaps, but it really doesn't stop them. They know their limitations and go for it. You should never do things that are beyond you, or push yourself too much at our age. Get physically fit first, get healthy, and then compete if that is an interest."

—*From Connie Goldman's "Late Bloomer" public radio series*

lower in older people (because of decreased activity and lower body weight), fat intake as low as 10 percent of total intake may be more appropriate. This can be achieved by limiting red meat, removing skin from chicken, eating more fish, avoiding cooking in fats (especially animal fats), and eliminating fat condiments such as butter and mayonnaise. Nutritionists recommend replacing fat in the diet with an increase in complex carbohydrates: cereals, fruits, vegetables, bread, rice, and pasta. Many dietitians urge 55 percent or more of the diet consist of carbohydrates.

Protein needs are diminished in older people due to a decrease in muscle mass, but the percentage of protein intake (30 percent to 50 percent) is similar to that of younger people. Carbohydrates in the form of complex sugars and starches (such as bread and potatoes) are preferred to simple sugars (such as table sugar and candy). Simple sugars are high in calories while providing little nutritional value, other than as a rapid source of energy in those older adults who are very active physically. High-caloric foods such as these should be avoided by older people who are prone to overweight.

Recent studies endorse diets plentiful in fiber. High-fiber diets may reduce the risk of certain intestinal cancers and promote regular intestinal function. (Whether this is as true for all age groups is as yet unknown.) Sodium restriction can lower blood pressure and reduce the risk of illnesses associated with hypertension, such as stroke and kidney disease. As most Americans consume far more sodium than is needed, a reduction in very salty foods can be recommended for all age groups.

Vitamin supplementation remains a controversial topic. While vitamin deficiencies should definitely be treated, the use of supplementary vitamins in healthy older persons without vitamin deficiency has inconsistent support. Certain vitamins have particular appeal to older persons because of their effects on the aging process. Vitamin E is an antioxidant and may have value in slowing down the aging process; oxidation of body cells is one of the theoretical mechanisms of aging. Vitamin E's reported ability to enhance certain body functions such as memory and sexual function has as yet not been proven. The long-term effects of high doses of vitamin E are unknown. High doses of vitamin C have

Julia Child

Cookbook author and television personality

SNAPSHOT

I never thought of retirement; it would never occur to me. Because I like my work, I continue to go on and on. I think young people should realize that they have to have a passionate occupation."

Julia Child's career might be described as an odyssey. Born Julia McWilliams in Pasadena, California, in 1912 she graduated from Smith College in 1934 and went to work in advertising and publicity. When World War II broke out, she joined the Office of Strategic Services, which later became the Central Intelligence Agency. In Ceylon, her first overseas assignment, she met Paul Child, served with him in China, and married him in 1946, after returning to the United States.

In those days, Child explains, if two people in government service got married, one of them was expected to quit—and it wasn't the man. She resigned and moved with her husband to France, where the U.S. Information Agency sent him after the war. Child discovered her true vocation in France. "I stepped off the boat," she remarks, "took one mouthful of French food, and I was hooked for life."

She studied at the Cordon Bleu and made two friends who became important collaborators: Simone Beck and Louise Bertholle. Post–World War II Paris housed many Americans, but few could speak French, making it difficult for women to take classes at any of the existing French cooking schools. In 1949 Child and her friends opened their own English-speaking cooking school, *Le Club des Gourmettes*, and began writing a book on French cuisine for an American audience. This book, the all-time bestseller, *Mastering the Art of*

French Cooking, was published by Alfred Knopf in 1961, after the Childs returned to the United States.

Nervous about their prospects for selling five thousand French cookbooks, Knopf arranged to feature Child in an hour-long TV book review show at WGBH in Boston. Child was momentarily stumped: "What was I going to do?" she wondered, "Read recipes for an hour?" Then she hit upon the notion of taking along something she could "whip up" on camera, as a demonstration. Since television studios in those days were not equipped with cooking facilities, Child thought of doing an omelette: All it required was a dozen eggs, a wire whip, a copper mixing bowl, an omelette pan, and a hot plate.

The omelette was a tremendous success and occasioned so many enthusiastic calls and letters from viewers the station asked Child to do her own cooking show, five days a week. Thus "The French Chef" was launched, and Americans, until then disdainful and suspicious of "foreign" food, embraced the cuisine. With her engaging and lighthearted manner, Child made French cooking fun and accessible.

After taping some two hundred episodes of "The French Chef," Child developed a new television series featuring a more contemporary cuisine, "Julia Child and Company," and in 1984, with WGBH, she produced six one-hour teaching videos, "The Way to Cook." Child also published companion books for these series, *Julia Child and Company* (1974), *Julia Child and More Company* (1980), and *The Way to Cook* (1989).

Today Child is still going strong at the age of eighty, with new books, a new TV series, "Dinner with Julia," and appearances on ABC's "Good Morning, America." She has had a career peak lasting thirty years—and it began at age fifty!

—*Lydia Brontë*

long been reported to prevent viral infections and may also improve the quality of skin and bone. Vitamin C has little or no adverse effects and therefore can be supported for general use in most older persons. Vitamin D deficiency is common in older persons who have little exposure to sunlight; vitamin D is produced in the skin when exposed to the sun. This deficiency is especially common in older people who reside in nursing homes or are unable to go outdoors because of illness or disability. Oral vitamin D supplementation is appropriate for these individuals.

Minerals such as calcium, magnesium, and other trace metals are commonly used as dietary supplements, but only calcium has been shown to be of proven benefit. Calcium supplementation in postmenopausal women can help maintain or improve bone density, and doses of one to one and a half grams per day combined with estrogens may prevent osteoporosis and fractures. Adequate water intake is very important for the older adult. Extra liquids should be taken to replace fluids lost during exercise.

Abuses

There is no doubt that abusive behavior takes its toll on the older adult, and the physical results of a lifetime of abusive behavior can manifest itself in both chronic and acute illnesses. What role, specifically, does each abuse play in the adult's body?

Smoking: The long-term risks of tobacco use are well known: cancer (lung, breast, bladder, and probably others), chronic lung disease, and heart disease. Quitting or never starting will decrease the risk of these problems in later years. The older person who stops smoking will also benefit in more immediate ways. Twenty percent of older adults are current smokers and are at increased risk for lung infections such as pneumonia and influenza. Because respiratory infections are the fourth leading cause of death in persons over age sixty-five, giving up smoking can reduce the likelihood of these serious and often fatal conditions.

Smoking is also associated with lower food intake and may contribute to weight loss in older people. Low body weight is an important marker for frailty and eventual death in older adults. In addition, quitting smoking will save money. This money could be used to purchase food or medication, which would have an even greater impact on the older person's health than quitting by itself.

Alcohol: Approximately 1 percent to 6 percent of older people have a problem with alcohol overuse, abuse, and dependency. While small amounts of alcohol (one to two ounces per day) might prevent some cardiac and vascular conditions, larger amounts are associated with liver disease and neurological problems. Alcohol can also predispose people to falls and is associated with suicide. Overuse of all forms of alcoholic beverages should be discouraged in older people to decrease their risk of encountering alcohol-related problems. Reasonable advice is to limit alcohol consumption to one serving in a twenty-four-hour period, and to avoid drinking daily.

Improper use of medication: The average older American uses 4.5 prescription drugs and 3.5 over-the-counter drugs annually. The older American uses medications even more often. The adverse effects of drug use are numerous and varied. Older persons are more susceptible because of body changes associated with normal aging, such as decreased kidney function, which in turn causes difficulty in the elimination of certain drugs from the bloodstream. Avoiding unnecessary medications and using the lowest possible dose can provide some protection for the older person. Physicians often contribute to adverse drug reactions by prescribing excessive and unnecessary amounts. Health promotion for the elderly must emphasize proper use of drugs, with the understanding that medications can improve health in the best of circumstances, but can cause serious and life-threatening problems when used inappropriately.

Obesity: Obesity in the older adult is a common problem. Approximately 30 percent of persons above the age of sixty-five are overweight (which is defined as weighing more than 30 percent above one's ideal). Obesity is associated with hypertension, stroke, heart disease, high cholesterol, diabetes mellitus, and osteoarthritis. Maintenance of ideal body weight is important in the prevention of these disorders and is an important facet of health promotion.

Calories should not be restricted to less than one thousand calories per day, however, as this energy requirement is usually needed by the older person to maintain proper body function and prevent illness. Exercise will have an additive effect on weight loss when combined with proper nutrition.

Abnormally low body weight and malnutrition are problems as significant in the elderly as overweight; they predispose to disease states and can predict poor health and premature death. For example, overly thin older women are at greater risk of fractures and falls, both serious and threatening events. Excessive underweight may indicate underlying illnesses or functional disturbance; social difficulties such as poverty or inability to obtain food may result in weight loss as well.

Sudden weight loss (defined as losing more than 5 percent to 10 percent of one's body weight in six months or less) is a problem that may have multiple causes. The most common in older persons is inadequate intake of calories for any of a multitude of reasons: depression, unavailability of food, chewing problems, or difficulties with meal preparation. Cancer causes weight loss in no more than 20 percent of cases. The assumption that an older person who loses weight must have a malignancy is incorrect. Other causes of weight loss include diabetes and thyroid disease, common at this age. The effects of digitalis on appetite and intestinal function must always be considered in case of malnourishment or weight loss.

Aging and Sexuality

Fears and myths abound concerning changes in older persons' sexual activity and experience. As a general rule, sexual interest and need continue into the later part of one's life. As with many other patterns of activity, frequency of sexual activity in earlier decades is the greatest determinant in later life.

One key limiting factor of sexual activity for many older people is the lack of a partner. Since widowers tend to remarry within two years of the death of a spouse, and older men have the availability of the large population of widows, divorced, and single older women, women are statistically disadvantaged. Also, their greater numbers means fewer men to go around.

Dr. William Cahan

Surgeon

I think that from the point of view of being physically and mentally able, I'm quite equipped and refuse to obey the numbers. Nothing bores me more than the chronological listing of people's ages as indications of their inability and ability."

Still a practicing surgeon at the age of seventy-eight, Dr. William Cahan has been at the forefront of several major advances in cancer surgery and treatment, while crusading for years against cigarette smoking. Born in New York City on August 2, 1914, the first day of World War I, Cahan was the only child of artistic parents: his father was an artist with *New York World*; his mother was an interior decorator. Cahan graduated from Harvard in 1935 with a bachelor of science degree, then earned his M.D. at Columbia Medical School. After interning at the Hospital of Joint Diseases, Cahan "walked into (Sloan-Kettering) Memorial Hospital January 1, 1942—twenty-four days after Pearl Harbor—and, except for the three years I went to war, I've been there ever since."

Sloan-Kettering was an ideal place for Cahan to conduct his cancer research, because of the wide variety of patients and conditions and the supportive research environment of the hospital. Cahan proved that radiation, used to treat diseases like tuberculosis, was cancer causing, and he developed treatments for various types of cancer, including cryogenics in the early 1960s. Using liquid nitrogen to freeze and "kill" tumor tissue, Cahan and Dr. Irving Cooper proved cryogenics to be very effective in treating bone cancer, treating skin cancers, treating benign and malignant tumors, removing cataracts, and reattaching retinas.

His crusade against cigarette smoking also began in the 1960s. In the belief that smoking is the number one cause of rapid aging and early death in America, Cahan devised experiments that proved conclusively that cigarette smoking causes lung cancer. Responsible in large part for getting cigarette advertising off television and radio, Cahan testified before Congress as the representative of the American Cancer Society to change the labels on cigarettes in order to alert the public, the society awarded him their distinguished service award in recognition of his contributions.

Cahan has been active as a teacher at Cornell University Medical College, and he has been affiliated with many hospitals in New York and around the country. When he reached seventy, Cahan fought Sloan-Kettering's attempt to retire him, because he had always dreamed of operating with his son, who was then a surgeon at New York Hospital, and he considered irrational any bylaw that required retirement solely for chronological age: "I would quit in two seconds if I thought I was technically unable to do it."

"I wrote a paper called 'Age and Cancer Surgery' in which I point out that the chronological age of people, if you take it without its context of the individual personality, is ridiculous. It's unscientific, first of all. Second, the people who are becoming septuagenarians and octogenarians are a different breed than they were a generation or two ago. I assure you, in another generation it will not be unique for nonagenarians to do remarkable things."

Cahan recently completed his autobiography, *No Stranger to Tears: A Surgeon's Story*. With many interests in addition to his medical pursuits, Cahan remains extremely active, needing only four hours of sleep a night.

—*Lydia Brontë*

Researchers have found that older people have the desire for sexual contact and that couples remain sexually active quite late into life—especially if there are no complicating illnesses. Sexual experience is clearly important for physical and psychological well-being, and achieving orgasm remains an important part of sexual satisfaction. For some older people, sexual experience actually improves with age. More flexible schedules, greater privacy from children, no fear of pregnancy, a more relaxing lifestyle, and increased appreciation of and knowledge about sexuality contribute to this enhancement.

Despite the diversity of personal attitudes and experiences, there are some generalizations that can be made about sexual changes that occur with age.

For men, the most common changes include the following:

- A longer period of direct stimulation may be necessary for full arousal and more time may be needed to complete an erection.

- An erection may not be as firm or large as in earlier years.

- There may be a reduction in lubrication before ejaculation.

- A decrease in the force of ejaculation may occur but an ability to delay and make love longer may also occur.

- The time it takes to achieve another erection after orgasm may increase.

Men who have continued a satisfying sex life over the years will likely experience less dramatic changes in their sexual functioning unless certain illnesses (such as those affecting the prostate gland) are encountered. A pattern of regular sexual activity helps to preserve sexual ability. Periods of impotence are not unique to older men since they may be triggered at any age by fatigue, stress, illness, or excessive use of alcohol.

Occasional impotence in males is more readily overcome if partners are aware of the normality of occurrence and the woman is understanding and supportive. Medical professionals have found that periods of impotence are generally not considered a medical problem unless they occur in more than 25 percent of sexual intercourse with the same partner. Where impotence is more frequent, medical evaluation is recommended.

While males reach a peak of sexual response in adolescence, and thereafter experience a gradual decline, females reach a peak of sexual response in their mid-thirties and generally stay at that level throughout the rest of their lives. Age alone generally does not trigger a reduction in sexual capacity for women. Changes that do occur are usually noticed many years after menopause. The most common changes in sexual functioning affecting older women are as follows:

- Reduction in vaginal lubrication and longer lengths of time are often required for lubrication.

- Thinning of the vaginal lining is common.

- Narrowing and shortening of the vaginal canal and reduced elasticity of vaginal tissue are common.

- There may be the increased possibility of infection in the vagina and bladder.

- Possible irritation of the bladder and urethra during intercourse is common.

Vaginal dryness is a common experience for some post-menopausal women. As with men, sexual discomfort or difficulty can often be remedied through an understanding and supportive male partner and with the use of simple aids. For example, many women find that the use of a water-soluble lubricant helps remove discomfort during sexual intercourse. Women experiencing severe vaginal atrophy may be treated with estrogen replacement therapy (ERT) once a physician has determined that there are no pre-cancerous conditions present. Benefits of ERT include reduction in heart disease and osteoporosis.

Some of the physical causes of impotence are connected with certain diseases, surgery, or accidental damage to certain blood vessels or nerves which, in turn, upset hormonal balance. Other possible causes include excessive use of alcohol (a depressant), tobacco (nicotine constricts blood vessels), and some medications such as those used to treat high blood pressure and depression. Among diseases, diabetes and vascular (heart) disease are prominent causes of physical impotence.

In many cases, impotence caused by the identified factors can be alleviated through medical treatment or counseling. A variety of mechanisms are available for men unable to achieve an erection. These include vacuum or suction devices that are placed around the penis to aid erection, and penile implants such as rod, inflatable, and self-contained prostheses.

It may seem awkward to categorize healthy mental activities as healthy life behavior. However mental wellness is related to one's physical wellness, and the benefits derived from socialization and stress reduction can greatly improve one's physical health. Lack of social contact has been linked to depression and can be a marker for underlying medical illness. While a high degree of socialization may indicate a healthier individual, increasing one's social contacts will not definitively improve physical health. It does, however, directly improve emotional health and can relieve symptoms such as anxiety and improve or prevent reactive depression. It is appropriate to encourage greater socialization among older persons to maintain emotional well-being, prevent psychological illness, and improve overall health.

Emotional Health

Stress is a response to physical and emotional demands often resulting in ill feelings and anxiety. Everyone experiences stress at one time or another; the ability to cope with the demand is what determines the intensity of the stress response. Common reactions to stress, both physical and psychological, include substance abuse (alcohol, drugs, tobacco) and eating disorders. Maladaptive responses can lead to mental illness in susceptible persons. Table 2 lists many possible physical and psychological reactions to stress. Methods to relieve stress include exercise, relaxation techniques, meditation, recreation, and other more personal actions.

Prevention as it pertains to health refers to a process or activity that is specifically intended to prevent disease/disability

Prevention and Wellness

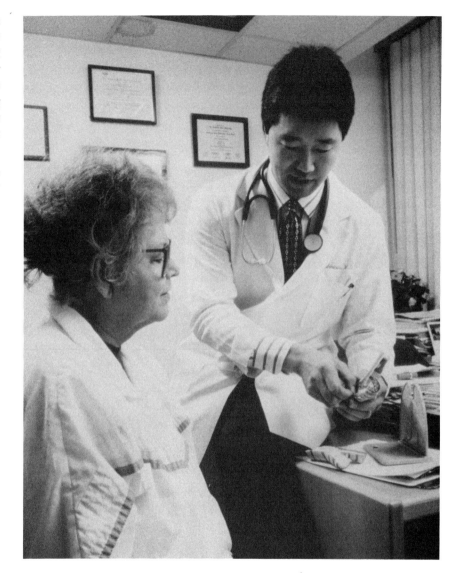

While seeing a physician regularly might serve to detect disease, it is unclear whether this practice will prolong life or improve outcome except in a few conditions.

or detect early disease so that it can be treated before it causes serious problems. Conditions or diseases that may be preventable generally meet the following criteria: (1) there is a known cause or associated circumstance, (2) and beneficial interventions are available, acceptable to the person, and have reasonable risk and cost.

Preventive measures for conditions common in the older adult can be divided into three categories:

Table 2: Reactions to Stress

Physical Reactions
Increased heart rate, blood pressure, respiration
Decrease in efficiency of immune system
Sweaty palms
Cold hands and feet
Headaches
Backaches
Constipation
Diarrhea

Psychological Reactions
Anxiety
Panic
Restlessness
Memory loss
Poor concentration
Irrational behavior
Poor self-esteem
Fatigue

Health Problems that May Result from Too Much Negative or Chronic Stress
High blood pressure
Insomnia
Ulcers and other disturbances in the digestive tract
Headaches
Poor circulation and restriction in breathing

1. Primary prevention: measures to prevent the occurrence of disease, such as the influenza vaccine.

2. Secondary prevention: measures to find hidden disease for early treatment, such as mammogram screening for early breast cancer. The benefit may be prolongation of life or relief of pain and suffering.

3. Tertiary prevention: measures to identify symptomatic disease or disability and use a treatment to improve the overall condition of the person, such as rehabilitation after a stroke.

Many conditions are amenable to preventive health measures. The following preventive measures are discussed in this section because of their particular importance to the older adult.

Relaxation Techniques

Neck and Facial Massage

Seated in a comfortable position, breathe in and out, close your eyes. Place your fingers behind your neck. Make five large circles on the back of your neck by moving your hands in an outward direction. Repeat this sequence with your chin, cheeks, temples, and forehead. Repeat the massage three times.

Clock Technique

While lying down, close your eyes; breathe in and out. Imagine that you see a clock in front of you, hand pointed at twelve o'clock. Inhale through the nose and imagine the clock's hand moves toward one o'clock, exhale as it reaches one o'clock. Repeat all the way around the numbers of the clock.

Immunization

Immunizations of known benefit to the older adult include the influenza vaccine, the pneumococcal vaccine, and tetanus. During epidemics of influenza A and B, older adults are the most frequently affected and are more likely to be hospitalized or die from the illness. Eighty percent of influenza-related deaths occur in persons over the age of sixty-five. Vaccination against influenza is recommended above age sixty-five, especially to the very old and those with chronic illness. The influenza vaccine is 60 percent to 70 percent effective in reducing mortality and can prevent hospitalization. However, older Americans are not routinely vaccinated; surveys have shown that only 30 percent to 40 percent of eligible elders are vaccinated in any given year. Predictably, older people of lower socioeconomic classes and minorities are the least likely to receive the vaccine, possibly because of limited access, cost, or insufficient knowledge of its benefit.

The pneumococcal vaccine is a once-per-lifetime vaccination which helps to protect against pneumonia due to certain common bacteria. It is recommended for all persons over the age of sixty-five, especially those with underlying lung disease or those who have problems fighting infections. It is 60 percent to 70 percent effective, relatively safe, and inexpensive.

The tetanus vaccination prevents tetanus, an infectious disease due to bacterial contamination of skin wounds. Primary immunization is given in childhood and a booster injection every ten years, every five years if a tetanus-prone wound occurs. Many older persons have never been vaccinated, since this vaccination was not mandatory in years past. Older people are also commonly behind on the timing of the tetanus booster and physicians rarely offer the booster unless a skin wound occurs. Greater efforts are necessary by public health organizations and the medical community to insure adequate protection against tetanus through routine and properly timed vaccination.

Routine Checkups and Physicals

There is inconsistent data to support routine checkups for older persons. While seeing a physician regularly might serve to detect disease, it is unclear whether this practice will prolong life or improve outcome except in a few conditions. The traditional visit to the doctor is probably less valuable than a personalized functional health assessment. This assessment typically includes a survey of daily living activities and an inventory of social supports, along with more traditional assessments of health and function. Using this approach, health counseling may have much more impact on quality of life than mere advice on physical health.

An innovative approach to health care suggests that telephone "visits" with a physician can improve function and reduce hospitalization in older adults when compared to traditional office visits. Thus, the regular checkup for older people may be replaced by addressing functional health issues as a priority. The encounter could be in the office or clinic but may also be effectively carried out by telephone or by family conference. It is not yet known whether regular assessments of this type are cost effective or beneficial in the absence of specific illness or functional problem. Of course, periodic physical examinations and health assessments (such as an annual physical) remain an important component of health care but may not be needed as routinely as previously thought. The timing of health surveillance should be based upon the older person's individual needs and wishes.

Preventive Measures for Cancer

The majority of cancers are age-specific diseases; that is, they are more prevalent in older persons, and most new cases occur in older age groups. Because of this tendency, preventive measures should be directed toward this group. Healthful behavior in young and middle years is actually the best way to prevent cancer in later years. Eating a low-fat diet helps prevent colon cancer; stopping smoking or never starting helps ward off lung, breast, and bladder cancer; and avoiding exposure to direct sunlight helps prevent skin cancer.

There are several cancers in the older adult population amenable to preventive measures, including breast, uterine, cervical, ovarian skin, colon, prostate, and oral.

Breast cancer: Breast cancer is more likely to occur as a woman ages; it is the most common cause of cancer death in older females. Mammography can detect early disease and improve the rate of survival when appropriately treated. Mammography is safe, well tolerated, and relatively inexpensive, so it is an important tool in improving health and prolonging life. Women over age fifty should be screened for early, treatable breast cancer.

Cancer of the prostate: Cancer of the prostate occurs almost exclusively in older men and has replaced lung cancer as the most common cancer in adult males. The increasing occurrence of prostate cancer in recent years may reflect improved ability to detect the cancer rather than an actual increase in the number of cases. Two screening tests are available to detect prostate cancer: the digital rectal examination (feeling for nodules or tumors) and a blood test for a prostate-specific antigen (PSA, a protein produced by cancerous prostate cells). Together these tests can detect asymptomatic cancer in as many as 85 percent of cases. Prostate cancer that is detected early will probably respond better to treatment, although this remains a somewhat controversial opinion. Nevertheless, digital examination and measurement of PSA should be done annually for men over age fifty.

Cancer of the cervix: Screening for cancer of the cervix with a pap smear is no longer recommended for women over age sixty-five provided they have been previously properly screened. The number of new cases of cervical cancer decreases markedly after age fifty, and the yield of screening women sixty-five and older who have had previously normal serial pap smears is low. Pelvic examination remains valuable and should be used to detect abnormalities of the female organs when appropriate.

Colon cancer: Colon cancer is a uniformly fatal disease when allowed to advance unchecked. The only reasonable chance for cure is surgical treatment of early lesions before the disease has spread outside the colon. Screening tests are available to find early disease: the digital rectal examination, testing stool for occult (hidden) blood, radiographs of the colon, and looking directly at the colon and rectum with an endoscope. While these tests can detect early, asymptomatic disease, there is no substantial evidence to show that early detection by these methods prolongs life. Drawbacks to routine use of screening tests for colon cancer include cost, risks of the procedure (including perforation of the intestine for endoscopy and radiographs), and possible patient discomfort. Thus it is appropriate to individualize decisions to conduct colon cancer screening in older people. The risks and cost of the procedures must be weighed against the potential benefits (prolongation of life and relief of pain and suffering).

Preventive Measures for Heart Disease and Cholesterol

The most common form of heart disease in our society is blockage of the blood vessels of the heart due to fat deposits. The condition is called coronary heart disease and the process is called atherosclerosis. Older adults are affected by this condition in epidemic proportions; it is the most common cause of death and disability in Americans today. However, there are no reliable preventive measures once atherosclerosis has been established. Coronary artery bypass, angioplasty, and other surgical procedures improve symptoms but do not prolong life except in very few specific situations. The key to treatment of coronary heart disease, therefore, is prevention.

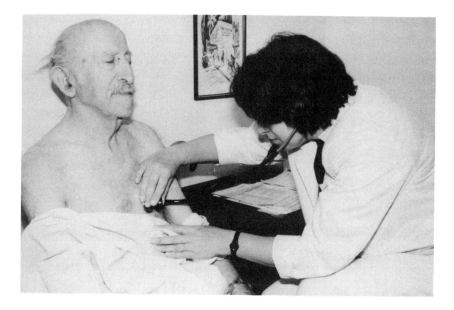

Cancer of the prostate occurs almost exclusively in older men and has replaced lung cancer as the most common cancer in adult males.

Risk factors for atherosclerosis include smoking, diabetes, hypertension, high cholesterol, and a family history of atherosclerosis. Healthful behavior such as a low-fat diet, smoking cessation, and exercise are appropriate preventive measures. Treatment of hypertension, high cholesterol, and diabetes are additional methods to prevent coronary heart disease. Hereditary factors pose a very significant risk.

There is controversy on how to approach these risk factors in older people. Conflicting data exist as to the benefit of lowering abnormal cholesterol levels in older adults, especially those over age seventy. No clinical trial has yet to show a clear advantage to aggressive treatment. In addition, dietary restrictions and the use of cholesterol-lowering drugs may be of greater risk to an older person than their potential benefits against heart disease. Decisions on treatment must be individualized, using known data on the benefits and judgment regarding the risks. There should also be agreement on the goals of therapy between the caregiver and the subject. Aggressively treating high cholesterol in persons over age seventy-five in order to prolong life or prevent atherosclerosis is probably inappropriate, though simple methods to improve blood cholesterol can be encouraged and advocated.

Smoking cessation in later years will likely have little if any effect in preventing heart disease; it is strongly recommended because of the potential benefit to respiratory function and prevention of lung infections. Treating hypertension in older persons is effective in preventing stroke and aggressive control of blood pressure is appropriate. In summary, coronary heart disease is a common condition in all age groups and is the most common cause of death and serious illness in our society. Preventive measures should be directed against behavior and conditions which predispose to atherosclerosis. Unfortunately, there are no definitive methods to prevent heart attack, heart failure, or death in those who have established coronary heart disease.

Preventive Measures for Osteoporosis

Loss of bone density is a uniform process after age thirty. The rate of bone loss remains steady in men throughout life, but increases dramatically in women after menopause. Bone strength and density in women is dependent on the female hormone, estrogen; as estrogen levels decrease during and after menopause, bone density cannot be maintained. Early on, this bone loss causes few problems. But with time (fifteen to twenty years on average) the cumulative losses can severely weaken certain bones (especially the hip, wrist, and spine) and make them vulnerable to fractures. The condition in which bones become weakened with age and subject to fracture is known as osteoporosis. Osteoporosis is the leading cause of fractures in older women. Risk factors for osteoporosis include female gender, postmenopausal status, cigarette smoking, sedentary lifestyle, Caucasian race, small body build, and a family history of osteoporosis. Fractures of the hip, spine, and extremities are the most serious complications of osteoporosis and are significant causes of pain and disability. Hip fracture is associated with an increased risk of early death and commonly leads to nursing home placement.

Techniques to prevent osteoporosis includes exercise, calcium supplementation with vitamin D, and the use of estrogen replacement therapy. Studies show that osteoporosis can be improved by taking part in a regular weight-bearing exercise program and by resistance training. Estrogen given in oral or topical form at the time of menopause will slow or stabilize the accelerated bone loss which would otherwise occur. It is generally accepted that women should be given estrogen replacement therapy for at least five to fifteen years after menopause, and possibly lifelong. Estrogen should be combined with calcium to give maximum benefit. It is not known whether women who are ten or more years past menopause will benefit from estrogen replacement therapy. Preliminary studies show some benefit, but conclusive evidence is as yet not available.

The most significant complication of estrogen therapy is an increased risk of uterine cancer. The risk is relatively small, and data have shown that there is no increased risk of death in women who develop uterine cancer while receiving estrogen therapy. The addition of a hormonal agent, progesterone, can nullify the risk of uterine cancer when added to estrogen therapy. Despite past concerns, there has been no convincing evidence that estrogen therapy causes breast cancer. An additional benefit is a statistical decrease in heart disease by 50 percent in women taking estrogen; this is likely due to estrogen's beneficial effect on cholesterol levels. All women at risk for osteoporosis should be considered for estrogen therapy at the time of menopause unless there are strong contraindications. Routine use in women more than ten years past menopause cannot as yet be recommended.

Preventive Measures for Sensory Deficits

Older adults are universally affected by progressive losses in vision and hearing. Sensory loss is part of normal aging and will manifest to differing degrees in each older person. Vision will be commonly altered by presbyopia (loss of near vision due to changes in the lens of the eye). Hearing is altered by presbycusis (loss of hearing high tones due to dysfunction of the nerves to the ear). Prevention in the context of normal sensory impairment is tertiary in nature; that is, it consists of finding the condition and designing adaptive measure to improve function and prevent disability.

Eyeglasses are the obvious corrective measure for presbyopia. However, many older persons with vision impairment go undiagnosed, especially in nursing homes. Other common causes of visual impairment in older people include cataracts and macular degeneration (a degenerative process of the retina of unknown cause). Cataracts cannot be prevented, but the resulting impairment can be cured by surgical removal with artificial lens implantation. There is no treatment for macular degeneration, so it is a common cause of blindness in older adults. Finding the visually impaired elderly is the most important step in preventing and treating the disabilities associated with this condition.

A hearing aid can greatly improve the functional capacity of older people with hearing impairment. It may allow independent living for persons who might otherwise require a more sheltered setting due to an inability to communicate. Hearing aids are very expensive and most health insurance (including Medicare) does not provide payment coverage. Finding and providing for elderly people who could benefit from a hearing aid is the preventive measure of choice. Besides presbycusis, the only additional cause which commonly occurs is ear wax impaction. The preventive measure is to detect the problem before it causes serious impairment, and to remove the wax obstruction as the definitive cure. Unfortunately, this condition is frequently overlooked, especially in nursing homes and among older people who cannot communicate their problems to caregivers.

Mental Wellness

Recent generations of retirees in the United States are probably the first to have expectations that well-being in later life may include more than avoidance of disabling physical diseases or mental impairments. The proliferation of health newsletters, magazines, and health promotion programs for older adults testify to dramatic increases in older people's awareness of their health potential. Conceiving of wellness as more than just the opposite or absence of illness is a relatively new idea. Until recently, health in all its forms has been the domain of the medical establishment. But wellness, both physical and mental, needs to be viewed as extending beyond the medical model that emphasizes healing and disease prevention, and include personal responsibility.

The following discussion of mental wellness draws from the expertise of mental health practitioners and researchers who attempt to go beyond an illness or clinical orientation. This view

Protecting Health

focuses on growth, change, and attainment of new ways of experiencing and relating to one's world in later life.

The discussion takes into account a central theme of aging, namely the experience of loss in later life. How individuals cope with, adjust to, and learn from experiences of loss—whether of a job, spouse, physical capability—is a critical feature of mental wellness. Responses to loss are examined from the viewpoint of several human development theories about later life. Also presented is a list of activities and programs which may foster psychological wellness. In short, the challenges and possibilities of psychological growth form the main topic of this exploration.

The Meaning of Psychological Wellness

HOW should psychological wellness be defined? One way is to say what it is not. Clearly, psychological wellness is not identical to happiness, normalcy, or freedom from worries and problems. Although a healthy person may experience happiness, it is also possible that to be happy in the context of real human problems may be little more than denial of reality. Psychological wellness may differ from normalcy or typicalness, since these terms assume certain norms as the standards of behavior. A certain maladaptive or dysfunctional style can become so typical in a society that it may appear to represent health. For example, disengagement from social participation and passive withdrawal into reminiscing were once considered to be normal and appropriate behaviors for older people. The rocking chair was synonymous with old age. Today, these attributes may be viewed as symptoms associated with depression, a reaction to forced retirement, or lack of social opportunities.

Psychological wellness is not identical with an absence of emotional distress. Mental illness is clinically recognized when an individual seeks help from a mental health practitioner and is diagnosed as having a specific disorder. The label and diagnostic category describe a person in a state of distress, wishing to make changes in his or her life. From this view, the individual could be regarded as demonstrating psychological wellness by seeking help as compared to the individual who needs it but fails to seek appropriate treatment. Sometimes the sense of felt distress is a result of another family member who creates stress as a result of destructive behavior patterns. Frequently, those who create stress fail to acknowledge their behavior. Thus, the person officially receiving the diagnostic label of mental illness may in fact turn out to be the healthier family member.

Positive mental health in later life refers to successful encounters with challenging conditions and situations in which the person gains insight and expands his or her capability for relationships.

The concept of psychological wellness describes a process rather than a static way of being. It describes a manner of relating to a complicated changing world and how the individual and the world interact in this dynamic process. Mental well-being is influenced but not necessarily determined by economic and social status, intellectual capacity, and other individual factors limiting attainment of optimal psychological well-being.

Positive mental health includes ideals of growth, realization of personal potential (self-actualization), and integration of personality. These set standards of what is possible—even though complete attainment of the ideal may be statistically rare.

Psychological wellness describes a process that is likely to change as an individual becomes older. The issues facing the adolescent and young adult differ from the issues of the older adult moving into the latter stages of life. Adaptations and transformations representing psychological wellness are also correspondingly different.

Within the field of psychology, humanistic psychologists have articulated a concept suggesting a nonillness orientation toward psychological wellness. For example, psychologist Carl Rogers, the founder of client-centered therapy, used the phrase "fully functioning person" to describe an active process rather than a static form of being. Rogers identified three main characteristics: first, the fully functioning person manifests increasing openness to experience rather than defensiveness; second, such a person lives fully in the moment; finally, this person places a basic trust in his or her own "organism as a means of arriving at the most satisfying behavior" for each situation.

Rogers's characterization may help define wellness in any particular age group of the population, but this definition is especially useful when applied to how older individuals relate to a significant characteristic of old age: loss. More specifically, when encountering loss, does the older individual come to the experience with an attitude of openness? Is there an effort to respond to the loss in the present moment? Is there trust in the individual's experience of making decisions about the loss? When an older person embodies the three attributes, he or she may be described as exhibiting psychological wellness.

Loss and Mental Wellness

Although individuals at any age may experience loss, those in the second half of their lives are faced with multiple losses. Barbara Silverstone and H. Kandel Hyman state in their book *You and Your Aging Parent* that "if any word can sum up the varied catalogue of problems that do appear in old age, it is the word loss." Those commonly encountered in old age include:

1. Physical losses: changes in the sense organs, nervous system, internal organs, bone structure, and depletion of the resources to cope with physical illness

Pauline G. and Pauline K.

Both retired school teachers who visit homebound individuals, these women speak of the gratification and pleasure of getting out and helping others:

"Everybody knows us, but they don't know our last names. They just know us as the two Paulines. We do our volunteer work together through our city's Red Cross. We are working more hours now than we did when we were teaching. It's good for your health when you're outside every day; you're not hemmed in.

"Everything we do is voluntary. We get more pleasure out of it and wouldn't have it any other way. It's just too dreadful and too dreary to sit all day and do nothing. We try to follow a regular schedule; if we don't we might have more than we can do in one week and nothing to do the next week.

"We try to do at least eighty hours a month of visiting. Usually we visit nursing homes where people are lonely and want us to come in and stay a while with them. We also go to the handicapped center once a week. We've always been received so well. There is a lady who is always so glad to see us on Monday morning. She lives in a home for the handicapped and says that we make her week by visiting on Monday.

"We just are going to do the best we can, as long as we can, as well as we can. And we're going to be happy while we're doing it. We aren't going to worry about any illness that we might have; we will live with it. As long as we can get out and be active, we know that we'll feel better."

—*From Connie Goldman's "Late Bloomer" public radio series*

2. Relationship losses: the reduction of social contact after retirement from employment, reduced contact with friends due to death or limitations resulting from illness or injury, and changes in the nature of friendships resulting from illness, pain, and death

3. Loss of a stable environment as the world continues to change

4. Loss of familiar roles: parent, breadwinner, homemaker, spouse, church member, athlete, householder

5. Loss of financial security in the context of inflation and rising medical costs

6. Loss of a sense of independence and personal power

7. Loss of mental ability and mental stability

In addition to these actual losses, the older adult often becomes keenly aware of the ultimate loss, which is the approach of death. The older adult who is psychologically well will suffer these losses just as surely as the elder who is psychologically unhealthy. The ability to respond effectively to these losses is perhaps the primary factor that separates psychological well-being from other states.

Adaptation and Transformation

Adaptation is a concept used in the field of aging to describe the manner in which older individuals respond to changing circumstances, especially losses. Professor and psychologist Robert J. Kastenbaum has categorized three main styles of adaptation: habituation, continuity, and conflict management.

Habituation is a process through which individuals gradually pay less and less conscious attention to ways of acting and thinking—they do them automatically. A person coping with intense loss may distract him- or herself from the experience by becoming absorbed in day-to-day routines. Continuity refers to the way that new life experiences are absorbed into a context of familiar and relatively persistent patterns of self-activity and interaction with the environment. Kastenbaum suggests that older individuals have a stronger sense of this continuity than younger

After retirement older adults may spend increasing time with friends, in activities around the house, or in hobbies.

people. As a result, a significant loss will be accommodated into larger patterns of experience and cause a smaller disruption in day-to-day functioning.

Conflict management is the process by which perception of impasses is changed from negative to neutral or positive. Examples of conflict management include the use of humor (defusing angry elements of conflict by focusing on resolutions), altruism (viewing one's own needs as secondary to other people's), sublimation (channeling energy resulting from a conflict into socially acceptable activities), and suppression (coping by putting the conflict out of one's consciousness).

Distinguished gerontologist Atchley has described patterns of adaptation for specific problem areas. For example, loss of income in old age typically results in an adaptation pattern of doing with less. For individuals used to having a surplus of resources, this loss is more psychological than physical. For those who are at or below the minimal level of economic survival, doing with less can result in inadequate care of basic needs. Loss of roles and activities is common for older individuals in retirement. They can respond by substituting new roles for earlier ones. As people move into their late seventies, it may become increasingly difficult for them to find substitutive roles because of limited mobility and declining energy.

Another strategy is to redistribute one's energy in the remaining roles. Thus, one who discontinues employment may spend increasing time with friends, in activities around the house, or in hobbies. No new roles are added, but increased time is spent in remaining roles. Still other individuals gradually disengage from activities as they get older. While for some there is a tendency to withdraw from the outside world and turn toward issues of a more inward spiritual nature, research indicates that some forms of disengagement are more likely to be a result of diminished opportunities rather than as a part of a natural process.

A form of coping that represents a less functional pattern than the adaptational styles above is escape. With escape, the problem remains but the individual chooses a reduced sense of self rather than a diminished sense of the problem. Forms of escape include isolation, in which the person withdraws from life as a way of coping with problems; the use of drugs and alcohol as a strategy for reducing the experience of loss; and suicide.

The concept of adaptation is based on a biological model of how plants and animals modify themselves in order to survive. Similarly, human adaptation in response to loss suggests self-modification or compensatory behavior rather than making changes to the environment or achieving personal new growth. Adaptation represents a higher form of psychological wellness when compared with escape, which attempts to ignore or deny the loss through activities that cannot actually diminish it.

Adaptation thus implies a continuum of change ranging from escape and denial at one end, stability in the middle, and positive growth or transformation in the quality of one's life experience at the other end.

Personal transformation is often discussed in the context of crises—identifiable with losses in later life. Crises may serve as a catalyst for development, leading to favorable outcomes rather than arrested growth or deficits. While no one consciously wishes to invite loss and crisis, such events may bring the person across a threshold to new experience, meanings, and psychological states. For example, the loss of a spouse may challenge the individual to reevaluate beliefs and assumptions about the world, to renegotiate an established social network, and to shift one's sense of self from "we" to "I." What is critical to these positive outcomes of loss is having a supportive, nurturing environment: friends, support groups, educational resources, and so on.

Transformations in later life are more often identified through subjective self-reporting as collected in interviews or reflected in books and articles written in testimony to experience. Often illusive, transformations do not readily lend themselves to scientific examination in ways that adaptational approaches can be studied. Nonetheless, important questions must be asked about the nature of transformation: What are the conditions under which it may occur? What are the probable outcomes? In what ways does transformation for older adults differ from transformations at other ages? The following section details some current thinking about the kinds of transformations that are likely in the life of an adult who exhibits psychological wellness. In addition, an attempt is made to explain the nature of transformation and why it applies particularly to older adults.

In a study of the bereavement process, researchers found that 27 percent of those recovering from the death of a spouse showed clear evidence of growth—"new behaviors, new ways of doing things, restructuring of the self in relationship to others. . . ."

Developmental Models of Transformation

A developmental approach to transformation has been a useful tool for examining transitions through life. Theorists and researchers have applied a developmental model to describe the aging process and to understand the ways mental wellness can be manifested as a result of changes in age. Social psychologist Erik Erikson developed the most widely known conception of transformational stages, and he continued to revise and incorporate information into this schema. Erikson proposed an eight-stage theory, of

Robert McNamara

Businessman and author

SNAPSHOT

I am over seventy-five, but I don't feel physically or mentally old. I have an intense interest in the learning environment; it is fun for me. I don't feel any desire to retire to Palm Beach or go to the baseball games."

Former secretary of defense (1961–68) and Ford Motor Company director and president (1957–61), Robert McNamara was born in San Francisco in 1916. Neither parent had gone beyond high school, but they encouraged their children to achieve at school from an early age. "My earliest recollection of childhood is of the home environment that was focused on providing for the children opportunities which my parents hadn't had," recalls McNamara. "And they expected the children to take advantage of those opportunites."

McNamara graduated Phi Beta Kappa from the University of California in 1937 where he developed a passionate interest in economics, and enrolled at the Harvard Graduate School of Business in 1938. At this time McNamara married former Berkeley classmate Margaret Craig. The marriage lasted forty years, until her death in 1978. McNamara worked as an instructor at Harvard until the outbreak of World War II, when he was asked to go to Europe as a civilian consultant to the War Department.

When discharged in 1945, he and his wife fell sick with polio, stationed at Wright Field on inactive service. McNamara suffered only a light illness, but his wife became seriously ill and remained hospitalized for eight months. McNamara soon realized that his teaching job at Harvard, to which he hoped to return with the war over, would not cover the hospital debts. A colleague had an idea to save Ford Motor Co. (which had been experiencing large financial losses at the time) by sending a group of ten ecomomists to help run the company.

McNamara began work at Ford in 1946, where he had a distinguished career, working there for almost fifteen years. In 1957 he was elected director, and by 1960 he became the first nonfamily member in the history of the company to be elected president. Five weeks later, McNamara was appointed secretary of defense by President Kennedy. He said it was not easy to leave Ford: "I recognized my responsibility to the Ford family and to the company, but it was very difficult to put personal or corporate considerations above those of the national interest." He served as secretary of defense from January 1961 to March 1968, when he became president of the World Bank Group of Institutions, where he worked until June 1981.

Since then McNamara has served on the board of numerous corporations and is associated with a number of nonprofit associations. He is the author of *The Essence of Security*, written while serving as defense secretary, and has written four other books. He engages in public speaking on such global issues as world peace and the environment and is the recipient of numerous honorary degrees and prizes worldwide, including the Albert Einstein Peace Prize.

Now in his seventies, McNamara is not phased by the aging process, and instead sees it as "a function of the mind." He explains: "I think the mind is a muscle. Therefore, the exercising of the mind is a way to maintain the strength of the muscle." Outside of his mental pursuits, he is an avid skier, tennis player, mountain climber, and runner. "I enjoy physical exercise," he admits. "Exercising the mind and the body is important to maintain both physical strength and mental capability."

—*Lydia Brontë*

which the later three stages are specifically related to midlife and old age. Each of these stages posits psychological tasks presented as opposing possibilities (such as trust versus mistrust, stagnation versus generativity). Under conditions of growth, the individual is able to accomplish the task, build on, and then move to the next developmental stage. Under conditions that do not favor growth, the individual is psychologically paralyzed at that stage.

Even as individuals age chronologically, they may respond to current situations from the unresolved viewpoint of an earlier developmental stage. As a result, older individuals may find themselves working through earlier stages. Although most of Erikson's work focused on childhood and adolescent stages, he believed that the later stages from young to older adulthood are the critical ones that encompass the "evolutionary development which has made man the teaching and instituting animal."

Erikson asserted that during childhood, healthy development would involve a child's acquiring a sense of basic trust in the reliability of his or her world, control over behavior, confidence in undertaking tasks, recognition of competencies, and a firm sense of identity. Assuming adequate accomplishment in these areas, Erikson believed that the main task of early adulthood is acquiring the capacity for intimacy. Healthy intimacy assumes that the person has a clear sense of self that allows him or her to enter into relationships with a capacity for commitment and the ethical strength of character to maintain closeness. The mentally well adult would be able to maintain intimacy without fear of losing his or her identity or without engaging in behavior that would be consciously or unconsciously destructive to the relationship.

The developmental task for middle adulthood Erikson termed "generativity," which he defined as the commitment to establish and provide guidance for the next generation. Generativity implies energy, mental growth, and absorption in others. Failure to achieve generativity is represented by stagnation—boredom, mental decline, obsessive pseudointimacy, and narcissistic self-indulgence. In the mode of generativity, older adults' relationships are characterized by growth, selflessness, giving, and involvement in the community. Their mental activity is open, flex-

Generativity is the commitment to establish and provide guidance for the next generation.

ible, and creative. Generativity brings about a realistic body image and a sense of being needed.

The contest of integrity or wisdom versus despair forms the basis for Erikson's last stage of development. He regarded the healthy elder as able to perceive and accept a pattern of necessity in his or her life that enables the individual to embrace the past as the only history that one could have lived—in a sense, the destiny that one has fulfilled. Failure leads to despair, which is characterized by anxiety, social withdrawal, disappointment, bitterness, and the sense that one's life lacks overall coherence and inner meaning.

Integrity in relationships is evidenced in the form of autonomy, rather than dependency, and an ability to provide solutions to problems presented by others. Mental activity implies continuing study, artistic expression, and service to others. Such older individuals will have realistic evaluations and acceptance of their losses and a satisfactory resolution of the illness experience.

Another approach to late-life development has been formulated by Allan Chinen in two recent books. Chinen expands upon his psychiatric training by drawing insights from over five thousand fairy tales from throughout the world. He notes that about 10 percent of the fairy tales focus on characters who can be identified as "middle-aged." Another 5 percent of the stories focus on characters who can be described as "elders" or people in their later years.

These stories, Chinen believes, convey psychological truths that can be helpful to individuals interested in psychological transformation. He claims that in preliterate societies, stories were told in small groups for the benefit of adults, who would recognize the symbolic or allegorical meanings of the tales. Chinen believes that these stories had the power to bypass rational thinking and touch the deeper aspects of consciousness. As a result, the telling of these stories provided a means for helping adults make necessary transformations in their lives.

Chinen's analysis shows that developmental tasks for youth differ from the tasks of adults in mid- and later life. The task of youth is to leave home. Almost all fairy tales about youth involve departing from home and going into a difficult and frightening world. The hero of the story seeks true love and great adventure. Frightening adversaries are met and defeated. Finally, the youth acknowledges the power that comes from having passed through these experiences.

In these middle-age tales, women acknowledge their talent and power and break out of their restricted social roles. Male characters begin to explore their feminine natures and recognize the importance of relationships. Having accomplished these important reversals, adults in middle age can tolerate ambiguity and no longer need to rely on arbitrary distinctions between good and evil. Middle-age tales show that a confrontation with death is a necessary developmental task at this time. Unlike the youthful hero, the middle-aged adult can face these fears. Often humor is the vehicle allowing for middle-aged adults to maintain their responsibilities, carry the burdens, and move toward their elder years without despair and cynicism.

Chinen identifies the task that defines the transformation from middle age to elder as the gaining of wisdom. Wisdom is often attributed to elders simply on the basis of being old, yet Chinen believes that wisdom is acquired through often painful experiences, and elders who have been unable or unwilling to face this pain may have no more wisdom than persons at any other age. When an individual undergoes an experience of pain and suffering and is simultaneously able to remain conscious of the choices that are being made, then wisdom is the likely result.

But wisdom is more than the accumulation of facts and the feeling of pain. Wisdom comes through an examination of the more recessive, less developed side of personality, which psychologist Carl Jung termed the "shadow" of the self. Jung described exploration of the shadow as a deepening process of development beginning in midlife. In Jung's view, individuals in their early years take on roles and responsibilities that become "masks" of the self. With the achievement of adulthood, there may be more freedom to take off the masks to discover or remember the fuller picture of one's inner life and to affirm the full range of experiences, positive and negative. This is the basis for wisdom.

Fairy tales involving middle-aged adults are quite different. In these stories, the main character is forced to give up the dreams and ideals of an earlier time. As these earlier visions are given up, the middle-ager takes on a pragmatism and responsibility that was previously absent.

A second major task for elders identified by Chinen is transcendence of self, which is a moving beyond immediate personal needs similar to Erikson's notion of generativity. Chinen notes that elder tales provide three forms of transcendence of self: (1) moving beyond self by turning one's focus toward family, community, and society; (2) moving beyond self through spiritual discipline toward a direct experience of God; and (3) moving beyond the limited egocentric sense of "self" to the larger "Self." Carl Jung contended that this higher Self is the experience of the fully developed personality. The person who has moved fully into the experience of Self is able to view the realistic limits of his or her capacity and at the same time see the potential that exists in humankind. As these two experiences are held simultaneously, the individual is able to recognize the full potential of humankind that exists in him- or herself. In this way the person transcends the smaller experience of self. Each of these three forms of transcendence requires the wisdom accumulated through earlier stages.

A third task for elders is a return to innocence and wonder. At this point of life, the elder has given up any notion of personal perfection. This allows for a return to childlike zest, spontaneity, and innocence. The elder takes delight in nature. In this stage the elder moves beyond social convention and is able to integrate the judgment and skill acquired in midlife with the newfound spontaneous experience of life.

Chinen maintains that the final task for the healthy elder is to bring the fullness of experience to bear on practical solutions to the world's dilemmas. Unlike earlier efforts, the elder does not need to force solutions on others. The elder provides a model of groundedness, knowledge, discipline, and patience. As a result of these skills the elder is able to provide transitions for younger individuals attempting to achieve their own transformations, to mediate between two viewpoints that appear to be entirely oppositional, or to bridge the gap between intergenerational conflicts.

For Chinen, the healthy older adult will be able to cope with loss in a transformational manner because the elder will have acquired wisdom, will have moved beyond the egocentric self, will possess innocence and wonder, and will have the capacity to mediate between opposing views. In sum, the older person will have gained a unified view of the life cycle. The portrait of the wise older person is an ideal of the possible but should be tempered with modesty and humility to avoid creating new, overidealized stereotypes to replace earlier negative ones. In today's Western societies, old age implies a loss of social status. But the ideal of older people contributing to a culture of wisdom may help point toward the future.

The Transformation Process and Aging

While transformation can occur at any age, the potential for transformational change in older individuals is increased by several factors. First, like all individuals, older adults have accumulated a lifetime of inevitable scars and wounds. Many of these wounds occurred at a very early age and resulted in unsophisticated strategies for coping with pain. While the aging process provides opportunities for personal growth, some individuals nonetheless arrive at old age with wounds that have not yet

healed. The potential for transformation for healthy elders is heightened because there is less reason for them to hide from these wounds or to deny the scars or the ineffectual coping mechanisms.

A second factor increasing the possibility for transformation in the older adult is that the magnitude of stress can be quite large as a result of the number and intensity of losses so likely at this time of life. Not only are these losses inevitable, but there is also an attitude of anticipating future losses, notably the final loss of death and the accompanying apprehension that becomes increasingly prominent as one becomes older.

Significant transformation occurs in ways that ease the stress of existing wounds. Just as an earthquake is likely to relieve existing stresses in the earth's structure, the psychological earthquakes also relieve stress. If individuals are able to tolerate the

Due to the rapid increase in health care costs, a great deal of effort and money is going into research on problems related to aging.

conscious experience of pain, then they will be in the best position to choose the manner in which the stress can be resolved. As a result, the transformation is likely to be in a positive way rather than a regression to earlier stages of development.

Personal transformation movement leader Jean Houston asserts that positive transformations are most likely to occur when an individual is able to move from the small personal story to a larger mythological one, which helps the individual understand the nature of loss and provide a pattern for living out the loss in a heroic manner. However, in our society there are few opportunities to learn about mythological potential. Enlightened individuals Joseph Campbell, Jean Shinoda Bolin, Carol Pearson, Robert Moore, Robert Bly, and Allan Chinen are at the forefront of those reintroducing this powerful perspective to our society. When elders have devoted themselves to enhancing their mythological world, the earthquakes are more likely to result in positive experiences.

Even if an older person devotes time to the mythological world, it does not mean that earthquake experiences can be avoided. Loss is a natural part of the life process. The manner in which a person responds to loss is the grief process.

The Grief Process

Grief expert and best-selling author Elisabeth Kübler-Ross was the first to detail the way individuals respond to their own process of dying. She identified five stages: denial, anger, bargaining, depression, and acceptance. Although initially identified in individuals who knew they had a terminal illness, the stages have also been extrapolated to anyone who is experiencing a significant loss. Not everyone experiences each of these stages, nor does each individual pass through them in a linear, sequential way, but the stages help validate reactions that are a normal part of the grief process. Although loss often produces the reactions characterized by Kübler-Ross, this process does not always involve only negative reactions. Individuals may also respond to loss with (1) relief and hope that the future will be improved; (2) curiosity about the nature of loss as a new kind of experience; (3) apathy about the loss; and (4) relief resulting from the end of negative experiences.

Each of these response styles can be a natural part of the grief process likely to occur with any significant loss. As an individual ages, there will be increasing opportunities to experiment with coping styles. Stephen Levine observes that some individuals approaching their death begin to live in a different way, closely resembling Carl Rogers's concept of the fully functioning person. This way of being seems to capture the essence of psychological wellness.

Levine notes that individuals who are dying often view pain and death as the enemy. Resisting their pain, they become disconnected from the fullness and entirety of their being. They are not open to experience, because they fear pain; and they are unable to stay in the moment, because the present seems so overwhelming. They have difficulty trusting that they can move through the experience in a satisfying way.

In contrast, some individuals are able to experience spiritual growth by opening their hearts to the conscious experience of pain and dying. Through meditation it becomes possible to stay in the moment and to notice the subtle and exquisite changes that occur even in the face of death. As a result, it becomes possible to once again place trust in one's basic organism.

Levine describes a series of meditations designed to assist the individual to move beyond the denial, anger, bargaining, and depression that are associated with intense loss. These exercises involve forgiveness, loving kindness, and mindfulness, in response to the experience of dying. Ultimately the person comes to a place where death can be experienced fully, and it is at this moment that life is also experienced fully.

Facilitating Mental Wellness

More than ever before, there are a number of different approaches and vehicles to achieving mental well-being, depending upon one's mind-set, lifestyle, creativity, and willingness to explore new options for healing. From the traditional to the New Age and beyond, older adults are finding solutions to their problems and constructive ways of working through their feelings, situations, and issues. Here is a sampling of some approaches that have heralded very real and sometimes miraculous results.

Psychotherapy

Psychotherapy may be regarded as a vehicle for facilitating transformational shifts. Psychotherapies vary as to what experiences or capacities they emphasize. Traditional psychoanalysis, for example, puts great emphasis on the unconscious, dreams, fantasies, and sex drives. Behavioral therapies focus more on patterns of actual response to conflicts and fears and on how these can be changed through a process of relearning. Very generally, psychotherapies can be classified into two groups: ego-oriented psychotherapies, which focus attention on the ego's ability to adapt to pain and stress; and soul-oriented psychotherapies, which focus on more philosophical and sometimes cosmic issues relating individual meanings to broader, perennial meanings of life. Psychotherapists trained in Jungian thought and its archetypal or mythological perspectives are more likely to encourage a therapeutic experience which seeks these deeper forms.

Another approach to facilitating positive change in the mental health of older adults can be found in the work of Mary Baird Carlsen, a therapist who works with and writes about creative potential in aging. Carlsen is influenced by schools of psychotherapy that emphasize ways that people make up or "construct" their realities. By helping people discover how they construct their world of values and perceptions, Carlsen is able to help them take responsibility for themselves, enabling them to tap their creativity as a process of "meaning-making." Carlsen recognizes that older adults may be especially inclined to explore their meaning-making potential, since they are able to perceive repeating and evolving patterns of experience in their lives.

Carlsen describes the goals and process of psychotherapy as a relationship formed between therapist and client, through which information is gathered and then reshaped into new patterns that validate the client's knowledge and sophistication. The final phase is a closure to the therapy relationship.

Carlsen believes that successful therapy introduces new possibilities, provides a model for cognitive flexibility and openness, and stimulates clients to arrive at new insights. These insights are instances of new meaning-making. This process is accomplished when the client is able to "go meta," which means to stand away from the problem and to view it from above. This is the transformational aspect of psychotherapy. Carlsen details a variety of particularly helpful techniques for older adults, including use of early recollections, representations of the family tree, memory exercises, visualizing new patterns, meditation, family therapy, and pet and gardening therapies.

A similar program has been developed in a workshop format and companion workbook entitled *Growing Wiser: The Older Person's Guide to Mental Wellness.* This program is organized in six parts:

1. Strategies for creating positive expectations and becoming a "sage"

2. Strategies for dealing with problems of memory

3. Strategies for maintaining mental alertness

4. Exercises for coping with personal grief and the grief of others

5. Techniques for establishing and maintaining communication with others

6. Techniques for fostering relationships in the larger world

Individuals interested in increasing their knowledge of mythology generally and of transformational mythology in particular can attend workshops regularly available in large cities by many of the authors mentioned in this section. Some of these workshops are primarily informational, but many of them require active participation by the attendees. For example, a mythological story may be told and explained; then the participants begin to enact the major roles of the story as a way of deepening the connection between the story and themselves.

Psychotherapy and growth-oriented workshops are expensive and beyond the budget or inclination of most older adults. Many individuals continue to associate a stigma with seeking treatment in psychotherapy. Although there is a strong movement away from the mental illness concept toward a personal growth orientation, it is likely that this narrower view of psychotherapy will persist. Regardless of the reasons for not electing psychotherapy, it is important to remember that there are other options.

Support Groups

Support groups in many formats have developed to facilitate the change process. The twelve-step movement that began with Alcoholics Anonymous has been expanded and adapted to deal with issues including substance abuse, emotional excesses, sexual disorders, and relationship problems. In addition there are increasing numbers of consciousness-raising groups for men and women. These types of groups vary in orientation, style, and effectiveness from community to community and even within one group over a period of time. When one chooses to work on personal issues in a support group (or with any therapist, mentor, or friend), it is important that the helper be more focused on the best interest of the helpee rather than in fostering a particular type of change.

Spiritual Institutions and Groups

The church has often been associated with the kinds of changes discussed in this chapter. Bible study, meditation groups, and focused discussion about spiritual matters is another prominent vehicle for transformational change. Increased interest in spirituality is reflected by the large number of spirituality-related courses listed in the Elderhostel catalog—an international learning and travel program attracting over 300,000 seniors each year. Also, the spiritual disciplines found within or derived from Eastern religions have provided opportunities for spiritual growth. These approaches provide a cognitive framework as well as a variety of disciplines, such as mindfulness meditation described by Levine and others.

Art Therapy

Art has often been used as a vehicle for transformational growth. Poetry, creative writing, drawing and painting, sculpture, and music can all be used as a way of developing a connection with the inner self. In fact, they are often integrated as a regular part of curricula at community colleges. Further, therapists also use forms such as art therapy and music therapy as ways of spiritual and psychological growth.

Community Programs

Older adults may also look for help through community agencies. Even small community agencies such as community mental health centers, hospitals, and hospice centers may provide opportunities for personal growth. In addition, colleges and universities provide an increasing number of educational options for older adults.

No matter what avenues a person chooses to explore as he or she makes a commitment to balance and health—both physical and mental—one thing is certain: the twenty-first century will be greeting an enlightened and dedicated group of adults. Many people will have embraced a "choice ethic"—that the good life is one that permits the individual the greatest amount of choices. Certainly the health care arena and its professionals gives people a greater range of choices as to how they will approach their future years.

—*Richard F. Afable, M.D., M.P.H.; Richard Johnson, Ph.D.; David R. Thomas, M.D.*

Having a sense of community with others remains a vital part of growing older. While some like to be with other people most of the time, and others prefer doing things on their own, the need to belong—whether it's to family, neighborhood, congregation, political group, or cultural heritage—may actually intensify through the middle and later years of life. Community means different things to different people. For some it's working for a charitable organization, for others it's being a part of a sports team, a political cause, a gardening club, or a lifelong learning program. These sources of fellowship and friendship help to extend the core of family ties to the extent that sometimes nonfamily relationships feel like kinship.

Feeling a part of a community, contributing to it, and benefiting from the support and fellowship of others is a major factor determining quality of life after fifty. For one, living longer means experiencing more changes. Community participation through family and friends can help improve elements of continuity and comfort. In addition, most of the important information second middle-agers receive comes through these channels.

The theme of finding community encompasses a broad range of topics, from various methods of social support to what it really means to establish one's niche in a neighborhood. An older adult's physical surroundings and the support vehicles available are critically important factors that determine whether older people experience old age as secure and meaningful or disabling and isolated. Changes such as moving from one home or one state to another, retirement from the workplace, or even loss of a spouse impact people's community participation in a wide variety of ways. Although recent data help to document important progress in meeting the basic needs of second middle-agers, the rapidly growing number of older households and communities will present new challenges to housing providers, policy makers, and, above all, midlife adults and their families in the coming decades.

Family support throughout late life is extremely important to the physical and mental well-being of midlife adults. However, the changing American family often leaves midlife adults unclear about sources of emotional and instrumental assistance. Families that remain intact have well-demarcated lines of assistance for midlife adults; this help can come from adult children, sisters and brothers, grandchildren, extended family, or fictive kin. Families no longer intact because of geographical mobility, divorce, remarriage, or death have greater difficulty in identifying who will help and in what way. Just as some midlife adults need to rearrange their lives in order to accommodate the divorce of one of their children, others have to face their own losses through divorce or widowhood. Throughout this era of rapid social change and individual differences, however, it is important to remember that the family in American society remains the central source of love and support for the older adult.

Many chapters of the story of older adult friendship remain unwritten. Although philosophers have pondered the meaning of friendship for centuries, researchers have just recently begun to examine the phenomenon. At first, scholars discussed older people's friendships only in passing, mainly in the context of discussions of retirement and widowhood. Since the early 1970s, however, many research projects have focused specifically on friendship in later life. In fact, researchers have paid more attention to older adult friendship than they have to friendship during earlier stages of adulthood.

We are only beginning to be able to answer questions posed about the friendships of midlife adults. Older people from different ethnic, racial, and class backgrounds, of different genders, living in different periods of history, and raised in different cultural contexts all have different friendship experiences. But while the definition of friendship varies across cultural and gender lines, and they do carry certain stresses, the rewards are easier to measure: love, loyalty, companionship, support, and concern are just a few.

During the past fifty years, the American family has experienced many changes. Some of these changes result from increased geographic mobility; others are caused by changing population characteristics. Simply put, the American family is different now than it was fifty years ago in terms of longevity and structure. The differences in families are especially evident to older people who were raised in two- and three-generation families living under the same roof and typically unaffected by divorce. During the past fifty years, midlife adults have witnessed radical alterations in their own family forms and in the generations within their families.

Family Relationships in Later Life

One of the causes of changing family composition is the aging of American society. The population is aging in large part because people are living longer. Four out of five people born in the 1990s can expect to live at least to age sixty-five, and 50 percent of the people who reach age sixty-five will live past age eighty. These demographic changes have had a powerful effect on the age distribution of the population and have resulted in a greater number and higher proportion of older people in the U.S. population than ever before.

As individuals live longer, they spend more time in their family roles and may experience different family roles than their parents did. For example, one of the most rapidly changing trends is that of the multigenerational family. According to recent statistics of people age sixty-five and older who have adult children, 40 percent live in four-generation families. Ninety-four percent of the people who head these families have grandchildren, and 46 percent have great-grandchildren. As the number of living generations per family increases, so too does the number of family roles

Family Roles in an Aging Society

available to midlife adults. More older people are currently grand-parents and great-grandparents than ever before.

However, older people are not the only ones to experience changes in their family roles. Adults have living parents for a much longer time than ever before. These proportions are remark-able, especially to older people who themselves may not have had a single living grandparent during childhood. These changes in family patterns are highlighted even more considering that 10 per-cent of all people age sixty-five and older also have a child who is sixty-five years of age or older.

The Rise of Multigenerational Families

Multigenerational families result in an increase in the number of years that most older people spend as grandparents or great-grandparents. The possibility of multigenerational family interac-tions is quite high for most elderly. But longevity also means that midlife adults have the potential for experiencing long periods of dependency during which they may need support from other fam-ily members. Extended life expectancy is a wonderful gift when the added years are healthy and happy, but it can be a burden for older people with chronic, debilitating illness. Whether an older person is healthy or not, the family plays a critical role for a much longer period of time than was true in the past.

Increasing life expectancy is not the only change affecting the population of the United States. Family size is another demo-graphic trend that continues to influence family structure. Although parents during the late 1940s through the mid-1960s had large families, their children (known as the baby boomers) are having, on average, substantially smaller families. This trend cuts across all social, economic, and race categories in this country. Gerontologist Vern Bengtson calls this consequence of declining birth rate the "verticalization" of the family. Instead of families with successively more members in younger generations, vertical-ization results in more living generations per family but fewer members within each of those generations.

Verticalization has an impact on the family life of older people in several ways. First, verticalization affects patterns of family interaction. Instead of interacting within generations (with siblings or cousins), family members typically interact between generations. Because fewer members exist in any single generation, family members must look up and down the family tree rather than just within generations to find people with whom they can share family bonds and establish important family relationships. Midlife adults will have fewer brothers and sisters, nieces and nephews, cousins, uncles, and aunts as the vertical families increase in number. This pattern may affect family members negatively as they search for potential family ties. For example, young children in smaller families may have few or no siblings; they may have no cousins either. These children might then rely only on grandparents and great-grandparents for family relationships.

Second, verticalization can affect patterns of support within the multigenerational family. The smaller number of members in any one generation may mean that dependent family members, especially midlife adults, cannot simply look to the next generation for support. For example, an older widowed man with serious chronic illness who has only one son and no daughters might have to ask his granddaughters or great-granddaughters to cook his meals or help him with personal care. Of course, these family members will be available only if his son has had children. Choices for support providers within the family are diminishing as generations become smaller.

The increasing numbers of older people in the population combined with earlier marital and childbearing patterns of many people age sixty-five and older have resulted in families that span three, four, and even five generations frequently living in separate households.

Finally, verticalization has affected the length of time women spend in different family roles across their lives. Men and women have different life expectancies, with women expecting at birth to live on average 7.6 years longer than men. Women continue to have an advantage in life expectancy at age sixty-five when they can expect to live 4.5 years longer than men. These differences, combined with the fact that men in older cohorts tended to marry younger women, result in the feminization of the oldest age groups. It is quite possible in a five-generation family to have the two or three oldest generations comprised entirely of widowed females. Advanced age and widowhood can result in inevitable dependency for these women, with aging daughters caring for even older mothers. The younger generations in families like this are often too small to meet the dependency needs of older family members. If current trends of extending life expectancy continue, the multigenerational family headed by a generation or generations of females may become even more prevalent.

Declining Birth Rate and Delayed Childbearing

Patterns of family establishment also have been altered because of the declining birth rate in this country. Delayed childbearing is one way in which individual families are affected by these demographic changes. Instead of marrying and having children in their early twenties, many young adults currently wait until their late thirties or early forties to start a family. This delay gives young adults opportunities to establish themselves in their careers and their marriages. But later parenthood means later grandparenthood as well, and older people find themselves waiting much longer before making the transition to grandparenting.

When delayed childbearing occurs in multiple generations in the same family, the result, according to researchers, is called an age-gapped family. First, age differences between family generations increase. Instead of twenty or twenty-five years between parent and child, the age-gapped family can have up to forty or forty-five years between generations. Eventually, this pattern will limit the number of generations living concurrently. But, more importantly, the age-gapped family has a potentially negative impact for older family members who need family support. In the age-gapped family, the pool of support providers for midlife adults is quite small at any given time. Some midlife adults who find themselves in an age-gapped family may have to explore community services or institutional care because of a shortage of family caregivers.

On the other hand, some families experience timing and sequencing between generations differently. According to Linda Burton, a researcher at Pennsylvania State University, sequential teenage pregnancy in multiple generations in a family causes an

Marital satisfaction in post-parental years is often higher than at any other time in the life course.

age-condensed family. Unlike the age-gapped family in which generations are spaced many years apart, the age-condensed family can have as little as fifteen years between generations, with a consequent blurring of generational lines or boundaries within a family. For example, a thirty-year-old mother and her fifteen-year-old pregnant daughter may relate to each other as members of the same generation (as two mothers) rather than in an intergenerational relationship. The age-condensed family bestows the role of grandmother on very young people. With fifteen-year intervals between generations, a woman could become a grandmother at age forty-five. The probability of four- and five-generation families is extremely high under these conditions.

Diversity of Family Forms

Several other social trends also have affected the family lives of midlife adults. The increase in women in the labor force has had a striking effect on traditional marriages and family forms, resulting in such phenomena as latch-key children. Often, grandparents find themselves with the responsibility for raising or providing day care for their grandchildren. Further, divorce is at an all-time high in this country, with about 50 percent of all marriages ending in divorce. Midlife adults usually find divorce of their adult children difficult, in part because the divorce may affect relationships with grandchildren. This is especially problematic for parents of the noncustodial spouse.

Divorce and remarriage can result in a blended or reconstituted family—that is, a marriage between two previously married spouses with children from the previous marriages. This combining of families is another way in which traditional family forms have been modified. It is difficult to maintain relationships with grandchildren and great-grandchildren when families remain intact for only short periods of time. Keeping family members emotionally invested in each other when they are no longer bound by legal ties is difficult. Further, integrating stepchildren and step-grandchildren into a family can be complex and can result in anger and rivalry. Family decisions, including divorce and remarriage, have consequences for all generations.

Reconstituted families have become more common as divorces and remarriages increase. Other family forms include increased cohabitation by unmarried couples as well as gay and lesbian relationships. Nontraditional families introduce many levels of complexity into multigenerational relationships within the family. Yet the impact of these changes is not well understood or well documented. Further research will be needed to measure the ways in which these changes affect family feelings of obligation, commitment, caring, and the ways in which midlife adults react to these changes. Most social scientists agree that this diversity is unlikely to be replaced by more homogeneous marriage and family patterns.

Marriage, Social Support, and Adult Children in Later Life

Many of the changes that occur during late life alter the ways in which older people interact with family and friends. Some of these changes are positive; retirement, for example, allows older people to pursue interests other than their careers. Having grandchildren is another positive change for midlife adults. However, some of the changes associated with late life may have a negative impact on social interactions. For example, widowhood and chronic health problems may limit opportunities for social exchanges and interpersonal involvement. One irony associated with late life is that even as negative changes occur that may limit sources of assistance, midlife adults may be in greater need of social support than ever before. Given that various personal circumstances may increase older people's need for assistance, older people often find themselves in an incongruous situation: opportunities for social support diminish while needs for support grow.

Regardless of its type or generational structure, the family is—and always has been—extremely important to midlife adults. In the eighteenth and nineteenth centuries, family ties were often economic in nature; for example, children in rural areas were expected to provide labor on farms. Today's families are bonded together more by emotional than by financial ties. Further, the intensity of bonds between multiple generations appears to have increased in the last fifty years. Although families are often far from agreement on politics, religion, and gender roles, many family ties are considered inviolate by multiple generations.

Informal Social Support

Informal social support includes assistance provided by family, friends, and neighbors for which midlife adults do not pay. Unlike formal services, such as those offered by health care providers or transportation and housekeeping services, informal social support focuses first on emotional reassurance and second on the provision of specific kinds of support.

Despite geographic mobility that may result in adult children moving some distance from their parents' home, most older people have multiple family members or close friends for whom they can provide support and from whom they can expect support in times of difficulty. For the most part, this network is one of reciprocity, with midlife adults exchanging support with network members. Although support given and received are not necessarily balanced, older people often feel they need to be able to provide whatever they can to others in their network for their own sense of reciprocity and self-worth. For example, if an older widow's grandson mows her lawn, she may bake him a pie in return. The efforts of mowing a lawn and baking a pie are quite different, yet they become a social exchange. Informal support can help midlife adults with tasks from the simplest to the most complex. Knowing that this support network exists provides peace of mind for many midlife adults.

As money for federal programs grows tighter and formal services are cut back, informal support plays an even more critical role in the lives of midlife adults. Neighbors, relatives, friends, and acquaintances can help midlife adults manage some of the negative consequences of chronic illness and loss. We know that those older people who have no informal social networks can experience problems with chronic illness, stressful life events, and bereavement or widowhood. Further, those older people without informal networks rely much more on formal services for assistance; these individuals are at higher risk of institutionalization as well.

The Role of Spouse in Late Life

Of all family relationships of midlife adults, marriage is the most important in terms of physical health, mental health, and overall well-being. Marriage provides crucial support for most older people; a spouse is a ready-made confidant and companion. Once responsibilities of parenting and employment decline, older people often turn to their lifelong companions for social interaction and intimacy. Not surprisingly, marital satisfaction in the postparental years is often higher than at any other time in the life course. According to the research team of Vern Bengtson, Carolyn Rosenthal, and Linda Burton, most midlife adults rate their marriages as either happy or very happy. A much larger proportion of older men are married than older women, partially reflecting differences in marital satisfaction. Men tend to report higher marital satisfaction than women; they also report having their emotional needs more fulfilled within the marriage than women do. On the other hand researcher Carole Holahan, in her longitudinal study of marital attitudes over forty years, found that older women often report a decrease in marital satisfaction. However, satisfaction of older women still tends to be higher than that of younger, more recently married women.

Holahan also suggests that there have been multiple changes in attitudes of midlife adults toward marriage during the last forty to fifty years. For example, contemporary men appear to be far more involved in family life and child care than married men were in the past. Further, men appear to recognize more equality in marriage than they did in the past. Yet Holahan still found some enduring sex differences about marital attitudes in her study. For example, women favored a wife's being fully informed about family finances, while men were less certain that this was important. Holahan notes that both aging and historical change contribute to these attitudinal changes.

Increased marital satisfaction in later life may result in part from children leaving home; the empty nest gives parents freedom and opportunity that are not available during childrearing.

Many investigators have found that a gender crossover occurs in late life in which men become more affectionate and less achievement oriented while women turn their interests and efforts outside the home. This crossover may bring spouses closer together in old age and appears to strengthen most late-life marriages. In one longitudinal study, social psychologist Erik Erikson and his colleagues found that most older spouses described their marriages as compassionate, companionate, affectionate, and supportive; they also saw these relationships as lifelong commitments.

Research has found that marriage is not only perceived as positive and satisfying but actually appears to improve quality of life as well. When married midlife adults are compared with their unmarried peers, married people seem happier, healthier, and longer lived. There is substantial evidence to show that married midlife adults report greater life satisfaction, morale, and social integration. Married people are also less vulnerable to health problems than are unmarried people, with widowed and divorced people less protected than the never married.

Marital satisfaction is the most important factor predicting life satisfaction for older women—more important than health, age, education, or retirement; for men, marital satisfaction is second only to good health in predicting overall life satisfaction.

Hume Cronyn

Actor

SNAPSHOT

"**T**here is a quotation I'm very fond of by I. J. Singer. He was changing careers, giving up journalism and becoming a professor of classical languages. He learned to speak both Latin and Greek. And somebody said, 'Mr. Singer, what do you have to look forward to?' And he said, 'I hope to die young, as late as possible.' Isn't that marvelous?"

For over sixty years, Hume Cronyn has successfully conducted simultaneous careers on stage, screen, and television. He has contributed his talents not only as an actor but also as a producer, director, playwright, screenwriter, and lecturer.

Cronyn was born in 1911 in London, Ontario, Canada in what he calls an "Edwardian" family. Though he never planned on becoming a professional actor when he was growing up, he spent his childhood days in "some sort of mad fantasy world," where he played the cowboys *and* the Indians.

He graduated from Ridley College in 1930 and entered pre-law studies at McGill University. "I went through my first two years and found I was doing absolutely nothing about law, but I was in every amateur theatrical project that was offered to the community." With his family's support, he left his legal studies and went to New York City. The first casting director he met told him frankly that "you don't look like anything"—he couldn't easily be typecast. This quality turned out to be an enormous advantage for Cronyn, allowing him to play a broad spectrum of roles.

In New York, Cronyn enrolled at the American Academy of Dramatic Arts, graduating in 1934. He made his professional stage debut in *Up Pops the Devil* at the National Theatre in Washington, D.C., in 1931. His Broadway debut soon followed in 1934 in *Hipper's Holiday*. Since then Cronyn has appeared in more than eighty plays. He made his stage directorial debut in Los Angeles with *Portrait of a Madonna*, followed by his Broadway directorial debut in 1950 with *Now I Lay Me Down to Sleep*. He has since directed many successful stage productions.

In 1942 he married Jessica Tandy. Tandy and Cronyn enjoyed performing together throughout their careers and became one of America's favorite entertainment duos. They worked together in hit plays, including *Foxfire* and *The Gin Game* (which he also coproduced with Mike Nichols), and on screen in the landmark film about aging, *Cocoon*. The couple even had their own television series in 1953 called "The Marriage."

Cronyn made his screen debut in Alfred Hitchcock's *Shadow of a Doubt* and has appeared in thirty-two major motion pictures. He made his television debut in 1939 in "Her Master's Voice" and has always remained involved with high-quality television productions as an actor, producer, and director. He co-authored (with Susan Cooper) *The Dollmaker* and *Foxfire*, both award-winning teleplays.

Cronyn has received numerous honors from the theatrical community. He has been nominated for a Tony Award four times, winning in 1964 for his performance as Polonius in *Hamlet*. He was also nominated for an Academy Award for his performance in *The Seventh Cross*. He won an Emmy for the television special "Age-Old Friends" (1989) and an Obie for *Krapp's Last Tape* (1973). In 1986 he and Tandy were honored together by the Kennedy Center for the Performing Arts for their lifetime achievement.

Cronyn describes the actor's life: "To go on being an actor, you need sheer animal energy. If you can't restock your energy, you have to hide your lack of it." As he continues to be involved in several projects at once, Cronyn exhibits no lack of energy, finding sufficient fuel in his work.

—*Lydia Brontë*

According to Robert Atchley, professor and director of the Scripps Gerontology Center at Miami University of Ohio, marriage encourages three major functions for midlife adults: intimacy, interdependence, and a sense of belonging. These functions enhance the possibility of positive health and well-being among married older people.

Married midlife adults have other advantages over the unmarried as well. The social support and social integration of married midlife adults is reportedly higher than those of unmarried people. Marriage leads to increased social status and economic security, especially for women of current older cohorts who may not have qualified for pensions in their own rights. As compared to married couples, widows and widowers both experience a decline in financial well-being. Little is known about the economic impact of spousal death on widows and widowers in rural areas or on minority widows and widowers.

Spouses and Social Support

Although marriage seems to protect midlife adults from some negative consequences of aging, that protection cannot continue indefinitely. Sadly, one spouse usually begins to experience physical, cognitive, or emotional declines as he or she ages. Unlike unmarried people who rarely have an identified support provider, married midlife adults can turn to spouses as a first line of defense against the dependence created by physical or mental illness. Provision of support can continue for long periods of time, even though the supportive spouse may also experience problems. Yet older spouses who are providing support must continue to contend with their own problems of illness, financial limitations, or legal burdens. Thus, although spouses are always there to provide support, the role is not without its own expensive costs.

Not only does the spouse as an individual provide support, but being married also appears to have an impact on the number of people available to give assistance. Women tend to have larger social networks than men; further, married people have larger networks than do nonmarrieds. Thus, being married not only insures the provision of support from the spouse but also from larger support networks and more possible sources of support outside the nuclear family.

The impact of differential life expectancies is seen once again as many more older wives provide support to their disabled or ill husbands than husbands providing support for dependent wives. These women are the hidden victims of family illness, for they often experience the loneliness, isolation, and overload of providing support. Stressful for all older spouses, supporting an ill or demented spouse may be especially difficult for those midlife adults who are recently married. Spouses in those circumstances do not have a lifetime of shared experience upon which they can call. But regardless of length of marriage, providing support for a physically or mentally ill older adult can take a tremendous toll on older spouses.

Adult Children and Their Relationships with Aging Parents

One persistent social myth suggests that older people spend most of their time alone and lonely. Yet research shows that this is not true, that midlife adults—even those without spouses—find that their adult children are important sources of contact and support. Although the popular press delights in reporting that bonds between generations have gotten weaker in the 1980s and 1990s, on the whole the relationships between midlife adults and their adult children are extremely positive. According to recent studies, about four out of five midlife adults have living children, but having children does not necessarily increase happiness in old age. It does increase the likelihood of older people having support providers.

Although midlife adults have frequent contact with many of their adult children, most older people choose to live independently. The American ethic cherishes autonomy and self-care, and many older adults feel that living with children might compromise their own and their children's privacy. According to the U.S. Senate Special Commission on Aging, less than 20 percent of older adults reside in their children's households; however, as parents grow older and become widowed, separated, or divorced, shared living arrangements become more common. Further, adult children who themselves become separated or divorced are more and more likely to return to their parental home for support and assistance. This may be especially true for single parents with children who find live-in baby-sitters and housekeepers beneficial. Older parents like living near their adult children, but just as they do not want to move into their children's households, older parents prefer not having adult children return to their homes.

According to one classic study by sociologist Ethel Shanas at the University of Illinois, approximately 80 percent of all older people with children live less than an hour from at least one child; 50 percent have at least one child living within ten minutes of their home; and 84 percent see an adult child at least once a week.

Are there race differences in the frequency with which midlife adults see, talk to, or write their adult children? Sociologists Jim Mitchell and Jasper Register hypothesized that older African Americans would see and receive help from their children and grandchildren more frequently than whites. Although their study showed that older African Americans were more likely to receive assistance from children and grandchildren, older whites were more likely to see their children and grandchildren. This finding contradicts findings of some earlier studies and indicates that additional research in this area is needed.

Most research on contact between midlife adults and their adult children has focused on relationships in which midlife adults are geographically proximate to their children. Relations with children living at a distance have been ignored, despite the fact that one study showed that over 50 percent of older people had at least one adult child living more than five hundred miles away. Emotional support might be one area in which distant children could provide help, yet no one has yet examined how that kind of assistance affects the lives of older people. Relationships between midlife adults and both nearby and distant adult children are important and need additional investigation as employment opportunities drive families geographically further apart.

Although geographic distance affects the frequency with which older people and adult children have contact with each other, it does not affect the quality of relationships between parents and their adult children. Even when they live far apart, most adult children report feeling close to their older parents. As noted, long distances between family members usually result from children's mobility in searching for employment opportunities. Differences in socioeconomic status appear far more powerful in creating barriers to close parent-child relationships than does geographic distance. Lower- and working-class families tend to remain geographically and emotionally close, while middle- and upper-class families may experience greater geographic and emotional distance. Parents and adult children with different socioeconomic statuses tend to drift apart; many feel that they have nothing in common. Given that the parent-child relationship is one of inherent inequality (one in which one member has a clear advantage in power over the other), some researchers suggest that contact within that relationship is driven by obligation rather than by volition.

Even if they do not share a home, midlife adults and their adult children engage in frequent and positive contact. Older people and their children experience close relationships, even at a distance.

Yet the fact that a number of studies that have found consistently that adult children feel close toward their parents makes the obligational expectation difficult to believe.

Social Support from Adult Children

After spouses, adult children are the single most important source of social support for older people. Even though most adult children work, care for their own families, and try to save for their own old age, they willingly provide support for their parents. As adult children improve their own financial positions, they may have access to more resources than their parents do; often later in life, support from child to parent becomes a normative and expected exchange.

According to recent studies, adult children provide three distinct types of support to their parents. First, they provide emotional support that includes listening to problems, providing advice, and giving comfort. Second, they provide instrumental or tangible support that includes goods and services, especially around the home. Additional instrumental support might be given in the form of transportation, home repairs, housework, or assistance with personal care. Third, adult children provide financial support, although many older people continue to give financial assistance to their children and grandchildren despite their own needs. Social class strongly affects patterns of intergenerational support, with lower- and working-class families giving more instrumental support, and middle- and upper-class families giving emotional and financial support. Women from blue-collar families become care providers themselves; women from white-collar families become care managers, identifying needed services and locating quality providers. Adult children with higher incomes have more options about how to provide support.

One consistent research finding relates to gender differences in support from adult children. Without question, women provide substantially more support to their parents than do men; daughters are the primary support providers in almost every situation, and when daughters are unavailable, daughters-in-law or granddaughters frequently take over support responsibilities. Researcher Elaine Brody found in her Philadelphia sample that about 80 percent of support providers to chronically ill midlife adults are women. Of that 80 percent, daughters represent approximately 30 percent of primary and secondary caregiving. When sons provide support, they tend to give money and supervision; daughters provide personal care and emotional support. Studies have consistently shown that men rarely provide the personal, day-to-day care given by wives and daughters.

Little is known about racial and ethnic differences in the provision of support to aging parents. Being both old and a member of a minority group creates a double disadvantage, according to some researchers. The family plays an important role in African-American and Hispanic culture, but how that role translates into actual support is not clear. Researchers suggest that older members of ethnic or racial minority families enjoy close relationships with younger family members and that support is mutual.

It appears, however, that African-American families and their elderly members are diverse. Many older African-American adults utilize their extended families as critical sources of support. Elizabeth Mutran suggests that both socioeconomic status and race have an influence on family support, but the way in which support is given and received in minority families has not been well documented. There is the need to learn a great deal more about the effects of minority status on the provision of social support.

Most families, regardless of minority status or socioeconomic class, make efforts to care for an aging parent in preference to institutionalizing that parent. Typically, adult children begin to consider placing a parent in a nursing home when the needs of that parent exceed the support capabilities of the children. Most adult children view nursing homes as negative environments. Therefore, the placement of a parent in a long-term care facility can be stressful for parent and child. Although institutionalization may provide relief from providing support on a daily basis, it does not necessarily relieve the stress that may be experienced by adult children. Many decisions to institutionalize are precipitated by a life event or crisis of the family member providing support (through widowhood or serious illness). Therefore, these decisions are often made under pressure, and careful selection of facilities may not be possible.

On average, men take part in personal care or instrumental tasks only when no female relative (such as a wife, daughter, daughter-in-law, sister, granddaughter) is available. Interestingly, sons appear to feel less stress when they provide support to parents than daughters do, even when they provide the same kinds of assistance.

Social Support from Friends and Neighbors

A great percentage of midlife adults have friends available to help them in times of need. For older people whose relatives live at a distance, friends and neighbors are the front line of support provision. When families are far away, friends and neighbors can provide assistance quickly in an emergency. Friends can also help older people in routine ways. For example, if an older individual needs help getting on the bus to go shopping, a friend who is going as well may be able to provide assistance.

Several studies have found that relationships with friends are more likely to lead to increased life satisfaction than are relations with adult children. Because people usually have more in

Formal Support Services

Most older people will experience times in their lives when use of formal support services becomes almost mandatory. Although assistance to older adults can be provided by families, friends, and neighbors, a continuum of long-term care services must include relevant formal services to impaired older adults. In these instances, family members may have to act as ombudsmen and assist older adults in contacting providers of formal care or arranging for necessary services. Bureaucracies of federal, state, and local governments may be too complex for midlife adults to negotiate alone. Thus, some combination of informal support and formal services may best meet older people's support needs.

Access services allow midlife and older adults to contact providers of necessary services. Access services include information and referral services as well as case managers who provide overall supervision and organization of the entire service community. Additional access services include transportation to help midlife and older adults travel to services.

For older people with serious physical problems, the *health care system* is one essential source of formal support. In addition to support received from physicians, many other health care professionals can contribute to the quality of life of older adults. Visiting nurses and home health aides may provide enough assistance to allow a partially disabled or dysfunctional older adult to remain in the community instead of being institutionalized. Physical and occupational therapists offer services which may be necessary for rehabilitation after serious acute problems or in ongoing management of chronic diseases. For those older adults who have had strokes or other health problems that disrupt their abilities to carry out activities of daily living, rehabilitation can assist them in returning to as near-normal a life as possible.

Nutrition services can be provided in multiple ways to the elderly. Meals on Wheels and other food delivery systems bring hot meals to those older adults who cannot cook for themselves. Hot lunch programs at senior centers or congregate meal sites also insure that those more mobile adults who utilize these services get balanced meals. Many older adults rely on these services to provide their basic nutrition.

Relaxation, leisure, and social and recreational services are necessary components of an older adult's life. Currently, senior centers provide probably the most consistent recreational and educational programming for older people. Programs such as adult day care and respite services for the cognitively impaired provide activities for midlife adults who cannot remain under twenty-four-hour supervision by family members. These programs allow many older people to remain in the community who would otherwise be consigned to nursing homes or assisted living programs.

Personal support services such as companions, choreworkers, and telephone reassurance programs help midlife and older adults who can remain independent but who may need assistance in an emergency. These services enable the elderly who otherwise might need institutional placement to remain in the community. Older people who have short-term illnesses, who are recovering from surgery, or who may be exceptionally frail can benefit tremendously from these services.

Finally, formal support can be provided in an institution such as a nursing home. At any given time, approximately 5 percent of all older adults live in institutions; this small percentage results from families providing support to their older members whenever possible. However, twenty-five percent of all older adults will at some time utilize institutional care. Nursing homes are the most typical providers of this formal service and may be an appropriate choice for those midlife adults who can no longer function independently.

The majority of nursing home residents are functionally impaired in some way, through physical illness, cognitive decline, or a combination of multiple problems. However, for every impaired older adult living in a long-term care facility, there are as few as two and as many as five equally impaired older adults living in the community. Strong social support systems are the most important factor in determining who can survive in the community and who must rely totally on formal services.

In the past, formal support services were primarily limited to nursing homes, and few community support services were available to older adults. Today, a broad range of community support services provide assistance to older individuals. These services have helped older adults to retain their independence in the community as long as possible. Further, community support services provide assistance not only for the older adult but for family members as well. Respite care can provide important relief to informal support providers, allowing them to continue to care for their older family members.

common with friends than with family members, friendship interactions may help midlife adults feel increased self-esteem. Further, because friendship is volitional instead of obligatory and because friends are often more able to bring older people into contact with the larger society than are adult children, friends play extremely important roles in the lives of midlife adults.

Also, friends often provide more intimacy than do family members other than spouses. Widows in particular find contact with friends extremely important after their transition to widowhood. Friendship provides continuing alternatives to other traditional roles (such as spouse or parent), and midlife adults can function effectively as friends long after roles such as worker, spouse, and childrearer are gone. In discussing the importance of friends, most midlife adults say that the quality of friendship is extremely important. For those older people who have only limited contacts with society at large, friends provide companionship and links to the outside community. Friends may be particularly hard to replace in late life because situations in which friendships frequently originate and blossom (such as at work, at voluntary organization meetings, in school) often are not part of the lives of most older adults.

Grandparents and Grandchildren

Most midlife adults view becoming a grandparent as one of the most positive changes in late life. Adults often become grandparents for the first time while they are in their middle to late forties and fifties. At that time they are still occupationally and socially engaged and often are enjoying the freedoms of having had their own children leave home and establish themselves as independent adults. The appearance of grandchildren often gives an older adult tremendous pleasure. The birth of that next generation assures that the family name will continue beyond the older adult's lifetime.

Increasing life expectancy frequently means that grandparents are not necessarily the generation closest to death in a family. In an ever-growing number of families, at least one older generation remains alive. Great-grandparenthood, once an extremely rare phenomenon, is occurring more frequently as people live longer. Of older adults who have children, 94 percent are grand-parents and 46 percent are great-grandparents. Nearly three-quarters of all grandparents see at least one grandchild on a weekly or biweekly basis. This pattern of contact is quite different from the one experienced by older adults and their grandparents. Many of today's children have four living grandparents and may have multiple great-grandparents still alive. In contrast, many midlife adults never met their own grandparents. As life expectancy continues to increase, more and more midlife adults will become both grandparents and great-grandparents.

Research in grandparent-grandchild relations has been inconsistent. Several different investigators have examined the perspective of grandparents, and some investigators have studied relations between children and their grandparents. But the role of grandparents in their grandchildren's lives is still not clear, especially when the grandchildren are adults. Although it might be assumed that grandparents who live with their grandchildren exert more influence on them, there is little empirical evidence to support this belief.

The classic study on grandparenthood was done by gerontologists Bernice Neugarten and Karol Weinstein at the University of Chicago. In it, the authors identified five different styles of grandparenting: the formal, the fun-seeking, the distant, the surrogate parent, and the reservoir of family wisdom. The names of these types characterize the kinds of relationships between grandparents and their grandchildren. Older grandparents tended to fall into the formal or distant styles, never establishing a close, interactive relationship with their grandchildren. Younger grandparents emphasized the closeness of their relationships, often looking to grandchildren as sources of interest and pleasure. The grandparent who became a surrogate parent had more of a parent-child relationship with grandchildren than a grandparental one. And the reservoir of family wisdom was seen as a person who could provide family history and personal knowledge for grandchildren.

Another study by sociologist Helen Kivnick suggests that grandchildren provide immortality to grandparents and that older adults live vicariously through this generation. It is credible that grandparents might see their grandchildren as the bearers of the

Magna S.

At age sixty-six, Magna S. received her master's in social work from Fordham University with a goal to ease life transitions for women in midlife and later year crises.

"I see a tremendous hope for older women, and I hope to convey that to my patients, to my surroundings, and to myself. I wanted to be in the social work field because I have lent broad shoulders for many, many years to many people in my long years of volunteer work with midlife and older adults. I've seen many places where they are getting excellent physical care; however, there is absolutely no support system, nothing to make their lives even tolerable emotionally. That disturbed me. When I decided to go into this field, I decided to work with the elderly and try to give them as much as I can.

"My focus is on working with women facing turning points in their lives. So much more is expected of women today. In reaction to this societal expectation, many women from the older generation suffer low self-esteem, because they see their lives as unproductive. They don't need to go out and develop a career, or get a job, or do something very meaningful in society. They have to do something meaningful for *themselves*. We all need to find our own path.

"I am aware of my mortality and am anxious to have a productive career as long as possible. In the back of my mind is the fear of how long I am going to be able to do it. Until I am unable, I would like to do what I feel will bring me pleasure. You can't just vegetate; you've go to do something. I love helping those I come in contact with. There is life after fifty, sixty, seventy, or even eighty!"

—*From Connie Goldman's "Late Bloomer" public radio series*

family name and family reputation. Although evidence of vicarious living through grandchildren is limited, only rarely has research indicated that the role of grandparent is not central to older people's lives and that the status of being a grandparent does not contribute to life satisfaction. For the most part, grandparenting is an important activity for older adults, one that provides ongoing pleasure. Instead of being a parent and having total responsibility for young children, older people can anticipate their interactions with their grandchildren, concentrating on sharing enjoyment rather than imposing discipline. Relationships between grandparents and grandchildren appear to be influenced by gender. Grandfathers are more closely linked to sons of sons while grandmothers develop a greater closeness with daughters of daughter. If grandchildren are carriers of family tradition and symbols of immortality and family unity, it is understandable for grandfathers to feel emotionally closer to male grandchildren and grandmothers to female grandchildren. Grandparents also can act as role models for their grandchildren, and the gender links here make sense as well.

One important correlate of the grandparent-grandchild relationship has not been examined closely: the importance of the middle generation, the children of grandparents and the parents of grandchildren. It is not yet known whether grandmothers with close relationships with daughters also have close relationships with their granddaughters. It is also unclear whether grandfathers who rarely interact with their sons also remain aloof from their grandsons. Additional studies will be necessary before these questions can be answered with any confidence.

Studies on grandparenting reveal that grandmothers have more influence over their grandchildren than do grandfathers. In part, this may result from the parenting experiences of today's midlife adults. In other words, fathers who took no active part in parenting may also distance themselves from their grandchildren. For whatever reasons, it appears that current grandparents have differential influence on their grandchildren by gender. The longer life expectancy of grandmothers may contribute to this phenomenon as well. The changing patterns of parenting for today's fathers may alter their experiences as grandfathers as well.

The rise of multigenerational families has extended the time people spend as grandparents.

COPYRIGHT MARIANNE GONTARZ

On the subject of the relationships between adult grandchildren and their grandparents, a recent study by L. G. Hodgson of a national sample of adult children age eighteen and older explored the relationships of these young adults with their grandparents. Hodgson found that the strength of grandparent-adult grandchild relations depended in part on the ages of grandchild and grandparent, their geographical proximity, the parent-child relationship, and the parent-grandparent relationship. But much is still poorly understood about grandparenting in general and grandparents and adult grandchildren in particular.

Finally, grandparenting can be disrupted by marital discord of young-adult or middle-aged sons and daughters. Divorce can upset the lives of young children and render their relationships with their grandparents ambiguous. Colleen Johnson in California interviewed midlife adults and their adult children on the topic of divorce. She found that grandmothers were often integral parts of their children's and grandchildren's lives, even after divorce. This was especially true when the middle generation—the adult children—were committed to facilitating grandparent-grandchild relations. Grandparents who respond to the divorce situation with compassion and assistance helped sustain family relationships on all levels. Without question, grandparents who were judgmental about their children's divorce were included less often in family activities and decisions.

The status of grandparents after a divorce is unclear as well. In many instances, relations between grandparents and grandchildren are stronger after a divorce. This is especially true when grandparents help the custodial parent with emotional or instrumental support. However, parents of the noncustodial child may be denied access to their grandchildren. The custodial parent can remove the grandchild geographically from grandparents or simply refuse to allow grandparents to visit. The legal status of grandparents in this situation is still unclear. In a few states, grandparents can have legal visitation rights with grandchildren; in most states, however, parents control visitation. These barriers to grandparent-grandchild relations may have a long-term impact on the grandchild, and grandchildren raised in these circumstances may find it difficult to establish relationships with their own grandchildren many years later.

Reconstituted families after divorce can also create problems for grandparents. This phenomenon occurs when two adults who have both been married before and have children from previous marriages decide to form a new family. In this instance, young children have "old" and "new" grandparents, the old from the first marriage and the new from the second. Grandparent relations with old and new grandchildren in this situation are unclear, and further research is vital to understanding the changes that occur when families are blended and reconstituted. However, the potential for conflict in this situation is high, especially for the noncustodial parent's parents.

Of all family interactions of midlife adults, those with siblings can be both the most rewarding and the most annoying simultaneously. Siblings share the most durable of family bonds,

Sibling Relationships

Bernice Neugarten

Gerontologist

SNAPSHOT

Development is like a fan. It opens as we age. People become more different from each other the older they become. If we want to look for similarities, we do best to look at people toward the beginning of the life span. There they are likely to be more alike."

Bernice Neugarten, one of the nation's leading authorities on aging, was born in rural Nebraska in 1916. She had what she terms "an odd childhood," where her above-average intelligence saw her skip grade after grade. While this proved helpful academically, Neugarten found it an isolating experience. "I was a child and everybody else was an adolescent," she explains.

Upon graduating from high school she swiftly moved to Chicago, where she attended the University of Chicago, gaining a B.A. in English literature in 1936. Not sure what to do after graduation, she became interested in the field of educational psychology and gained her master's in education the following year. She then entered a newly formed program called the Committee on Human Development to work toward her Ph.D. When she gained her degree in 1943 she was the first person to do so under the Committee.

Neugarten married in 1940 and decided to take time off to raise a family. She returned to the University of Chicago a decade later to work part-time as a counselor. "I wanted something to do out of the house," she explains. "I had no motivation about building a fancy career. I needed something that was interesting intellectually and I wanted it on my terms."

In 1952 Neugarten was asked to teach the course "Maturity and Old Age." "I was invited to join the research team that was beginning a study of middle-aged and aging persons in the metropolitan area of Kansas City," she recalls. "Had it been a course in child development that needed an instructor, I might well have wound up today as a child psychologist."

Neugarten's pioneering work in the then fledgling field of human development saw the committee "boom in size" over the following years. By 1960 she was named associate professor and in 1964 she became a professor. From 1969 to 1973, she served as chairperson of human development, and from 1969 to 1970 she chaired the first Committee on University Women.

During these years she also became a prolific researcher. She sought to challenge psychologists of the time who believed that personality ended when a person completed adolescence. She also challenged other traditional ideas such as the notion that nearly all people experience a midlife crisis or regularly timed transitions. Her major publications began with a monograph that she co-authored in 1957 and later turned into a book cowritten with colleagues. That work, *Personality in Middle and Late Life* (1964), became a classic in the field of aging. In it she discusses her findings that personality continues to develop and change throughout the life span.

She then went on to work in the study of grandparenting and retirement, co-authoring *Adjustment to Retirement* (1969) and *Social Status in the City* (1971) and editing *Age or Need? Public Policies for Older People* (1982).

Neugarten contends that because of the wide variety of differences in the way people grow old, age is a poor predictor of an adult's needs and physical, social, or intellectual competence. For this reason, public policy should be based on people's needs and not their ages, she says.

She also identified distinctions within the elderly population, defining "young-old" as people who, though technically senior citizens, retain an active, involved lifestyle, and "old-old" as those who behave as if they are elderly.

In 1981 Neugarten was named deputy chairperson of the White House Conference on Aging, a position she says accelerated her interest in the relationship between scholarship and public policy. That interest also led her in 1980 to accept an appointment at Northwestern University, as a professor in the School of Education and Social Policy.

Throughout her long career Neugarten gained many honorary degrees from universities around the world. In 1992 she was one of one hundred women featured in the Women's Heritage Exhibit at the American Psychological Association's centennial conference in Washington, D.C.

While she planned to retire in her mid-sixties, Neugarten found herself "talked into" joining the Center on Aging, Health and Society at the University of Chicago. She continues to work there as a Rothschild Distinguished Scholar.

—*Lydia Brontë*

potentially lasting from shared childhood experiences through the death of one sibling. Sisters and brothers often share more with each other than with anyone else, including family heritage, cultural background, and lifelong experiences. Ambivalence about siblings often may be generated in childhood and sustained throughout adulthood. Siblings may be viewed as concurrent allies and competitors throughout the life course. Despite feelings of sibling rivalry, childhood typically signals closeness and sharing with siblings. Midlife adults reminiscing about their sibling relationships classify childhood as a time of close and positive relations. Because only 10 percent of midlife adults are only children, the vast majority of older people have experienced the social role of sibling.

Adolescence is a time during which most sibling relationships become less involved. Traditional developmental theory states that adolescence is focused on independence and autonomy, and the need to find an individual identity affects sibling relationships strongly. Many siblings have little or no contact during these years and may continue to diverge in young adulthood, a time traditionally reserved for establishing a career, getting married, and starting a family. These major changes often leave little time for nurturing sibling bonds. The exception to this weakening of sibling bonds occurs between sisters who have children at approximately the same time. These sisters use each other as mentors and sounding boards, asking advice and providing suggestions when crises over children occur.

If young adulthood is the time of establishing family and career, middle age is the time of peak responsibilities in these areas. Career demands may be strongest at this time; family may be equally demanding. In early middle age, siblings often continue the separation of earlier years. If older parents need care, middle-aged siblings may be brought together to solve this problem. However, this area is rife with the potential for serious conflict among siblings if they disagree on major decisions about parent care (such as institutionalization). Concern over aging parents can be either a positive or negative influence on midlife sibling relations.

In late middle age, sibling bonds begin to be reforged. The first parental death can be a strong stimulus for sibling closeness; an even greater closeness may occur when the second parent dies. These incidents may bring siblings together as they realize they now belong to the generation in the family that is closest to death. Other major life transitions such as the empty nest (children leaving home) and retirement often stimulate interest in sibling relationships.

Like childhood, old age is a time of positive sibling relations and strong sibling bonds. Over 80 percent of older adults have positive relations with brothers and sisters, and many have some contact with siblings at least once a week. Throughout life, the sibling relationship is based on equality and reciprocity. Unlike the parent and child relationship in which one person clearly has authority and power, siblings share a balance of power and operate from norms of equity. Further, the sibling relationship is more voluntary than are other family relationships. Nothing forces adults to interact with their sisters and brothers except their own

For childless elderly, nieces or nephews often provide contact with the next generation and may also provide needed instrumental support.

COPYRIGHT MARIANNE GONTARZ

wishes, and it is rare that the ties between siblings are those of obligation. These feelings of choice and free will often result in more positive and supportive interactions.

According to sociologist Deborah T. Gold of Duke University Medical Center, the sibling bond is central to well-being in later life for a large proportion of older adults. Her studies of siblings across the life course suggest that five different types of late-life sibling relationships exist. The first is the intimate relationship, categorized by intense closeness and total sharing. These siblings are best friends and feel that their sibling bond is stronger than that with their spouses or children. Congenial siblings are friends rather than best friends but still share a tremendous amount of time and support with sisters and brothers. Although confidences might first be shared with a spouse, congenial siblings confide both positive and negative feelings to each other. Loyal siblings are always there when needed. They attend family weddings and family funerals with equal regularity and can be counted on to provide emotional and instrumental support in times of difficulty. Although loyal siblings may not see or talk to each other on a regular basis, each sibling knows that the other is there and available when necessary.

Unfortunately, not all sibling relationships in late life are positive and supportive. Apathetic siblings have little or no contact, not even at special occasions. They are not angry with each other; they are simply indifferent. These siblings report that their lives took different directions in adolescence and young adulthood; further, there appears to be no interest in reviving the sibling bond later in life. The most negative relationships of all are the hostile sibling relationships that are filled with hatred and disgust. These siblings feel betrayed or misled by the other and would not, under any circumstances, provide support for each other. It is interesting to realize that hostile and intimate siblings spend about the same amount of time thinking about each other. The difference is that intimate siblings empathize with and support each other while hostile siblings focus on negative aspects of their relationships.

Shared reminiscence is something that late-life siblings engage in frequently. Robert Butler identified the life review as an important part of the aging process. He defines the life review as the process of sorting through the memories of life and putting them together into a coherent whole. For most midlife adults, siblings are the only living people who knew them during childhood and adolescence. Brothers and sisters are valuable links to the past and validate each other's life review by mutual remembering. This assistance is invaluable in completing this major psychological task in late life.

Do different gender pairs of siblings have different kinds of relationships? Study after study has shown that sisters are the closest of all sibling pairs, and that this distinction holds true across the life course. Sisters frequently report deepest intimacy and closeness, sharing all aspects of life. Many brothers of brothers, on the other hand, report feelings of animosity and competition, especially when parental comparisons were made frequently in childhood. Somehow, the fact that parents held one brother up as a model to another is never forgotten, and issues such as family size, income, prestige in employment, and children's education perpetuate rivalry through adulthood.

Brother-sister sibling pairs are more like pairs of sisters than brothers. Researchers suggest that it is the presence of a woman in the sibling pair, rather than having two sisters, that leads to closeness and sharing in sibling relationships. Brothers report that they can confide in sisters more than in brothers; they also report greater interest in hearing the confidences of sisters than of brothers. However, some pairs of brothers capitalize on the increased emotionality of men in late life and are able to establish relationships of intimacy and caring.

Midlife adults who are widowed, divorced, or never married find that siblings are especially important sources of emotional support. For childless elderly, nieces and nephews often provide contact with the next generation and may also provide needed instrumental support. Researchers predict that those born between 1945 and 1960 will find siblings more important in late life than have other older people. As older adults, the baby boomers will have more siblings than children. Therefore, when they need support or care, they may have to find a sibling rather than a child to help.

But what of the children of the baby boomers? Many will be only children and will not learn sharing and cooperation from brothers and sisters; others will have only one sibling. The lack of sibling relationships may encourage this generation to have slightly larger families so that their children can have sisters and brothers.

Extended Kin Relationships

Primary family relationships are of greatest importance in American culture. These relationships include those with parents, children, spouses, and siblings. But most midlife adults also have active relationships that extend beyond the nuclear family. Feelings of family solidarity or family unity can be promoted by keeping a network of extended kin relationships invested in family interactions. Of all family relations, those with extended kin are most dependent on geographic proximity and family tradition for continuing closeness. Parents who interact with their own cousins, aunts, uncles, nieces, and nephews will influence their children to do the same. Midlife adults without spouses or children often turn to extended family members for social contact and support. Extended kin engage in family rituals, reunions, remembering holidays or birthdays, and reminiscing about past family events. Cousins, nephews, and nieces take the place of primary family members in family traditions.

Often, one person in the extended family network is identified as the kinkeeper, who keeps in touch with all family members and organizes family activities. Typically, the kinkeeper is female and responds to suggestions about potential family interactions from different network members. At some point, the older generation will not be able to continue this monumental effort, and kinkeeping responsibilities are passed down to the next generation. In this way, the extended family is kept alive and connected.

Sisters are the closest of all sibling pairs, and this distinction holds true across the life course. Sisters frequently report deepest intimacy and closeness, sharing all aspects of life.

Alternatively, there may be an identified head of the extended family who can be male or female. If the head of the family is male, the task of keeping in touch with family members may be delegated to someone else. Many families adopt a bureaucratic structure, especially as the size of the network increases. As with the kinkeeper, the head of the family will, at some point, need to step down and may identify his or her successor prior to doing so.

Because siblings are approximately the same age and may have many of the same needs, they tend not to exchange tangible support. For example, a sister whose chronic illness prevents her from doing her own housework will not be able to help her brother with his. However, sisters and brothers are important sources of emotional support. Siblings are the only kin who have the potential for lifelong relationships and who fill dual roles of family members and age peers. This combination makes brothers and sisters exceptionally qualified to provide emotional support.

One psychological task of late life is called the life review, a process by which midlife adults examine their past and reconstruct their lives into orderly and complete memories. Siblings are uniquely equipped to assist each other in the life review, pulling together shared memories from childhood onward. This support, and other forms of emotional support as well, can be provided as easily at a distance as it can be in person via telephone calls or letters. Therefore siblings need not be geographically close to help each other.

Never-Married Midlife Adults

About 5 percent of current midlife adults have never been married and therefore will experience aging with a unique set of needs. Future groups of older people will have higher proportions of never-married members. Two different kinds of never-married adults exist: those for whom being single is a choice, and those who wanted to get married but never did. It is as yet unclear whether those types of single midlife adults age differently.

Research indicates that the vast majority of never-married midlife adults are not lonely, although they may feel socially isolated. The emphasis in our culture is on the nuclear family, and key roles associated with that family (such as parent or spouse) are never available to single people. Extended kin relationships can be very important to those who have not married, and family ties with siblings, aunts and uncles, and nieces and nephews tend to be strong.

Those midlife adults who never married are also typically childless. Although this, too, may change as people become more accepting of single parents, the lack of children can be problematic for midlife adults who need care. Social psychologists Linda Beckman and Betsy Houser found that childless midlife adults tended to have fewer social contacts than older people with children; however, this held true for both the married and unmarried childless. In addition, childless midlife adults with health problems are more likely to become socially isolated. These people turn to siblings, nieces, and nephews for support when needed. The childless, never-married older adult is, in some ways, in double jeopardy; he or she has neither a spouse nor children to provide assistance. Other researchers found that childless unmarried older adults were much more likely to use nursing homes and other social services than married childless older adults. And unmarried childless older adults are at higher risk of institutionalization than either married midlife adults or older parents.

However, many never-married older people realize that their independence may create future difficulties and that support is essential. These single older people establish strong social support systems to assume responsibilities for care ordinarily taken by a spouse or adult child. In these networks, extended kin can play an important part. However, support networks can also be comprised of friends, neighbors, members of the same church, or other informal contacts. These nonfamily support networks appear less viable as older people become impaired or disabled

Because never-married midlife adults have spent all of adulthood independently, they report much less loneliness than do widows. Further, they establish relationships with fictive kin to replace missing family relationships.

and have increasing instrumental support needs. At that point, unmarried older people may need to utilize many more community services in order to meet their support needs.

The proportion of each generation that remains unmarried seems to be slowly increasing; further, current young adults appear to be marrying later. But if that trend continues, strong informal networks and accessible community services will be a necessity for independent living.

Little research has focused on homosexuality in late life, but research shows that relationships between gay and lesbian midlife adults are diverse. Existing research also suggests that about 10 percent of people age sixty-five years and older are gay or lesbian, the same proportion that is found in the adult population at large. Many of these people have strong, committed relationships with members of the same sex. But gay and lesbian relationships are not identical, and it is important to examine patterns of family relations among gay men and lesbians separately.

Gay and Lesbian Relationships in Later Life

Typically, older lesbians have had either one or a series of intimate relationships throughout their adult lives. Older lesbians without partners continue to hope to find a new mate. Despite the importance of sex in the relationships of older lesbians, it is not the factor that keeps lesbian couples together. Shared interests and long-term commitments are much more important to lesbian couples. Although lesbians remain sexually active, frequency of sexual interaction declines in later life.

Patterns of relationships of gay men in later life are somewhat different from those of lesbians. During middle age (forty-six to fifty-five years old), the number of monogamous partnerships between gay men peaks at approximately 59 percent; however, gay couplehood decreases after age sixty because of death of one partner or because some older men may reject monogamy in late life. Raymond Berger, author of *Gay and Gray*, found that the majority of older gay men reported satisfaction with their partners and indicated a greater sense of well-being and life satisfaction than did younger gay men. Although older lesbians generally do not fear the physical changes that result from aging, many older gay men show great concern about physical appearance in late life. Like older lesbians, gay male couples continue to report sexuality as important in their relationships despite reduced frequency of sexual interactions.

The gay community may function for gay men and lesbians in the same way that extended kin networks function for heterosexual midlife adults. If this is true, the support networks of gay men and lesbians can provide as much help in times of crisis as do spouses or adult children. Society's increasing acceptance of homosexuality over the last twenty years may suggest that future older homosexuals will be more socially accepted than they have been in the past.

Divorce and Widowhood

A variety of changes in late life can result in the end of marital relationships. From separation and divorce to death of a spouse, circumstances may require older people to establish independence in all walks of life. Sometimes this independence is not possible, and nursing homes or other institutional care is essential. But those older adults who find themselves without a spouse in later life for one reason or another face a difficult adjustment.

Although divorce and widowhood both have the same ultimate outcome—that is, the end of a marriage—adjustments may be quite different for those who face these two transitions.

Divorce and the Older Adult

Most married older adults report having high marital satisfaction in late life. However, there are some late-life marriages that simply do not work. Today, divorce is considered an acceptable means of ending an unhappy marriage, and more midlife adults are choosing divorce than ever before. Although the number of late-life marriages ending in divorce is still relatively low compared to other age groups, between 10 percent and 13 percent of midlife adults have been divorced at some point in the life course. This rate is slightly higher for males than females and declines as age increases.

In the future, both the number and proportion of older people experiencing divorce will increase. Researchers predict that one-third of those reaching age sixty-five between 2010 and 2014 will have been divorced at least once during their lives. For those born between 1950 and 1954, researchers estimate that 45 percent will have been divorced

In 1960, 1 percent of divorces involved someone age sixty-five and older; in 1980, this proportion had increased to 3.4 percent.

from at least one spouse. One contributing factor may be the increasing economic independence of women. Further, because people are living longer, and death is not terminating as many marriages before the participants reach old age, the divorce rate will continue to rise for older adults.

One reason for increasing numbers of divorced older adults may be the social acceptance of divorce as an alternative to an unhappy marriage. Further, the number of people who remarry after divorce is also increasing; this trend may make divorce more acceptable to those who still believe in marriage and want a marital relationship. However, remarriages are more likely to end in divorce than are first marriages. Thus remarrying does not necessarily increase the likelihood of success in marriage.

People who are divorced in late life often suffer serious economic and social consequences. Women are more likely to have these problems than men, especially if they have not qualified for Social Security or pensions on their own. Furthermore, the loss of a spouse to divorce is also the loss of a potential source of support. There is also evidence that late-life divorce may also weaken relationships between older parents and their adult children. If some or all children take sides in a divorce between older people, children may be lost as a potential sources of support as well. Divorce may also compromise the quality of relationships between older people and their grandchildren and great-grandchildren; legal guidelines for grandparent-grandchild contact are unclear.

Those older adults who readjust successfully from divorce have greater resources including money, education, and strong social support networks. But older people have fewer alternatives than do young people after the end of a marriage. This is especially true for older women for whom remarriage may be an impossibility. Thus late-life divorce results in unhappiness and loss of family and social networks for some divorcing couples.

Widowhood

Throughout late life, older adults face major changes. Of all the role changes older people experience, moving from spouse to widow is perhaps the most difficult. Widowhood requires greater readjustment by an older adult than does any other stressful life event in old age. Yet by age seventy, most women have been widowed already. Men, on the other hand, may not experience widowhood at all because their life expectancy is typically shorter than that of their wives.

The trend of men marrying younger women also makes it less likely that men will be widowed. If widowhood does occur for older men, it is likely to happen at age eighty-five or older. However, men's widowhood rates never come close to those of women. Race plays an important part in timing and frequency of widowhood as well. Twice as many non-white women experience widowhood as do white women, and those non-white women are likely to be widowed at an younger age. Further, while Hispanic and Asian widows frequently move in with others, African-Amer-

ican and white widows remain alone. This living pattern may have implications for support as widows continue to age.

Widows are more likely to cope successfully with spousal death if that death occurs "on time"—that is, late enough in life that one might expect to be widowed. "Off time" deaths of spouses are substantially more difficult to manage because there has been no time for emotional preparation either for the death or for the widowhood that follows. The widow who is often best prepared is the one who has cared for a chronically or terminally ill spouse. In this instance, the widow has had ample time to accept the idea of the death of the spouse, to mentally rehearse widowhood and changing roles with family members, and may have even begun the grieving process prior to the death itself.

Widowhood requires greater readjustment by an older adult than does any other stressful life event in old age.

COURTESY OF CHAUTAUQUA INSTITUTION

Other factors influence how great an impact widowhood has on midlife adults. In addition to gender, age, race, and "on time" or "off time" widowhood, social class, health, and living situation also affect the individual's response to this major life transition. Because there are five widows to every widower in American society, most research on widowhood has focused on women and their adaptation.

Do women cope with widowhood more effectively than men? The answer to that question is complex. For example, income and socioeconomic status help widows cope and encourage independence and continuing social participation; however, male widows are more likely to have higher incomes than are women and therefore might cope better. Some older women may have great difficulty in facing the economic consequences of widowhood. Financial repercussions may be especially problematic if the deceased spouse has been chronically ill and the widow has been serving as caregiver. Health services and long-term care can erode any family's resources, and widows in this situation may be left with little or no financial security. Nearly 40 percent of widowed women live in or near poverty, and the needs of these women have not yet been addressed by public policy.

In terms of health following bereavement, Larry Thompson and his colleagues report that recently widowed older people were more likely to report new illness or exacerbation of an existing condition than were nonwidowed peers. The widows also reported more new medication use than did nonwidows. Earlier studies had shown that men were more likely to experience illness after bereavement than women.

Kenneth Ferraro compared widows and widowers and found that bereaved men visited doctors more frequently and used more medications than bereaved women. Some studies found that widowers have worse physical health, greater isolation and loneliness, less social support, and fewer confidants than widows. Thus the negative consequences of widowhood can be damaging regardless of gender.

Although the financial arena of widowhood appears to favor men, women are better off in terms of friendship and support. Older women tend to have much larger and more supportive social networks than men, and women are more likely to accept both emotional support and instrumental help from network members. Because these networks can and do provide companionship and assistance for widows, widowed women often have little interest in remarriage. As noted, the differing life expectancies of men and women make the available group of older men very small, and almost 60 percent of all older women who are widowed remain unmarried and live alone. In one large study, 36 percent of widows reportedly liked being single and the independence that was part of the single life. Some widows chose not to remarry because they idealized their late husbands; others said that they did not want additional caregiving responsibilities. In all, the combination of few potential partners and preferences for independence means many widows remain unmarried for the rest of their lives.

In contrast, most older widowed men are not only interested in remarriage but are likely to remarry relatively soon after bereavement. Widowers complain much more about loneliness than widows, often a reflection of their lack of social networks. For a man whose confidante is his wife, widowhood can be especially devastating. Furthermore, because men are socialized not to betray their emotions, they may have difficulty in expressing feelings of grief and bereavement. When a wife dies, her husband has not only lost his best friend and confidante, but he may have lost his housekeeper and support provider as well. However, men's social networks may not be able to provide eligible candidates for remarriage quickly. As a result, widowers often report greater isolation and experience difficulty with simple survival tasks such as cooking, cleaning, and caring for the household.

Widowhood has well-documented mental health effects for both men and women. In a large study, researchers found that all widowed persons reported higher levels of mental impairment than did age-matched married people. In California, Gallagher and her colleagues report equal levels of difficulty in adjustment to widowhood for men and women. In particular, Gallagher reports that the mental health consequences of widowhood are high for both men and women. Suicide rates, incidence and prevalence of chronic illness, and other negative events can accompany widowhood. However, widows who have supportive family members can adapt more effectively to life changes.

As noted, widows with strong social support networks are more likely to experience bereavement successfully and to restructure their lives to meet current needs than are isolated widows. Adult children can play an important role during this process, providing emotional support and tangible help when necessary; they can also provide entertainment and distraction for their widowed parent. It is equally important, however, for widowed people to have social contact with people their own age. For widows, becoming socially involved with other widows is extremely important. Rather than try to interact in a couple-based social network, groups of widows often gather and share social and recreational activities. One widow is usually more able to accept help from another widow than from married couples or professionals. Of course the most likely people to participate in groups like this are women; widowers, even when groups are available, tend to remain isolated.

Friendship and Aging

For many years researchers and society alike accepted the common perception that as people age their friendship circles gradually become smaller. Certainly aging can contribute to social losses. Almost every midlife adult lives to witness the death of lifelong friends. When older people relocate to be near family members or to live in a warmer climate, they leave friends behind. Upon retirement, work-related friendships sometimes dissipate. The departure of children from the home makes contact with the parents of the children's friends less likely. Becoming a widow or widower can make it difficult to socialize with couples. Failing health or inadequate financial resources sometimes make it difficult to accept or to reciprocate invitations. Those who live dependently often receive very few visitors.

Thus, it is not surprising that many younger people hold the erroneous view that older people have few or no friends. However, the social losses and constraints on friendship that accompany the aging process are only part of the story. Each role change associated with aging creates opportunities for friendship as well as constraints on it. Retirement, the departure of children from the home, and even widowhood often mean that older people have more time for friendship. In addition, they often feel less bound by social expectations and exercise their newfound freedom by developing different types of friendships than they had previously.

Each role transition affects the social lives of midlife adults differently, depending on their specific circumstances. The effects of widowhood are different for young women than for older ones, mainly because when widows are older, they are in the majority. Among middle-aged people, socializing tends to be couple centered. Women who are widowed relatively early in life are often excluded from social gatherings, perhaps because a single woman is perceived as a threat or because a widow is a reminder to married women of what is to come.

Aging and Friendship Patterns

In contrast, widowhood can be a liberating experience for an older woman. Husbands, especially chronically ill ones, often interfere with their wives' social lives. This situation can be frustrating for the older woman whose widowed friends are free to socialize whenever they want. Older women are often embarrassed by the sense of relief they experience when their husbands die. They enter the society of widows expectantly, establishing new friendships and reestablishing old ones.

Very little research has been done on the effects of retirement on friendship. Scant evidence shows that the effects of retirement are different depending on the social class of the retiree and on what proportion of the retiree's friends were work based. Retirement does not appear to affect the friendships of middle-class men, but it does reduce contact for women and working-class men. People who depend on work as a primary source of identity and of friendship experience declines in social life upon retirement. People with interests and networks outside of the workplace often experience the same feeling of liberation when they retire that many women experience when they become widows.

Although relocation means leaving old friends behind, it can also provide an opportunity to make new friends. This is espe-

Friendships in Literature

Mr. Silver and Mrs. Gold, Dale Fink's 1980 children's story about friendship, accurately depicts the type of companionship involved in many older adult courting relationships. When they are together, Mr. Silver and Mrs. Gold play music, take walks in the park, share conversation, garden, bake, and drink tea and coffee.

---

cially true when the older adult moves into a neighborhood or apartment complex mainly or exclusively occupied by his or her age peers. Some recent research shows that older adults even establish new relationships in nursing homes.

Declining health can make it difficult for the older adult to maintain contact with friends, but it does not necessarily lead to the termination of relationships. In close relationships, the inability to reciprocate is not an important factor. Furthermore, one must view reciprocity over the entire life course. Sometimes, even though a friendship seems one-sided at a given moment, an examination of its history might reveal that an accumulated debt is being paid. In addition to the continuation of long-term friendships, older people in poor health who live among their age peers often attract good Samaritans as friends, people who enjoy helping those less fortunate than themselves.

More research is needed on why people respond to these age-related role changes in different ways. We know very little, for example, about how gender, ethnicity, race, and class background affect friendship. Gerontologists argue that older women probably fare better in friendships than older men, because women are more numerous among the elderly, because they have better developed interpersonal skills, and because their friendships are less likely to be work based and activity oriented. Researchers have not yet designed studies to test this hypothesis.

Maintaining Friendships

Certainly making and maintaining friendships comes more naturally to some people than to others, regardless of their gender, ethnic group, race, or class background. Not everyone is good at maintaining old friendships across long distances by writing letters, keeping in touch by telephone, and occasional visiting. Some people have never developed the relevant social skills or habits; they have relied on others or on routine interaction to make friends and maintain relationships.

For other people, their ability to keep in touch is determined by their access to resources. Midlife adults who have adequate finances for entertainment, travel, and telephone bills, who have access to transportation, or who have someone who can help them with correspondence often have an advantage.

The immediate circumstances in which older people live also affect their ability to make friends and maintain friendships as they age. Such factors as how isolated their home is, whether they live independently, how dangerous they perceive their neighborhood to be, how available support services are, and how easy it is to keep their home presentable for visitors can all affect the way people's friendships evolve as they age.

Common sense suggests that broader societal and cultural circumstances also influence older adult friendship patterns, but very little information is available about this topic. When the people who are currently old were young, they learned different friendship styles and abided by different social rules than young people do today. What they learned in their youth surely affects the friendships they have today. Given recent trends, the next generation of older women may be more likely to name men as friends than the current age cohort.

The opportunities for and constraints on midlife adults' friendships today differ from those of even just a generation ago. Since more people survive into old age now than in the past, they have a greater number of age peers from whom to select their friends. Cultural and social changes also influence friendships. The growth of senior centers, improved attitude toward aging, relatively better health of today's midlife adults, and the tendency of people to retire younger have affected older adult friendship patterns, and will continue to do so into the twenty-first century.

David Brown

Film producer

SNAPSHOT

| became more productive in my seventies than I ever had been before in my whole life."

David Brown achieved his greatest successes in the last ten years. With careers in journalism and publishing behind him, Brown produced hit movies and Broadway smashes, including *Tru*, *A Few Good Men*, and *The Cemetery Club*, and the award-winning television program "Women and Men." He has also published several best-selling books and is currently working on one about the 1930s.

Born in New York City in 1916, Brown was interested in journalism before he could even read. He loved to listen to radio broadcasters Lowell Thomas and Edmund C. Hill, and from the age of five he pored over newspapers—"I looked at the advertising and the drawing and the pictures," he recalls; "I was interested in the world outside and I was interested in how it would impact on me."

He studied social sciences and psychology, graduated from Stanford, and received a Master of Science degree from Columbia University; his first job was at Fairchild Publications for twenty-five dollars a week. Over the next few years he worked for *Women's Wear Daily* as a drama critic and copy editor, wrote horoscopes, and did some free-lance writing. In 1940, newly married, he decided he had to get a "real" job.

He worked for his father, doing public relations for the milk industry, but his father fired him in short order. "I couldn't keep regular hours," Brown admits. He next became the nightclub editor of one of the burgeoning picture magazines, *PIc*. "I covered nightclubs, cabaret, and theater. That's how I got interested in show business," he recalls.

Brown began writing skits for comedian Eddie Cantor, which led to a job with the weekly magazine *Liberty*. After the army, Brown returned to *Liberty* and then became managing editor of *Cosmopolitan*, until Darryl F. Zanuck called him to Hollywood in 1951.

At Twentieth Century Fox, Brown rose from story editor to producer to head of the scenario department. When the studio went bankrupt in 1963, Brown returned to New York and fell into yet another profession: book publishing. He founded New American Library, which boasted Ian Fleming's James Bond books on its list. But two years later he was back in the movie business.

In 1964 Brown purchased the film rights to the popular play *The Sound of Music*, which put Twentieth Century Fox back on the map. In six years, he became executive vice-president of creative operations, but in 1970, in a political coup against Darryl Zanuck, Brown and Richard Zanuck were fired. Brown learned from this experience: "It convinced me that I was never going to let a company control my destiny again—except my own company, which controls my destiny on a daily basis."

Brown and the younger Zanuck formed their own company on July 28, 1972. The Zanuck-Brown Company produced such successful films as *Jaws*, *The Sting*, *The Verdict*, and *Cocoon*, a landmark film that examines attitudes about aging. Brown was also executive producer for the Academy Award–winner *Driving Miss Daisy*, which proved that a story about an aging person could garner critical acclaim. After a long and fruitful partnership, Brown started his own development and production company, the Manhattan Project.

In 1991 the Academy of Motion Picture Arts and Sciences presented Brown and Zanuck with the Irving G. Thalberg Award, the highest honor for a film producer.

At seventy-eight, Brown attributes his physical, mental, and emotional well-being to the fact that he has never stopped working. "I'm healthy and energetic because I work. I take pleasure in my work. I still work seven days a week, and I enjoy it. As Tennessee Williams said, 'Make voyages. Attempt them. That's all there is.' "

—*Lydia Brontë*

How Active Are Midlife Adults as Friends?

Contrary to the stereotypical image of midlife adults as lonely and friendless, almost all older people do have friends. Estimates of the average number of friends older people have range from none to twelve, depending on their circumstances. In one study, researchers observed nursing home residents interacting with up to six friends. Those who had greater lucidity and better vision and speech had more friends. In another study, older female residents of a middle-class suburb named an average of twelve friends. Participation in social activities and employment both lead to larger social circles.

Comparing the findings of studies of adult friendships of various ages suggests that older people tend to have approximately the same number of friends as younger people. This evidence is not conclusive, though, because almost all of these studies were of a specific age group, took place in distinctive settings, or were of people who were socially similar to one another. No one has ever done a study of friendship in which a representative sampling of people of all adult ages, from all over the country, and from all walks of life were interviewed. For this reason, any statements comparing older adult friendship to friendship during the earlier stages of adulthood are tentative.

Not only do older people have friends, they see them quite frequently. Some researchers have found that older people see

each of their friends an average of several times a month, and others have found that they tend to see them more frequently than that. They tend to see their close friends more frequently than their more casual ones and to spend more time with these close friends than with their casual ones when they do see them.

Values in Friendships

Members of our culture, regardless of their ages, define friendship in a variety of ways. Although social conventions and circumstances influence our understanding of "friendship," we are allowed a great deal of freedom in interpreting the meaning of the word. Some people use the term "friend" to refer to mere acquaintances, and others reserve it for intimates. Each older adult thus has a slightly different concept of what friendship is and has developed a distinctive friendship style during his or her life. Furthermore, most older individuals have a variety of types of friendships, ranging from intimate to casual and from activity oriented to helping relationships. Because of this variation, it is difficult to describe in general terms what friendship means to midlife adults. Nonetheless, despite this individual variation, some general statements are relevant.

Friendships in Literature

The lack of need for close friends to reciprocate favors is aptly illustrated in William Stegner's 1987 novel *Crossing to Safety.* On the evening of Charity's death, her husband, Sid, their best friends, Larry and Sally, and the rest of the family gather at their summer home. Larry reflects on the lifelong friendship of the two couples. Charity and Sid met Larry and Sally when the two men were both young faculty members at the University of Wisconsin. When Larry's contract was not renewed and Sally became ill, Charity and Sid came to their aid. Sally and the baby spent the summer with them in Vermont at Charity's family's home. Larry would remain in Wisconsin to work on his novel while house-sitting for Charity and Sid. When Sally and Larry protested that they would never be able to repay the kindness, Charity clearly stated that "friends don't have to repay anything."

Although life led the two couples down different paths, Larry and Sally and Sid and Charity remained close, often spending summers together. Larry's account of their friendship makes it clear that much of the credit for its endurance belonged to Charity. Charity was better equipped to maintain friendships than others, because of her personality, characteristics, social skills, and financial circumstances.

Older women, for example, tend to define "friendship" affectively. In one study, they mentioned feelings of concern, caring, kindness, warmth, love, liking, compatibility, intimacy, acceptance, openness, sincerity, honesty, or closeness. The friend's willingness to help was mentioned by almost half of the women, and about a quarter of them referred to the length of time they had known the person. No one has conducted a similar study of older men's perceptions of friendship, though research on younger men suggests that they would emphasize shared activities and time spent together more than older women do.

In her retrospective study of friendships across the life course, gerontologist Sarah Matthews discovered that people had one of three conceptions of friendship that were related to whether they were able to acquire new friendships as they aged.

The independents are people who have such an idealized concept of friendship that almost no one qualifies. They associate with people who happen to be available, without expectations that the relationships will continue. The discerning have a small circle of close friends and emphasize their friends' specific qualities. Their friendships are mainly long term and thus impossible to replace when friends relocate or pass away. Acquisitive people, on the other hand, are likely to have made and committed themselves to friendships throughout their lives, in whatever circumstances they found themselves. Although they do not necessarily maintain these relationships when circumstances change, they consider them important at the time. The acquisitive thus hope their current friendships will continue and are open to forming new ones as opportunities present themselves. One can find compelling examples of friendship types among older people in film and literature. Examples drawn from the contemporary short story, the novel, and children's literature are offered in this section.

Clearly some types of relationships are more satisfying to midlife adults than are others. In general, the closer friends feel to one another, the more satisfied they are with the relationship. Several researchers have found that reciprocity, giving and taking equally, is important for satisfaction in more casual relationships, but not important in close ones. When older people feel very close to a friend, they do not keep track of who owes whom what. They do what they can for their friend and do not feel imposed upon if the friend does not repay them.

On the other hand, if willingness to help is part of an older woman's definition of friendship and if her network is relatively nonsupportive, she is less satisfied with her relationships as a whole. This finding is not inconsistent with a lack of concern about reciprocity in specific close relationships. The same woman might feel very satisfied with a specific close relationship in which she helps the friend more than the friend helps her, but dissatisfied with her friendships in general because of the lack of support she receives from her circle of friends as a whole. Some research has shown that this general perception of lack of support of friends leads to feelings of loneliness among midlife adults.

Friendships in Literature

Richard Bausch's 1984 novel *The Last Good Time* provides portraits of people with three distinct friendship styles. Edward Cakes, a widower in his seventies who lives alone, has a discerning friendship style. His best friend, Arthur Hagood, lives in a nursing home. Edward visits him often, spending whole afternoons. When Arthur appears to be dying, Edward utters "not now." It would not be possible to replace Arthur, his lifelong friend. Mary, a young woman who abruptly enters Edward's life, leaves just as abruptly when her circumstances change, with no apparent regrets. She illustrates the independent friendship style. Ida Warren, Edward's new elderly neighbor, pursues a friendship with him despite his reluctance. Her acquisitive style is effective; the book ends when Arthur dies, and Edward puts on a clean shirt and his good wing-tip shoes to visit Ida.

Older People's Friends

Older people have accumulated their friends over their lifetimes. Research has shown that midlife adults have known their closest friends for an average of twenty-three to thirty-nine years and their less close friends for an average of nineteen to twenty-four years. Because their oldest friends tend to be their closest friends and their newest friends tend to live nearest to them, older people's closest friends tend to live farther away from them than do their more casual friends. The need to maintain important relationships across great distances is a common artifact of a long life.

Not all of the friendships of midlife adults have endured for decades, however. The authors of one study reported that within a period of ten months, some of the friendships between midlife adults who had moved simultaneously into a newly constructed retirement community involved more liking, loving, and commitment than others. Another study showed that women who previously worked most of their lives took advantage of opportunities during retirement to become active in senior centers and social clubs and, for the first time in their lives, to supplement their enduring close relationships with casual ones. Other women who previously had community-based and family-centered friendships expanded their networks to include people outside of their neighborhood.

People tend to accumulate friends who are socially similar to themselves. Most middle-aged adults tend to have friends who are similar to themselves in terms of level of education, occupational status, ethnicity, age, marital status, income, gender, and religion. Although elderly people also tend to have friends of similar social status to themselves, they are less socially similar to their friends than their younger counterparts are in terms of marital status, education, and age. Friendships people establish in old age are more likely to be with people who are socially different from themselves than are those they establish earlier in life.

Why might this be? Older people are more likely to be widowed and less likely to be high school or college graduates than younger adults. Because there are fewer people with the same marital status and level of education available to be friends with them, widows, widowers, and older people with relatively little formal education are less likely than those in majority statuses to have friends who are socially similar to themselves. Furthermore, the older someone is, the fewer age peers are available. This lack of peers provides midlife adults with motivation to establish relationships with people junior to themselves. Though people exercise a great deal of freedom in selecting their friends, the characteristics of the people in the social context in which friendships are formed may limit the extent of choice.

Researchers have not closely examined older people's relationships with people having different levels of education or different marital statuses than theirs, and they have only examined intergenerational friendships in passing. The scant evidence suggests that the midlife adult is often a mentor to the younger person. The younger person, in return, helps the midlife adult with everyday tasks. Other times intergenerational friendships are not reciprocal. Older people sometimes report friendships with professional helpers who consider the older adult as a client rather than as a friend or with a member of their church or a neighbor who visits them out of a sense of duty rather than as a result of affection.

Older people and younger adults are equally unlikely to have friends who differ from them in terms of race and gender. Although researchers have not examined the cross-race friendships of midlife adults, they have begun to study their cross-sex

Friendships in Literature

Fictional accounts of intergenerational relationships are plentiful. Fannie Flagg's 1987 novel *Fried Green Tomatoes at the Whistle Stop Cafe* describes the friendship between Evelyn and Mrs. Threadgoode. Through conversations with Mrs. Threadgoode, Evelyn gains perspective on her own life. She learns to be more assertive and not to fear death. Mrs. Threadgoode, a nursing home resident, looks forward to regular visits from her young friend, who often brings her sweet treats.

Clyde Edgerton's *Walking Across Egypt* (1987) tells the story of the friendship between Mattie Rigsbee, an independent, strong-minded senior citizen who is slowing down just a bit, and Wesley Benfield, a young delinquent. Mattie decides that Wesley is one of "the least of these my brethren" and that in doing something for him, she will be doing something for Jesus. She cleans him up, takes him to church, and decides to adopt him. He thinks that she must be his grandmother and submits to her affection, lured by her mouth-watering pound cake. The consequence for Mattie is that she no longer lives alone and no longer has to depend on her biological son and chance visitors to do the chores that have become difficult for her.

In the children's book *The Treasure Hunt* (1980), about intergenerational friendship, Christopher Wilson describes a treasure hunt designed by the midlife adults in a community to bring them together with the local children. The children realize they have much to learn from senior citizens, and the midlife adults experience pleasure while teaching them.

---

relationships. Men are more likely to report friendships with women than women are to report them with men. This finding can be interpreted in two different ways. On the one hand, it provides further support for the notion that types of people in the minority are more likely to have friends who are socially different from themselves than types of people in the majority. Due to the greater longevity of women, during old age they have more gender peers of their age to choose as friends than men and thus a higher proportion of their friendships are with members of the same sex. On the other hand, the difference could be attributable to a gender difference in the informal social rules regarding cross-sex relationships. Because members of the older cohort were taught to view cross-sex relationships as romantic, older women who have friendships with men are sometimes stigmatized as being improper. Older women may thus be more hesitant than older men to report cross-sex friendships.

Very few of older women's cross-sex friendships are actually courting relationships, however. One study showed that most of their cross-sex friendships are actually friendships with couples or with younger people who help them in a professional capacity or as a favor to someone else. About an eighth of the older women studied did have courting relationships. Although some of these courting relationships were sexually intimate, the women emphasized that companionship was more important.

Gerontologists have repeatedly found that having com-

panions and confidants is important for the mental health of midlife adults. In fact, they have found friends to be more important than family members to the psychological well-being of midlife adults. Researchers have suggested many explanations for this finding. Because midlife adults have no rigid expectations of friendship, they are grateful for signs of affection and small favors. They expect more from their family members; therefore, they evaluate them more harshly. Helping friends can also protect the older adults from negative self-esteem. Also, because friends often have more in common with midlife adults than their family members, they are more likely to involve the older adult in activities that keep them engaged with the larger community and society. Furthermore, the freedom of choice in selecting friends is important for feelings of autonomy during old age.

Although friends are not as likely to be full-time caregivers as family members are, they do help midlife adults in many practical ways. Friends are more likely to help some midlife adults than they are to help others. Retired people report more confidants and are more likely to have someone to rely on in emergencies than employed people are.

Friends are more likely to help elderly people with certain types of tasks than with others. The most common type of help

Older people who have no family members living near them are most likely to name friends as helpers. Widowed elderly women receive more help from friends than married elderly women do.

friends give midlife adults is emotional support and companionship. Because of demographic similarities, midlife adults are likely to consult friends during role transitions such as retirement or becoming a widow. Because their age peers are likely to have gone through similar adjustments, they are the preferred source of support in these instances. Friends are likely to be asked for help with tasks that do not take too long, require only intermittent help, and are not too personal. Older women often ask friends for help when it is convenient for the friend to help them or when they had an emergency. Close friends are more likely to help midlife adults than casual friends. Intimate relationships that involve confiding are more likely to involve material and service resource exchanges than less intimate ones.

The amount of help provided to midlife adults by friends may be underestimated in the research literature. In studies of the support midlife adults receive from friends, kin, neighbors, and others, researchers have usually asked hypothetical questions ("Who would you turn to for help if . . .") rather than questions about actual behavior. Hypothetical questions tend to elicit socially acceptable responses. Possibly because people typically turn to their families for help rather than to their friends, responses to hypothetical questions lead researchers to underestimate the amount of help that is actually provided by friends. Researchers also tend to ask midlife adults to name only the person who gives them the most help with a given task. In many cases, the help friends give midlife adults supplements more extensive help from family members.

Strain in Older Adult Friendship

Although friendship is mainly a positive experience for midlife adults, it is not without its problems. Researchers have studied the problematic aspects of family relationships more than they have studied the problematic aspects of friendships. Karen

Friendships in Literature

Interracial relationships, such as the one described by Hennie Aucamp in her short story "Soup for the Sick" (1991), are relatively rare among people of all ages. Tant Rensie had health problems. The only help she received was from her lifelong nurse and friend, Sofietjie. Sofietjie continued to care for her, even though she too had heart problems. Tant could not reciprocate, both because of her own health and because of the racial status differences between them. Sofietjie died before her friend did. Tant Rensie requested that Sofietjie be buried in her garden. When the town council would not allow it, she was buried in a cemetery near the "colored" location. When Tant Rensie died, she left the town money to build a hospital on the condition that she be buried near her friend. She wanted to be near the woman who had helped her selflessly throughout her life.

Rook argues that neglecting to recognize the existence of strain in friendship is unfortunate, because problematic exchanges between friends become more frequent as relationships progress, can be extremely potent, and are potentially critical to older adults because of the importance of friendships in their lives.

Older people sometimes get irritated or feel betrayed by their friends just like younger people do. One study reported that older women were occasionally irritated by a tenth of their friends and often by another tenth. They criticized their friends for having ideas different than theirs and for being temperamental, snobbish, sloppy, bossy, plainspoken, too reserved, too talkative, hard of hearing, too heavy a drinker, too nosy, unfriendly, senile, unreliable, a complainer, and impossible to change.

In a review of the limited research literature on the negative aspects of older adult friendship, Rook concluded that strains have numerous origins. Possible sources of strain include: being expected to divulge personal information as the relationship deepens, failing to communicate or to interpret expectations accurately, deficient social skills, problematic personality characteristics, failure of family to meet their obligations and subsequent inappropriate impositions on friends, competition with other network members, and disruptive external events, such as age-related role

Friendships in Literature

Most close friends tend to age at a distance. In contrast to this typical situation, Alice Adams's 1988 novel *Second Chances* describes a group of lifelong friends who relocate to the same town when they become older. One of the central relationships in the story is the friendship between Dudley Venable and Edward Crane, which is based on a lifetime of shared experiences. They first met at summer camp as adolescents. During their old age, the old friends often walk and talk. Dudley supports Edward when Edward's gay lover leaves town. Edward provides Dudley comfort upon the death of her husband. On one occasion, Dudley exclaims, "Darling Edward, whatever in the world would I do without you?"

transitions. These strains can change the course of the friendship, lead to the dissolution of the relationship, affect other relationships, and have an adverse effect on psychological well-being.

Improving Older Adult Friendships

Older people's social lives are influenced every day by institutions, family, service providers, and policymakers. For example, midlife adults may attend senior recreation centers and meetings of organizations to make new acquaintances. Their children or spouses may influence or even control the visitors they receive. For some, therapists help them develop interpersonal skills and to overcome personality problems. Architects design age-segregated housing to facilitate social interaction. Policymakers sometimes pass laws that encourage midlife adults to rely on their friends and relatives for help rather than on formal agencies.

Whether or not these interventions are intentionally designed to change an older adult's friendship patterns, they might have myriad consequences. They might increase or decrease overall satisfaction within friendships. Other, less direct consequences might be changing the older adult's behavior, resources, attitudes, values, health, or mental health.

Interventions can be designed to affect the social life of one individual, to alter the relationship of a pair of friends, or to transform interaction in an entire social circle, building, community, or society. Before such interventions can be designed and implemented effectively and responsibly, however, researchers need to study the consequences of different types of friendship patterns much more extensively. In other words, they need to know what needs to be changed and why before they implement strategies that affect older people's social lives.

—*Deborah T. Gold, Ph.D.; Rebecca G. Adams, Ph.D.*

Where we live and how we get from place to place are of critical importance to everyone. But housing and transportation needs take on special significance in middle and later life. And they encompass more than matters of shelter and mobility. A person's home is an expression of selfhood. Transportation is an exercise in freedom of movement. How we think about, and plan for, the place we call home, and our means of getting to and from it, require careful consideration. They are vital aspects of living smarter.

As we get older, we spend more time inside our dwellings. The physical space of the home—be it apartment, condo, cabin, or mansion—is a world of familiar surroundings that represents memories and community. Moreover, for the majority of people over fifty, the home is the most valuable asset. For others who rent a house, apartment, or condo, the cost of housing may be their biggest expense. Housing is critically linked to transportation. Home location determines the ease or difficulty of reaching important places like the office (for those still working), the doctor, the hair salon, the supermarket, a favorite restaurant, a local church or synagogue, and, for many, their grandkids' homes. Most people continue to drive into their eighties and nineties, so safe driving and auto upkeep are important. In urban areas where many people rely on public transportation, ease, safety of use, and cost can be limiting factors.

The impact of a growing middle-aged society on transportation is, literally, easy to see. Highway and street signs are getting larger, car instrument panels more legible. Moreover, cars are being redesigned to make getting in and out safer. With increases in the aging population, new types of housing designs and arrangements are hitting the market. The patio home, condo, retirement community, and assisted living facility are some of the new options, while new technological advances are being integrated into the Smart House, a home of the future that will electronically monitor and control heating, air conditioning, lighting, and security systems—automatically.

While our homes and our cars may look and think smarter, we still have the major responsibility to monitor and control our environment to the best of our ability. Part of living smarter means having accurate information and exercising options.

Housing for Older Persons

In general the housing situation of midlife and older people has markedly improved over the past few decades. This improvement is likely to continue for the immediate future as more resources become available. Home repairs and adaptations are most likely to see substantial growth as older homeowners seek to "age in place." Older individuals and couples who move are most likely to do so out of substantial needs related to disabilities or declining financial resources. Housing facilities, such as assisted living or types that promote caregiving in a residential environment, such as elder cottage housing opportunity (ECHO) units, are the most likely to see substantial growth.

By 2020 the older population (sixty-five years and over) will have grown to 52.1 million, a 65 percent increase from the 31.6 million in 1990. As a percentage of the total population, the older population will have grown from 12.6 percent to 17.7 percent. Yet important changes in the age structure of the older population are occurring. Between 1990 and 2000, as the older population grows by 3.3 million, 41 percent of the growth will be among those eighty-five and older. In contrast, the population of sixty-five to seventy-four-year-olds will actually decline marginally during the same period, reflecting the "birth dearth" during the Great

By 2020 the older population (sixty-five plus) will have grown to 52.1 million, a 65 percent increase from the 31.6 million in 1990.

Depression. The decade of the 2010s will see explosive growth in the older population as the baby boomers begin to turn sixty-five—12.8 million people age sixty-five and older will be added during the decade. More than three-fourths (78 percent) of that growth will occur among the sixty-five to seventy-four-year-old age group, with an 18 percent growth among those seventy-five to eighty-four, and a flat 4 percent growth rate among those eighty-five and older.

Successive waves of individuals entering old age, which gerontologists refer to as "age cohorts," will have very different experiences of aging due to differing historical experiences. For example, today's "old-old" group is made up of cohorts who generally came of age during the Great Depression. These oldest individuals and families generally have lower incomes and assets, both because they have outlived many of their resources and because their career patterns suffered at the outset from the timing of trying to get a job in the midst of the depression.

The American Association of Retired Persons (AARP) Public Policy Institute recently commissioned the Urban Institute to develop a profile of the housing conditions of older Americans, comparing data from the 1980 and 1989 American Housing Surveys (AHS). These data indicate a dramatic increase in the poverty rate for those seventy-five years old and older, from 19.9 percent to 25 percent. In addition, the proportion of older households with incomes below $5,000 (in constant 1987 dollars) increased from 8.6 percent to 14.2 percent (1.38 million to 2.79 million households)—most of this increase is among the old-old.

Also reflecting the unfavorable economic times for household formation and launching a family during the Great Depression, the cohorts that make up the old-old during the 1990s have the highest rates of childlessness in American history.

These data indicate that a major demographic crunch is already facing the country. The 1990s will witness the most rapid growth in the oldest-old, who are most likely to experience significant disabilities, who have lower incomes and fewer assets than any age group (save, perhaps, the very youngest families,) and who have the weakest set of informal supports because of a high rate of childlessness. All of these factors increase the risk of nursing home use for long-term care needs.

Expanding housing options to accommodate an increasingly diverse range of needs among older persons and managing the transition between the cohorts of old-old and young-old will require foresight and planning on the part of developers, home builders, policy officials, and advocates. Meeting the challenge of a rapidly aging population will require increasing attention to promising new technologies to improve the safety, convenience, efficiency, and affordability of housing designed for a "life span."

The living arrangements of older people have changed dramatically over the past few decades, generally reflecting an improved ability to remain independent longer. Opinion surveys on the preferred living arrangements of older people have invariably documented a desire to live independently apart from children or others who might be inclined to caregiving responsibilities. Changes in living arrangements since 1960 indicate that increasing numbers of older people, especially women, are able to live independently. According to census data, 45 percent of all Americans age sixty-five and over lived with people other than their spouses in 1960—a figure that declined dramatically to 15.2 percent by 1989.

Reflecting longer life spans, the tendency to marry older men, and the lower likelihood of remarriage after widowhood or divorce, older women are much more likely than men to live alone—41 percent for older women versus 16 percent of older men. Similarly, older women are much more likely than men to live with people other than their spouses—by a margin of 19 percent to 10 percent. Conversely, the vast majority of older men (74 percent) live with their spouses, versus only 40 percent of older women, a number that declines to only 9 percent for women over age eighty-five.

Living arrangements also differ according to the ethnicity among older adults, reflecting both economic and cultural differences. Older whites are only half as likely to live with relatives as older African Americans or Hispanics—12 percent for whites versus 24 percent for older African Americans and 26 percent for older Hispanics. Because of higher widowhood rates, only 39 percent of older African Americans live with a spouse compared to 50 percent of older Hispanics and 54 percent of older whites.

The stability of older households, always at a high level, is increasing. Between 1980 and 1989, the percentage of older homeowners residing at their current address for twenty years or more increased from 50.6 percent to 58 percent. In contrast, 40 percent of

Living Arrangements and Location of Older Americans

nonelderly homeowners had moved within the last five years. Even older renters tend to stay put—only 42 percent reported moving in the last five years compared to 82 percent of renters under sixty-five.

During the 1980s the older population tended to grow in small towns at the expense of rural areas. Between 1980 and 1989, the older population grew by an impressive 80 percent in small towns. Reflecting the move to suburban areas by the cohort that formed households in the post–World War II era, the great majority of this growth (59 percent) was among the young-old—those age sixty-five to seventy-five.

The age profile of households in rural areas changed dramatically in the opposite direction. Between 1980 and 1989 the population over age seventy-five remained almost exactly the same—declining by 0.01 percent. On the other hand, the sixty-five-to seventy-four-year-old population declined by a substantial 18 percent in rural areas. Major metropolitan areas were in between rural areas and small towns—with the population over sixty-five growing 22 percent.

Older Homeowners

Of all age groups, older households have the highest rate of home ownership—78 percent own their homes, 84 percent own them mortgage free. Accumulation of equity is a major source of savings, and high home ownership rates are a bulwark of financial security for older homeowners. While the quality of housing of older persons generally improved during the 1980s, problems persist among the following subgroups of older homeowners:

Minorities: In 1989, homes of older African-American owners were almost four times more likely to exhibit severe or moderate quality problems as the homes of older white owners. In comparison, 13.4 percent of older Hispanic households had a similar level of housing problems.

Single person households: Three-fifths of severe housing inadequacies occurred in single person households compared to less than one-quarter in married households.

Rural elders: According to the 1985 American Housing Survey 57 percent of severe inadequacies among all older adult households occurred in rural areas. Older households in nonmetro areas were more than twice as likely as metropolitan households to experience housing inadequacies.

Central-city dwellers: Seventy-one percent of housing inadequacies in urban areas are concentrated in central cities. Despite higher average incomes than renters, older homeowners represented 63 percent of older households with incomes $5,000 and below in 1989. Real estate taxes, utility costs, and insurance are often a substantial burden, even though the vast majority of poor older adult households own their homes free and clear. According to the AHS, half of all poor older homeowners spent at least 46 percent of their income on housing in 1989. Housing expenditures, when combined with the older adult's high out-of-pocket medical expenses, limit the cash resources available for maintenance, repairs, and modifications to assist with mobility problems.

Federal programs to deal with the maintenance, repair, and modification needs of older homeowners have been inadequate and badly coordinated. Only a tiny program run by the Farmers Home Administration has focused on older homeowners.

While most older people do not view themselves as functionally impaired, many experience problems with activities of daily living. Older homeowners overwhelmingly prefer to stay where they are as they grow older. The ability to remain in their homes, however, often depends on the adaptability of the home environment. The location of the home and its characteristics can aid in the provision of in-home, long-term care services—or make such services nearly impossible. Home modifications can diminish problems related to reductions in physical functioning (such as sight, hearing, mobility) and may reduce the incidence of withdrawal from activities, premature institutionalization, accidents, and fatal injuries.

The Community Development Block Grant program and Title III of the Older Americans Act have funded some home

Colter H.

A seventy-seven-year-old gentleman farmer and innkeeper, Colter H. relates his belief that changing his lifestyle saved his life:

"I have lived in this part of the world for seventeen years. When I came up here, I couldn't walk without crutches. I had high blood pressure and was supposed to be dead in about six months. I retired, thinking I had little time to live, and have fooled everybody including myself. I purchased the farm and surrounded myself with livestock, birds, and pets. This life was a lifelong dream and welcome change after thirty years in the American Foreign Service. I think the farm cured my ailments. I feel at home with animals, and I think that made me well. If I had them, I had to feed them, whether I was on crutches or not. Eventually I didn't need my crutches, and eventually I didn't need much in the way of medicine for my blood pressure. It came down and stayed down pretty well.

"After a time I opened my remodeled home as a bed and breakfast inn. I manage the fifteen-room house, cook everyone's breakfast, do the laundry, make the beds, and tend to the daily chores of feeding the animals on my own. I enjoy each guest and at times can be helpful to some by drawing on my personal experience of working with hospice and dealing with my loss of a wife and child. I have been able to help some men of my own age who are facing issues about death.

"I don't think of myself as a very religious person, but I am grateful to the great I AM, whatever that great I AM is."

—*From Connie Goldman's "Late Bloomer" public radio series*

repairs, though resources for both programs has stagnated in recent years. The National Affordable Housing Act of 1990 authorized home repairs for older and disabled homeowners under the newly created HOME block grant, though no funds have been spent under the program. No federal program authorizes the full range of repairs and modifications needed to address both substandard housing conditions and adaptations needed to promote mobility. Older homeowners, especially older minorities, are underserved by these programs relative to the extent of deficiencies in their housing.

Home Modifications to Extend Independence

Home modification refers to adaptations to the home environment that can assist older or functionally impaired individuals to maintain independent living. Modifications may range from structural changes, such as lowering cabinets and doorway thresholds, widening door frames, and installing ramps, to material adjustments like rearranging furniture and storage of essential items for easy access. Special equipment like grab bars, bath benches, and railings can prevent falls and other serious accidents.

A recent survey by AARP indicates that the most common home modifications undertaken by older persons are installing additional lighting, confining living quarters to one floor to avoid stairs, using lever faucets in place of knobs, and installing additional hand rails or grab bars. Modifications used less frequently are installing emergency response systems, replacing door knobs with lever handles, replacing stairs with ramps, and widening doorways.

Relatively simple modifications can reduce stress from routine activities of daily living and allow older occupants to continue to enjoy many activities such as bathing, cooking, and entertaining. By adjusting the home environment to more closely fit the physical capabilities and social needs of the older occupant, home modification is one option for fulfilling the desire of most older persons to remain in their current residence.

For instance, Illustration 1 shows Ms. Benton in her kitchen. She likes to have friends over in the late afternoon several

Illustration 1. Ms. Benton in her kitchen—before modifications.

COURTESY OF THE AMERICAN ASSOCIATION FOR RETIRED PERSONS FROM *THE PERFECT FIT: CREATIVE IDEAS FOR A SAFE AND LIVABLE HOME*

times a week. She is well known in the neighborhood for her hot spiced-apple cider in the winter and iced mint tea in the summer as well as her special peach cobbler. She has found, however, that because of her arthritis, it is harder to prepare the food, serve her guests, and clean up.

Illustration 2 shows Ms. Benton after some modifications were made to her kitchen. The numbers correspond to recommended modifications.

1. Trays: Install roll-out trays to make base storage more accessible.

2. Faucet: Install a single lever-handled faucet that is easy to turn.

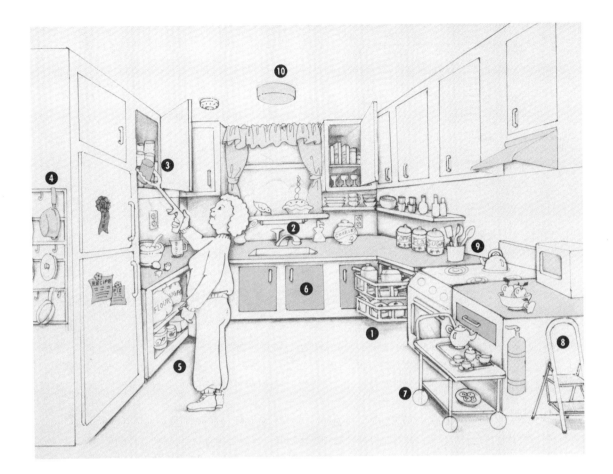

Illustration 2. Ms. Benton in her kitchen—after modifications.

COURTESY OF THE AMERICAN ASSOCIATION OF RETIRED PERSONS FROM *THE PERFECT FIT: CREATIVE IDEAS FOR A SAFE AND LIVABLE HOME*

3. Reacher: Use a long-handled reacher for lightweight items on high shelves.

4. Additional shelves: Add additional shelves and hooks under cabinets to store objects used regularly, or use a wall rack.

5. Heavy objects lower: Keep heavy objects on bottom shelves or cabinet tops; put lightweight or least-used objects on top shelves.

6. Replace knobs: Replace knobs with lever or U-shaped pulls or handles.

7. Trolley cart: Use a trolley cart instead of a tray to transport food.

8. Step stool: Obtain a solid stepladder with high railings to hold onto.

9. Objects over stove: Move objects over stove to another location to avoid potential burns.

10. Illumination: Install good ceiling illumination and additional task lighting where food is prepared.

The preference among older individuals for staying in their current homes can be attributed to numerous factors. Respondents to an AARP survey most often mentioned location, comfort, the neighborhood, the size of their residence or property, the attractiveness of their property, and the floor plan or the lack of steps. Present or expected lifestyle, health status, and financial resources are also key considerations. For many older persons, home ownership symbolizes independence and personal achievement. The reluctancy to relinquish their present homes for less private or independent living arrangements is a common feeling. In addition, the prospective loss of familial contact and treasured possessions makes relocation difficult and emotionally traumatic.

Diminishing physical abilities and chronic illnesses, however, often make it difficult for older persons to continue to live independently in their present environments. More than four out of five people age sixty-five and older have at least one chronic condition. According to the survey, approximately 13 percent of older persons living in the community had difficulty with one or more activities of daily living such as walking, bathing, transferring, dressing, using the toilet, and eating. Instrumental activities of daily living posed difficulties for 17.5 percent. Such activities include doing light housework, preparing meals, use of the telephone, getting around the community, shopping, and handling money. A very high proportion of older persons who live alone suffer from chronic health problems and have difficulty performing daily activities. By the year 2020, this population is expected to increase by 57 percent.

Illustration 3 shows Mrs. Klein preparing for a bath. She has always enjoyed bathing—she finds it relaxing, therapeutic, and hygienic. But recently, she slipped getting out of the bathtub

Illustration 3. Mrs. Klein in her bathroom—before modifications.

COURTESY OF THE AMERICAN ASSOCIATION OF RETIRED PERSONS FROM *THE PERFECT FIT: CREATIVE IDEAS FOR A SAFE AND LIVABLE HOME*

in her apartment. Luckily she didn't hurt herself, but it was a frightening experience. She has known several friends who have broken their hips in such falls and she doesn't want that to happen to her. At the same time, she wants to keep using the bathtub.

Illustration 4 shows Mrs. Klein after some modifications are made to her bathroom. The numbers correspond to recommended modifications.

1. Rug: Secure rug with nonskid tape or remove all loose rugs.

2. Grab bars: Add grab bars, either attached to studs in the wall or portable over bathtub ledge.

3. Bath mat: Add bath mat or nonskid strips to bottom of tub.

Illustration 4. Mrs. Klein in her bathroom—after modifications.

COURTESY OF THE AMERICAN ASSOCIATION OF RETIRED PERSONS FROM *THE PERFECT FIT: CREATIVE IDEAS FOR A SAFE AND LIVABLE HOME*

4. Toilet: Add grab bar by toilet.

5. Bath bench: Add bath bench in tub if necessary.

6. Shelf: Install small corner shelf over tub for bath supplies.

7. Shower: Install a hand-held shower.

Homes purchased when older occupants were raising families may now stress their physical abilities and financial resources. According to the latest American Housing Survey, 81 percent of older homeowners live in traditional single family detached homes, and almost two-thirds of these homes were built prior to 1960. These older homes can be more expensive to heat and maintain. In addition, very few have been modified to compensate for the increased frailty of their occupants.

A recent study notes that just 10 percent of older households with at least one member having a health or mobility limitation made any design modifications to their homes. The most common modification was the addition of hand rails and grab bars. Adjustments to sinks, cabinets, and light switches were found in little over 1 percent of the homes surveyed. Less than 1 percent of the households incorporated modifications to allow wheelchair access.

A high rate of fatal and disabling accidents reflects the increasing imbalance between the demands of the home environment and physical abilities of older occupants. For example, falls make up two-thirds of all accidental fatalities among older persons. Approximately 85 percent of all stair-related deaths occur among persons age sixty-five and older. Research indicates that two-thirds of these deaths could be prevented through home modifications or design changes.

Despite the fact that many modifications are relatively low-cost and easy to accomplish, significant barriers exist to wider modification activity. For example, Medicare and Medicaid will not pay for nonmedical equipment such as grab bars. A confusing array of federal, state, and local programs provide some assistance for low-income homeowners, but the services offered vary considerably and funding has been inadequate. Medical and other service providers often overlook home modifications that could assist older clients, and few communities have programs to assist older persons or their families in assessing the home environment. Finally, older persons may be reluctant to acknowledge that their capabilities have diminished, are unaware of how home modifications can improve quality of life, or do not know where to obtain assistance in getting home modifications installed.

A number of states have initiated programs using state moneys to foster home repair and modification. For instance, Maine established a low-interest loan program for adaptive equipment, and Ohio included home modification as part of a $75 million aging services initiative. Much of this activity has been implemented through the network of area agencies on aging. These agencies can often provide information to consumers on available services and programs. Preliminary results from a demonstration program funded by the Robert Wood Johnson Foundation show the potential for a successful private pay market for home modifications using home health agencies. Under the demonstration, 45 percent of clients offered home repair services purchased them, and over half the revenues of participating agencies were derived from home maintenance and handyman services and installation of grab bars.

Recent surveys by AARP indicate that older persons are planning more for future housing needs and have become increasingly aware of the impact of health limitations on household activities. In response, the Association has published *The Do•Able Renewable Home: Making Your Home Fit Your Needs* and *The Perfect Fit: Creative Ideas for a Safe and Livable Home.* These booklets are available free and contain suggestions for home modifications; they list available assessment guides as well as sources of products and information. They also provide useful tips on hiring a contractor to complete repairs and modifications. (To order single copies, write: AARP Fulfillment, 601 E Street, NW, Washington, DC 20049. Indicate stock numbers D12470 and D14823.)

Reverse Mortgages

The National Affordable Housing Act of 1990 also contained a provision to expand a mortgage insurance demonstration for home equity conversion from 2,500 to 25,000 loans over five years. Home equity conversion allows older homeowners to use the equity in their homes to meet needs such as home repair and support services without having to move or sell the home.

At present, Federal Housing Administration (FHA)-insured reverse mortgages are being offered by private lenders in at least thirty states. Eligible borrowers must be over sixty-two, own and occupy a single family home with little or no mortgage balance, and maintain the home as a principal residence for the duration of the reverse mortgage. Counseling by an independent third party is required of every borrower prior to submitting a loan application. Four types of payment options are available under the FHA demonstration:

1. Term: Monthly payments to a homeowner for a fixed period

2. Tenure: Monthly payments to a homeowner for as long as at least one borrower remains in the home

3. Line of credit: Draws permitted on an as-needed basis up to the loan limit

4. Combination: A line of credit plus either form of monthly payment as described above

The FHA demonstration imposes a maximum loan amount limit that ranges from $67,500 to $101,250 depending on geographic area. Insurance premiums, which are 2 percent of the loan amount, paid by the borrower at closing and 0.5 percent annually on the increasing loan balance, insure the loan and provide protection to both the lender and the borrower. Repayment is not due until the borrower dies, sells, or permanently moves from the home.

The program is not without flaws. Consumers are often shocked by the cost of reverse mortgages, as high as $9,000 on a loan of $125,000. Lenders, on the other hand, feel the origination fee is not high enough to cover their costs. In addition, the availability and quality of the required counseling has been uneven.

Recent data compiled from both public and private programs by the National Center for Home Equity Conversion indicate that the average reverse mortgage borrower is a single woman in her mid-seventies with an annual income of about $12,000.

According to the National Center for Home Equity Conversion, almost all reverse mortgage borrowers use their loan advances to pay property taxes or repair their homes. A recent survey of older homeowners by AARP found potential borrowers cite health needs and long-term care as the most likely reasons for considering a reverse mortgage.

The potential for increased use of home equity conversion is considerable. Nearly 25 percent of low-income older homeowners have at least $50,000 equity in their homes. Research has indicated that almost 75 percent of poor single homeowners age seventy-five and over could raise their incomes above the poverty line by converting home equity into spendable income.

Until recently, reverse mortgage lending has been mostly a public sector activity. These programs often place limits on the use of funds or the amount of the loans. For example, owners of high-valued properties cannot receive as high a payment, either monthly or on a lump sum basis, from an FHA-insured loan as they might from other private or public sector programs. However, the reverse mortgage industry is poised for major expansion. Private companies are now engaged in raising capital through public stock offerings, securing of debt by institutional investors, and negotiation with major pension funds to finance reverse mortgages for their members. In addition, federally insured mortgages are expected to be offered shortly by multistate lenders on both coasts and new regional lenders. AARP recently issued a model state statute on reverse mortgages to encourage additional lending by state housing finance agencies.

Neighborhood Environment and Alternative Housing Options

Most older households are choosing to reside in their current homes and are staying in these homes until late in life. However, the housing stock and land use patterns of suburban communities, where most older people now live, were not intended for an aging population. Large single family homes can be difficult and expensive to maintain. Zoning ordinances and subdivision regulations often define as "incompatible" the small neighborhood retail and commercial establishments that older residents find convenient and reduce their dependence on the automobile. Further, these regulations tend to exclude multifamily housing and the use of alternative housing forms such as shared housing, accessory apartments, manufactured housing, and ECHO units.

Diversity of housing options, accessibility to retail and social services, personal security, proximity to family members and close friends, and availability of assistance with household maintenance and repairs are characteristics of neighborhoods that work successfully for older residents. Fortunately, workable strategies are available for helping existing communities create a supportive environment for increasing numbers of older residents.

Regulatory Reform and Community Planning

Former U.S. Department of Housing and Urban Development (HUD) Secretary Jack Kemp appointed an Advisory Commission on Regulatory Barriers to Affordable Housing, which produced the report "Not in My Backyard," and it has rekindled debate over the purpose and effect of local zoning and other land use regulations. Senior advocates have noted that the impact of zoning on senior housing options and community improvements is often a two-way street. Some "age inclusive zoning" permitting older homeowners to construct accessory apartments or establishing "retirement community districts" achieve a legitimate public purpose and have been upheld by the courts. Other restrictions such as those related to density and parking requirements, restrictions on mixed uses, housing types, or occupancy by unrelated persons can create obstacles. For example, parking requirements established when a neighborhood housed younger working couples or families with children who own more autos than older households, can add significantly to development costs of senior housing, since more land is needed to provide the required (and unnecessary) parking spaces. Similarly, density requirements can make construction of housing for older adults economically unfeasible. Research by the American Planning Association indicates that allowing developers greater flexibility in meeting local zoning and planning requirements can be important in reducing housing costs.

An additional impediment is the narrow definition of family in many local ordinances, which tends to exclude nontraditional households and prevents the conversion of elderly owned single-family homes into shared residences and group homes. These ordinances often exclude group residences from residential neighborhoods most suitable for older persons. However, a number of landmark cases in both the U.S. Supreme Court and various state courts have undermined the legal basis for such restrictive definitions. In addition, the Fair Housing Act of 1988 has strengthened the rights of the disabled, including older disabled persons, to equal access to housing.

Meeting the needs of a growing population of older residents is often a new activity for local governments. Community planning activities such as revisions of local comprehensive land use plans and development of comprehensive housing affordability strategies (CHAS) can be one avenue for making needed changes in zoning, land use, and housing policies. Under the CHAS process, communities are required to assess regulatory barriers to affordable housing and develop action plans to remedy such barriers. The recent AARP report entitled "A Change for the Better" provides a number of recommendations for senior advocates to become involved in the community planning process. In addition, AARP has published a model local ordinance for ECHO housing, a planning guide for local elected officials and housing advocates, and a number of zoning related reports dealing with shared residences, ECHO units, and accessory apartments.

Adaptive Reuse

Older structures such as closed schools can often be refurbished to serve as housing and/or service centers for older persons. Such conversions are particularly useful in suburban jurisdictions, because they are centrally located in neighborhoods composed almost entirely of single-family residences. Abandoned factories, hotels, and hospitals in urban areas can often service a similar purpose. Historic structures have an additional advantage of being eligible for a number of federal and state tax credits. A survey by the U.S. Conference of Mayors noted that nearly 150 cities had completed or started adaptive reuse projects for older persons.

Accessory Apartments

Accessory apartments are independent living units built into or attached to an existing single-family home. At most they share an entrance, yard, and parking. Accessory apartments may be an appropriate housing option for an older person. Older homeowners may wish to continue living in their current residences but would benefit from having tenants to provide additional income and assistance with household maintenance, chores, and security. Accessory apartments promote independence, privacy, and extended family living by allowing homeowners to live adjacent to, but separate from, tenants who may be related.

At an average cost of $16,500, some older homeowners may not be able to afford construction of an accessory apartment.

However, the major barrier to greater use of accessory apartments are restrictive zoning ordinances and covenants in deeds. A number of localities are now permitting accessory units to be constructed by older homeowners.

Shared Housing

Shared housing refers to two or more unrelated persons living in the same housing unit, sharing living space and expenses. According to the National Shared Housing Resource Center, some 2 million persons are sharing homes. Approximately one-third of those sharing residences are older persons.

Home sharing has the advantage of allowing persons with limited incomes to remain in their home communities while making efficient use of the existing housing stock. According to the Shared Housing Resource Center, some five hundred matching agencies now exist to assist homeowners and prospective tenants. A recent national survey of older households indicates that over one-fourth of older persons have shared a home with an unrelated adult, and nearly one-half would consider some form of home sharing. One difficulty with this living arrangement is finding a partner who is compatible. However, as mentioned earlier, the major obstacle to wider utilization of home sharing is local zoning regulations. AARP publishes *Consumer's Guide to Homesharing,* which provides guidelines for developing a home share lease.

ECHO Units

ECHO units are small, manufactured homes that can be installed in the back or side yard of an existing single-family residence and removed when no longer needed. ECHO units are specially designed for older and disabled persons and are especially attractive to persons who wish to remain independent but live closer to supportive family members or friends. Such units are much less costly than traditional housing units and allow the owner to extend current financial assets, including equity in an existing home. However, the concept has only been attempted experimentally in the United States. ECHO units often encounter the same regulatory barriers placed on manufactured and modular housing. In 1985 AARP issued a model ordinance designed to assist localities in modifying their existing statutes to accommodate ECHO housing.

The National Affordable Housing Act of 1990 included a provision to permit the use of Section 202 funds to finance the purchase of ECHO units. However, HUD has not issued regulations to implement the provision.

Independent Retirement Housing, Congregate Housing, and Assisted Living Facilities

Popular with many of today's over-fifty set (especially empty nesters) are self-contained apartments designed for the independent, active adult (single or couple). Mainly found in urban and metropolitan areas, these are typically midrise building of one hundred to three hundred units. The apartments are moderately priced, but offer no additional services, as do congregate housing and assisted living facilities.

Congregate housing developments provide some communal services in addition to the basic independent housing units. These may include communal areas for socializing, and help with certain daily activities such as cleaning and shopping. Communal dining for one or two meals a day is a central feature of congregate housing. A variation is the congregate care facility, which adds some direct personal care. In most cases, congregate residents must be mobile and not bedridden.

Assisted living is similar to congregate housing and has become increasingly popular with people who have some disabilities, need a safe and secure environment, but who lead a fairly active lifestyle that may include driving, vacation travel, and the ability to cook and do light housekeeping. Many assisted living units are like independent retirement apartment buildings with the addition of congregate meals, the option to cook for oneself in a small kitchen featured in each unit, emergency on-call systems, communal entertainment and educational programs, and some transportation services. Again, there are variations, and some assisted living facilities include personal care services related to dressing, washing, and cleaning.

These three types of housing and their variants reflect the wide diversity of lifestyle and health situations among older people. The larger number of post-fifty individuals means a greater market for new types of housing that more appropriately align with personal situations. We can expect an even broader array of housing options in the future.

Over 2 million older persons, 6 percent of older households, live in manufactured housing, more commonly referred to as "mobile homes." According to HUD older households account for 23 percent of all households residing in this type of housing.

Manufactured Housing

An average retail price of $19,800 for a new single section and $36,600 for a new multisection home makes manufactured housing particularly attractive to retired persons. Many older persons also enjoy the close-knit atmosphere and amenities of some manufactured home communities developed specifically for older persons.

While over 90 percent of older mobile home households own their homes, over half rent a site in a mobile home park. Park management practices have become a major political issue in state legislatures. Without oversight, the unique combination of home ownership and site tenancy can result in a number of unfair practices, including frequent and excessive rent increases, "tie-ins" between home sales and park rentals, excessive and unreasonable fees and park rules, and inadequate park maintenance.

Older mobile home park residents are particularly vulnerable to increases in park rental fees and other costs associated with mobile home park living, because of their limited financial resources, increased medical costs, and the rising costs of maintaining an older home. According to the latest American Housing Survey in 1989, 43 percent of older households residing in manufactured homes have annual incomes below $10,000, and 80 percent have incomes below $20,000.

Unlike site-built housing, manufactured homes must be transported and installed at the intended site of consumer use. Many homes are improperly installed by dealers or subcontract installers. According to the National Conference of States on Building Codes and Standards (NCSBCS), improper installation is a significant problem and can lead to major structural failure. However, only thirty states have an installation standard, and these are inadequately enforced. NCSBCS and the Manufactured Housing Institute recently formed a task force to develop a certification program for installers.

Local zoning commissions have often excluded or relegated manufactured housing to less desirable and nonresidential sites. Some local communities exclude manufactured housing by regulating items not addressed by federal construction standards. Prohibitions on single siting of homes effectively exclude the less costly single-wide homes that might be suitable as ECHO units for older persons. Many states have attempted to eliminate such requirements by passing special legislation. As of 1989, twenty-two states have enacted statutes prohibiting discriminatory zoning practices.

Since 1976 the federal government has established construction and safety standards for manufactured housing. However, the states play an important role in implementing the program by acting as design and production inspection agencies and investigating consumer complaints. In 1990 Congress authorized a National Commission on Manufactured Housing to review the need for additional and revised standards and recommend

SNAPSHOT

"Retirement never occurred to me. I need to be active, doing something, feeling that I can make a difference, even as little as it might be. How could I retire? I wouldn't know what to do!"

Labor and consumer administrator Esther Peterson was born in 1906 in Provo, Utah, to a Mormon family, attended Brigham Young University, and majored in physical education. After two years of teaching in Utah, Peterson attended Columbia University for her master's degree. This is where she met her husband, Oliver Peterson, then a sociology student and a socialist.

Through him, Peterson became involved in the labor movement, volunteering for the YWCA's industrial department and the National Consumers' League in Boston and teaching at Bryn Mawr Summer School for Women Workers. From the early 1930s to 1961 Peterson worked for the International Ladies Garment Workers Union, was the assistant director of education for the Amalgamated Clothing Workers, and was the legislative representative for the industrial union department of the American Federation of Labor and Congress of Industrial Organization. Nine years of this period she spent overseas with her husband, who was a foreign service labor attache, and raised four children.

As a lobbyist in Washington Peterson knew Senator John F. Kennedy. When Kennedy came to the White House, he appointed her director of the Women's Bureau of the Labor Department. She organized the President's Commission on the Status of Women and established Status of Women Commissions in every state in the country. Then Kennedy appointed

Peterson assistant secretary of labor, a position she kept when Lyndon Johnson took office. He also made Peterson his special assistant for consumer affairs, but as her opinions on consumer issues were controversial, she resigned from the consumer post in 1967 to work at the Labor Department full-time.

During the Nixon administration, Peterson worked for Giant Food Corp., a supermarket chain in the region around Washington, D.C., where she established many reforms, including open dating, unit pricing, nutritional and ingredient labeling, and safety programs. When Jimmy Carter became president in 1976, he asked Peterson, at seventy, to resume her previous office as special assistant for consumer affairs. She convinced President Carter to reauthorize the Consumer Product Safety Commission and to sign an executive order restricting the export of hazardous products banned in the United States, which the Reagan administration revoked a few short weeks after its institution.

Out of the White House again, Peterson hosted television and radio shows on consumer issues for two years, then worked at the United Nations as a volunteer lobbyist. Once again at the forefront of the battle for consumer affairs, she hopes the fight will "go global." Peterson predicts, "The international consumer movement is going to be a new big force, just like the labor movement has been and the women's movement." Peterson's latest project is a Code of Conduct for multinational corporations. She also moderates between industry and consumer disputes, most recently the insurance industry and the manufactured housing business.

On the subject of growing older, Peterson reveals: "I didn't realize at a young enough age, how important the financial aspects were. If I had, I would have done certain things differently. Most women don't realize that their husbands may die earlier than they do. As a result they're less well-prepared than they should be to manage their own affairs."

—*Lydia Brontë*

improvements in the current system of inspection and enforcement. Issues before the commission are expected to include improved energy efficiency standards and strengthening warranty protections, service, and installation requirements.

A Continuing care retirement community (CCRC) offers a combination of residential, personal, and health care services. These services are secured by a contract usually requiring a substantial entrance fee and a monthly payment. In return, the CCRC facility guarantees fulfillment of the resident's housing and service needs for the term of the contract. The duration of the contract and extent of services may vary considerably. Some facilities extend lifetime contracts and offer a full range of services, including nursing care. Others provide a much more limited menu of services. CCRCs are often attractive because they offer potential residents psychological and financial security and a wide range of services in a single location.

Approximately seven hundred CCRCs are in operation, and about 10 percent have been built since 1986. Fees and charges can be expensive, with entrance fees ranging from $40,000 to $200,000 and monthly charges from $400 to $1,500. Because of the unpredictability of health care costs, many facilities are moving away from the total life care concept toward a more limited array of services.

The CCRC concept does entail some risks for potential residents. More than 10 percent of all facilities have gone bankrupt or experienced extreme financial difficulties. A review of 1983 data from 109 facilities indicates that as many as one-third exhibited either a negative net income or negative net worth profile.

Thirty states have enacted legislation to regulate the financial management of CCRCs. Regulations generally address reserve requirements, refund policies, escrow accounts, marketing, audits, and financial procedures. Many of the statutes, however, rely primarily on consumer disclosure to regulate industry practices, and regulators often lack staff and oversight authority. Therefore, it is extremely important for prospective residents to carefully review the contract prior to signing and seek the advice of a competent independent financial adviser.

CCRCs meeting strict national standards for financial practices and quality care can apply for accreditation by the Continuing Care Accreditation Commission (CCAC). Established by the American Association of Homes for the Aging, the CCAC maintains a list of accredited facilities.

**Table 1: Advantages and Disadvantages
of Selected Alternative Housing Options**

A = Advantages   D = Disadvantages

Accessory Apartments
A   • Provide additional income for older homeowners
D   • Initial construction cost to homeowners

A   • Provide companionship and security
D   • Neighborhood concern about lowered property values

A   • Increase the supply of affordable rental housing
D   • Have zoning restraints

A   • Provide personal support services
D   • Are possibly in violation of housing and building codes

Board and Care Homes
A   • Provide a homelike environment
D   • Are not licensed or concerned with standards and treatment of residents

A   • Afford fragile, isolated older adults opportunity to interact with others
D   • Often lack trained owners/operators

A   • Are economical
D   • Have few planned social activities

Congregate Housing Structures
A   • Provide basic support services that can extend independent living
D   • Often oversee the needs of tenants, promoting dependency

A   • Reduce social isolation
D   • Expensive to build and operate

A   • Provide physical and emotional security
D   • Those without kitchen facilities restrict tenants' independence
D   • Expensive for most older adults without subsidy

Elder Cottages, Granny Flats
A   • Facilitate older persons receiving support from younger family members
D   • Potential to lower property values

A   • Provide the option to remain in individual home

D   • Attitude of and impact on neighborhood

A   • Are smaller housing units, less expensive to operate

D   • Concerns about housing and building code violations

Home Equity Conversion

A   • Converts lifetime investment into usable income

D   • Risk that homeowner will live longer than term of loan

A   • Allows older adults with marginal incomes to remain in familiar surroundings

D   • Homes of lower value (often type owned by older adults) may not provide monthly payments large enough to be worth cost of loan

A   • Can be used to finance housing expenses, e.g., make necessary repairs, utilities, taxes

D   • Reluctance by homeowner to utilize due to lack of information, concern for lien on property, and/or impact on estate for heirs

Life Care Facilities

A   • Offer prepaid health care

D   • Are too expensive for many older adults

A   • Provide security and protection against inflation and financially draining illness

D   • Questionable protections should the facility go out of business

A   • Provide a wide range of social activities with health support systems

D   • Older person receives no deed to property

D   • Provide no guarantees that monthly payments will not rise

D   • Location is usually rural, isolated from community services

Shared Housing Facilities

A   • Less expensive due to shared costs for household operators

D   • Problems with selection of individual to share home

A   • Offer companionship, security

D   • Reduced privacy

A   • Promote intergenerational cooperation and understanding

D   • Do not meet medical and personal problems

A   • More extensive use of existing housing

D   • Added income may mean owner is no longer eligible for public benefits

A   • Program inexpensive to operate

D   • City zoning ordinances may prohibit shared housing

Source: Katz, Rosalyn, Ph.D. *A Manual of Housing Alternatives for the Elderly.* Vol. 1. Pittsburgh, PA: Health and Welfare Planning Association; American Association of Retired Persons, *Housing Choices for Older Homeowners.* West Virginia Commission on Aging. Reprinted with permission from *Generations* (American Society on Aging, 833 Market St., Suite 512, San Francisco, CA 94103: 1992).

Older Renters and the Production of Rental Housing

Just as the demographic and economic profile of older Americans has changed, the profile of older renters has changed significantly in recent years. According to data from the AHS, older renters became a great deal older and poorer over the decade of the 1980s. Between 1980 and 1989, the number of renters age sixty-five to seventy-four actually declined by 4.6 percent, while the number of renters age seventy-five and over increased by 21.2 percent.

During the same period of time, older renters became dramatically poorer—the number of older renters with incomes under $5,000 (1987 dollars) rose by 86.7 percent, while the number of older renters with incomes over $5,000 declined by 5.8 percent. Older renters with incomes over $35,000 declined 41.5 percent during the decade. As a result, 60 percent of older renters spent more than 30 percent of their incomes—the federal standard for excessive rent—on rent.

The profile data on older renters indicate a high needs-driven market—largely concentrated among the oldest, poorest, and frailest of the old, and the private market and federal housing programs have made some attempts to meet the needs of older renters.

The Private Market

The production of any multifamily rental housing by the private market in the United States has been stymied in recent years by the combined effects of changing tax policy, earlier overproduction, wary credit markets, a slowly developing secondary market for multifamily mortgages, the withdrawal of federal credit enhancement, and the collapse of the financial institutions that have provided mortgages for multifamily housing. Tax advantages for investment in rental housing contributed to an overproduction of rental housing in the early 1980s—especially for rental housing geared to the relatively well-off. When those tax advantages were largely removed by the Tax Reform Act of 1986, investment in rental housing declined dramatically. Savings and loan associations, traditionally the major mortgage originators for multifamily housing, have decreased their loan activities—in no small part because of the enormous losses suffered by the industry during the late 1980s. The federal government, which insured over 30 percent of multifamily mortgages at the beginning of the decade, retreated in the face of losses to the FHA mortgage insurance fund to insure only 6 percent of multifamily rental housing by the end of the decade.

The earlier overproduction may have moderated rent increases for renters with middle and upper incomes but did very little to ameliorate a precipitous decline in rental housing affordable to low-income renters in recent years. Between 1974 and 1985 the number of unsubsidized rental units in the private market that were affordable to a family with poverty-level income declined by one-third—a loss of 2.9 million such units. This loss can be explained in roughly equal measures by the deterioration of units no longer inhabitable and the upgrading of units that are no longer affordable to low-income families.

The growth of rental housing among the oldest and poorest of the old indicates that the market is highly needs driven. When coupled with a widely expressed preference for staying put, the general experience with rental housing for older persons is that consumers are wary and move only when the need to move is driven by strong health or economic concerns. Combined with the factors just mentioned, which have dampened the production of all kinds of rental housing, the private market for rental housing for older persons has been very slow in recent years.

Federally Subsidized Rental Housing

In the face of dwindling rental housing resources affordable to low-income older persons on the private market, federally subsidized housing has played an increasingly important role. Over time, federal housing assistance has been increasingly targeted to older renters for three reasons:

1. Older adult renters have had lower incomes, fewer assets, and poorer housing conditions than nonelderly renters.

2. Long-term residents of subsidized housing programs "aged in place."

3. Several new programs were created to serve older people, in part because older people have been viewed as the more "deserving" poor.

However, the range of federal housing programs serving older people is often bewildering for the average layperson seeking housing assistance. In any given market area, the consumer is likely to find federally subsidized elderly housing projects operated by for-profit developers, nonprofit sponsors, or public agencies—each with different facilities, services, and even eligibility criteria. The only way to understand the differences among the programs is to place them in historical context. Since housing projects typically operate under long-term contracts that define their amenities and eligibility standards, to understand programmatic differences requires understanding the evolution of American housing policy.

The first federal housing program to assist low-income renters was the public housing program. Created by the 1937 Housing Act, the public housing program provides housing owned and operated by local public housing authorities (PHAs). Federal grants to local PHAs finance construction and provide annual supplements for operating expenses and modernization.

No distinct program for older adults has ever been authorized under the public housing program, but public housing authorities used the 1956 eligibility definition of "elderly family" to begin a major construction program of elderly projects—the first of which opened in 1962. HUD estimates that 45 percent of the units of public housing—over 500,000 units—are currently occupied older adults, making public housing the largest single housing program serving older people in the United States.

In 1959 Congress created the first housing program specifically designed for older adults, known widely by its section number in the National Housing Act, "Section 202." Section 202 originally provided direct, low-interest loans to nonprofit sponsors (mostly religious) to provide housing targeted to moderate-income tenants who were ineligible for public housing. Under current financing arrangements, Section 202 sponsors receive construction grants and operating subsidies and must use the same very low-income eligibility standards as public housing. While Section 202 projects generally have more amenities, such as congregate spaces, than elderly public housing, residents who have not been able to function independently have generally been expected to move on to more supportive settings such as nursing homes and board and care homes. The National Affordable Housing Act of 1990 (NAHA) clarified the ability of Section 202 to serve very frail older persons and authorized, for the first time, funding for a services coordinator and 15 percent of the cost of services to frail individuals. A total of over 240,000 units of Section 202 housing have been built to date.

Mortgage insurance programs to stimulate the private production of multifamily housing were enacted during the 1950s and 1960s (especially Sections 221, 231, and 236). Though not specifically targeted to older adults (except Section 231), each of these programs produced a disproportionate number of projects for older people. A rural counterpart to Section 202 was established by the Farmer's Home Administration's Section 515 program, a program that has since been expanded to all multifamily housing but continues to finance a large number of elderly projects.

According to the U.S. Congress, single individuals were not eligible for public housing until 1956 when a definition of "elderly family" was enacted to include single older individuals as eligible residents of public housing.

The Housing Act of 1974 created the Section 8 rental assistance program, which originally could be used either as "tenant-based assistance" through certificates issued by PHAs to individual renters, or as "project-based assistance" to subsidize the construction or rehabilitation of multifamily projects. While the tenant-based assistance tended to be used by older people roughly in proportion to their numbers in the general population, as much as 70 percent of the project-based assistance may have been used for elderly projects.

The most recent approach to funding housing projects has been through the tax code. Enacted as part of the Tax Reform Bill of 1986, the low-income housing tax credit (LIHTC) has produced over 100,000 units of low- and moderate-income housing per year for the past three years. How much of the tax credit has been used for elderly housing is unknown at this point. Finally, NAHA created the HOME program, a block grant to state and local governments to be used for a wide range of housing purposes, but the first funds from this program have yet to be awarded.

The sum of these programs represents a substantial invest-ment in older adult housing. Though no government agency can give an accurate count, the number of federally funded older adult housing projects probably exceeds 20,000 nationwide. In all, over 1.5 million older Americans are served by federal housing subsi-dies. In 1988 older households represented 36 percent of the renter households receiving federal assistance, even though they made up only 27 percent of the low-income renter households in the country, a significant targeting of housing subsidies to low-income older renters.

Transportation Issues

Fueled by congestion, energy costs, environmental con-cerns, and limited fiscal resources, the visibility of the transporta-tion issue has risen dramatically in recent years. As the country's median age rises, the relationship between older transportation users and our transportation systems and services is also receiving increased attention. Moreover, demographic trends relating to population, longevity, place of residence, and personal safety suggest that new challenges will likely surface in the near future.

The personal mobility associated with transportation has a major impact on the basic quality of life of older people. As people age and eventually retire, most do not move into retirement communities, where compact development and the physical design promote easy circulation. Rather, most people age in the urban, suburban, and rural communities in which they worked and have lived for years. In these communities, they continue to depend on the automobile as the primary transportation (including rides from friends and family) and public transit as the secondary means.

The Mobility Continuum

Transportation services which meet the mobility needs of older persons exist along a continuum. At one end, people enjoy the freedom and independence of unlimited and unrestricted driving in a private automobile. Over time, however, many are likely to experience difficulty with driving due to functional decline and will eventually discontinue driving. On the other end, consequently, people are totally dependent on public and private transit services.

An often-cited problem with transportation services for second middle-agers is that movement along the mobility continuum does not occur very smoothly. For instance, current driver testing, screening, and licensing practices are based largely on chronological age rather than functional age. Few states offer a driver's license that is specially suited to the particular needs of a driver. Oftentimes, safe and capable drivers are tested more strenuously because they are older, while old and young drivers most at risk for accidents continue driving. In other words, the current system does not allow for the individual variability that occurs as people age, and tests, for the most part, do not accurately predict who will have accidents. Another often-cited problem is that transit services for the non-work trips of older suburban dwellers are scarce. And many people are simply unaware of the transit services that are available.

Other problems exist: (1) the roadway system is inadequate to accommodate the changing functional capabilities of a growing number of road users; (2) transit services are uncoordinated and expensive to provide; and (3) transportation facilities, including vehicles and terminals, are not physically accessible to the mobility impaired. In many ways the transportation system has been developed to accommodate a young, working, auto-oriented society. Over time, an increasing median age of the population and the number of retirees will necessitate some change in this approach.

Transportation Mandate

Most older people consider transportation to be one of their greatest needs. According to surveys of older people in states such as Alabama, Colorado, Oklahoma, Pennsylvania, and Rhode Island, transportation is the service most requested of social service providers by older people. Transportation is a critical link to nutrition and health care facilities and shopping, as well as to social, work, recreation, community, and adult day-care activities. Mobility is also critical to a person's independence, well-being, and overall quality of life. The isolation imposed by restricted mobility can adversely impact physical, mental, and spiritual health.

Other recent legislation and research demonstrate the increased importance of the transportation issue:

- A 1988 landmark report by the National Academy of Sciences concerning the mobility of older Americans ("Transportation in an Aging Society: Improving Mobility and Safety for Older Persons")

- The 1990 passage of the Americans with Disabilities Act (ADA), a landmark civil rights law guaranteeing access to public facilities, including transportation

- The 1991 establishment of the National Eldercare Institute on Transportation by the Administration on Aging to address the mobility needs of at-risk elders

Trends

The advent of the automobile during this century has dramatically affected older persons. Consider this story of a granddaughter offering to drive her grandmother to the store. Getting in, she needs to adjust the seat forward. "Grandma," she asks, "do you always sit this far back?" Her ninety-year-old grandmother replies: "Well, I always did like a long stirrup."

While most second middle-agers and those older probably did not grow up on horseback, more likely in a Ford or Chevy, the vast majority will continue to drive well into life. For example, almost 90 percent of men and 53 percent of women over seventy continue to drive. And 95 percent of men and 82 percent of women fifty-five to fifty-nine are drivers who average 12,595 miles each year, according to a U.S. Department of Transportation 1990 report. With more people living well into their eighties and baby boomers entering their fifties, the mature drive is a trend that is here to stay.

Drivers

In 1970 most older Americans lived in central cities. By 1980 the trend had changed; a majority of persons over sixty-five lived in suburban communities. By 1990 that majority as well as the proportion of the general population living in suburban communities had grown. The low densities and physical design of suburban communities promote the use of automobiles, not public transit. As older Americans continue to age in place, their transportation needs will move along the transportation continuum. Also in 1990 more than 22 million people over the age of sixty-five were licensed to drive, according to the Federal Highway Administration. Over the coming decades, the number of drivers over sixty-five is expected to increase. On average, 85 percent of Americans eligible to drive do so. If present trends continue, it is estimated that as many 50 million persons over the age of sixty-five could be driving by 2020.

Transit Users

As an alternative to driving, transit provides mobility to many. It is estimated that more than 50 percent of those over eighty use transit services. It is also estimated that the number of nondrivers, or potential transit users, will grow to 14 million by 2020. There are more than five thousand transit service providers in the United States. In 1990, those systems provided over 9 billion passenger miles, 77 million of which were demand-responsive trips (a segment certain to grow if the transit-dependent, frail elderly population increases as expected). In addition, human service (as opposed to transportation service) providers, such as area agencies on aging, provided more than 63 million trips.

Pedestrians and Cyclists

Another transportation option available to many older persons is walking. Most walking trips are for social, recreational, or health reasons. Americans over sixty-five years walk about twenty-eight miles per year. Walking accounts for one-tenth of all trips taken. Generally, people with lower incomes who live in central cities make larger numbers of walking trips. Also, shopping trips constitute the vast majority of destinations for pedestrians, particularly those over eighty-five years. Far fewer people use bicycles as a primary means of transportation, and little information exists on the level of use. Nevertheless, to increase the availability and use of all modes of transportation, greater attention will need to be given to the environmental barriers, such as no sidewalks, inadequate curb cuts, rapid crosswalk signal timing, and driver awareness and consideration of pedestrians.

How Aging Impacts Transportation Choices

As a process, aging is highly complex and varies tremendously among individuals. Very often, age-related changes are confused with signs of specific diseases, and, to the degree that changes occur, it is not easy to attribute the source. Factors such as general health, heredity, lifestyle, and environment tend to have a greater influence on how one ages than age itself. Nonetheless, as people age, functional limitations are more likely to appear, and these can impact transportation choices greatly. Yet, people who reach sixty-five years of age can now expect to live into their eighties. Those over eighty-five are most likely to experience difficulty with the driving task and to use public transportation services.

In fact, many older drivers also report having to work harder at the driving task than their younger counterparts. Some commonly reported problems include traffic sign legibility, reduced night vision, turning, reaching, merging, and exiting. At

To increase the availability and use of all modes of transportation, greater attention will need to be given to barriers such as driver awareness and consideration of pedestrians.

least some of these problems can be attributed to the effects of normal, healthy aging. Regardless of the source, however, perceptual, cognitive, and physical changes can cause problems with driving.

Vision

Studies of the visual abilities of bus travelers show that factors such as static, dynamic, and low-illumination acuity, motion in depth, contrast sensitivity, glare recovery, target detection, and depth perception have been linked to accidents and to problems with reading schedules and identifying landmarks during bus travel. But as to car drivers, driver license agencies do not test for and transit providers do not consider many of these factors.

Hearing

Generally, people first lose the ability to hear high-pitched sounds. So sounds such as sirens, horns, whistles, and announcements on buses may be obscured. There is also evidence that hearing is correlated with selected attention. However, no definitive research has linked these problems to driving performance. Further, no license agency screens or tests drivers on these factors.

Cognition

In the driving environment the ability to attend, recognize, and respond to stimuli is crucial. There is a growing body of knowledge on how to assess a person's visual and cognitive abilities as they relate to attention and reaction—the concept is generally known as useful field of view—in the driving environment. Research has shown that performance on a battery of tests measuring useful field of view is correlated with factors other than chronological age.

Physical Agility

Physical agility tends to be limited as people age. The result can be slower, more cautious movements. Hence, the reported problems with reaching and turning, and boarding and exiting.

All of these aging factors having been considered, there is still great variability among older people, and none of these changes occur in the same ways or to the same degrees in everyone.

Accidents

Any reported or actual problems are tempered by several positive influences, which frequently include: increased behind-the-wheel experience and applied decision making (exposure to and practice with driving's many circumstances); cautious approaches to driving situations (more fully recognizing the significance of the driving dynamic); and greater ability to control when driving must occur (less bondage to work-related timetables and destinations). The net result is a category of drivers with favorable overall accident frequency rates when compared to their younger counterparts. This comparison indicates the value of experience, caution, and ability to limit exposure to accidents in high-risk situations. However, older drivers' accident experience increases when exposure is considered. Persons sixty-five and older typically travel far shorter distance than others—an average of 12.2 miles per day as compared to 27.5 for those younger than sixty-five.

As a group, older drivers and pedestrians are more vulnerable to injury or death in traffic accidents than other age groups. For instance, older drivers have proportionately fewer car crashes than their younger counterparts but are more likely to be killed or seriously injured. Between 1980 and 1989 the number of people killed in auto accidents dropped more than 8 percent. At the same time, drivers over sixty-five years experienced a 43 percent increase in their death rate. Of the 8,000 annual pedestrian fatalities, more than 1,800—22.7 percent—are older persons. Pedestrian accidents are exceeded only by falls and motor vehicle accidents as a cause of accidental death. As mentioned, older people represent 13 percent of the population, but are involved in only 7.7 percent of the 70,000 annual pedestrian accidents. Again, the higher rates among older drivers and pedestrians compared with their younger counterparts most likely reflects the higher susceptibility to injury and greater likelihood of complications following injuries.

As people age, they need more information about how functional impairments can affect the driving task and how to compensate for any deficiencies. Through better self-awareness of abilities and limitations, older adults can more effectively regulate their travel and the circumstances in which they travel. In addition, older people and their families and caregivers need to understand whether the transportation system accommodates that change and how to insure that it is responsive. Education efforts should also note that mobility is not always dependent on driving and should offer more information about public transportation options.

Driver Education

Many organizations are active in older driver education, and the hope is that many others will become involved as well. AARP, the American Automobile Association, and National Safety Council each administer classroom refresher courses for drivers fifty and older. AARP's eight-hour defensive driving course, "55 Alive," reaches several hundred thousand older drivers each year with information about the aging process, interacting with traffic, safety restraints, accident prevention measures, other road users, and deciding about when not to drive.

The growing body of knowledge regarding medical conditions and pharmaceuticals and their impacts on mobility provides greater opportunity for the medical community to participate in older driver and pedestrian education. Select physicians currently serve on medical advisory boards for state licensing agencies. All practitioners (doctors, nurses, pharmacists) have increasing information from which to recognize individual capabilities, diagnose conditions, and make recommendations to older people and their families and caregivers.

Driver Licensing

There is little consistency among state driver license policies regarding older drivers. A few states require older drivers to take added tests or to renew more frequently (Alaska, Arizona, California, District of Columbia, Hawaii, Illinois, Indiana, Iowa, Louisiana, Maine, Maryland, New Hampshire, New Mexico, Oregon, Pennsylvania, Rhode Island, and Utah), but most treat all drivers equally. For the most part, the ages designated by these policies are arbitrary. Chronological age alone is no predictor of driving performance.

Few states are prepared to assess meaningfully the abilities and needs of drivers as they age. At this juncture, there is no cost-effective and efficient battery of tests—states are already cutting costs and reducing lines at motor vehicle agencies. There is growing evidence that assessing functional age might be a better predictor of driver performance than chronological age. Some drivers at age seventy-five or older are as capable as ever, making up in judgment and attitude whatever they may have lost in sensory abilities and reaction time. Others, however, may likely contribute to the increase in accidents that is well documented for those over seventy-five. Between these two extremes are people who can safely drive, given a license that is compatible with their needs.

Graduated Driver Licensing

Greater use of accurate functional assessment tests could give rise to more flexible driver licenses, such as graduated licenses. A graduated license requires the holders to restrict their driving in some well-specified way, such as by type of vehicle, time of day, destination, or routes. A few states, such as Oregon and Washington, have developed effective graduated driver license programs. In these programs, problem drivers regardless of age are identified through police reports, insurance companies, personal physician, family, or others, and through accident and violation records or a report from an examiner at license renewal or reexamination.

Once identified, drivers can either take a regular reexamination or go through a special reexamination evaluation program. In the latter, medical history and medications are assessed; special reaction-time, vision, and road tests are administered. Once tests are completed, the driver could continue as an unrestricted driver; a driver improvement course or rehabilitation could be mandated; periodic medical examinations required; a graduated license issued; or driving privilege revoked. More and more states are looking seriously at functional assessments and graduated driver licenses.

Transit

As people age, drive less, and rely on (or choose to use) transit more, not only will systems need to be physically adapted to accommodate new users, but, more importantly, transit service providers will need to look at delivering new services that are more responsive to the mobility needs of well and frail elderly. Furthermore, existing and potential transit users and the families, caregivers, and representatives must be empowered with information about public transportation options. Before a discussion of transit service can begin, it is important to consider the impact that the Americans with Disabilities Act is having on service delivery.

Americans with Disabilities Act

The ADA was signed into law July 26, 1990. Modeled after the Civil Rights Act and Title V of the Rehabilitation Act, the ADA prohibits discrimination against people with disabilities in employment, public services, public accommodations, transportation, and telecommunications. Disability under the ADA is defined as:

1. Having a physical or mental impairment that substantially limits that person in some major life activity

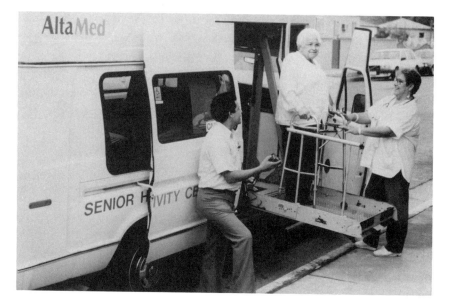

As people drive less, transit service providers will need to look at delivering new services that are more responsive to the mobility needs of well and frail elderly.

2. Having a record of such an impairment that causes discrimination based upon a past disability, or

3. Being regarded as having an impairment because of physical appearance

Needless to say, many older persons are considered disabled under the ADA, and this has many implications for transportation services. The ADA prohibits discrimination in transportation provided by public entities. Further, public entities that operate fixed route transportation systems are required to provide paratransit and other specialized transportation services; the intention is to furnish individuals with disabilities a level of service that is comparable to the level of transportation service provided to individuals without disabilities on the fixed route system.

The ADA also requires that new transportation equipment (buses) and that special transportation services, such as paratransit, be made available for those who cannot use mainline transportation. New transportation facilities must be accessible, and existing facilities must be retrofitted. Intercity and commuter rail coaches and stations must also be made accessible or retrofitted.

As the ADA is implemented, many older persons with disabilities are entitled to new and better services. At the same time, those without a disability are being forced to mainstream onto fixed route systems so that limited dollars can fund more expensive special transportation services. Note that the ADA is civil rights legislation and made no additional financial resources available for implementation. Although the ADA presents improved access and opportunity for some, others may be adversely impacted.

Transit Service: Key Terms and Descriptors

The transit programs described earlier finance a number of different kinds of transit services. These are some key terms and descriptors common in transit service:

Traditional transit services: These services include buses, rail, and commuter systems that primarily serve work trips in urban areas.

Fixed-route service: A bus service that operates on a regular route at specified intervals between common stops.

Paratransit: A general term for transit service that includes smaller vehicles, which are usually accessible to people with mobility impairments, and provides demand-responsive service to special populations, such as older adults and people with disabilities.

Demand-responsive services: Transit services available on a limited basis to special populations, such as older adults and disabled, which provide transit service at the request of the user; usually a telephone call and a reservation secures the service; also known as "dial-a-ride" service.

Subscription services: Demand-responsive services provided to a user on a regular basis, at specified dates and time, for the same purpose or destination, such as dialysis or shopping.

User-side subsidy: Reduced or free transit fares, provided through vouchers, tokens, or card systems, for use on taxis and paratransit service.

Supply-side subsidy: Financial operating or capital assistance provided to a government or nonprofit transit service provider; usually occurs in areas, such as rural locations, where providers are scarce and service is expensive.

Accessibility: This includes buses, vans, airplanes, trains, bus stops, transfer stations, and airports, which can accommodate a variety of sensory, cognitive, and physical impairments experienced by users.

Transit Demand

The problems with transit are availability, affordability, and accessibility. The need for the most demand-responsive transit services far outweighs the supply. One study estimates that 5.6 million people over sixty-five are without private transportation. The implication is that they rely on, but don't necessarily have access to, public transportation. The deregulation of the intercity bus industry has made the problem of public transportation particularly acute in rural portions of this country.

Approximately $100 million from all sources are spent annually on rural transit services. Because smaller populations do not support public transportation services, rural dwellers rely more heavily on their automobiles. Because of decreasing populations, other services are also decreasing, and rural people are being forced to travel longer distances to access medical care, shopping, and other activities.

Specialized Transit

Most communities deliver traditional specialized transit services, such as paratransit, demand-responsive, subscription, and taxicabs. There is usually a combination of all in each community. Although specialized transportation operators use more than 50,000 vehicles to meet mobility needs of the transit-dependent, many problems exist in urban areas. For instance, many services are located in places with no public transportation. Besides the rise in population of the transit-dependent, the low densities of most communities present a formidable barrier to greater transit use. Some communities are attempting to address this problem by creating new services.

Service Routes

One such form of transit is service routes. This service provides buses along regular routes, with specific stops and regular schedules—similar to fixed routes. But also it employs vehicles that are smaller than typical buses, fully accessible, routes planned to minimize walking, drivers sensitized to the needs of the riders, and travel to and from places of interest and need to older persons. The service is experiencing widespread use in Europe and is being piloted in the United States.

Given what is known about the population, housing patterns, and transportation opportunities, an increasing number of transportation planning decisions are made at the state, regional, and local levels. Participation in the decision-making process extends to those using the system. As the interests are broadened, meaningful community transportation must address needs assessment for older transportation users, older persons with disabilities, and frail elderly. Hopefully, middle-age and older adults themselves can become stronger advocates for present and future service needs.

Across the country more than 1,200 counties provided no transit services. Further, for every federal transit $1.00 spent on rural residents, $27.00 more are spent on their urban counterparts.

—*George Gaberlavage, M.A.; Don Redfoot, Ph.D.; Steve Lee*

Returning to school has become increasingly popular with midlife and mature adults. Education plays a new role in the flexible life course. For some who are still in the workforce, it means learning the latest computer applications, management techniques, or even a new language for an overseas assignment. For others, a master's degree in liberal arts serves as an evening renewal project to broaden one's horizons. For those who have left the world of paid employment, enrolling in one of the hundreds of new programs for older learners may mean the chance to explore a subject that was of great interest earlier in life but set aside because of the pressures of work and family obligations. Gaining knowledge, intellectual stimulation, and making new friends through common educational interest are all part of lifelong learning today.

Lifelong learning activities can be group-oriented or solitary. Many public libraries offer reader's advisory services to those who like to learn on their own. Libraries provide lists of recommended books (or records, tapes and CDs) on a variety of subjects. Computerized self-paced learning modules are available for purchase on everything from typing to symbolic logic. In many cities, people can join organizations of independent scholars that sponsor roundtable discussions for individuals who carry out scholarly studies and research while holding jobs outside the academic world.

In institutions of higher education, lifelong learning is often administered through departments of continuing education. Not uncommonly, these continuing education programs enroll more students and bring in more money than the traditional undergraduate and graduate programs. Education is simply not limited to the period of youth. Education adds vitality to life at any age.

Education involvement for retirement-age people may also provide new coping skills, ranging from learning how to mange financial affairs to finding more productive ways of communicating with adult children and grandchildren. Many programs in health promotion and physical fitness help to remain self-reliant, and maintain self-esteem, strengthen mind and body, and find channels for satisfying participation in the larger society.

Lifelong learning goes by several other names: adult education, continuing education, learning in retirement, and so on—all are types of learning opportunities across the life course. To understand how these programs came about, a little historical review is useful.

A Bit of History   Adult educational opportunities in the United States date back to the 1700s when coffee houses functioned as adult educational institutions, mainly for disseminating political propaganda. The potential for influencing the thinking of a larger number of adults was recognized by political parties such as the Whigs, who oftentimes owned the coffee houses. Many of the coffee houses in New York City also provided writing and reading materials for their customers.

The early colonial leaders believed that democracy depended on the educability of the citizenry, and that through widespread educational efforts, the public decision-making process could be improved. American statesman Benjamin Franklin, a great believer in this theory, established one of the first adult education activities in the colonies, called Junto. Established in 1727, Junto was a weekly study group of twelve people who met to discuss community and social issues and was responsible for the formation of the first local lending libraries. Junto lasted for thirty years. Almost one hundred years later a lecture series, given the name Lyceum (in ancient tradition, an association providing public lectures, concerts, and entertainment) was established. The Lyceum series introduced adult citizens residing in small towns and rural areas to scholarly knowledge. These lectures attempted to raise the educational levels of participants who had not completed an elementary level education. For well over one hundred years the lecture series brought intellectual stimulation to many of the rural areas of the country. Approximately fifty years later the Chautauqua movement began introducing adults to religious studies, liberal arts education, and the performing arts. Established at Lake Chautauqua, New York, in 1874 by the Methodist Episcopal Church, it was basically nondenominational and drew audiences from throughout the United States to the summer assembly tent performances. Similar "tent Chautauquas" were held across the country. Still in existence today, Chautauqua attracts thousands of older adults each year. The program offerings have expanded to include vocational/personal education and civic/community education as well as programming designed specifically for older adults.

In 1949 a Committee on Education for Aging was established under the Department of Adult Education of the National Education Association. In 1951 this committee became a part of the Adult Education Association of the U.S.A. For the first time in history, a descriptive book on educational programming for older adult learners, *Education for Later Maturity: A Handbook,* was developed by this committee. Yet, until the early 1950s, a cultural bias toward youth exerted a detrimental effect upon the growth of educational programs for older adults. An emphasis on youth was prevalent in the majority of publications in the field of education. From 1950 to 1960 only a few educational administrators were considering offering educational programs for older adults. The very few programs that were in operation were experimental in nature with no research base. In the early 1960s, gerontological researchers devoted considerable energy to examining links between aging and intellectual functioning. The combined empha-

Emergence of Older Adult Education

Midlife and mature adults gain knowledge and make new friends through common educational interests.

sis on the youth culture and research on age-related cognitive declines continued to have a negative impact upon attitudes toward older adult educational programs.

During this period, the trend that emerged for program planners was to segregate older learners because their integration in ongoing adult educational programs was deemed undesirable. Most practitioners pointed to the differences, not the similarities, between young and old.

By the mid-1960s small inroads were made in removing the educational bias toward the young while attitudes toward older adults began to change. For example, social workers trained during the 1940s and 1950s had been instructed to discourage reminiscing among older people because it was viewed as a form of pathology—the person denying or having lost contact with the present. However, between the late 1950s and early 1970s this view changed dramatically. The work of Pulitzer Prize–winning author (*Why Survive?*) and psychiatrist Robert Butler helped educators and social service providers recognize a universal "life review" process that occurs normally in mid and later life. The writings of Harvard-based developmental psychologist Erik Erikson helped them to understand the mature person's struggle to integrate life experiences into a coherent and meaningful whole.

These two tendencies could serve as the basis for reminiscence groups and educational programs that built on people's life stories. Some researchers and educators went even further, recognizing elements of wisdom and creativity in the life review process.

Many educators have addressed the importance of past experiences in enhancing the older adult's learning experience. Education was defined by American philosopher and educator John Dewey as the "continuous reconstruction of experience." Adult educator Malcolm Knowles further contended that life experience distinguishes child learning from adult learning.

A summary of the last forty years of older adult education can be found in philosopher and gerontologist Harry Moody's view of the changing attitudes toward older adults and the value of education in their lives. He identified four stages, each with its own underlying presupposition about older adult education held by professionals and educators. The first presupposition (stage one) or attitude is *rejection* of older adults. This attitude contends that since older people are socially obsolete, it would be a waste of time and financial resources to provide adult educational programs. The second stage emphasizes the problems and needs of older adults and suggests these must be altered by a change in public policy. Education is regarded as one among many *social services* for the dependent older adults. With an emphasis on providing access and opportunity, older adults passively receive services rather than learning the skills necessary to initiate new programs. Many social service programs lead to the segregation of older adults, because such programs are designed to keep older adults busy, rather than providing opportunities that will assist older adults in improving their lives. All of this changes in stage three, in which the *participation* view maintains that older adults should be encouraged to actively continue in the mainstream of community life and to develop self-sufficiency— the mind-set being that the older adult's skills and abilities become instrumental in helping them overcome personal problems as well as some of society's. *Self-actualization*, the fourth stage, emphasizes psychological growth and spiritual concerns as the major objective of educational programs for older adults. Based on humanistic psychologist Abraham Maslow's theory of the hierarchy of needs, self-actualization can only be realized through a combined psychological and spiritual quest for meaning and insight. Old age, being the last stage in the course of life, may be viewed as an attempt to explore the meaning of one's experiences and integrate an understanding of these experiences acquired throughout a lifetime.

One can find elements of all four stages in current practice, though variations often depend on the situation and functional status of older adults. Hence, self-actualization may be the predominant goal in programs for and with the well, mobile older adult, while a more therapeutic, social work approach may prevail in a nursing home setting. Nevertheless, poetry writing and creative dramatics courses are not uncommon in care centers.

National Policies and Older Adult Education

The change in societal attitudes has had significant impact on federal policies regarding the education of older adults. The first major development came with the creation of the Older Americans Act in 1965. This act established the Administration on Aging and provided needed funding for training and research at colleges and universities, which, in turn, opened the door for new educational opportunities for older adults and extended educational gerontology, work force training, and multidisciplinary graduate programs as well as research in addressing the needs of older adult learners.

Another departure from prevailing attitudes occurred in 1971 when the White House Conference on Aging advanced recommendations that paved the road for educational programming for older adults. The national event had significant impact on the attitudes of educators and gerontologists. Education received special attention at the conference, which called for increased funding and manpower to provide older adult educational programs in the private and public sector. The conference can best be summarized by the comments of educational gerontologist Howard Y. McCluskey: "Education is a basic right for all persons of all age groups. It is continuous and henceforth one of the ways of enabling older people to have a full and meaningful life and a means of helping them develop their potential as a resource for the betterment of society." The 1971 White House Conference on Aging served as a benchmark in the history of older adult education.

Although the expression "lifelong learning" has been in use for many years, it is only recently that the concept has been applied to the older adult learner.

COPYRIGHT BENJAMIN PORTER

Congress enacted the Older Americans Comprehensive Services Amendments of 1973 to strengthen the Older Americans Act. Under this act the Administration on Aging was reorganized under the U.S. Department of Health, Education, and Welfare, and the Federal Council on the Aging was created, as well as the National Information and Resource Clearinghouse for the Aging. Grants were awarded by the commissioner on aging to state governments for special library and education programs for older adults. Research in the field of aging and grants for training personnel to work with older adults was also encouraged by the commissioner on aging.

In addition to federal policies concerning older adult education, many states began to establish guidelines within their statutes to allow or require a waiver or reduction of tuition fees for older adults who are enrolled at a state-supported institution of higher education.

The private sector also became involved in the educational pursuits of older adults during the 1970s. The private sector took the initiative to design projects that would enable older adults to become involved in new careers, to further their knowledge so that they might continue to contribute to society. Private sector programs established to meet the needs of the aging included those of the American Association of Retired Persons, National Retired Teachers Association, National Association of Retired Federal Employees, National Association for the Spanish Speaking Elderly, National Center on the Black Aged, The National Council on the Aging, National Council of Senior Citizens, National Farmers Union, and the National Indian Council on Aging. The Edna McConnell Clark Foundation funded many research projects to determine the best utilization of services for older adults. One of their projects included a grant to the American Association of Community and Junior Colleges to extend the career opportunities to older adults by assisting them to prepare for further careers before and after retirement.

As older people comprise an increasingly large percent of the U.S. population, eventually every individual and institution will be affected. Education can no longer be associated exclusively with young people. In fact, the number of so-called traditional college students (eighteen to twenty-two) continues to decline, while that of nontraditional students (over age twenty-two) is increasing. Higher education institutions have expanded efforts toward establishing nontraditional learning programs, though opportunities for and impact on older adults are still modest.

Intellectual Functioning of Older Adults

Maintaining intellectual functioning and capacity is one purpose of education in later life. However, a popular stereotype still prevails that decline in intellectual functioning is usual with advancing age. Gerontologists explain that often we make the observation that older people tend to function intellectually less well than younger people. If one draws the conclusion that the intellectual maximum peak is reached in the years of young adulthood, then it is not surprising that we assume there is a decline that accelerates during old age. In taking this point of view, one would need to explore whether the developmental change in intelligence is a uniform phenomenon. Intelligence is a construct that is measured by an intelligence, or I.Q. test. The intellectual behavior of an individual is based on an index number arrived at by examining various dimensions that are important for effective mental functioning.

When examining the results of these studies, one must take into consideration that people who differ by age frequently differ by other characteristics. Differences in age mean differences in life experiences. Gerontologists contend that it does not follow that all older adults have declined intellectually. Individual differences must be taken into consideration—such a significant and chronic physical illness that may impair learning or limited and static environments (such as substandard housing and lack of food and clothing) which may result in limited educational opportunities.

Social Scientists John Riley (a consultant for the Equitable Life Insurance Society and the International Association of Aging) and Matilda White Riley (senior scholar at the National Institute on Aging) have explored a series of studies on intellectual functioning that shows improvement with age under certain conditions. The researchers found that life situations must continue to be stimulating and challenging and people must use their skills. It is also important for the social environment to provide incentives as well as opportunities for learning. Experiments involving people with a mean age of seventy have focused on intellectual skills such as spatial orientation and inductive reasoning, in which older adults have been most likely to show declines in test performance. The results of these experiments have shown that intellectual performance does improve when the social environment has provided incentives and opportunities for learning. Test subjects in many studies have shown improvement following training. Some longitudinal studies have also shown that many remarkable individuals gained in level of performance from age seventy to eighty-four.

Researchers agree that no significant loss of intellectual functioning need be associated with older adults if they are cognitively stimulated throughout their lifetime. A report from the Panel on Behavioral and Social Sciences Research, National Advisory Council on the Aging in the U.S.A., explains that education may actually slow the onset of some consequences of old age. The standardized tests used to measure intellectual functioning have been designed for the young, primarily for use in school settings. And there may be other areas of intelligence that do not develop until middle or later in life, including experience-based decision making, interpersonal competence, and the wisdom to evaluate, set priorities, and take appropriate action. For years, the strengths and potentials of older learners have been grossly underestimated. Only now are researchers and educators beginning to understand the importance of providing productive and rewarding roles to older citizens.

The Purpose of Education for Older Adults

Adult educator Howard McClusky in his presentation to the 1971 White House Conference on Aging identified five categories of older adults' educational needs: coping, expressive, contribution, influence, and transcendence. McClusky describes *coping* needs as those enabling an older person to survive by adapting to changing social conditions. Educational programming that addresses coping needs provides older adults with the skills necessary to deal with societal change, such as basic skills in reading, writing, and math, and life skills like nutrition, health care, and family adjustment. *Expressive* needs are those met by participating in an activity for the sheer value or enjoyment of the experience. Education can provide opportunities for meeting expressive needs when programming is fun, intellectually challenging, and interesting. Participation in the arts and humanities are examples of expressive needs that lead to creativity and improved self-image. *Contribution* needs include the desires of most people to assist others with their problems and concerns, which is based upon the fundamental need to give something that is of value to others in order to become self-fulfilled. Education may be a means by which older adults realize their potential contribution in the most meaningful ways. *Influence* needs are not unique to older adults. People of all ages have a need to make a difference in the world. Educational programming can help in the fulfillment of these needs by helping older adults to identify appropriate roles, develop personal or group skills, and provide social support to assist them in having an impact on the issues and problems. *Transcendence* needs stem from the desire for a deeper understanding of life. These

needs are experienced at all ages but become more acute in the later stages of life. Education can assist older adults in meeting these needs by providing insight into people of other ages and cultures and offering a supportive setting for life review. By meeting and talking with others, older adults may examine the insights of others and come to conclusions about their own life meanings.

Researchers report that educational programs for older adults increase self-esteem, feelings of personal worth, and renewed social participation. Sixteen community colleges across Texas taking part in the Community College Program for Elderly Texans have touched and perhaps changed the lives of many older adults residing in their service area through the imaginative presentation of academic courses, methods and procedures in arts and crafts, and needed social activities.

With the growing evidence that people can continue to learn at any age, one can expect the interest in lifelong learning to grow in the future.

COURTESY OF THE NATIONAL COUNCIL ON THE AGING, INC.

Helen H.

A graduate student at age eighty-five, Helen tells how her pursuit of learning on a college campus keeps her mentally alive and in contact with others:

"When my husband retired, we moved into a retirement community that provided a life care plan. After he died, I moved to the Phoenix area and bought a house with my son, who was recently divorced. I gave up a secure lifestyle that provided complete medical coverage for the rest of my life and made a firm decision to keep learning. I did wonder what people would think of my going back to school at my age. And they do ask me if I am still taking classes and what am I going to use them for. I answer, 'For me, for me.'

"I will take as many courses as my stamina will allow. My goal is not knowledge. My goal is increasing my awareness as I go along. I want to keep mentally alive for my own satisfaction. I like to go up on campus and talk to anybody, everybody. Young people know me: There's that old lady with the umbrella, they say. People ask me if I am an instructor or on staff. I tell them that I am just here going to school because I like it.

"When I began my course work, I attended classes five days a week. My biggest handicap now is arthritis. I cannot tell from one time to another if I will be able to make the walk to campus. I used to be able to walk there in ten or twelve minutes. Now it will take me at least twenty, sometimes thirty, minutes, and I'll have to stop partway a get my breath a little bit. But I am still going. And you know what I am learning? The more you learn, the less you know. So, it will never end."

—*From Connie Goldman's "Late Bloomer" public radio series*

With the growing evidence that people can continue to learn at any age, one can expect the interest in lifelong learning to grow in the future. The educational attainment of the current population is changing. According to the U.S. Senate Special Committee on Aging, in the 1950s the median years of school for people sixty-five and older was 9.0. By 1989 that level had reached 13.0.

Harry Moody asserts that older adults are not necessarily interested in degree programs because tests, grades, and competition may hold little interest for them. Rather, most older adults prefer participative learning that allows them to be involved and active by drawing on knowledge, life experiences, and interests. The most effective educational programs are those geared to the diverse interests of older learners. These programs may take many forms.

Theorists point to three types of learning that may be applied to older adult educational programs—instrumental, expressive, and adaptive. The source of the terms instrumental and expressive can be traced back to the 1951 work of Talcott Parsons, a leading sociologist of the structural-functional school of analysis. Parsons wrote of the gratification people receive when they participate in activities as they strive to meet their goals. Those activities that yield immediate gratification simply by participating in them are termed expressive. Those activities which provide delayed gratification upon completion of some future goal are termed instrumental. Adaptive learning involves acquisition of practical skills that help people to achieve what McCluskey has defined as coping needs. Basic skills in reading, writing, and computation, as well as education on good nutrition, health care, income security, and family adjustment, assist older adults in adapting to an ever-changing world. Instrumental and adaptive learning are overlapping concepts.

The rise in educational attainment is significant because research has shown that individuals with higher levels of education are more inclined to enroll in educational programs upon retirement.

Adult education researcher Caroll Londoner argues that instrumental educational activities should be given priority over

John Gardner

Author, educator, and founder

SNAPSHOT

I discovered that I like to fight! It was a big surprise. I enjoyed taking something on. It's very odd to discover that when you're in your mid-fifties. These are interesting things to learn about yourself."

Born in California in 1912, John Gardner read a great deal while he was growing up and wanted to be a novelist. The writers of this era provided dashing, adventurous role models for the young men of the time, including Gardner.

At sixteen Gardner entered Stanford University, but he found it difficult to engage in any of his courses, so after two years, he interrupted his studies to write. Being a novelist didn't suit him either. Enrolled again at Stanford, Gardner discovered that psychology seemed "more like the study of literature than anything else," so he "settled" for psychology, taking his B.A. and M.A. at Stanford and his Ph.D. in the same subject at Berkeley.

During World War II, Gardner worked in Washington, D.C., for the Federal Communications Commission on propaganda analysis. Put in charge of six people, he began getting positive comments about his gift for management. Because he always thought of himself as a loner, he claims: "No one could have been more surprised than I. I didn't even respect managers. It wasn't on my chart."

Later Gardner served in the Marine Corps and then in the Office of Strategic Services (OSS), ending up as executive officer of the OSS in Austria after the war. While in Austria he received a letter from Henry A. Murray, a professor at Harvard, saying that a job was waiting for him at Carnegie Corporation of New York. Gardner did not know anyone at Carnegie Corporation, and he thought the letter was a joke. However, he met with Murray and discovered that it was *not* a joke. Gardner met the corporation's officers and took the job. He remained at Carnegie for nineteen years. For the last decade of his tenure he was Carnegie's president, and by all accounts an exceptionally fine one.

While at Carnegie, Gardner began using his writing ability again in an unexpected way: as a result of taking part in a Rockefeller Commission on the future of the nation, he wrote a slender book called *Excellence*, which has shaped the American debate about quality versus equality for almost thirty years. *Excellence* was followed within a few years by *Self-Renewal*, Gardner's reflections on the individual's need for continuing growth.

In 1965 Gardner was appointed secretary of Health, Education, and Welfare (HEW), which opened a period of learning and expansion in his life. "I didn't have the faintest inkling of the growth that lay ahead," Gardner says of his move to Washington. "I didn't know that I would enjoy politicians. I found I liked journalists," Gardner adds with a twinkle, "as much as you can like journalists."

When Gardner stepped down from HEW, he founded an organization called Common Cause. Once it was established, Gardner saw another space in American life that needed to be filled: he created Independent Sector, an organization for nonprofit organizations where those that fund and those that seek funds could come together under one umbrella and work toward the increased improvement of institutions.

Gardner left Washington for Stanford University Business School in 1990, where he was appointed centennial professor of business. He recently published another book, *Leadership*.

—*Lydia Brontë*

expressive activities because they provide needed coping and growth skills. Earlier findings indicating that older people actually prefer instrumental over expressive educational activities has strengthened Londoner's thesis that instrumental activities provide the essential skills for survival and growth when interacting with the social environment. The goal of instrumental education for older adults is to enhance life. Under instrumental education four types of skills may be taught: financial, health care, work, and familial.

Education is also seen as the tool for changing the learner's situation. Expressive activities provide learning in which the goal lies within the act of learning itself. Researchers have found that a person's occupation prior to retirement, educational attainment, and previous participation in adult education programs usually determines whether instrumental or expressive educational activities are preferred. Expressive motivators are described as the desire for general knowledge or to become more well rounded. Instrumental motivations include a desire to learn skills for hobbies, to meet new people, to better understand community and political issues, to improve family life, to learn skills for a new job, to improve the ability to read, write, speak, or do math, to help plan retirement, and to get a high school diploma, general equivalency diploma, or college degree.

In 1981 the National Center for Education Statistics reported that reasons for taking adult education courses were either job related (suggesting instrumental inclinations) or non-job related (more likely to include expressive inclinations). Males fifty-five to sixty-four showed preference for job-related activities, and females fifty-five to sixty-four, as well as sixty-five and older, showed preference for non-job-related educational activities. Researchers argue that both types of educational activity, expressive and instrumental, are important to older adults and should be used in assessing how best to meet the needs of the older adult learner.

Institutions and Exemplary Programs

Currently the U.S. elderly are the best educated and most prosperous generation of older adults in the nation's history. Older adults are mixing work, leisure, education, and personal growth in new ways in an educational milieu that varies from the traditional to the avante-garde. According to some experts, in the years ahead older people's accomplishments will be even more surprising, partly spun by their own initiative and partly due to the myriad programs and institutions available all over the country, where a new creative and innovative spirit is hard at work for those adults fifty-five and older.

Colleges, Universities, and Community Colleges

In the 1990s institutions of higher education are confronted with difficult economic challenges. Since the 1970s there has been a significant decline in the proportion of full-time, traditional-age students (eighteen to twenty-two years of age). Along with this decline in the traditional-age students, costs for providing education continue to rise. In the 1980s educators predicted that the decline in enrollment of traditional-age students would also have an impact on the use of facilities, need for faculty, and the relevance of curriculum. Today, institutions of higher education may not be having as many problems in terms of enrollment as once expected. Non-traditional-age students in their thirties and forties are making up for the decline in enrollment of traditional-age students. Older students are welcomed in the regular academic programs, but the thirty- and forty-year-old students have outnumbered them considerably.

Researchers have found that until the past ten to fifteen years, older adult education was an issue of speculative discussion rather than practice. Currently, higher education institutions have begun to recognize that the college campus is no longer reserved for the young adult.

Degree and Non-Degree Programs

In a 1976 survey conducted by the Academy for Educational Development of a selected sample of 814 colleges and universities believed to be offering programs for older adults throughout the United States, researchers found that colleges and universities offering educational programs for older adults fell into three categories:

1. Courses specifically designed for older adults

J. William Fulbright

Senator

SNAPSHOT

I never had any idea of being a politician."

J. William Fulbright, senator from Arkansas for thirty years, was born in Missouri on April 9, 1905, and moved with his family to Fayetteville, Arkansas. During his senior year at the University of Arkansas, Fulbright won a Rhodes scholarship to study at Oxford University in England for three years.

Fulbright returned to Arkansas and worked briefly in his father's business, then studied law at George Washington University, completing his degree in 1934. During his law school days, he married Elizabeth Williams. He spent a year as a special attorney for the U.S. Department of Justice and taught law for a year at George Washington, followed by three years of teaching law at the University of Arkansas.

Then in 1939, at the age of thirty-five, Fulbright became the youngest man ever elected to be president of the University of Arkansas, but was fired two years later by the newly elected governor, whom Fulbright's mother's newspaper had opposed. He ran for U.S. Congress from Arkansas's Third District in 1942, won unexpectedly, and served for a single term, then ran for the Senate against the governor who had fired him from the university presidency. Despite a difficult race, Fulbright won by a reasonable majority, and held the Senate seat for the next thirty years. During his years of political service, Fulbright pushed to revitalize the concept of the League of Nations, which ultimately led to the creation of the

United Nations. In 1954 he served as a delegate to the 9th General Assembly of his realized dream, the United Nations Organization.

Another of Fulbright's most notable contributions was legislation authorizing the construction of the Kennedy Center for the Performing Arts in Washington, D.C. Money for its construction was raised through private contributions, and Edward Durrell Store, an architect from Fulbright's hometown of Fayetteville, designed the center.

The achievement for which Fulbright is known throughout the world is the Fulbright scholarship for American students, initially funded by loan repayments made to the United States by foreign countries after World War II. Made in foreign currency, the payments provided for travel and tuition of American students overseas. Although the loans have long since been repaid, the scholarship still exists, with funds appropriated from the U.S. budget and the contributions of thirty foreign countries.

Since leaving the Senate in 1974, Fulbright has been associated with Hogan & Hartson, a Washington, D.C., law firm, and is the honorary chairman of the Fulbright Alumni Association, with thousands of members worldwide.

—*Lydia Brontë*

2. Regular or continuing education courses either for credit or on an auditing basis provided free or reduced tuition to older adults

3. Courses of special interest to older adults offered through a continuing education program

In 1981 a Louis Harris survey sponsored by the National Council on the Aging found that adults sixty-five and over are most often enrolled in older adult educational programs at colleges and universities as opposed to their place of business, high school, community or senior center, church, library, museum, or by correspondence. In another survey conducted by the National Center for Education Statistics (NCES) in 1981 concerning the location preferred by older adults, NCES reported that 32 percent of the courses taken by people sixty-five and over were taken in educational settings: elementary or high schools, two- and four-year colleges, business, trade or vocational schools, and particularly community colleges.

The National Center for Education Statistics reported in fall 1987 that 238,029 students fifty to sixty-four years of age, and 94,875 students sixty-five and older were enrolled in undergraduate credit programs at higher education institutions throughout the United States.

In 1989 the League for Innovation in the Community College and the American Association of Retired Persons (AARP), conducted a national survey of league member institutions (community colleges). From the approximately six hundred community colleges responding to the survey the researchers found:

1. Most older adult educational programs come under organizational units such as community services, adult education, or short courses.

2. The majority of the colleges conduct noncredit courses with fees ranging between twenty-five and fifty dollars per course.

3. Some colleges allow students sixty and older to audit credit courses with fees waived.

4. Half of the League colleges have a special program and/or center for older adults at their college.

5. Three-fourths of the colleges reported offering noncredit classes to older adults.

6. Full-term credit courses are often taught at off-campus sites.

Catherine Ventura-Merkel, senior education specialist in the special projects section of AARP, and Don Doucette, associate director of the League for Innovation in the Community College, reported in 1991 that through the 1980s the types of courses offered in the community colleges were the traditional classes in exercise and nutrition, avocational arts, crafts, hobbies, and trips; and financial management programs on retirement and estate planning. The courses least likely to be offered were, in fact, the ones demographers and other analysts contended were most needed by the older adult population. These courses included skills training for second and third occupations, personal development courses, and health care programs. Ventura-Merkel and Doucette concluded that only a small number of community colleges offer programs and services designed for retired groups of seniors. Colleges reported that lack of funding was a major obstacle in offering more programs and services for older adults. Ventura-Merkel and Doucette proposed that the most logical explanation for the few programs offered for older adults by community colleges was that this particular population did not realize what community colleges could offer to them. Older adults were only likely to demand such programs when they began to realize their need for new skills, which would assist them in adapting to a fast-changing world and to the personal changes of aging and retirement.

Several community colleges provide outstanding programs and services designed specifically for older adults. Cuyahoga Community College in Warrensville Township, Ohio, provides a comprehensive range of educational services, including seminars, workshops, and special events; courses in the humanities, social, behavioral, and biological sciences; and courses on a variety of special interest topics related to health and well-being in the later years. The program, designed for adults fifty-five and older and offered in forty locations throughout the county where older adults live or meet, is held in cooperation with the Office on Aging, Title III nutrition sites, and community and senior centers and residences. A special program, Elder's Campus, is a day-long, weekly program held on the eastern and western campuses of the college. The participants in that program assist in planning and implementation, serve as the advisory committee, and function as teaching faculty.

Overcoming Barriers to Participation in College and University Programs
Many kinds of barriers, real or perceived, may prevent older adults from participating in educational opportunities. These bar-

Education can provide opportunities for meeting expressive needs when programming is fun, challenging, and interesting.

riers may be categorized as situational, dispositional, and institutional. Situational barriers may include a lack of mobility or knowledge about available educational opportunities or the cost of programs. These barriers pertain to one's situation at the time of the educational offering. The dispositional barriers include how the person views him- or herself as a learner. For example, many adults believe they are simply too old to learn. Some older adults have limited educational backgrounds. As a result of this limitation the older adult may have a lack of interest in further education, feelings of insecurity concerning the ability to learn, and lack of ability to see the need for education at this time in his or her life. Institutional barriers are practices or procedures within an institution that may discourage participation. Inflexible schedules, expensive fees, inappropriate course offerings, complicated application and registration procedures, inaccessible buildings, and lack of communication concerning what educational opportunities are available are all examples of institutional barriers.

Ruth Weinstock, author of *The Graying of the Campus*, believes institutions can remove many barriers to education for older adults. For example, admissions procedures and registration for college credit courses is a difficult experience for all students and should be modified specifically for the older adult learner. When an applicant has to request permission to audit a course from a professor, the professor's office location, telephone number, and office hours should be readily available. Weinstock suggests other modifications for the older adult learner such as campus orientation and publication of an older student handbook.

There are many strategies that may be used by educational programs for increasing older adult's participation: reduced or waived tuition, courses designed specifically for older adults, support services (orientation workshops and counseling), and outreach strategies to include older adults. As the need for educational programs for older adults continues to grow, educational institutions and community organizations are attempting to meet these demands by developing programs to serve this special population. At many institutions these barriers are simply not understood; therefore, efforts to overcome them are not universal.

Elderhostel

Elderhostel is an international educational network providing opportunities for adults over sixty to live with other students and participate in noncredit educational activities on college campuses and in other educational settings.

Founded in 1975 by Martin Knowlton as a short-term residential college program, Elderhostel originally operated under the auspices of the Center for Continuing Education at the University of New Hampshire in Durham. The first elderhostel programs in 1975 were run by a small group of colleges and universities in New Hampshire, with 220 older adults participating in course offerings. In 1977, Elderhostel became an independent, nonprofit organization with the full support of the University. A national office was established in Boston to coordinate all Elderhostel activities. In 1979, a computerized national mailing list system was installed, and the national office began registering participants for any Elderhostel program anywhere in the country by phone or mail.

Since 1986 Elderhostel has grown at a rate of 15 percent to 25 percent. The program is operating in more than 1,800 sites in the United States and Canada and in forty-five countries worldwide. The enrollment averages 250,000 annually. The sponsoring institutions are largely four-year colleges and universities, but environmental study centers, scientific research stations, and conference centers also host programs. Variations in programming also allow the participants to bring their recreational vehicles to programs offered in state and national parks in the United States.

Elderhostel's international activity provides opportunities for Elderhostelers to study abroad. The catalog of courses for studying abroad is published three times a year. Catalogs of the courses in Canada and the United States are published four times annually.

Participants are responsible for their room and board, transportation, and course fees. The cost of an average one-week stay in the United States varies somewhat, and includes a campus dorm room, cafeteria meals, three college-level courses, and extracurricular activities.

AARP's Institute of Lifetime Learning grants two hundred scholarship awards annually for attendance at Elderhostel programs in the United States. Applicants must be sixty years or older, a member of AAUP, and have given a significant amount of volunteer time in their communities. Special consideration is given to those who could have difficulty paying the Elderhostel fee. Applications are available from the AAUP Fulfillment, Elderhostel Application Form D 12309, P.O. Box 2400, Long Beach, California 90801.

A notable aspect of Elderhostel is that none of the courses offered take old age as the subject matter. This is based on the view that courses that deal with aging teach people to be old. The program mainly focuses on the expressive needs of students, using a liberal arts curriculum that is preselected by the institution's administration. The courses are generally designed for a one-week period. Three courses are offered in each of the one-week programs, and the courses do not require homework, grades, or a prior knowledge of the subject matter. The noncredit course offerings enable students to participate for the sheer enjoyment of learning.

Elderhostel programs range from exploring the Alaska mountain range to studying the culture and society of China. At Denali National Park, location of Mt. McKinley, Elderhostel class sessions include lectures, slide presentations, and guided tours of the wildlife, natural history, history and management, and glaciers and glacial geology of Denali. Participants are housed in two-room cabins on the banks of the Nenana River.

The Elderhostel program in China is organized in cooperation with the Chinese American Educational Exchange based at the City University of New York. The "Chinese Culture and Society" program is designed so participants may achieve a deeper understanding of the Chinese people, their lives, and their cultures as reflected in the differences dictated by the history and traditions of the various geographical areas in which they live. The programs are offered in the provinces of Hebei and Shandong. Each program is three weeks long and held in university settings. All programs offer the opportunity for observing both rural and city life and for studying a large, "modern" city and a smaller, ancient city, as well as the chance to view various aspects of country life through visits to agricultural villages.

These programs are just a few of the examples of diverse and stimulating educational opportunities available through Elderhostel.

Learning in Retirement Institutes

A learning in retirement institute (LRI) is an organization of retirement-age learners dedicated to meeting the educational needs of its members. LRIs generally fall into one of two general program categories: institution driven or member driven. Francis A. Meyers of the Association of Learning in Retirement Organizations in the Western Region, a consortium of LRIs, defines the institution-driven model as an educational offering traditionally designed by professional staff and taught by the regular higher education faculty. The member-driven model is developed, designed, and taught by the members with the cooperative sponsorship of a higher education institution. The members also take an active role in governing the organization, with elected directors and officers.

A set of common characteristics has been identified in LRIs:

1. LRIs are typically designed to meet the educational needs of older adults that live within commuting distance of the program.

2. The offerings are varied and cover a broad spectrum, with the majority consisting of college-level material.

3. LRIs are sponsored by accredited colleges or universities, by institutions or organizations working in collaboration with an accredited higher education institution, or by an organization or institution sponsoring a comparable college- or university-level program.

4. The institutes are nonprofit organizations charging a modest tuition or membership fee.

5. A needs-based scholarship program is available.

6. Affirmative action goals are of utmost importance.

7. Members often serve as volunteer teachers or course leaders.

8. Social, cultural, and physical experience are a part of the offerings.

9. Participants are encouraged to be involved in planning, evaluating, teaching, and (when appropriate) administering the program.

The New School for Social Research in New York City is often cited as beginning the LRI movement in 1962 when it established the Institute for Retired Professionals (IRP). During the 1960s and 1970s colleges and universities began replicating or adapting the IRP model. Many national conferences have been devoted to the institute concept, and the number of LRIs is steadily increasing.

In 1989 Elderhostel established the Institute Network to advance and promote LRIs. This voluntary association of independent institutes is dedicated to extending the institute concept to new people in new institutions and strengthening and supporting the effectiveness of established institutes. In 1992 there were over 130 LRIs in existence in the United States.

The LRI programs include core courses and classes in the humanities and liberal arts. Literature, history, public affairs, and music and art appreciation have proven to be most popular among participants. Many times the core curriculum is supplemented by classes in computer science, foreign languages, painting, and writing. Recreational and physical fitness programs are also offered. Classes are not limited to the traditional classroom setting. Cultural events and field trips, including one-day or overnight travel to museums and historical sites, are part of the LRIs' offerings.

During the past few years the Institute Network began offering national study/travel opportunities. These programs include such opportunities as exploration of the myriad aspects of Rome; a naturalist's study in Costa Rica, a naturalist's paradise;

Recreation and physical fitness programs are often enjoyed by older adults.

architectural studies in London and Dublin; the study of European unification, focusing on the position of smaller countries like Belgium and Holland; and numerous other ventures.

There are many outstanding LRIs in the United States and Canada today. One example is the College for Seniors, established in 1988 at the North Carolina Center for Creative Retirement, University of North Carolina at Asheville (UNCA). This member-driven institute provides life enrichment courses to anyone fifty-five and over who pays the required membership fee (some scholarships are available when needed). There are no educational prerequisites and no exams or grades. The program was founded on the desire of adults to pursue learning for pleasure and stimulation, and to do so in the company of others similarly motivated. Participants are involved in more than taking classes. From teaching to working on a newsletter, from registering participants to designing curriculum, there is much to become involved in. The curriculum provides a variety of exciting courses in almost every field—music, literature, history, fitness and wellness, art, religion, environmental issues, psychology, philosophy, computer science, political science, foreign language, and current events of interest to the older adult population. The College for Seniors is an organization that welcomes participant involvement in the shaping and creating of its offerings and thus is able to offer a full and varied program because of its members, people who give freely of their time and knowledge.

The Senior Academy for Intergenerational Learning (SAIL) matches retired civic and professional leaders with undergraduate students and UNCA faculty to work together on learning projects. The SAIL "Senior Fellows" volunteers share their time and expertise with students. For example, senior adults work with university athletes sharing career interests, and retired physicians serve as mentors for premedical students. The SAIL program provides an opportunity for retirees to continue their contributions to their professions and community.

The Leadership Asheville Seniors (LAS) program provides an intensive learning experience for its older adult participants. Local political leaders, agency directors, and civic leaders share information about community issues through lectures and problem-solving sessions, enabling the LAS participants to improve their leadership skills and to contribute meaningfully to the community.

The life journey program provides outreach humanities programming through reading and group discussion led by trained volunteers at churches, community centers, and other sites in the rural areas of western North Carolina. In cooperation with the National Endowment for the Humanities, the center provides other humanities programs led by paid, trained scholars, including a program entitled "The Carolina Special: Railroads through the Carolinas and Beyond as Reflected in Literature and History," cosponsored with public libraries in North Carolina, South Carolina, Tennessee, and Virginia.

In addition to the College for Seniors, the Center for Creative Retirement conducts programs in leadership, intergenerational collaboration, research, volunteerism, wellness, and retirement planning.

The center's retirement planning program offers corporations and individuals retirement seminars. The research institute has studied the economic and social impact of in-migrating retirees in the western North Carolina and conducted a national survey of older adult educational programs. The latter study provides a national perspective on certain forms of educational programs for older adults in the United States, examining critical variables in the success of these programs and highlighting organizational features that might lend themselves to replication in other programs, whether already existing, in the planning process, or simply as ideas in the minds of senior leaders, college administrators, or administrators of community organization.

The center serves as a laboratory for North Carolina and the nation by designing, implementing, and evaluating innovative educational programs, and its long-range mission is to encourage an age-integrated society.

Established in 1977, Duke University's Institute for Learning in Retirement is another good example of programming for people age fifty and older. Older adults participate in peer-taught academic classes in a year-round program. Numerous benefits are available to students enrolled in the program including use of the library, swimming pool, language labs, and the faculty dining room. The class offerings range from drama to religion to literature to science. Approximately forty courses are offered each semester. These classes meet once a week for ninety minutes over a twelve-week period. The class offerings are determined by faculty availability, student interest, and variety. Students volunteer in such activities as teaching some of the courses, leading study groups, acting as teaching assistants, and assisting with administrative tasks.

Certification

While LRI participants are pursuing educational courses for the sheer enjoyment of learning, some older adults require programs to retrain them for second and even third careers. Certification programs provide this type of training.

Many colleges and universities are establishing special programs and making the older learner's transition back into the educational environment more appealing as well as preparing them for new careers or new job challenges. One such program is Kingsborough Community College's "My Turn." This special tuition-free college education program has waived all admission requirements with the exception that students must be residents of New York State and sixty-five years of age by the first day of class. Many students are working toward a general equivalency diploma while others are working toward an associate degree.

The University of Massachusetts, Boston campus, offers a program to qualified students over sixty who are preparing to serve as professionals in the fields of gerontology. The educational backgrounds of the students vary. Not all have high school diplomas, and only one-third have college degrees. The university has sought diversity in the backgrounds of the students as well as age and ethnicity. Classes are scheduled during daytime hours and are held in easily accessible buildings. Tutoring services and administrative assistance is provided to students when needed. Upon completion of two terms of intensive study, an equivalent of thirty undergraduate hours, students receive a State Certificate in Gerontology. Graduates of the program have found job opportuni-

ties in government agencies serving the aging, nursing homes, working for political candidates, and administering programs for the aging. These programs all facilitate job-market competitiveness for older adults.

The Role of Public Libraries

Many older adults find themselves with increased leisure time, reduced income, and declining health at a time when their information needs are increasing. As they become more socially isolated, older adults have fewer opportunities to seek answers from daily communication with other people and other traditional sources. The public library is a community service that may fill this void.

The older adult is one of many publics that the library serves on a regular basis. Established to serve the community as a whole, from preschoolers to the oldest citizens, public libraries purpose to facilitate informal self-education of all people in the community; to enhance the subjects being undertaken in formal education; to meet the informational needs of the total population; to support education, civic, and cultural activities of groups; and to encourage recreation and constructive use of leisure time.

For many years special programs from public and state libraries have provided library services to the aging via bookmobiles, cable TV, and books-by-mail delivery. Many bookmobiles are more user friendly, with hydraulic lifts to raise patrons into the bookmobile. Books-by-Mail connects the older learner to selected readings, including large print materials, by way of free, prepaid mailings. Regular, on-site library programs enable older adults to participate in discussions, films, videos, arts and crafts demonstrations, exhibits of older adults' hobbies, concerts or forums on consumer issues and health concerns, and life enrichment programs. Many of the library programs are brought directly to retirement and senior centers, while transportation is provided to the library for other programs.

Librarians and volunteers make visits to the homebound, to residents of nursing homes, and to other institutional settings to provide reading materials and many times to read to their audience. Talking books and closed-captioned video tapes are also provided by public libraries. These materials are excellent resources for the visually- and hearing-impaired older adult.

Public libraries also serve as an information and referral service for educational opportunities. Older adults may acquire information on where to learn a specific skill, who teaches desired courses, where to get a specific type of educational program, and what the eligibility requirements are for the program.

Many library programs are available to older adults today. The Brooklyn Public Library's Service to the Aging (SAGE) program for older adults is a nationally recognized example of what can be accomplished. The SAGE project's older adult volunteer program sends older people into the community to establish library-based senior groups, organize educational programs using films, lectures, and television, oversee trips to cultural events, and expand the homebound service. These volunteers recruit older adults to teach minicourses on crafts, art, music, and photography. They also organize intergenerational projects that bring older adults in touch with young children.

The Monroe County Library System (MCLS) in Rochester, New York, provides a program of live entertainment for and by older adults. Older adult performers include magicians, pianists, and collectors. MCLS also helps older adults learn advocacy skills on their own behalf. The older adult advocates present their views to local, state, and federal offices on various issues. MCLS publishes a directory of services for older adults, nursing homes, and housing for seniors and a newsletter, *Sunburst*, written by older adult MCLS patrons.

As the older adult population grows, so does the emphasis to educate librarians to provide library and information services for older adults to meet the needs of the aging as well as the needs of their service providers.

In 1987, the American Library Association's Library Services to an Aging Population Committee of its Reference and Adult Services Division prepared "Guidelines of a Library Service to Older Adults," emphasizing the growing importance of designing library services for older adults as this population grows in numbers. Libraries can meet those needs by exhibiting and promoting a positive attitude toward older adults. Information and resources on aging and its implications must be promoted to older adults, their family members, professionals in gerontology, and persons interested in the aging process. The library services provided must reflect cultural, ethnic, and economic differences. The potential of older adults (paid or volunteers) as liaisons should be utilized in reaching other older adults and as a resource in intergenerational programming. Older adults should be employed at professional and support staff levels for general library work and older adult programs. Older adults should be involved in the planning and design of library services and programs for the entire community as well as older adults. A good working relationship should be promoted and developed with other agencies serving older adults. Preretirement and later-life career alternatives programs, services, and information should be made available. Library design improvements and access to transportation should be implemented to facilitate library use by older adults. The library's planning and evaluation process should incorporate the changing needs of older adults. An aggressive funding effort should be implemented and a portion of the library budget committed to older adult programs and services.

Humanities Programs

Humanities programs are learning experiences based on the study of history, literature, philosophy, and criticism of the arts. "Life-long Learning for an Aging Society," prepared by the U.S. Senate Special Committee on Aging in 1991 cited David Shuldiner's definition of humanities programs as educational programs that explore and interpret the human experience. Shuldiner contended that good humanities programs involve participants in lively discussion, critical thinking, and life review, all of which add information and insight to the topics at hand.

A major development in this direction took place in 1976 with the establishment of the "Senior Center Humanities" program by the National Council on the Aging (NCOA) with a grant from the National Endowment for the Humanities. The program was designed to provide life enrichment and self-discovery through the humanities. The program became known as "Discovery through the Humanities" in 1984 and is organized around informal discussion groups initiated in local communities.

The NCOA lends their "Discovery" materials on literature, history, philosophy, and the arts to any group or organization that serves older adults. Anthologies are used as a basis for discussion, inviting participants to explore the works of distinguished writers and artists, to relate what they read and hear to their own experiences, and to consider issues of profound meaning for every generation. At the local community level, older adults meet on a regular basis to reflect on the readings and to share their responses with the guidance of discussion leaders. Today, the NCOA humanities program is offered free of charge at libraries, community colleges, retirement communities, senior centers, nutrition sites, nursing homes, adult day-care centers, housing complexes, churches, and synagogues. For a small fee to organizations, NCOA provides the program materials, discussion leader guides, publicity materials, and audiotapes for conducting the program.

With the Federation of State Humanities Councils, program administrator Esther Mackintosh compiled *Humanities Programming for Older Adults,* which reports that many state humanities councils have begun to recruit older adults into humanities programs. In her literature Mackintosh contends that older adults

are a ready and growing audience for these programs; they have the time to devote to humanities activities as participants and volunteers, and they are a responsive and interested audience because they seek out intellectual stimulation. The lifetime of experience that older adults bring to these programs enriches and enlivens them. No other age group can provide the oral history as older adults may. Older individuals have political influence, but as a large group that political influence becomes magnified. Homebound or institutionalized older adults may also benefit from the intellectual and social qualities these humanities programs offer.

In New York City, for the past twenty-three years, Hospital Audiences, Inc. (HAI) has brought arts and humanities programming to over 7 million people including the frail elderly. HAI is supported by city, state, and federal agencies as well as the private sector. HAI has three components: (1) community, (2) institutional, and 3) advocacy. The institutional component brings live music, dance, and theater by professional artists into institutions. Its Senior Composers program enables composers to share their talents and experiences as performers for the aged, and its community-oriented access program provides an opportunity for thousands of homebound frail elderly to attend cultural events throughout the year. These events include the New York Philharmonic and Metropolitan Opera concerts in the parks, the Delacorte Theater, and Macy's Fourth of July Fireworks and Thanksgiving Day Parade. Daytime appearances of renowned artists at auditoriums selected for accessibility are also available. In its advocacy role, HAI has formed the Arts Access Task Force, a consortium between HAI, the Arts and Business Council, and the New York Foundation for the Arts. The mission of the task force is to make the arts more accessible to people with disabilities. A guide to neighborhood restaurants, movies, and other leisure sites for and by consumers with disabilities, *Access NY,* is available from the HAI office.

Another unique program is Museum One, offering arts and humanities programming to thousands of older adults sixty years of age and older in the Washington, D.C., area, at more than one hundred facilities, including nursing homes, retirement communities, senior centers, adult day-care centers, and senior apartment complexes. Programming includes courses on impressionism, American heritage and traditions, Renaissance artists, modern art, African-American art, art and aging, American women artists, and Latin-American art. Special courses and workshops are designed for intense geriatric rehabilitation of the mentally ill, hearing impaired, and the blind and visually impaired older adults in hospitals, senior centers, and retirement communities.

For professionals working with older adults, Museum One has developed educational and training materials, "Enriching Life through the Humanities: Workshops for Practitioners in Aging," focusing on how staff can utilize the arts to better communicate with their groups and clients.

Senior Centers

A senior center is a physical facility, resulting from a community planning process, that offers a wide variety of services and activities for older adults. They are an outgrowth of senior clubs that can be traced back to 1870, which served as associations of peers providing social support for their members. The first senior center, the William Hodson Community Center, was established in 1943 for low-income elderly in New York City, by the Public Welfare Department under the direction of social workers Harry Levine and Gertrude Landau. Social workers in the community have been credited with the idea of senior centers because they recognized the need for human contact and communication required by their older clientele. These social workers concluded that older adults could benefit from a setting that would enable them to socialize and participate in activities with other older adults. Since Hodson's founding, other centers opened in San Francisco (1947), Philadelphia (1948), and Bridgeport (1951). By the late 1950s there were approximately two hundred senior centers nationwide, established by local resources and sponsored by nonprofit organizations and/or local government agencies (such as departments of social service or recreation). No federal or state legislation existed yet to fund the senior center concept.

During the following decade the multiservice senior center concept began to flourish. Activities and services available at these centers included nutrition, health, employment, transportation, social work, education, creative arts, recreation, leadership, and volunteer opportunities. In the 1970s, federal legislation funded development of senior centers. Title V, Section 501 of the Older Americans Act was amended to include the new "Multipurpose Senior Centers" title and provided funds to renovate or construct senior centers. Title III of the act then made operational monies available to develop and deliver specific services.

In 1970 the NCOA sponsored the National Institute of Senior Centers (NISC), a network of 1,200 centers in all parts of the country. By the late 1980s the NCOA reported 9,000 senior centers in existence nationwide. In 1991 the NISC reported approximately 8 million older adults participating in senior center. The NISC classifies senior center services into individual, group, and community categories. The individual services include counseling, employment, and health maintenance. Group services involve recreational, nutritional, and educational activities, as well as group social work. The participants in the senior centers provide services to the local community through volunteer work in community institutions or organizations. Services available through senior centers depend on their resources, facilities, and community supports; many are provided by the center staff, by appropriate agency staff assigned to the center, or by agencies on rotation through the center.

While some senior centers provide a wide range of offerings, many provide mainly recreational and educational activities. The recreation-education component of senior center programming varies with availability of community resources and participant interest. Some of the more common activities include arts and crafts, nature, science and outdoor life, drama, physical activity, music, dance, table games, special social activities, literary activities, excursions, hobby or special interest grouping, speakers, lectures, movies, forums, round tables, and community service projects.

At one senior center in Brooklyn, New York, off-campus instruction in the liberal arts has been conducted under the auspices of the Institute of Study for Older Adults. Under institute direction, members of local senior centers help design courses, and the local community colleges provide faculty to teach them at the senior centers. Liberal arts courses and self-help instruction are popular among the clientele that attend these centers. The Iowa City/Johnson County Senior Center in Iowa City, Iowa, recorded serving 75,000 older adults in 1991. Educational offerings included applied arts, performing arts, art appreciation, crafts, exercise, and computers. Special workshops also featured topics varying from medication to chair caning.

In the 1970s at the Siouxland Senior Center, Sioux City, a program called "Talk Show" provided opportunities for older adults to meet newsmakers, discuss current events, or talk with professionals from a variety of occupations. Although the program has made many changes over the years, it is still held weekly, from 10:30 A.M. to 12:00 P.M., with approximately sixty-five older adults meeting to hear about and discuss the day's topic.

Older Adult Service and Information System

The Older Adult Service and Information System (OASIS) is a consortium between business and nonprofit organizations designed to challenge and enrich the lives of adults fifty-five and older. Educational, cultural, health, and volunteer outreach programs are offered at OASIS Institutes, providing participants opportunities to remain independent and active in community affairs. OASIS strives to empower adults, fifty-five and older, to live independently and continue to expand their knowledge and remain productive individuals.

Marylen Mann, executive director of OASIS National, and Margie Wolcott May established OASIS in St. Louis, Missouri, in 1982. The May Department Stores Company, the major national sponsor, furnishes the meeting and activity space in many of its stores. Initial support for the program came from the Administration on Aging. The program is administered nationally from St. Louis. The national office establishes program-quality requirements and overall management and operations guidelines; it also supplies management training, new programs and materials, and ongoing support to local program directors.

Currently there are OASIS Institutes in Portland, Los Angeles, Long Beach, San Diego, Escondido, Phoenix, Tucson, Denver, Houston, San Antonio, St. Louis, Chicago, Indianapolis, Akron, Cleveland, Rochester, Buffalo, Pittsburgh, Hyattsville, Boston, Enfield, and Waterbury, with over 129,000 members participating. Each institute has permanent and specially designed space for offices, student lounges, and meeting rooms. In addition to May Company support, in many cities, local hospitals and nonprofit community agencies sponsor institutes. People from all socioeconomic, cultural, and educational backgrounds are invited to participate. OASIS membership is free, and the programs have minimal or no charge. Courses, which last from one to twelve weeks, are scheduled by calendar quarters or trimesters, and classes are held once a week during daytime hours. Course offerings include visual arts, music, drama, creative writing, contemporary issues, history, science, exercise, and health. The collaboration of local cultural and educational institutions benefits many courses.

Volunteer outreach is an important component of the OASIS program. The Older Adult Peer Leadership (OAPL) program trains participants to teach classes in the community and to work in intergenerational programs helping young children. In 1990 more than two thousand volunteers gave over 110,000 hours of their time to run OASIS sites.

The OASIS Institutes in St. Louis are housed in Famous-Barr Department Stores and other area locations. The programs are sponsored by Famous-Barr and its parent company, the May Department Stores Company, by Jewish Hospital of St. Louis, and Washington University School of Medicine. Volunteers are on duty from 10:00 A.M. to 3:00 P.M., Monday through Friday, to enroll students sixty years of age and older in the classes. All health-related classes are free of charge, and most other programs require a nominal fee of one dollar. The courses include wellness, liberal arts, and vocational training. OASIS/OAPL are provided to older adults throughout the St. Louis Metro area by the OAPL Outreach program. Volunteers are trained in subject matter and leadership skills and conduct these classes at libraries, churches, residential and senior centers, and other sites. In 1990 the St. Louis OASIS institutes established the OASIS Award to recognize outstanding volunteer contributions to the St. Louis community made by the area's older adults.

Special events and travel programs are also an integral part of the OASIS Institutes in St. Louis. Special events, such as the Opera Theatre St. Louis, Picnic at the St. Louis Zoo, and an Evening at Queeny Pops, provide OASIS participants an opportunity to participate in local cultural activities free or at a nominal charge. Travel programs to the Winston Churchill Memorial, Inn of the Ozarks, McDonnell-Douglas Aerospace Center, a cruise on the *Belle of St. Louis;* and other places of interest provide adventure and new learning experiences for OASIS members.

Chautauqua

The Chautauqua Institution is a 750–acre complex on the shores of Chautauqua Lake in southwestern New York state. Established over a century ago, the institution provides educational, religious, recreational, and cultural opportunities for persons of all ages from all parts of the United States and abroad.

Chautauqua Institution's "55 Plus" Weekend, established eighteen years ago, is an important component of the multifaceted Chautauqua experience. Each weekend program presents topics through discussion, workshops, lectures, films, cassette tapes, or any other appropriate means. Cultural programs are scheduled for Saturday evenings. Weekend themes and discussions have included topics on socialism to capitalism and the presidential campaign and election year. Housing and meals are available on site. The registration fee covers all programs and accommodations. In addition to the weekend programs, a special one-week program, "The Chautauqua Experience," introduces older adults to lectures, music, recreation, drama, and group fellowship.

A Shepherd's Center is a nonprofit community organization sponsored by a coalition of religious congregations committed to the delivery of services and programs for older adults.

Shepherd's Centers

In 1972, the first Shepherd's Center was founded by the Reverend Dr. Elbert C. Cole in Kansas City, Missouri. Twenty-three churches and synagogues joined in an interfaith effort to provide a ministry by, with, and for older adults. In 1972 the original center began with only six volunteers. Today, eighty-seven Shepherd's Centers in twenty-five states comprise a network of 15,000 volunteers serving over 175,000 older adults. The services and programs of the Shepherd's Center are designed to empower older adults to lead creative, productive, meaningful, and interdependent lives. The Shepherd's Centers are controlled and operated by older adults.

Dr. Cole reports that Shepherd's Centers are an expression of congregations in a defined area. By working together the congregations may accomplish what can not be done alone. The Shepherd's Centers focus on neighborhoods or specifically defined territories. The participants develop an attitude of ownership, empowering them to take responsibility for their well-being. Governed by a self-perpetuating board of trustees appropriately representative and ecumenical, with age-relevant skills and interests, the board is committed to the overall concept of the centers. Church and synagogue property is used for office space and major programs and services. Duplication of services is a problem that Shepherd's Centers seek to avoid. The center encourages partnerships with other agencies serving older adults, always giving credit and recognition where due. Congregations, participants, friends, businesses, civic organizations and clubs, United Way, public funds, and foundations are the funding sources for the centers. The Shepherd's Center concept is a new social model with a healthy view of life after retirement. The idea is applicable to any ethnic, economic, or cultural group of older adults.

One of the many offerings of the Shepherd's Centers is the "Adventures in Learning" educational program, utilizing older adults as both teachers and students, as planners and participants. Classes are normally held weekly, biweekly, or monthly and provide an environment where older adults may share their knowledge, talents, skills, and new interests with their peers.

A committee of volunteers makes the program decisions regarding curriculum, faculty, marketing, and evaluating. This committee is composed of faculty and students with background experience in education, public relations, administration, the arts, health, and clerical services. Most of the teachers are older adults who volunteer their time, knowledge, and skills. The educational program allows students to choose their own subjects. If the student finds a course that does not meet his or her needs, the student may then try a different class. Many classes may require advanced registration due to space limitations.

"Adventures in Learning" program students participate for the joy of learning without the pressures of tests, grades, and academic credits. Courses are organized on an academic semester or quarter basis with classes being held during the daylight hours. Some centers close during August and between sessions. During the long breaks some centers offer alternative programs, such as short-term classes, picnics, trips, or fairs to provide an opportunity for those who count on the friendship and stimulation of the center's activities. All classes are held on one day of the week in the same location, usually a church or synagogue. Every hour courses are offered in intellectual pursuits, current events, or history; philosophy, humanities, religion, or art; needlework, crafts, or painting; exercise, yoga, nutrition, or health information; and travelogues.

Noontime fellowship is a very important part of the "Adventures in Learning" program. Students, teachers, and volunteers share a meal and friendship, at which time the program coordinator makes announcements, recognizes teachers, celebrates accomplishments, and welcomes and introduces new participants in the program. Musical entertainment, a theater presentation, an address by a community leader, or a presentation by a guest speaker on a topic of student interest rounds out the program. The planning committee of the "Adventures in Learning" program has Protestant, Catholic, and Jewish persons serving on the committee.

Workplace Education

Workplace education or training programs are not new. For years, preservice and in-service training for workers has taken place in the private and public sectors. Traditionally these programs were reserved for the younger worker, because the older worker was forced to retire at or before the age of sixty-five. Social policy has promoted retirement instead of employment for older adults. Yet, over the past twenty-six years a new policy has evolved, encouraging older adults to stay in the labor force rather than retire early. The current belief is that working beyond "traditional" retirement age will help older adults feel better while they continue contributing to society.

These trends are evident in recent legislation concerning age and the workplace. In 1967 Congress passed laws prohibiting age discrimination in employment. By 1978 the mandatory retirement age for older workers was pushed back to seventy, and in 1986, mandatory retirement at any age was abolished for almost all workers.

Today employers are facing new problems. The Committee for Economic Development, a private, nonprofit, and nonpartisan

Education helps older adults realize their potential contributions and assists them in implementing those contributions in the most meaningful ways.

research and education organization made up of 250 top business executives and university presidents, has stated that the nation has now entered a time when there are fewer young job entrants into the work force and an increasing older adult population. It urges business and policymakers to develop qualified workers to fill the increasing number of knowledge- and technology-driven jobs. The tight labor market could provide incentives for employees to encourage older workers to remain in the work force.

With the changes in laws regarding age and employment, higher costs of living, reduced labor market of younger workers, and an increasing older population, many corporations are implementing programs to bring in older workers. McDonald's Corporation has the "McMasters" program, which provides skills training and job placement for persons fifty-five and older. Annually eighty to one hundred employees are trained in each McMasters program. General Electric has a special "Technical Renewal Program" in its Aerospace Electronic System Department, which provides training to engineers to update their skills and stay current with new technology. The public sector also has programs to train its older workers. One program on a local level has been established in Union City, New Jersey, training older adults to take care of children in training centers. The program has been accredited by the National Association for the Education of Young Children, an organization responsible for accrediting child-care programs. In Boston, Massachusetts, Operation ABLE (Ability Based on Long Experience), is a consortium effort between industry, government, and private foundations, which provides computer training to older workers for competing successfully in the workplace.

Many older workers are still choosing to retire before the age of seventy, but for those who wish to remain in the work force, business and industry have major responsibilities to train these older workers. For older workers who wish to remain in the work force, AARP has developed the booklet *Using the Experience of a Lifetime,* which provides an in-depth look at creative programs and opportunities for older workers.

Support of Older Learners

In the 1990s, there is no central system supporting or monitoring educational activities for older adults. Programs have developed around the preferences of administrators and/or the needs of the local community. This process has responded to the immediate needs of the older adult learner but has not provided program categories or models that could be easily described or replicated in other sites. The federal government has encouraged public and private sector employers and community organizations to offer educational opportunities to assist older adults in holding or gaining contributive roles in society.

A number of major federal statutes currently authorize provision of federal assistance for adult and continuing education. Much federal assistance is channeled through appropriate state agencies which in turn disperse the funds at the local level. The following is a brief description of a few of the programs available.

The Older Americans Act authorizes state agencies on aging to provide education and training to adults sixty and older in the areas of consumer education, continuing education, health education, preretirement education, financial planning, and other education and training services. The Adult Education Act provides a means by which all adults (young and old) may obtain basic educational skills.

There are federal as well as state policies to waive tuition fees of older adults, and researchers have conducted many studies of these tuition waiver programs. The minimum age requirement varies from sixty to sixty-five. Many institutions offer credit, others specify audit only, and many limit enrollment on a space-available basis only. According to educational researchers Moyer and Lago, cost is neither a barrier nor an incentive to older adults participating in education programs. Twenty-nine states have established some guidelines on this subject of tuition waiver programs. Nine additional states have state policies to waive or reduce tuition mostly on a space-available basis. However, Alabama, Arizona, Colorado, District of Columbia, Iowa, Maine, Mississippi, Missouri, Nebraska, Pennsylvania, Vermont, West Virginia, and Wyoming have remained silent both in their statutes and in their written state policies.

More information about the older learner is needed to assist government and institutions of higher education in meeting future needs appropriately, as more older adults demonstrate increasing interest in educational pursuits.

Lifelong Learning and Links to Other Generations

Midlife and older persons have a multitude of new education avenues to follow and more are likely to be developed as the baby boomer generation, with its high percentage of college grads, reaches the over-fifty stage of life. Lifelong learning for the second middle age and later can help people rethink, regroup, and refurbish their lives while exploring how personal development might relate to the well being of others. One model of the older learner sees him or her enjoying discovery of new ideas and skills while making new friendships and using increased leisure time to play leadership roles through community service.

Intergenerational service and learning is another new and growing part of lifelong learning. There are intergenerational drama groups and theater companies, music groups, special school programs, and even corporate retirement groups "adopting" schools and special project helping handicapped children.

One new ideal of the good life for the second middle-ager is the person whose learning career incorporates self-improvement with service to others, thus uniting virtue and leisure.

—*Diane Moskow-McKenzie, M.A.*

Through volunteerism older citizens make enormous contributions to their communities, to charitable and cultural organizations, and to individuals who benefit from their altruism. Older volunteers provide loving care to children who are starved for attention; they provide transportation, homemaking, caregiving, and a whole range of other kinds of help to frail elderly; they run cultural programs at museums, theaters, and music centers; they are mentors for university students; they repair leaky faucets for poor people—and the list goes on and on.

Millions of older adults in this country serve as volunteers; even many people who are in their eighties and nineties continue to volunteer. According to a national estimate, older volunteers contribute about 3.6 billion hours of voluntary service to organizations every year. If valued at the minimum wage, this amounts to a contribution to American society of about $15.3 billion. And this does not even count all of the hours that older people spend in "informal" services, helping their neighbors, friends, and relatives.

During the last twenty years or so, volunteer programs for seniors—both public and private—have developed and flourished. Locally and nationally, there are now thousands of senior volunteer programs organized through church and interfaith groups, health care institutions, and a broad range of cultural and social service organizations. The Senior Companion program and the Foster Grandparent program were initiated in the 1960s. Many other programs are even newer, including experimental programs to integrate education and volunteering for retirees, to link nurturing older persons with troubled teenagers, to offer caregiving to isolated and frail elderly, to provide mentors for children in inner-city schools, to serve as companions for homeless children.

The development of these programs has meant that there has been a tremendous increase in opportunities for older persons to volunteer, as well as in services provided by older volunteers. Even so, many successful programs are found in only a few local areas, while elsewhere older adults with comparable interests and skills have no such volunteer opportunities. Moreover, many fine programs have very small budgets, which constrict their services and limit their ability to recruit and work with older volunteers.

How Many Volunteers?

It may be surprising to learn that older people seem to be *less* likely to volunteer than other adults. A number of surveys have found a U-shaped curve for the relationship between volunteering and age: People in their thirties and forties are the most likely to volunteer. Both younger people and older people have lower rates of volunteering.

But studies of volunteering have been based on differing definitions, and the wording of questions has varied from one survey to the next. There is enormous variability in estimates of how many Americans volunteer. Even surveys conducted in the same year report different numbers of volunteers. Among people ages eighteen to sixty-four, somewhere between 14 percent and 55 percent volunteer. For older adults, the estimates range from 11 percent to 52 percent.

The various studies are also consistent in another way—older people do not volunteer more than working age adults. An important rationale for recruiting older volunteers is that retirees ought to have more time to do volunteer work than younger people, who are in the paid work force. Retirees, it would seem, should be more likely to volunteer than younger people. But this does not seem to be true. Moreover, studies have shown that most

Some types of volunteering require private and face-to-face involvement with other people.

COPYRIGHT BENJAMIN PORTER

older volunteers do not spend large amounts of time in their volunteer work. One study, for example, found that only 5 percent of older adult volunteers work more than six hours a week.

There are a number of significant barriers to volunteering by older people. Older adults are much more likely than others to give the following two reasons for not volunteering: poor health and lack of transportation. Another problem is income level. Low income is likely to restrict a person's ability to volunteer time, as well as to give money to charity.

According to national surveys, older people are much more likely than working-age adults to have only enough money for basic necessities. However, most older adults are healthy and capable of volunteering. Moreover, people age sixty-five and over give the highest proportion of their income to charity. A recent report on charitable giving in the United States notes: "Among the 56 percent of contributors who worried about having enough money in the future, only respondents sixty-five years of age or older gave an average of 2 percent or more of their household income to charity." Even if rates of volunteering decline with age, there are still substantial numbers of older adults, even among the very old, who continue to volunteer. About an eighth of Americans over age eighty are volunteers.

Volunteering

397

However, the age curve may be changing so that the decline in volunteering occurs at much later ages. Previous surveys indicate that there was a substantial decline in volunteering at around age sixty. In more recent surveys, the drop-off in rates of volunteering seems to happen much later—*after* age seventy-five or eighty.

This suggests that postretirement "careers" (including volunteer careers) may last for many years, suggesting the following implications:

- There is ample time for "career development" among retired volunteers.

- Periodic retraining may be important.

- Retiree volunteers may need opportunities for growth and advancement to sustain a long-term involvement in volunteering.

- There may need to be provisions made for "retiring" older volunteers.

Types of Volunteer Work

The types of activities included under the term volunteering are extraordinarily diverse. A volunteer might be the president or chair of a charitable foundation, an usher for a church function, a campaign worker who stuffs envelopes for a political candidate, a driver who delivers "meals-on-wheels," or a friendly visitor at a hospital. People who do any of these types of jobs might be called volunteers, and this is just a small sample of types of volunteer jobs or positions. There is also "informal" volunteering—that is, helping neighbors and friends, as individuals, but not through an organization. If a volunteer for a church, for example, gives rides to her neighbor as part of a church-sponsored transportation program, why should the same type of service (giving a ride) not be counted as volunteering if this service is offered without any organization?

A list of all the different types of voluntary services would be long and quite varied. One way to think about the different types of volunteering is to group volunteer jobs or roles according to the following criteria:

- Is the voluntary service "formal" (arranged through an organization) or "informal" (arranged by individuals)?

- Does the activity require a regular (ongoing) time commitment or an occasional (once or twice) commitment?

- What is the nature of the activity? Working with the public? Working with objects? Helping individual people?

Formal versus Informal Volunteering

Formal volunteering refers to services arranged through or for organizations—churches, social welfare agencies, museums, hospitals, and so forth. In informal voluntary service, there is no organizational affiliation. Informal helping includes services for friends, neighbors, and other individuals in the community. Many of the same volunteer activities may be arranged either formally or informally.

Time

The time-commitment issue is important because there are fundamental differences between regular and occasional volunteering. In formal volunteer organizations, volunteers who have ongoing responsibilities have jobs that are often very similar to paid jobs. In informal volunteering, regular voluntary service is similar to responsibilities typically done in families.

Serving the Public

Some kinds of volunteering require interactions with the "community" or with large organizations or groups of people. Leadership roles such as the president or treasurer of a charitable organization fit this type. But there are also other volunteer jobs that largely entail contacts with people in the community—for example, an usher at a cultural event, the editor of a newsletter, the salesperson at a hospitality shop, or a performer at a charity concert. Public roles, almost by definition, involve formal rather than informal arrangements.

Working with Objects

In some kinds of volunteering, although the service is intended to help a person or group, the actual work centers on manipulating

Shirley Brussell

Job agency founder

SNAPSHOT

The trend of older people working past the age of sixty-five is only going to keep growing. We don't have to sell older workers anymore. Our problem is matching them to the right job. We have far more jobs than we can fill—the demand is so great."

Chicagoan Shirley Brussell started Operation Able, an employment agency for persons over forty-five, in the summer of 1977. Since then, Able has grown into a nationally acclaimed program that has found jobs for more than 60,000 Chicagoans over forty-five. Born in Chicago in 1920, Brussell earned a college degree and did graduate work at the University of Chicago. After an internship in the Secretary of War's office in Washington, D.C., Brussell became civilian personnel officer in Detroit, where 2,300 engineers were preparing military vehicles for the invasion of North Africa. After a transfer to the War Labor Board, she served as director of personnel in Detroit and Washington.

After the war she returned to Chicago and went into private industry, becoming the personnel manager of a mini-conglomerate food and restaurant chain with 2,200 employees. Three years later she married Judge Abraham Brussell. Though Brussell left work to have a family, she still managed to run a staggering list of volunteer projects.

When the children left home twenty-four years later, Brussell finished a master's degree in community organization. Volunteer work at the university involved her in creating employment programs for older people, and in 1974 she created the first temporary agency for older people, Re-Entry. By 1977 the Chicago Community Trust asked Brussell to direct a program called Life Options which was the start of Operation Able.

"There was nothing at 'Able' when I started," Brussell remembers. "There were some bylaws. The Metropolitan Welfare Council had given it some space. There were three of us: I had an assistant who was a gerontologist ex-nun with a Ph.D. who had left the church a few years ago, and I had a secretary. And a lot of good advice from the Trust; and a very supportive and involved board."

Brussell has built Operation Able into an organization with a staff of 346 people, including 70 permanent staff, 125 temps, and 100 independent career counselors, and a yearly budget of over $4 million. The tightening economy and increasing use of early retirement by large corporations has only increased Able's clientele and usefulness. Able offshoots have formed in seven American cities; in 1990 Sears asked Able to go into five additional communities and create "baby Ables" there.

Brussell has advised the International Labor Organization of the United Nations as well as countless older worker programs throughout the United States. In 1991 she received the YWCA's Outstanding Achievement Award for Community Leadership.

"I didn't retire at sixty-five because I thought I was only getting started," explains Brussell. "I don't think of retirement; I think of what other area would I like to help in or grow in. It's corny, but it's fun as you get older to grow. If you can feel growth and development, you don't feel old. It's when you feel you can't learn anything or do anything new that it's the end of the road."

—*Lydia Brontë*

Volunteers in Action

objects. This type of work includes stuffing envelopes for a charitable organization or political campaigns, bookkeeping, baking a cake for a bake sale, housecleaning for a church or neighbor, fixing a car, or mowing a lawn. The service may or may not lead to contact with others (one can stuff envelopes alone or with others), but the performance of the work is oriented toward contact with objects rather than people.

Helping Individuals

Some types of volunteering require private and face-to-face involvement with other people. This type of service work may be arranged on an informal basis or may be organized through a church or other organization. One obvious example of this type of service is caregiving, which can be formal or informal, regular or occasional. Other person-to-person services, not necessarily as intimate as caregiving, include personal services such as providing transportation, serving food, baby-sitting, and tutoring.

For a person who is considering volunteering, it is useful to think how each of these types matches his or her individual preferences. People who like to spend their time interacting with people are not likely to be very satisfied with jobs that mainly involve working with objects—or vice versa. Someone who is unwilling to make a regular commitment for a volunteer job can volunteer for occasional events. Conversely, a retiree who wants an ongoing commitment needs to look for regular volunteer opportunities.

There is a special type of volunteering that needs its own explanation and discussion—a service exchange program. The incentive system for this type of program is rather different from most other volunteer activities. A few such experimental programs have been tried. For example, there is a program in Missouri in which volunteers earn "service credits" by providing respite care and other services, primarily to the elderly. In an intergenerational neighborhood exchange program in a suburb of Los Angeles, older neighbors offer baby-sitting services in exchange for help with transportation.

The service credit concept is especially interesting as a way to provide long-term care at home for frail elderly who are at risk of institutionalization.

Time Dollars Network founder Edgar Cahn, a major proponent of the service credit system, asserts that an exchange program can generate a considerable amount of service for a modest set of administrative costs and is attractive to legislators, who can satisfy service needs without having to raise large revenues. He estimates that service credits cost about $1.50 per hour of service. Four states have enacted service credit laws, and nine other states are considering such legislation.

Long-term care is expensive and does not necessarily require a high level of skill. The use of volunteers through a service credit program or through other types of volunteer programs both serves the needs of older adults, who usually want to continue living in their own homes, and also potentially can reduce public expenditures on long-term care.

But administrating service exchange programs can be complicated. An exchange program is only valuable if there is an adequate tracking system and if the program continues. Otherwise a donor risks getting no payback for time volunteered. An exchange program becomes increasingly valuable as the range of services grows. The larger the program, the more complex it is to administer and the greater the administrative costs.

Cahn notes that until service credits establish a track record, their extrinsic value will be regarded with skepticism, making it a catch-22 type of problem: An exchange program has little value unless it is functioning; but it can only attract participants—volunteers, clients, and stable sources of funding—if it has value!

Who Volunteers: A Demographic Profile

Demographic factors seem to influence who volunteers. For example, people with more education, higher incomes, a higher occupational status, and better health are more likely to volunteer than other people. However, research findings on demographic characteristics of volunteers are not entirely consistent across studies.

Social Class

Among demographic factors that are associated with rates of volunteering, social class seems to be the most significant. Among volunteers, the more affluent and the better educated are the most active and give the most time. One researcher observes, "We also know from an earlier study asking about all volunteer work—for organizations or relatives—that income dominated the explanations, so much so that, surprisingly, the single best predictor was the number of modern appliances in the home."

People with higher incomes, with more education, and with professional types of occupations are not only more likely to give money to charity, but more likely to volunteer their time to organizations.

Among the older adult population, income and education also affect the amount of volunteering. Various studies suggest, in fact, that social class has much more of an impact on volunteering than age. It is possible that older persons are less likely to volunteer than working-age adults, in large part, because older adults tend to have less education and lower incomes.

Gender

Do women volunteer more than men? Certainly there is the perception that volunteering is an avocation for women who are homemakers. In fact, a major reason for rising concern about the supply of volunteers and the need to recruit older volunteers is that women have been entering the paid labor force in increasing numbers. Research findings on the effect of gender on volunteering, however, are somewhat mixed. Some studies have found that women volunteer more. Others have found no gender difference in rates of volunteering but have reported that women spend somewhat more hours volunteering than men. According to some research, women no longer do more volunteering than men—thus much of the growth in volunteering has come from increased participation by men. Whether men or women are more likely to volunteer, it is quite clear that volunteering, like the paid labor force, tends to be gender related—that is, men and women often do different kinds of jobs as volunteers—with the differences largely conforming to gender role expectations.

Marital Status

Married people are more likely to volunteer than unmarried people. This has been found both in general populations and in studies of older adults. Married people tend to have more income than unmarried people, and the gap in income level may be enough to explain the difference in volunteering by marital status.

Health

Poor health is a significant barrier to volunteering. This has been reported in a number of studies of volunteering among the older adult population. In fact, when nonvolunteers are asked why they do not volunteer, poor health is given as one of the two most common reasons; lack of time is the other.

Work and Retirement

An important rationale for recruiting older volunteers is that retirees ought to have more time to do volunteer work than workers, raising expectations that older retirees would be more likely to volunteer than older adults who are still working. In fact, the reverse appears to be true—that is, the older adults who remain in the labor force are more likely to volunteer than retired older adults. Surveys have found that older persons who are working part-time are more likely to volunteer than either full-time workers or those who have retired completely. But studies also show that, among older volunteers, those who are retired spend somewhat more time in volunteering than those still in the paid work force. Comparisons between retirees and older workers point out the substantial age and health differences between these groups. Older workers, on average, are considerably younger than retirees, and they are much less likely to have health and functional problems.

Race and Ethnicity

The research on how racial and ethnic factors affect volunteering is very limited, and the conclusions are controversial. Some data show that certain minority groups have substantially lower rates of volunteering than the white majority. Other studies, however, have found no difference or even the converse of these trends. It is clear that income and education are confounding factors in assessing the relationship between volunteering and race or ethnicity. In fact, middle- and upper- income African Americans are more likely to volunteer than poorer African Americans.

Why and how do these demographic factors determine whether or not someone volunteers? It seems that the most logical explanation is that virtually all of these demographic determinants are resources of various types. Income and health are obvious resources. Education is another kind of resource—in terms of knowledge and skills (education also is connected to status, which is another resource). Marital status is a personal resource, in that being married means having a spouse—that is, having a roommate, a financial partner, a confidant, and a companion in leisure activities. Being employed means having an income and also having regular contact with other people. These various resources affect both the costs and the opportunities for volunteering in a variety of ways.

An absence of these resources raises the cost of volunteering. For example, a volunteer who does not have good health must expend a much larger portion of his or her available energy on volunteering tasks than would otherwise be required. For a person whose income is very low, the direct and indirect expenditures associated with volunteering (such as transportation or foregone wages) might be an insurmountable obstacle.

Conversely, having resources expands opportunities for volunteering in many ways. For example, having many social contacts increases the likelihood that a person will be invited to volunteer. Thus, for example, being employed (in contrast to being retired or being a homemaker) exposes an individual to many relationships and opens up possibilities for a variety of activities, including volunteering.

Education is a particularly important resource. It is likely that well-educated persons have the most interesting and attractive volunteer opportunities. Among older volunteers, retired executives and other professionals may be in a uniquely advantageous volunteer position. Their skills and expertise are valued, and they are able to offer volunteer services that are both useful to others and meaningful to themselves.

Newer experimental programs link nurturing older persons with troubled teenagers.

Volunteers in Aging

Retired engineers, from a very successful corporate volunteer program, work as a team at a residential facility for disabled persons. They design and manufacture mechanical devices for people with handicaps. Most of the people they have helped never could have afforded such devices without their donation of talent and time.

To what extent do these demographic factors "determine" whether or not someone volunteers? A recent survey on volunteering found that "volunteers and nonvolunteers are very similar with respect to sex, age, marital status, annual household income, the presence of children under the age of eighteen in the household, and region of the country in which they live." From the research evidence to date, it is apparent that demographic factors operate as predispositions in volunteering. But demography, by itself, cannot explain who volunteers—or why.

Who Volunteers: The Personality Factor

There are some people who are helpers—women and men who seem to have a natural talent for doing good. Everyone knows such a person. There is the man who cleans driveways for all his neighbors with his snow blower; he never allows them to pay him, and he is embarrassed when they bring him Christmas gifts as a way of saying "thank you." There is the woman who has been cooking for her church for years and years; whenever there is a special event, she is in charge of the kitchen. There are the people who volunteer for a dozen worthy causes and who always say yes when they are asked to make a charitable donation.

Why do some people help and volunteer more than others? Laboratory experiments reveal that people with altruistic or "other-oriented" personality traits, according to psychological test scores, are more likely to help others, if presented with opportunities.

An important component of the altruistic personality is the capacity for empathy. People behave altruistically when they feel empathy for the person in need of help. People who are inclined to volunteer seem to have a high emotional IQ—that is, a well-developed capacity for empathy.

It also appears that when people believe that they are altruistic, they develop an altruistic identity and are more likely to behave generously. This has been found in research with both children and adults. A study of blood donating found that people who give blood begin to identify themselves as donors, and this identity motivates future donations, year after year. Conversely, being rejected as a blood donor affects the potential giver's self-image negatively. People who are rejected, for whatever reason, develop an identity as nondonors and tend not to try again.

A number of studies have revealed an association between doing good and good feelings. Optimism, positive mood, self-esteem, and extroversion all seem to increase altruism and volunteering. Thus, people who feel good about themselves are more likely to help and give to others. Furthermore, people are more likely to help others when they are in a good mood than when they are in a bad mood. Potentially there is a positive reinforcement loop: good feelings create a positive identity—which is both created and reinforced by altruistic behavior.

> *Research suggests that there is an altruistic personality. That is, some people are inclined to be helpers because of their moral character, their capacity for empathy, and their particular configuration of personality traits.*

Older people who volunteer tend to be joiners. Older volunteers, most commonly, have volunteered in the past and have high levels of activity in most other areas of their lives as well. It may be that volunteers are people who are energized by contact with other people. They have recreational activities, spend time with and care for their families, do things with their neighbors and friends, and attend church regularly. In other words, there tends to be a "general activity syndrome"—so that volunteering is one type of activity for generally active people.

A very large proportion of volunteering is through religious organizations. This is particularly true for older volunteers, who have high rates of church membership. Thus, a large portion of volunteering by older persons is church work.

Religion and Volunteering

Volunteers in Action

A one-hundred-year-old woman, living in a residential facility in a small town in New York State, started doing volunteer work about six years ago. Although she needs help herself, she offers telephone outreach to other older people who are homebound and isolated.

Religion is very strong in this country. Most Americans say they belong to a church or synagogue and the great majority (about 90 percent) say they believe in God. Scarcely any American is more than a few miles away from a house of worship. In an essay on "Religion and the Voluntary Spirit," Robert Wuthnow asserts that "despite changes in the nature of faith and in the wider society, religious organizations remain one of the most effective mechanisms in our society for motivating, organizing, and disseminating charitable giving."

Why is it that churches are so important in fostering volunteer work? One reason may be that volunteer work is simply a part of everyday church work. Churches, as nonprofit organizations, are bound to rely heavily on unpaid labor. Thus, it ought not to be surprising that a large portion of church members say that they are volunteers. But there may be other factors as well. Religions are likely to encourage altruistic values and behavior. Religious values also tend to foster a sense of community responsibility. This may be why church members are more likely to volunteer, in general, not just for church-sponsored activities.

It is also possible that churches offer another indirect impetus to volunteer work—that is, they provide a way to organize volunteers. Religious organizations are in a particularly advantageous position to locate and recruit older volunteers. They can provide potential volunteers with a spiritual rationale for their services. They can offer recognition within their congregational community. Churches also can help to develop a lay leadership among older volunteers. For all these reasons, church work has important implications for volunteering that go well beyond services provided to or through individual churches or particular religious organizations.

What do people get from volunteering? Some research and many personal anecdotes have suggested that people who volunteer enjoy certain benefits—like better health, more positive self-esteem, and having more friends. In *The Healing Power of Doing Good*, Allan Luks with Peggy Payne argue that volunteering brings a "helper's high," which comes from the release of endorphins into the bloodstream and actually makes people feel healthier.

It may be that the potential benefits from volunteering are especially important for older persons confronting the hazards of old age. Some studies have suggested that people are healthier and happier in old age if they remain socially involved and participate in productive and meaningful activities. An older volunteer, who helps a child from a troubled family, says:

> I get out more. I have lost weight. I have played games and rode a bicycle since I started visiting Johnny, and I had not done much outside for a long time until me and Johnny started visiting each other. We take walks, play ball, ride bicycles, swim and go fishing. We also go out to eat a lot. Johnny is a wonderful friend. . . . I think this program is what every child and old person needs. It gets your time clock started again. I think it gives new meaning to my life, and also to Johnny's.

But it is difficult to get convincing evidence that volunteer work *causes* older people to be healthier and happier—because healthier and more active persons are the most likely to choose to be involved in volunteer work, as well as other activities. Although some research indicates associations between volunteering and good health, greater life satisfaction, better friendships, and so forth, other studies have not shown these effects. In any case, *causality is extremely difficult to prove.* Possibly volunteering does make people healthier and happier. But these benefits have not yet been adequately demonstrated.

Much of the research in volunteerism—especially on older volunteers—suggests that the most important benefits are intangible, or "spiritual." In his theory of life span development, social

Does Volunteering Make Older People Healthier and Happier?

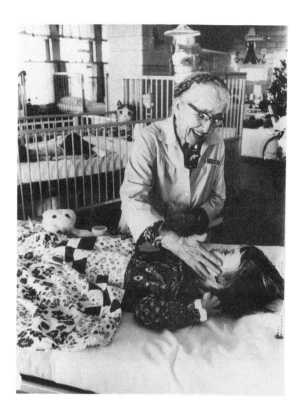

psychologist Erik Erikson argued that a central theme in later life is generativity—the human need to be productive and creative, to have meaning in one's life, and to be connected to others, across generations. If an individual does not have meaning and a sense of connection with others, his or her life may seem empty and purposeless. Without a sense of purpose, Erikson said, adults will have a "pervading sense of stagnation and personal impoverishment." Erikson's theory points out that in later stages of life people become increasingly aware of their own mortality. The great fact of human life is death. Young people may deny, ignore, and even disbelieve mortality. The old, however, struggle to find meaning in life—especially when confronting the fact of death.

By giving to others, people connect to society and become part of something much larger than their individual lives. People's "spiritual wealth," however, allows them to confront death with some prospect of immortality. Robert Wuthnow writes in *Acts of Compassion*: "When someone shows compassion to a stranger, it does set in motion a series of relationships that spreads throughout the entire society. Even if the chain is broken at some point so that no direct benefits come back to us as individuals, the whole society is affected, just as an entire lake is affected when someone pours in a bucket of water."

Why Volunteer?

When people are asked why they volunteer, they often say something about wanting to help, wanting to be useful, having a sense of social responsibility, or wanting to do good. Virtually every study of volunteer motivation has found that most volunteers give such altruistic responses. In a recent national survey, 97 percent of volunteers gave "I want to help others" as a reason for volunteering. Altruism—just doing good—is rarely the only motivation; most people give multiple reasons for volunteering.

Some volunteering is for personal, materialistic, or "selfish" reasons. For example, some people volunteer in order to expand their career opportunities, with the ultimate goal of paid employment; a business executive may donate time and money to a charitable or arts organization to benefit his or her business through publicity, public goodwill, and opportunities to network with other influential persons in the community; a person who volunteers in a cooperative neighborhood group or for the Parent-Teacher Association at his or her child's school is providing a service to the family, in addition to serving others. Of course, the fact that individuals receive personal benefits from volunteering does not entirely answer the question about why these particular people—and not others—have chosen to volunteer.

Retired volunteers tend to have little interest in volunteering for the sake of enhancing or developing their careers. In this sense, older people tend to be less motivated by the possibility of material benefits. Conversely, older volunteers are more attracted to volunteering as an opportunity for socialization, learning, and personal growth.

A noted authority on volunteerism has suggested that it may be futile to try to understand motivations for volunteering. Jone Pearce writes, "Perhaps we should accept the inherent mys-

Samuel A.

A retired attorney and literature teacher, at sixty-eight years Samuel A. volunteers his time and scholarship to teach public school children.

"I don't feel that I am fully retired; I feel that I am engaged as much as I ever was. When I look back, I wonder how I found time to go to work. When I retired I joined the Reading Aloud program as a volunteer in the Boston school system. I talk to the students about outstanding figures in black history: Harriet Tubman, Frederick Douglass, and a number of others. I find there is a great deal of interest in this subject among the kids. I also enjoy reading poetry to them—some pieces I have written. One I often read to them is about the great baseball player Satchel Paige: 'Sometimes I feel like I will never stop, just go on forever till one fine morning I'm gonna to reach up and grab me a handful of stars, swing out my long lean leg, and whip three hot strikes burning down the heavens and look over at God and say, "How about that." '

"A marvelous aspect of being older and free of some of the responsibilities you had before is to contemplate, to meditate, to reflect upon things. I think that's an important part of aging. One reason that I rejoice is that I have this time to involve myself in those things."

—*From Connie Goldman's "Late Bloomer" public radio series*

tery of volunteer motivation—recognizing its benefits as well as its costs—rather than searching for an 'explanation' that will never really fit." Apparently there are certain topics—such as love and religious belief—for which scientific research can only nip around the edges. It does not yet fully convey why humans love one another or why humans help one another.

The Good That Volunteers Do

(ertain circumstances encourage and inspire helping behavior. In effect, the more favorable the social conditions, the larger the numbers of people who would be inclined to help and volunteer. Imagine the following scene:

> It is evening and you are taking a walk in your neighborhood. You look up and see a woman lying in the road. She seems to have been hit by a car. In the moonlight, you think you notice blood staining the road, and she seems to be moaning in pain. It is a quiet neighborhood and, although there are lights on in some of the houses, you see no one else on the street. What do you do?

And here is another scene:

> In the early evening, you are walking along a city street. The street glitters with neon lights, and there are many restaurants and a few shops open. You pass a woman and a child, squatting in the doorway of a shop. They are both dirty and shabbily dressed. An old blanket and a pair of adult-sized crutches are lying on the cement sidewalk beside them. The woman, looking up at you, asks for money. "We need money to eat," she says. What do you do?

These are both situations in which an individual may help someone in need. But they seem quite different. Emotionally, morally, and legally they elicit different levels of responsibility. It is not likely that the two situations would provoke identical responses.

In the first situation it is hard to imagine not helping. In fact, to simply notice and walk on might be considered, morally if not legally, as negligence—since there is no assurance that someone else would help, and the woman could die. Yet the woman and child in the second vignette may also be in peril. They seem to be lacking a basic necessity—food—without which they also could die. Even so, many people who pass them probably will turn away and give nothing.

Experts on altruism contrast two kinds of conditions that elicit helping behavior: "strong" versus "weak" situations. In strong situations, the following conditions apply:

- There is a pressing need.

- There no alternative source of help.

- There is a strong likelihood of a direct and positive impact.

All of these conditions are met by the first scenario; they are arguable in the second. In the case of the woman lying injured on a lonely street, the vulnerability is clear: there is an ostensible risk of immediate death. Since the street seems to be empty, there is no one else to take responsibility for this woman's life. There is also a strong probability that intervention by a passerby will be useful—at the very least, an ambulance can be called. Moreover, what is called for is a one-time service. The passerby has no reason to suppose that, after this one act, he or she will be called upon for any ongoing responsibility or rescue service. A quick and spontaneous "altruistic calculus" will show that the cost (to the helper) is relatively modest, while the benefit (to the woman on the street) is substantial.

With the situation of the woman begging on the street, the first condition is partially met: the woman asking for help is vulnerable and in need. Even so, the need is not so immediate that she would actually die if the passerby does not help her. In fact, one of the most critical factors here is the presence of other alternative sources of help. Numerous studies of the "bystander effect" have shown that the number of people nearby strongly affects the choice to help or not. In this case, a passerby can rationalize that there are many others on the street to give her money, and/or there are other sources of help (government funds and private

By giving to others, individuals connect themselves to society and become part of something that is larger than their individual lives.

COPYRIGHT BENJAMIN PORTER

charities), and/or perhaps she could help herself (get a job). There is, finally, the issue of the impact of help. At best, the benefit will be temporary. In a short while, this same woman and child will again need money for food. Moreover, donating to these two people will make virtually no dent in the overwhelming problem of hungry and homeless people in our cities. There is a risk, in fact, that a passerby who gives to one person with a tin cup will be seen as a "mark" by others on the street, and the demands could be limitless. Therefore, the cost-benefit assessment in this case is very different from the first situation.

Regular volunteer work for organizations is more likely to approximate a weak than a strong helping condition. In regular volunteering, there is more likely to be a muted than a critical need for help. In many kinds of volunteer work, the impact is subtle rather than obvious. And, most important, it is very rare for a potential volunteer to believe that he or she is indispensable for the service to be provided.

Studies of natural and human-caused disasters have found that in such situations there are often more volunteers than needed. These are situations with obvious vulnerability and a clear benefit to those in need. When a situation is viewed as a crisis, then there is inherently a perceived shortage of volunteers, since

A West Coast museum has three hundred or so paid staff and over six hundred volunteers. About half of them are older adults who serve as guides and teachers, working in every department. About eight thousand people visit the museum each day.

there is little time to recruit helpers. Similarly, personal crises also function as strong helping situations. Kidney donors are more likely to volunteer if there are no other possible donors. Moreover, donors, particularly if they are relatives, tend to decide instantaneously, without having to think about the decision. Such situations meet all the conditions of strong helping situations: there is immediate vulnerability (risk of kidney failure), no alternative helpers (the relative has, by far, the best tissue match); and there is a direct, positive impact (the probability of saving a life).

Even if regular volunteering constitutes a relatively weak helping situation, there are still matters of degree. For example, sometimes potential volunteers offer unique contributions, so that alternative sources of help either are not available or could not be nearly as effective. Often, there are immediate and critical needs for help (such as for AIDS patients, teenagers using drugs, older adults at risk of losing their independence).

A very important factor is the probable impact of a volunteer's efforts. The "warm afterglow of success" reinforces helping behavior, while failure and frustration make people want to quit. As one researcher notes: "People do not volunteer if they perceive that their time and efforts will be wasted."

Special Issues of Older Volunteers

In many ways, the factors affecting who volunteers and why are essentially the same for younger and older volunteers. And yet, there are several special issues for older volunteers. First, there are-related concerns. Second, there are access issues, because of changes in work and family life. Third, there are scheduling issues related to the time frame of postretirement lives. Finally, there is the experience factor—that is, older persons have accumulated many years worth of experiences that potentially affect their interest in volunteering and the value of their contributed time.

Older persons, especially if they are retired, are likely to have more time to offer as volunteers than people who are working age—but there are also more barriers. Older people have more health and functional problems; their incomes tend to be some-what lower; and access to trans-portation is more likely to be a problem. Volunteers may become frail or, even without serious health problems, they may sim-ply have less energy as they enter older and older ages. Their eyesight may become impaired, and they may no longer be able to safely drive a car. Not all or even most older volunteers are incapacitated, but, quite simply, there are more risks of health and functional problems with older volun-teers, which present special challenges for organizations that have many volunteers in their late seventies and over.

A number of studies have shown that people are more likely to help if they feel compe-tent and effective.

Age affects access to volunteering in a paradoxical way: Older people potentially are more accessible as volunteers because they have diminished responsibilities in work and family roles and therefore have more time for volunteering. But without these roles, older persons are less accessible for recruitment, because they are not associated with the institutions and organizations from which volunteers are commonly recruited. Many volunteer programs are associated, directly or indirectly, with careers and occupations. Two of the most common types of voluntary associations to which indi-viduals contribute their time are trade groups and civic organiza-tions; both of these tend to attract memberships through their occu-pations and professions. There are also many programs associated with family roles. Parent-teacher associations, Boy Scouts, Girl Scouts, and church youth programs are several obvious examples of organizations that recruit volunteers primarily because of parental ties. According to a survey by the Gallup Organization, almost a quarter of volunteers indicated that they were motivated to contribute their time because they had a "child, relative, or friend who was involved in the activity or would benefit from it."

Through volunteerism older citizens make enormous contributions to individuals who benefit from their altruism.

COPYRIGHT MARIANNE GONTARZ

Corporate and executive retiree programs are *unusual* in attempting to recruit older volunteers because of their special affiliations and past work experience. There are also a few experimental programs that recruit grandparents to volunteer in school and other youth programs because of commitments to their own grandchildren. But such programs are exceptions. Most older volunteers are recruited despite their lack of such ties through family or work. There is one notable exception to this lack of institutional affiliation: large proportions of older persons are members of religious organizations. Church work has a unique place in volunteerism, particularly for older persons, in part because it offers communal affiliations outside of work and family roles.

Access to older volunteers is also related to scheduling issues. Retirees are potentially more accessible because they do not have work commitments during daytime hours. On the other hand, many older volunteers are unable or unwilling to volunteer after dark, either because of problems with night driving or fear of crime. The implication is that not only are many older volunteers available during the day but they may be available *only* during the day. In the winter months this may cause some scheduling problems for volunteer programs. There is also another winter problem: in January and February, volunteer programs in cold-climate states sometimes lose many of their regular volunteers who go as "snowbirds" to Arizona, California, Florida, and other states with warmer winter climates. Older persons are able to be snowbirds because they lack time commitments imposed by work or school schedules. It is their relative freedom from such schedules that makes retirees both accessible and, in some ways, irregular, as volunteers.

Older volunteers are especially valuable to volunteer programs when they are given opportunities to use the particular skills and abilities that they have gained over their lives.

There is at least one other age factor: Persons in later life have accumulated many years of experience and, in a number of ways, these past experiences affect the recruitment of older volunteers. For example, consider the issue of whether or not a person has previously volunteered. At age twenty, it would not be unusual for a person to have had no experience as a volunteer; yet this person is more likely to be considered as not-yet-a-volunteer rather than a nonvolunteer. Conversely, if by age seventy an individual has never volunteered, he or she has missed various opportunities for volunteering in middle age, for whatever reason. Surveys have shown that both young persons and older adults have relatively lower rates of volunteering than people in their middle years. But these patterns have different meaning—because past experience is a more significant factor for older persons. Similarly, older persons have had many experiences over their lives—in family, work, friendship, and so forth.

An Untapped Potential?

According to Edgar Cahn, "When a society has vast unmet needs at the same time that there are large numbers of healthy, energetic, productive human beings for whom the society can find no use—even though they would like to be useful—then something is wrong." Does our society provide adequate opportunities for older persons to continue in productive activities? Is there an untapped potential for recruiting older persons as volunteers? Many older people who do not currently volunteer say they would like to. Many current volunteers say that they would be willing to spend more time volunteering. Is this evidence that many more older adults would or could volunteer?

Actually, it is not easy to extrapolate based on what people say they might or should do. Motivations for volunteering are complex. When people say that they might or they should volunteer, it is hard to know what this means. Moreover, it is unrealistic to expect that all older adults will volunteer. Many older persons either are not interested in volunteering or have health and physical limitations that seriously limit what they can do. When older nonvolunteers are asked why they are not volunteering, by far the most common reasons they give are health problems and their age.

It is also clear that an elder volunteer force does not offer a cure for shortages in public funding for human services. Even if it were possible to recruit millions more older adults as volunteers, their work would largely complement rather than supplant other health and social services. An older volunteer force, by itself, cannot be expected to solve serious social problems confronting American society today—like poverty, drug abuse, crime, and teenage pregnancy.

Nonetheless, much more could be done. Many volunteer programs—especially service-oriented programs—are small because their funds are very limited. When public and/or private monies are available to support volunteer programs, these programs thrive and grow. The implication is clear: To the extent that more opportunities are developed and more funds are invested in programs for older volunteers, the "payoff" should be more older volunteers and increased services by older volunteers.

Studies have found that a major reason that many older people give for not volunteering is that *no one asked them.* Volunteer organizations rely heavily on word-of-mouth recruitment, in part because this is an effective method of recruitment but also because they do not have the funds to develop larger programs.

The implication is intriguing: With systematic recruitment efforts, many more older persons, from diverse backgrounds and experiences, could be recruited as volunteers.

There is also both theory and research to support the importance of "productive aging"—that older persons are interested in and can benefit from opportunities for productive activities, including volunteerism. According to theorists like Erik Erikson, the human need to be productive and to have meaning in life becomes increasingly poignant as people age. Most older people believe strongly that "life is not worth living if you can't contribute to the well-being of others." Even so, older people spend much of the extra time that they have gained through retirement in passive activities, such as watching television. There is, thus, the implication that there are many older people who could be attracted to enhanced opportunities for productive activities through volunteerism.

> *Volunteers tend to be recruited from closed networks, and many people who are different from the people in these networks are simply never asked to volunteer.*

Over their lifetimes, older persons have developed and accumulated knowledge, skills, experience, abilities, and talents. Much of their knowledge is practical—how to soothe a child, how to drive nails into a corner beam, how to make chicken soup, how to adjust a pair of eyeglasses, how to teach someone to read. What structures or opportunities are readily available for older persons to make use of the full range of their accumulated talents and skills? Since the investment in volunteerism has been rather limited, the conclusion seems obvious: The accumulated life experiences and skills of older persons are not being as well utilized as they might be.

This century has witnessed a miracle of survival, as life expectancy has increased by as much as 50 percent in the last fifty years or so. Of all the revolutions in recent times, the age revolution is in some ways the most miraculous, the most dramatic, and possibly the most significant in its impact on everyday lives. But, according to many gerontologists, current social policies are out of step with the "age revolution." Sociologists Matilda White Riley and John Riley argue that, while about twenty-eight years have been added to the life span, there is a problem of "structural lag, because the age structure of social opportunities has not kept pace with the rapid changes in the ways people grow old."

Current social policies and most public expenditures on aging focus on old age as a terminal stage. The problems of old age—frailty and sickness—cost hundreds of billions of dollars. The lion's share of the aging budget, both federal and state, is for health and long-term care. While there are some publicly supported programs to provide activities for senior citizens, the budget for these projects is almost negligible.

It may be time to refocus—to develop social definitions and public policies that are future focused, that offer meaningful futures to older citizens, and that use their capacities to help shape a better future world for everyone. This will require broadening social visions, expanding public-private investments in programs for older volunteers, and developing social policies that redefine the meaning of the last third of life.

Where to Begin   For readers who are interested in learning more about volunteer opportunities, here is a list of organizations that serve as resource centers on volunteering. Most of these organizations are national, but many have local affiliates that should be listed in telephone directories. Since there are many different types of volunteer programs, this list is not comprehensive but rather is intended as a representative sample of places to contact.

American Association for Museum Volunteers
1225 Eye St. NW, Ste. 200
Washington, DC 20005
(202) 289-6575

Formerly the United States Association of Museum Volunteers, this membership organization holds its annual training conference in conjunction with the American Association of Museums. Periodicals: *Museum News; AVISO.*

American Association of Retired Persons (AARP)

601 E St. NW
Washington, DC 20049
(202) 434-3200

A nonprofit, nonpartisan organization whose members are all fifty years of age and over. AARP offers a wide range of membership benefits and services, and education and advocacy materials. The AARP Volunteer Talent Bank matches volunteers age fifty or older with suitable volunteer positions nationwide, in both AARP programs and other organizations. Periodicals: *Prime Time, Modern Maturity; AARP News Bulletin* (monthly), and *Legislative Report*.

American Red Cross (ARC)

National Headquarters
17th and D Sts. NW
Washington, DC 20006

The Red Cross brings together trained volunteers and paid staff to help prevent, prepare for, and cope with emergencies. The ARC is chartered by the U.S. Congress to provide disaster relief at home and abroad. It collects, processes, and distributes voluntarily donated blood and involves 1.4 million volunteers.

Habitat for Humanity International

121 Habitat St.
Americus, GA 31709-3498
(912) 924-6935

Habitat for Humanity is an ecumenical Christian housing ministry whose objective is to eliminate poverty housing from the world and to make decent shelter a matter of conscience. Over 40,000 volunteers have helped build or rehabilitate over two thousand homes for low-income families in the United States and in developing countries.

Independent Sector (IS)

1828 L St. NW, Ste. 1200
Washington, DC 20036
(202) 223-8100

IS is a national membership organization formed through the merger of the Coalition of National Voluntary Organizations (CONVO) and the National Council of Philanthropy (NCOP). It works to preserve and enhance the national traditions of giving, volunteering, and nonprofit initiative. Periodical: *Update*.

Minnesota Office on Volunteer Services (MOVS)
117 University Ave.
St. Paul, MN 55155
(612) 296-4731

The Minnesota Office of Volunteer Services, Department of Administration, strives to improve the quality of life in Minnesota through voluntary action. It works with both public and private organizations. MOVS is involved in the following activities: advocacy for volunteers and volunteer service; publishing a bimonthly newsletter; operation of a resource library; technical assistance and information; research on special volunteer issues and projects; convening meetings of volunteer groups and leaders and providing training opportunities. Membership is not required for MOVS services. Periodical: *Volunteers Move Minnesota*.

National Assembly of National Voluntary Health and Social Welfare Organizations
1319 F St. NW, Ste. 601
Washington, DC 20004
(202) 347-2080

The National Assembly is an organizational membership association formed to facilitate cooperation and communication among voluntary organizations and to pursue mutual goals and convictions. It also acts as a clearinghouse and resource center.

National Association of Partners in Education (NAPE)
209 Madison St., Ste. 401
Alexandria, VA 22314
(703) 836-4880

NAPE (formerly National School Volunteer Program—NSVP) is a membership organization comprised of those involved in or interested in school volunteer programs. It functions as a resource for its members and as an advocate activity within the educational field. Periodical: *Partners in Education.*

National CASA Association
2722 Eastlake Ave. E, Ste. 220
Seattle, WA 98102
(206) 328-8588

A membership organization for court-appointed special advocates formed in 1982 to provide coordination, technical training, and assistance to CASA/guardian and listen programs nationwide. CASA is a nationwide movement of community volunteers who speak for abused or neglected children in court. The National CASA Association represents more than 377 CASA programs and 13,000 CASA volunteers in forty-seven states. Periodical: *CASA Connection.*

The National Council on the Aging (NCOA)
409 3d St. SW, 2d Floor
Washington, DC 20224
(202) 479-1200

The NCOA is a resource for information, training, technical assistance, advocacy, publications, and research on every aspect of aging. The membership organization offers various networking opportunities and sponsors an annual conference.

National Retiree Volunteer Center
607 Marquette Ave., Ste. 10
Minneapolis, MN 55402
(612) 341-2689

The National Retiree Volunteer Center is the catalyst that empowers retirees to be a contributing force in their communities through the investment of their skills and expertise. It initiates, develops, and expands retiree volunteer programs, for community benefit, in cooperation with corporations, government, educational institutions, and professional associations.

Points of Light (POL) Foundation
1737 H St. NW
Washington, DC 20006
(202) 223-9186

The mission of the POL Foundation is to make community service aimed at serious social problems central to the life of every American. The foundation works to stimulate new initiatives and build on and enhance the efforts of existing organizations in addressing its goals. These goals include: enlisting the media in making people aware of the benefits of engaging in service; persuading businesses, unions, schools, civic groups, religious institutions and other organizations to mobilize all of their members for community service; and identifying and disseminating community service ideas that work.

The National Volunteer Center (VOLUNTEER), created in 1979 through the merger of the National Center for Voluntary Action and the National Information Center on Volunteerism, is now under the POL umbrella. It serves as the only national voluntary organization whose sole purpose is to encourage the more effective use of volunteers in community problem solving. VOLUNTEER helps to improve the effectiveness of volunteer management skills by providing information sharing, training and technical assistance services; operates special projects to demonstrate new, unique, and innovative ways to get people involved; and serves as a national advocate for volunteering and citizen involvement. Periodicals: *Voluntary Action Leadership; Volunteering; Volunteer Readership Catalog.*

The National Council on Corporate Volunteerism (NCCV), a corporate membership organization, promotes volunteerism by serving as a national resource for the development and expansion of corporate employee volunteer programs. The council also serves as a clearinghouse for the exchange of information on corporate volunteerism and produces a quarterly newsletter as part of VOLUNTEER's "Volunteers from the Workplace" service. NCCV president is Jill Ragatz, who is manager of corporate volunteer programs, Honeywell, Inc., Minneapolis, Minnesota. Periodical: *Corporate Newsletter.*

Service Corps of Retired Executives (SCORE)
409 3d St. SW
Washington, DC 20024-3212
(202) 205-6762

SCORE is sponsored by the Small Business Administration, but it is an independent nonprofit organization. SCORE's primary purpose is to render a community service by providing, without charge, the expert assistance of its volunteer counselors in solving the problems encountered by small businesses.

United Way of America (UWA)
701 North Fairfax
Alexandria, VA 22314-2045
(703) 836-7100

UWA provides leadership and service to over 2,200 local United Ways in fund-raising, fiscal, and program management. It is also engaged in research and liaison activities with other national organizations and the government. Periodical: *Community*.

—*Lucy Rose Fischer, Ph.D.*

Most Americans now entering later life can expect to become members of a "new leisure class," due to the massive social and demographic changes over the twentieth century. Because leisure looms so large in the lives of all but the poorest older Americans, it deserves more than a cursory examination. Free time is important not only because retirement provides so much of it, and so suddenly, but because aging well depends in large part on making this time meaningful.

Living longer, fuller, and healthier lives, most Americans now look forward to a postwork time span of approximately nineteen to twenty-five years. The French call the period the *Troisieme Age,* or Third Age, in the life cycle, following the broad stages of learning (youth) and working (adulthood). As a people, Americans have decidedly mixed feelings about what, for most, will constitute the Third Age: leisure and retirement. On the one hand, after leading busy lives raising and supporting a family, the prospect of finally having plenty of time seems like a gift; on the other, cultural conditioning carries with it guilt feelings about leisure that may diminish its pleasures.

While no discussion of leisure time can be fully comprehensive, the chief choices older Americans make about how to spend their time will dictate whether they are, to paraphrase a Middle Eastern proverb, heading into the winter of their lives—or into the harvest.

Changing Attitudes Toward Leisure

Ancient cultures—chiefly the Greeks and Romans—elevated leisure to the highest status. Greek philosopher Aristotle rated it "better than work and its end." But since the Reformation, the work ethic, also called the Protestant ethic, has dominated and shaped the attitudes toward work (and play) of all Western societies, including the United States. Leisure, according to the Puritans who settled this land, was the work of the devil. Making a living, being productive, was the accepted goal.

The generation now facing retirement grew up believing that recreation and leisure were highly marginal—fine for kids but to be taken in small doses by adults. It was only the "idle rich" who possessed limitless leisure.

Sometime in the middle of the twentieth century, thanks to industrialization and hard work, Western societies were producing more goods than they could consume. The relationship between the job and leisure time began to change. If work was the seed of progress, its fruits included the shorter work week, the paid vacation, the pension, and the long period of retirement.

It has been said that a measure of civilization may be the degree that people perceive the use of time to be a problem. The problem, typically, doesn't emerge the morning after retirement. To most new retirees, still fit and energetic, the first few months are euphoric, full of the delight of children just sprung from school for summer vacation. Eventually, however, many experience a down side to the freedom that has replaced alarm clocks, commutes, and rigid schedules: the challenge of how to fill it.

Thus the "honeymoon" phase of retirement is usually followed by a "disenchantment" phase. People with feelings of guilt about retirement sometimes compensate by cramming their calendars with a multitude of projects. In effect, they exchange the work ethic for the "busy ethic." Cautioning against this, behaviorist B. F. Skinner advised: "To keep busy just because you feel you should . . . is not likely to be of much help. You must get more out of what you do than an escape from feeling guilty because you are idle. Instead of trying hard to enjoy what you are doing, try hard to find something that you like better."

Other older adults accept late-life leisure as an earned privilege, as "bonus time" to which their labor has entitled them. This more relaxed approach reflects a fairly recent trend in theory that views leisure as an avenue to self-realization and, as such, as an end in itself—not only for seniors but for all Americans. Writing of leisure's current role, French theorist Dumazedier observes, "Part of what used to be considered sinful by religious institutions is now recognized as the art of living."

Regardless of how leisure is perceived by older people, the exchange of the routines and rituals of work for leisure is one of life's most abrupt transitions. Retirees must deal with the suddenness of the change along with the feelings of emptiness and disorientation that often accompany a major life transition. Some find that time stretches before them "like the open sea"; this can be frightening or exhilarating.

A large AARP survey of older adults found that disposing of leisure was their third most significant problem, after health and finances.

What people fear in retirement, as well as the challenge of filling time, is the sense of diminished self-respect and purpose. Other losses—real or perceived—include loss of income, status and recognition, job perks, a sense of accomplishment, and—perhaps most crucial—social contacts. Author/business guru Peter Drucker has stated, "Work, since time immemorial, has been the means to satisfy man's need for belonging to a group and for a meaningful relationship to others of his kind." The challenge of retirement is replacing these losses with meaningful leisure activities. Sociologist Stephen Cutler assigns an even loftier role to leisure, proposing that "it is through leisure that new and renewed selves may be produced."

The Meaning of Leisure

How, then, to define the multifaceted condition that is leisure? A good, working definition by the late A. Bartlett Giamatti, university president and commissioner of major league baseball, called leisure "that form of non-work activity felt to be chosen, not imposed." He maintained that the use of freely chosen leisure reveals more about an individual—or a culture—than does

Numerous studies show that participating in excercise programs can improve memory, reduce anxiety and fatigue, and even alleviate depression.

its labor, for "to pursue leisure is to use freedom, our most precious possession." More simply, leisure is the time left over after life's necessities have been attended to. It is uncommitted time.

In one sense the notion of leisure is subjective, for the attitude toward the activity, not the activity itself, defines its nature. Making ceramic pots or analyzing the stock market, for example, may be leisure-time hobbies for some but businesses for others.

Leisure time and recreation are closely related but not identical concepts. Leisure refers to time availability, while recreation is the use of that time to refresh one's mind or body. In her autobiography, actress Helen Hayes summed up the positive outlook an older person needs in dealing with both of them: "To feel refreshed and ready for the next plateau, there must be some genuine eagerness to get there—a plan, a reason, a goal, a commitment . . . enthusiasm, productiveness, stimulating activities, intellectual progress—these are the ingredients for avoiding an enervating retirement routine."

All human activity, including leisure, may be classified broadly into physical action, social action, and mental action. It is the quality of leisure that lends it meaning, not the type. To realize the potential for late-life growth in free time, it must be used "meaningfully." Psychologist Charlotte Buhler defines meaningful use of time as that which contributes to the fulfillment of life. Such fulfillment is highly individual, and may be found in active or contemplative pursuits. (Social scientists often use the terms developmental and disengaged.) Active leisure runs the gamut from home-centered projects such as gardening, needlework, and refinishing furniture, to taking part in countless organizations and volunteer projects, working part-time or perfecting a golf game. Each of these activities provides some meaning to the participant. Contemplative use of time is equally valid. Seeking self-knowledge through meditation or prayer, selective reading, corresponding with old friends, writing one's memoirs, conducting a "life review"—are all quiet but highly meaningful pastimes. They form a common pattern especially among the "oldest-old."

> *Whatever the type of leisure, researchers have found that retired persons tend to seek the same values and satisfactions from these pursuits as they once did from their work.*

In the Third Age of life, many people feel a strong desire to give something back. The reflections of the older adult can enrich their lives but may also enrich society. Their insights and experiences are uniquely able to build a bridge from the past to the present. In a culture that has been called "throwaway," it is particularly important to recycle the wisdom of the elderly and preserve it in some form.

Interestingly, the values and meanings people seek from their leisure do not appear much affected by age, by social class, or by gender. They do vary, however, according to the personality of the individual.

Some gerontologists note that retirees, often unconsciously, divide their leisure time between self-chosen projects or "assignments" leading to a goal, and "R & R" activities that are pure relaxation. This helps maintain the rhythm of alternate work and play that has characterized one's earlier years and appears to promote a positive adjustment to retirement.

Every day *is* a holiday for retirees, hence the need to redefine some of one's activities. Linked to the work ethic again, it is a

Retirement appears to foster both latent and active artistic ability.

major reason why so many seniors spend so much time in goal-oriented volunteer work. Even after they retire, most Americans still struggle to fit into a culture shaped by industrialization; they are what philosopher Hannah Arendt called "a society of laborers without labor."

Table 1: The Meaning of Activity

The same activity can mean quite different things to different people. The following is an incomplete list of some of the meanings activities can have:

- A source of personal identity—I am what I do
- A way to make money
- A way to be with people
- A way to get the "vital juices" flowing
- A source of personal development
- A way to focus creativity

- A source of sensory experience
- A source of prestige or status
- A source of new experience
- A way to be of service to others
- A way of passing time
- Something to look forward to
- A way to exercise competence
- A source of peace and quiet
- A means of escape
- A source of joy and fun
- A source of feelings of accomplishment

Source: Robert C. Atchley, *Aging: Continuity and Change.* 2d ed. Belmont, CA: Wadsworth, 1987.

Retirement Planning

Only a minority of Americans make detailed, thoughtful plans about retirement well in advance, despite the growing field of leisure counseling and the fact that many large companies, as well as government employers, offer some form of preretirement advice, workshop, or seminar. Much of this counseling, however, is financial and doesn't help older adults deal with leisure time.

The level of middle-aged involvement is generally an accurate predictor of involvement after retirement.

The best preparation for retirement, of course, is lifelong. If during youth and middle age people considered how to make old age both active and meaningful, it would be more likely to happen. Studies show that most people who have had active non-work interests before retirement continue to enjoy them afterward.

According to researchers, people fall into three main categories at retirement age:

1. Those who do not retire: the self-employed, artists, professors, homemakers, who may scale down their work, and those who keep working out of financial necessity or choice

2. Those who retire to a new life fully anticipated and planned for

3. Those who leave the work force with little or no advance planning

Adele D.

Adele D., age eighty-one, speaks about self-reliance and looking on life as a creative adventure:

"If I put up a sign in front of my house, it would say: Herb plants for sale, lectures given, groups welcomed, palms read on Thursday between 1:15 and 2:45, Tarot card fortunes, figure drawing classes on Tuesday nights.

"I don't feel eighty-one. I don't even know what eighty-one is supposed to feel like. One of the real hazards of aging is not aging itself, it's believing what people tell you about old age. I think the main thing to remember is don't believe a word anybody tells you, even me.

"I believe your life is what you expect. I think we are co-creators of our lives, and if we think things are going to happen that we like, they will. If we think bad things are going to happen, they will. I know lots of miserable people who are famous and lots of miserable people who are very rich. You see, they talk about acquiring money and fame for security. There's no security in that. Who knows what's going to happen next? There's only one security and that's a feeling you have inside yourself that whatever comes up, you can handle it. It doesn't take money for that. I have very little money and mainly exist on my Social Security income.

"Every year at the end of summer I rent my house and am off to see the world. I've traveled to Japan, China, Mexico, Guatemala, Spain, France—all over. You've got everything in the world to do, all the things you always wanted to do and didn't have time because you had to do other things. Do them now, and enjoy them.

"Every day, when I get up, I think of millions of projects I want to undertake. I'm so happy to have the chance to take them on."

—*From Connie Goldman's "Late Bloomer" public radio series*

For the first group, use of leisure is not a problem. It is the third group—the largest category—whose adjustment may be difficult. Without some game plan for their lives, retirees may wonder whether "a Sunday evening is robbed of its pleasure if there is no anticipation of work on Monday." There is little doubt that planning eases the adjustment, but those whose work was especially rewarding or was closely linked to their self-image are likely to miss it more than those whose jobs were physically demanding or boring.

In all likelihood the number of hours of freedom will be between 2,000 and 2,500 hours a year. Converting this freedom windfall into hours of satisfaction is the business of later life. There should be room within the hours of freedom for pure relaxation, for activities where pleasure is an end in itself. Dr. Joyce Brothers says that fun should be savored: "When we are truly having fun, we briefly drop out of time, focus on the moment and lose ourselves in it . . . so long as we abandon ourselves to the possibility of delight of what is around us right now . . . we look past the serious problems; they'll still be there. . . . We are left refreshed and relaxed with a new perspective and a sharper focus."

Limits on Leisure

While the scope of leisure is broad for most older Americans, they are still limited by a number of factors: health, economic resources, family situation, location (urban versus rural), climate, living arrangement, transportation access, even by socioeconomic status and ethnic background.

Francoise Gilot

Artist and writer

SNAPSHOT

B eing an artist is a continuous ascent, rather like mountain climbing. There can be particular moments of achievement in the art itself. Outward recognition always follows much later, so it is not felt as strongly as a breakthrough in the work itself."

Painter and author Francoise Gilot was born in Paris in 1922. Exposed to literature and art from an early age, she recalls having her portrait painted in oils on a commission from her grandmother and being fascinated by the colors, smells, and processes of painting. On New Year's Day after her fifth birthday, she woke up bursting with the knowledge that she wanted to be an artist; shortly afterward her mother enrolled her in her first drawing class.

But in time Gilot's father decided she should acquire a practical skill that would enable her to earn a living: she should go to law school. Though she enrolled in law school, she left after two years, determined to live her own life and become an artist. Gilot was selling and exhibiting her work by the age of twenty-one. "I could not conceive of a woman not living through the fruits of her own efforts. For an artist it is the way to become a professional artist," Gilot says.

Gilot met artist Pablo Picasso, and they began living together and had two children, Claude and Paloma. Meanwhile Gilot continued to draw and paint, receiving favorable critical attention and mounting several shows. As her career bloomed, Picasso became more jealous because it distracted her from him, and he began to be unfaithful.

In 1954 feeling the situation was hopeless, Gilot left Picasso. She is the only one of Picasso's companions to leave him; in every other case—except for his last companion, Jaqueline Roque, whom he married—Picasso was the one who left.

In Paris Gilot tried to reestablish herself alone but discovered that Picasso, in his fury at her departure, had told every dealer he knew that if they handled her work he would never give them any of his. The technique was partly effective, although she was able to work around it over time and largely diminish it. Seeking a wider geographical range, Gilot attended the Tamarind Workshop in Los Angeles several times. On one such visit, mutual friends introduced her to Dr. Jonas Salk, and they were married some six months later. They live in La Jolla, California, not far from the Salk Institute, and periodically travel to New York and Paris.

Always a writer, Gilot published *Life with Picasso* in 1964, which became an international best-seller. Author of two versions of the book, Gilot actually wrote the book twice: once in English, once in French. She has published a number of other books, including several volumes of poems and the recent memoir *Matisse and Picasso: A Friendship in Art*.

Gilot also continues to paint, write, lecture, and exhibit widely. When asked about retiring, she declares, "Art is not a career, it's a lifetime calling."

—*Lydia Brontë*

Health is of course the most important factor limiting leisure choices. Energy and physical vigor vary widely among individuals and inevitably decline with age. Most recent research shows, however, that mental alertness is far more stable than was previously thought. Serious mental impairment among Americans over sixty-five is less than 5 percent. And that decrement is found chiefly in those over eighty-five.

Evidence indicates that those who achieved competence in various mental occupations in early life can maintain it as they age, though speed for learning new things declines somewhat. The motivation to learn is strong well into the Third Age, and extending intellectual growth is one of its most hopeful aspects. The financial limit on free-time activities is less important than in the past because leisure has been democratized. Many types of leisure are publicly provided or low in cost, such as activities at community and senior centers, parks, libraries, and local American Association of Retired Persons chapters. Seniors of all economic classes attend the same movies and sports events, for example, at relatively low prices.

Time and Older Americans

Both personal experience and research reveal that time is subjective. The elderly perceive it differently; it seems to pass more quickly for older adults than for the young. Some older adults report spending half a morning on ordinary activities they used to rush through, such as balancing a checkbook or buying groceries. This is partly because they can afford to be prodigal with time. A widow can bake "from scratch" and lavishly decorate a birthday cake for her granddaughter. An elderly woodcarver crafts an entire zoo of miniature animals. Each task can be given the time it deserves; time no longer equals money.

Some moments in time are much more significant than others. Time studies of how people allocate their leisure, which began in the 1930s and continue today, are only partially instructive, because they can't measure *quality time*. A six-minute long-distance call from an old high school pal has far more meaning to an older man than three hours of watching television—but both are leisure.

The pace of life slows for physical reasons as people move through the life stages from young-old (fifty-five to sixty-nine) to old (seventy to eighty-four) to oldest-old (eighty-five and over). Chosen activities become less strenuous and often more introspective. Arthritis in the shoulders might dictate a change from playing tennis to taking nature hikes. If vision fails, perhaps gardening can replace needlepoint. Satisfying uses for leisure can yet be found.

Older Americans recognize that most of their lives are past and the future is limited. Nevertheless, late life can include expansion and growth for seniors who have basic economic security and reasonably good health. The first generation to enjoy both for extended periods, today's elderly are also the first to enjoy the potential in old age. They practice a broader spectrum of lifestyles than any other age group.

Continuing to Work

Those whose lifestyles change the least with aging are the many older Americans who continue to work at their regular jobs, at least on a part-time basis. In 1989, 12 percent of the American work force was age sixty-five or older. But many opt for a very different second career, or a less demanding one, and some, with expertise in a specific area, turn to teaching. Others start their own businesses. While being one's own boss can realize a longtime dream, it can be a dramatic change in lifestyle, with the potential both for risks and rewards.

A variation of entrepreneurship that fits the modestly adventurous is starting a minibusiness. Forming a partnership for a minibusiness or a larger one can bolster morale and spread management responsibilities. Small service businesses that fill a real need but require little initial investment are probably most likely to succeed. These range from pet-sitting to resume writing to a telephone wake-up service.

A growing number of seniors, many of them women, are discovering that a small-scale business has big advantages: it can be tailored to the interests and pace of a retiree, it often can be run out of the home, and it requires less than full-time commitment.

Hobbies

Sometimes a favorite hobby can be metamorphosed into a business, though this entails a risk that "going commercial" may take the joy out of it. All sorts of craft items—jewelry, quilts, wooden toys, pottery, T-shirts, table mats—can be designed, produced, and marketed. Most older hobbyists will simply enjoy the ample time in which to expand their lifelong hobbies. A cherished hobby, such as birdwatching or researching the family tree, can become the centerpiece of later life.

While hobbies are as personal as fingerprints, there are three main types: doing, making, and collecting hobbies. "Doing" is the broadest category, including such diverse activities as going fishing, visiting Civil War battlefields, playing cards, and learning to square dance.

"Making" covers the full spectrum of creativity and can be a most meaningful use of leisure hours. Seniors in great numbers practice creative hobbies. A National Council on the Aging survey conducted in 1980 reported that 42 percent of older Americans do handiwork, weaving, or needlepoint; 31 percent enjoy photography; 38 percent play a musical instrument or sing in a choir (making music); 8 percent make pottery or ceramics; 15 percent paint or draw; and 12 percent write stories or poetry. Many do two or three of these things.

Older adults also take lessons and attend workshops in arts and crafts. Retirement appears to foster both latent and active artistic ability. Such activity has the power to transform because, according to researcher and leisure expert Max Kaplan, it "can go on indefinitely, thus directing the older participant to anticipate and visualize the future. . . . He develops a feeling of becoming and of growing."

One effort to bolster creative expression in seniors is the "Writing: Yarns of Yesteryear" project, headquartered at the University of Wisconsin at Madison. It encourages the writing of memoirs and reminiscences through correspondence courses and workshops. Another is the Dance Exchange, a Washington, D.C., program that fosters creative dance in older adults through classes and performances of its troupe of elderly dancers, named "Dancers of the Third Age."

Many older people also find creative outlets through community theater groups at various levels of professionalism. This hobby is a popular one, whether it is considered doing something or making a performance.

Collecting things continues to fill time constructively for seniors, according to hobby magazines. The number of different items considered to be collectibles is nearly three thousand, and there are publications and clubs for almost all of them. Displaying, mounting, and cataloguing a collection extends the hobby beyond simple acquisition.

Social and Religious Participation

While many hobbies are home centered, others lead to social interaction through clubs, hobby fairs, and conventions. Seniors also build social contacts by joining fraternal organizations, civic groups, clubs, and religious bodies.

Participation in job-related organizations predictably drops after retirement, but membership in other associations holds up fairly well until late age. The American Association of Retired Persons (AARP), founded in 1958, is undoubtedly the most popular senior organization, claiming 33 million Americans fifty years

Will Barnet

Artist

SNAPSHOT

For painters, maturity is more important than being young ... if you study the history of art, you will find the greatest painters were those who were trying to understand their language and develop it as they grew older. That's what it's all about."

Born in Beverly, Massachusetts, in 1911, Will Barnet remembers going to the library throughout his early childhood. When he was about six, he picked up a book filled with fantastic, wonderful colored drawings. He was entranced by these illustrations and declared, "That's what I want to do." With exceptional determination for someone so young, he set about shaping his education so that he could become an artist. His parents had very little money and knew nothing about art, and there was no art instruction in Beverly, so, at fifteen, Barnet won a fellowship to the School of Fine Arts at the Boston Museum to begin his formal artistic training and complete his high school degree.

After three years of study in Boston, Barnet grew restless. He had become a young revolutionary artist, no longer wanting to be limited to classical techniques. "We used to have fist fights over art!" Barnet says about his group of classmates at the art school. He had been studying modern artists such as Gauguin and Modigliani and decided to move to New York to better explore his avant-garde interests. So he wrote to the Art Students League and was awarded a fellowship. To support himself during the depression, Barnet drew cartoons for the *New Yorker,* worked as a librarian, and became a lithograph printer. The Art Students League hired him as the school's printer for students, outside professionals, and the graphics instructors.

Within two years, he became the youngest instructor ever at the Art Students League, teaching both printing and graphics. The Art Students League was the focal point of the art world in America at the time; the most famous artists came to the League to exhibit, to work, and to teach. And the students were top-notch as well: young Jackson Pollock was studying at the League during this period. The League also acted as a meeting place for the artists, who were deeply concerned with the social and political issues of the day.

By the early 1940s, Barnet was developing his own work and showing in galleries around New York. Most of his work consisted of oil paintings; but in 1939 he did a woodcut called "Early Morning," one of his most important prints of the period. "That was the beginning of the development of my work toward a more abstract concept," explains Barnet.

During the war he was recruited to work in a lithograph company, printing secret war documents at night, while continuing to teach during the daytime. When the war ended, veterans flooded his classroom, and Barnet began to shape the younger generation of artists. Throughout his career Barnet made mentoring other artists a priority, and many of his former students have gone on to achieve world fame. He also continued making both prints and oil paintings, showing and selling some of both.

In the 1950s, Barnet began to do more representational work that was still heavily influenced by his understanding of abstract forms, a style which Barnet calls "figurative abstraction." He became known for this style, and by the 1960s, he had achieved recognition within the art world as one of the most accomplished contemporary painters. But it was in the 1970s that a renaissance in prints gave him much wider recognition. He continues to paint and teach in New York. His works are exhibited in public collections at our nation's greatest museums and can also be seen at the Library of Congress and the New York Public Library.

—Lydia Brontë

Elderly lower-income individuals tend to concentrate leisure pursuits around home and family; higher incomes correlate with wider interests.

lar senior organization, claiming 33 million Americans fifty years and over as members in 1992.

Overall, those with higher education levels who live in cities participate more in clubs and organizations than do rural and blue-collar Americans. Those who need social contacts the most—solitary older people—tend to be less active in communal activities than those with companions, a spouse, a family member, or a close friend. Transportation problems are often the biggest barrier to participation by older adults in organizations of all sorts.

Several studies over the past few decades have attempted to determine the life satisfaction of retired Americans. It appears that a sense of well-being correlates strongly with health, with financial security, and with marital status, but also with the level of participation in social events outside the family.

Attendance at churches and synagogues peaks somewhere around age sixty. Older people are often leaders in church-related activities and, in general, hold more memberships in church or synagogue than other generations. Studies on aging and religious activity tend to be inconclusive; some show a rise in attendance at services while others find participation drops slightly with age but religious feelings increase.

Older Americans who regularly attend senior centers—currently less than 5 percent of those over sixty-five—typically are middle class, with a strong attachment to the community. In addition to social services, such centers offer varied educational and recreational programs and informal companionship. Their purpose is to support both independence and community involvement among older adults.

Following the Older Americans Act of 1965, the senior center movement spread rapidly. Today there are well over nine thousand centers in the United States, offering services ranging from income tax counseling to bridge tournaments to courses in defensive driving.

Card games are just one of the leisure activities enjoyed by those who attend senior centers.

COPYRIGHT MARIANNE GONTARZ

Activities for the elderly are also offered through Golden Age clubs, community and neighborhood centers, and parks and recreation departments. However, in a 1981 survey only 9 percent of people over sixty-five said they had attended any of these within the past two weeks. But a larger percentage (27 percent) said they would like to attend such a facility; the most interest was reflected among elderly African Americans.

Minorities and Leisure

Retirement—in the conventional sense of abundant leisure supported by adequate income—does not apply to most ethnic minorities. Many continue to work, or to look for work, and many live in real poverty. Overall, poorer educational opportunities and discrimination have yielded smaller retirement incomes than whites enjoy. Few African Americans, Chicanos, or Native Americans have pensions, and fewer own their own homes than do whites. But because their jobs were less rewarding, some research indicates they miss them less at retirement. This easier adjustment is usually only temporary, and later on they report greater disappointment with retirement.

Life expectancy is less for most minority groups than for whites. Minority elderly have less access to health services and generally inferior health conditions than their white counterparts. Older African Americans are less likely than whites to have cultivated hobbies. They take part in fewer activities outside the home. The little research done in this area shows, not surprisingly, that their morale, or life satisfaction, also tends to be lower.

Ethnic minorities generally take pride in caring for their own ill or aging members, and very few live in planned retirement communities. Informal networks such as the family, the extended family, and friends are the chief source of social support for elderly minorities.

Because discriminatory barriers to participation in certain sports and access to travel accommodations have now been lowered for African Americans, these leisure activities have increased slightly. Church-related activities are important, though African Americans also attend movies, sporting events, classes, and club meetings. Historically the church has been a strong support for African Americans, but while the elderly attend church in high numbers, they are not necessarily more religious than the elderly in other ethnic groups.

One recent study focused on predictors of mortality among older African Americans. It found a higher risk of death among those with little family contact who did not take part in activities or attend church.

Elderly Japanese Americans are far less secure financially than their offspring; some 20 percent live below the poverty level. The older generation, having grown up in highly structured families where the elders were revered, now must struggle with changing attitudes of filial piety. Their expectations of total support and respect from their children are often disappointed. Most older Japanese Americans cling to religious observances for stability as well as for social interaction.

Housing and Activities

Where older Americans live affects their leisure lifestyles. Most seniors choose to live in independent households, but multiple living arrangements are on the rise. Age-congregated living features a potpourri of activities and recreation as part of the expected lifestyle. Housing arrangements vary from small retirement homes to senior apartments to huge retirement complexes such as Leisure World and Sun City.

The planned retirement community (RC) offering safe, attractive, communal living is a post–World War II, largely white phenomenon. By 1984 there were approximately 2,300 RCs, mostly in the Sunbelt. An RC offers flexible living, from small apartments in a central lodge to townhouses and cluster homes.

Two of the oldest and largest RCs are Sun City and Sun City West, near Phoenix, which together house some 75,000 people. Facilities include several recreation centers, multiple golf courses, pools, bowling alleys, and tennis courts, chapters of national service organizations, and activity clubs in mind-boggling variety. Table 2 lists the leisure choices of one RC.

The activity levels of elderly people living in multiple unit housing are higher than those who live in dispersed housing.

Sports and Fitness for Older Adults

As Americans advance in age, their participation in sports decreases. This will be less true of future generations who have been taught to view physical fitness as a major goal. Still, seniors in the 1990s have heard, loud and clear, the repeated warning that Americans in general do not get enough exercise. Unlike younger working people, retirees cannot use the excuse of insufficient time. Further, longevity and better physical condition are decidedly linked.

How are they responding? Particularly among the young-old, taking part in sports and exercise is an escalating trend. They are keeping pace with other Americans in purchase of home gym equipment, exercise videotapes, and jogging shoes. They are flocking to classes in aerobics and water aerobics. Probably still not as active as optimum fitness dictates, the elderly are moving in the right direction.

The importance of exercise for older adults is underscored by copious research. Demonstrated benefits are both physiological—increased flexibility, strength, endurance, bone mass, cardio-

Table 2: Sun City West Chartered Club Activities

(Number after a club indicates more than one club)

Art	Greenhouse	Quilters
Astronomy		
	Horseshoes	Rhythm tappers
Ballet		Rock-hounds
Basketeers	Knitting (machine)	Rosemaling
Bicycle riders	Knitting and macramé	RV club
Billiards		
Bocce	Lapidary	Saddle club
Book review	Laugh-in club	Sewing
Bowling (10)	Lawn bowling (3)	Shuffleboard
	Leathercarvers	Silk flowers
Calligraphy	Library friends	Silver craft
Card clubs (13)		Singles social club
Ceramics	Mah jongg	Softball (2)
Chess	Mini golfers	Sportsmen (5)
China painting	Metal-craft	Stained glass
Chorus (Westernaires)	Miscellaneous chartered	
Clay-craft	activities (20)	Tennis (court, platform
Coin and stamp	Model railroad	and table)
Computers (4)	Musicians club	Theater (drama)
Copper-craft		Tole-craft
	Needle and craft	
Dance clubs	Newcomers coffee	Weavers
		Women's social club
Español club	Organ and keyboard	Woodworking
Exercise clubs (10)		Writers club
	Photography	
Garden clubs (2)	Prides (street cleaners)	
Golf (10)		

Source: Sun City West Chartered Club.

vascular fitness—and psychological. Numerous studies show that participating in exercise programs can improve memory, reduce anxiety and fatigue, and even alleviate depression. Becoming more proficient in a sport or exercise can also lift seniors' self-esteem.

Which sports do older Americans prefer? A survey taken in 1989 by the National Sporting Goods Association ranked these as the favorite sports activities for those over sixty-five: (1) exercise walking, (2) swimming, (3) fishing, (4) bicycle riding, and (5) golf. Bowling followed closely in sixth place. Older Americans play an estimated one-third of all rounds of golf; the National Golf Association says about 3.2 million people over sixty enjoy the game. Some 14 percent of seniors go fishing or hunting.

Special organizations to encourage sports participation among the older adult population abound. One of the most successful programs is the Senior Games, sponsored by the U.S. National Senior Olympics. Held

In sports as gentle as croquet or as demanding as parachute jumping, there are seniors, somewhere, who are participating.

every other year in participating states (currently in thirty-five states), the games classify participants in five-year age brackets. Standards for judging are professional but appropriate to older abilities. Among the games are tennis, swimming, golf, table tennis, bowling, shuffleboard, horseshoes, badminton, and track and field events. They provide a formal structure for participation and recognition of fitness in older adults. In 1989, 200,000 senior athletes took part in the local qualifying games for the Second Biennial National Senior Olympics. Roughly half that number participated in the National Senior Olympics member game events. More than one-third of all participants were women. The success of these types of programs is helping to shatter the myth that seniors are too frail for fitness.

Many other frameworks for senior competition exist. The Senior Softball World Series, with five age divisions beginning at fifty, has held annual tournaments since 1989. To promote tennis as a lifetime sport, the Senior Games Development Council launched a "Condo Tennis" program in south Florida. Geared to the area's large retired population living in condos with tennis courts, the program offers free tennis lessons to participants.

There are organizations for seniors built around virtually every sport, from skiing (the Over the Hill Gang International and the 70+ Ski Club) to mall walking. Older swimmers join associations such as San Francisco's Dolphin Club, whose members take a four-mile swim in the bay every New Year's Day. Many YMCAs, park and recreation departments, and community centers have

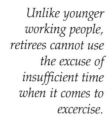

Unlike younger working people, retirees cannot use the excuse of insufficient time when it comes to excercise.

COPYRIGHT MARIANNE GONTARZ

sports and exercise programs for seniors, at different skill levels—and more are being organized all the time.

Whether or not they participate, older Americans are frequent spectators at sporting events of all kinds. Following favorite teams and studying the players and statistics can consume quantities of free time.

Watching one's team, whether it's the Yankees, the Bulls, or the grandson's Little League, can be a very special experience, offering a shared moment of leisure. The communal aspect adds to the pleasure when, reacting together to some play or triumph, the crowd becomes a community.

For sports fans who also like to travel, the National Senior Sports Association organizes trips, usually off season to keep prices down, to senior tournaments in golf, tennis, and bowling at elegant resorts.

The benefits of excercise include increased flexibility, strength, endurance, bone mass, and cardiovascular fitness.

COURTESY OF THE NATIONAL COUNCIL ON THE AGING, INC.

Not only are older people pursuing the arts as participants, they are increasingly rating cultural institutions as important to the quality of life. Older adults continue to attend cultural events as they age, and the over-sixty-five contingent reflects greater gains in attendance than do other groups. Ten percent of this group attend a play at least once a year, and 13 percent attend a musical. Classical music performances attract 13 percent of the group, and art museums and galleries draw 16 percent. These figures are based on a 1985 survey for the National Endowment for the Arts. The Endowment in recent years has made major strides in extending access to cultural programs. Its outreach initiatives both bring arts programs to people in nursing homes, senior centers, and rural areas, and facilitate bringing people to programs through subsidized transportation and special tickets for seniors.

Older people go to movies for entertainment and rent them on videotape to enjoy at home, read all kinds of periodicals, both read and subscribe to daily newspapers in higher numbers than younger people, and particularly enjoy the more than two hundred publications geared to older audiences. Having grown up with radio, they still listen to it. "Mature Focus Radio," produced by AARP for the Mutual Broadcasting System, is especially popu-

Entertainment: The Performing Arts and the Media

Among those over sixty-five, surveys show that from 92 percent to 95 percent watch TV regularly. As a segment of the total viewing audience, seniors watch more than forty hours a week, more than any other age group.

lar. More than 160 radio stations carry it in English and 170 stations in Spanish.

It is television, however, that accounts for a huge bite out of an older adult's free time. Both a curse and a blessing to the aging, TV is always readily available, requires no physical effort or special transportation, and is inexpensive. It entertains—or at least distracts. It can simulate companionship for the lonely and provide a link to the larger world. Further, it offers structure in an existence that often lacks it.

Occasionally, TV presents fine fare in drama, music, nature, news, and public affairs. Its critics, however, would agree with philosopher Harry R. Moody, who has said that for older people television threatens "the domination of late-life leisure through one-way communication that reduces the last stage of life to silence."

Prior to the 1980s, the images of older people presented on TV were too often inaccurate or inappropriate. For the past ten years, the situation has improved: there were many more portrayals of seniors, and they were far more positive than in the past. Credit goes to such innovative shows as "The Golden Girls," "Mr. Belvedere," "Matlock," and "Murder, She Wrote."

Travel

One of the most popular pastimes for retirees is travel. Seniors take all kinds of trips, from a short drive to a neighboring town to visit their children to ambitious round-the-world voyages.

A market survey of older travelers revealed their five favorite vacation choices: national parks, historic sites, beaches (and other warm weather spots), fall foliage trips, and special events or festivals.

Cruises are enjoyed by the older adult, whether by luxury ocean liner, freighter, barge, or paddleboat steamer; seniors make

John Forsythe

Actor

D ynasty stars were the same ages as their characters."

Born in 1918 in Penn's Grove, New Jersey, actor John Forsythe grew up wanting to be a baseball player, then a sports writer and play-by-play announcer. He attended the University of North Carolina at Chapel Hill, majoring in writing, but in his junior year he dropped out of college to be the announcer for baseball games at Ebbets Field.

But baseball announcing had one disadvantage Forsythe had not anticipated: It was only a summertime occupation! Looking for an off-season job, he auditioned to do radio dramas for WNYC radio in New York. He found he loved this job more than sports announcing. He went on to a job with a children's theater in Chappaqua and then worked with a Shakespearean company for a year. This led to Broadway appearances in *Vickie* and *Yankee Point* and a contract with Warner Brothers, debuting in *Destination Tokyo* with Cary Grant.

While serving in the army during World War II, Forsythe acted in *Winged Victory,* Moss Hart's stage musical using only servicemen. Other stage roles followed, including the Pulitzer Prize–winning *Teahouse of the August Moon.* Forsythe worked in early live television, including "Studio One," "Philco Playhouse," "Kraft Theater," and "World of Survival," a national wildlife series.

Movies occupied Forsythe as well, among them *Captive City, The Trouble With Harry, Topaz, And Justice For All*, and most recently *Scrooged*.

But the TV series "Dynasty" made Forsythe a major star. A sensation when it first aired, "Dynasty" kept millions of Americans enthralled with its high-powered portrayal of the life and business dealings of Forsythe's hard-driving but attractive character, Denver oil magnate Blake Carrington. One of the series' greatest accomplishments was that it depicted mature adults whose lives were eventful, glamorous, and exciting—and the stars who played the roles were the same ages as their characters. "Dynasty" broke age barriers in television, an industry that until then created few attractive and interesting roles women over forty or men over fifty. Forsythe, a happily married man in his sixties, became a sex symbol for millions of women. Forsythe was honored with two Golden Globe Awards as best actor in a dramatic television series and an Emmy nomination for his performance on "Dynasty."

In 1991 Forsythe became Senator Powers in a new comedy series called "The Powers That Be," a satire on American political life in the 1990s. He has also completed a romantic comedy for NBC, entitled "Opposites Attract," and has directed, produced, and narrated a documentary on the life and career of jockey Bill Shoemaker, called "Nice Guys Finish First."

—*Lydia Brontë*

up 30 percent of all cruise passengers. They are also getting hands-on sailing experiences via sailing schools and windjammer cruises.

One of the appealing features of travel, for people of all ages, is the element of adventure. This comprises the joys of exploring and learning, common to any new experience, and the excitement of taking risks. While the majority of older travelers insist on comfortable beds and confirmed reservations, others are anything but timid travelers. Those who have traveled extensively in earlier years are particularly apt to seek such exotic forms of travel as camel expeditions, river rafting, balloon flights, and wildlife safaris.

Consider these challenging trips, all undertaken by people over sixty:

Of all passport holders, 44 percent are over age fifty-five. Older adults represent 22 percent of all travelers and 30 percent of domestic travelers.

- A five-thousand-mile expedition by canoe and kayak, starting at the mouth of the Mackenzie River in Canada and ending thirty-three months later at Cape Horn, Chile. The couple who made this trip had to cope with snakes, black bears, and killer bees along the way.

- A trek up Tanzania's Mt. Kilimanjaro—the especially rugged Machame Trail—by an eighty-five-year-old woman.

- An eight-thousand-mile flight following the Alcan Highway in a home-built biplane. A World War II bomber pilot built the plane in his Kansas garage, then made the trip to Fairbanks, Alaska, with a seventy-one-year-old buddy as co-pilot.

- A river rafting trip down the Colorado by a group of grandmothers.

- A leisurely camping trip through Alaska—not by lavish RV, but by four-wheel-drive pick-up truck. A resourceful husband and wife built a deck on their truck to fit their tent; this gave them flexibility at rock-bottom cost.

- A solo round-the-world flight in a small Cessna. The pilot, age seventy-four, got his pilot's license ten years earlier and made some fifteen flights, including one to Australia, before attempting the worldwide trip.

Special interest, or theme travel, is a rapidly growing part of the travel market for all travelers. Trips built around such interests as archaeology, gardening, or birdwatching are popular with older adults who have had enough of conventional travel. Almost any interest can be the centerpiece for such a trip, either planned by a travel agent or by the travelers themselves. Older adults with plenty of time often relish the fun of researching and planning a trip, down to the last detail.

Because the older market is such a fertile one for the travel industry, in recent years a number of organizations have focused on tours specifically for seniors. The pace is a bit more relaxed, and comfortable accommodations can be counted on. Two of the larger companies geared to foreign trips for the elderly are Grand Circle Travel and Saga International Holidays. Another is the AARP Travel Service, which arranges both foreign and domestic escorted tours for its members.

Some special tours emphasize international understanding as one of the pleasures of the trip. Seniors Abroad arranges three-week home visits in one of six foreign countries for those over fifty. The Friendship Force, another organization emphasizing the people-to-people aspect of travel, places travelers of all ages in homes in some forty countries, then arranges exchange visits that bring foreigners into American homes.

Also noteworthy is Grandtravel, an organization that plans domestic and foreign tours for grandparents and their grandchildren.

Trips that mix learning with travel, both in the United States and abroad, are growing in importance for seniors. The largest and oldest organization is Elderhostel, which began in 1975 and has been hugely successful; another is Interhostel.

Research expeditions, such as Earthwatch, offer the chance to take part in scientific research along with travel. Some of these unusual trips carry academic credit for participants.

Discounts for older adults are available in virtually every facet of travel, from transportation to accommodations to services. Not only are they too wide ranging and numerous to list here, they also are changing constantly in response to the needs of the industry. Older Americans considering any sort of trip are well advised to investigate such bargains either through a travel agent or by individual research well in advance of the departure date. Newspaper advertisements, for example, sometimes list last-minute travel clubs, or travel clearinghouses, that offer big discounts on unsold accommodations. Some are legitimate, others are not, but the reliable operators may be ideal for retirees who can be flexible about timing their trips.

There is a wealth of information catering to wanderlust: travel magazines and newsletters, including several slanted to the

The reflections of the elderly can enrich their lives but may also enrich society. Their insights and experiences are uniquely able to build a bridge for the past to the present.

older adult, as well as practical guidebooks and books by travel writers that accurately convey the atmosphere of a destination. Libraries and bookstores have many shelves of literature on travel. State departments of tourism, Chambers of Commerce, travel agents, private tour companies, and even the U.S. government are valuable sources of information. There are also video and audio tapes that highlight various travel destinations. Public libraries usually have some; others can be obtained free from travel agents or rented from video stores.

Older Americans travel by car 80 percent of the time, and they make 72 percent of all trips made in recreational vehicles. Whether the RV is a motor home, trailer, truck camper, van conversion, or folding camper trailer, its appeal to seniors is that it combines transportation and overnight accommodation in one. One favorite RV owners' motto is "Home is where we park it." Many are in the young-old age group and represent all economic backgrounds. What they have in common is a desire to see the country and to do so in a more flexible way than conventional trips allow.

Some RV owners travel and live full-time in their vehicle. Others become nomads for a few weeks or a season. RVs can also be rented so people can test the lifestyle before making a big purchase. Living expenses for full-time RVers are usually lower than for those making home mortgage payments, but costs for health care, food, and services may be higher because they are less familiar with the community.

Staying in one of the growing number of RV parks gives second middle-agers valuable social contacts and the opportunity to network about travel destinations. Some belong to RV singles groups such as Loners on Wheels and Loners of America. In addition there are countless clubs for RV owners that sponsor caravans, campouts, and state, regional, and international rallies.

Camping is a leisure activity related to travel that counts some 5 million Americans over fifty-five among its devotees. Some 39 percent of campers prefer RV camping, and 20,000 campgrounds in the United States will accommodate RVs. Many large campgrounds cater to older campers, especially in the Sunbelt states. Retired campers can often utilize camp facilities off season when they are not in demand by younger campers.

Most older campers camped in their younger days and still enjoy the outdoor setting. However, the chance to develop skills and the simple living that camping provides makes others recent converts to camping.

—*Lyn Teven; Fred Lee; Alice Lee*

GENERAL BIBLIOGRAPHY

A

Abramson, Leonard. *Healing Our Health Care System.* New York: Grove Wiedenfeld, 1990.

Achenbaum, W. A. *Social Security: Visions and Revisions.* New York: Cambridge University Press, 1986.

Adams, R. G., and R. Blieszner, eds. *Older Adult Friendship: Structure and Process.* Newbury Park, CA: Sage Publications, 1989.

Alexander, Jo, Jr., et al., eds. *Women and Aging: An Anthology by Women.* Corvallis, OR: Calyx Books, 1986.

Altman, Maya, and others. *How Do I Pay for My Long-Term Health Care? A Consumer Guidebook About Long-Term Care Insurance.* Berkeley, CA: Berkeley Planning Associates, 1988.

————. *The Nursing Home and You: Partners in Caring for a Relative with Alzheimer's Disease.* Washington, DC: AAHA, 1988.

American Association of Retired Persons (AARP). *The Age Discrimination in Employment Act Guarantees You Certain Rights: Here's How . . . .* Washington, DC: AARP, 1987.

————. *Before You Buy: A Guide to Long-Term Care Insurance.* Rev. ed. Washington, DC: AARP, 1991.

————. *Business and Older Workers: Current Perceptions and New Directions for the 1990s.* Washington, DC: AARP, 1989.

————. *Ideas for Helping a Friend in Crisis.* Washington, DC: AARP, Social Outreach and Support Program Department, 1989.

————. *Knowing Your Rights: Medicare's Prospective Payment System.* Washington, DC: AARP Fulfillment.

————. *Look Before You Leap: A Guide to Early Retirement Incentive Programs*. Washington, DC: AARP Worker Equity, 1988.

————. *Miles Away and Still Caring: A Guide for Long-Distance Caregivers*. Washington, DC: AARP, 1986.

————. *The Perfect Fit: Creative Ideas for a Safe and Livable Home*. Washington, DC: AARP, 1992.

————. *Understanding Senior Housing for the 1990s*. Washington, DC: AARP Consumer Affairs, Program Coordination and Development Department, 1990.

————. *Work and Retirement: Employees Over Forty and Their Views*. Washington, DC: AARP, 1986.

————. *Your Home Your Choice: A Workbook for Older People and Their Families*. Washington, DC: AARP Consumer Affairs Program Coordination and Development Department, 1992.

The American Cancer Society Cancer Book: Prevention, Detection, Diagnosis, Treatment, Rehabilitation, Cure. New York: Doubleday, 1986.

The American Heart Association Heartbook: A Guide to Prevention and Treatment of Cardiovascular Diseases. New York: E. P. Dutton, 1980.

————. *Sex and Heart Disease*. Dallas: American Heart Association.

Atchley, Robert C. *Aging: Continuity and Change*. 2d ed. Belmont, CA: Wadsworth, 1987.

————. *Social Forces and Aging*. 6th ed. Belmont, CA: Wadsworth, 1991.

B

Bass, Scott A., Elizabeth A. Kutza, and Fernando M. Torres-Gil, eds. *Diversity in Aging: Challenges Facing Planners and Policymakers in the 1990s*. Glenview, IL: Scott, Foresman, 1989.

Beauvoir, Simone de. *The Coming of Age*. New York: Warner Books, 1973.

Beresford, Larry. *The Hospice Handbook*. Boston, MA: Little, Brown & Co., 1992.

Berg, Robert L., and Joseph S. Cassells, eds. *The Second Fifty Years: Promoting Health and Preventing Disability*. Washington, DC: Institute of Medicine, National Academy Press, 1990.

Berman, P. L., and K. Goldman. *The Ageless Spirit*. New York: Ballantine, 1992.

Berman, Philip L., ed. *The Courage to Grow Old: Forty-one Prominent Men and Women Reflect on Growing Old*. New York: Ballantine, Del Rey, Fawcett, 1989.

Bianci, Eugene C. *Aging as a Spiritual Journey*. New York: Crossroads, 1982.

Billig, Nathan. *To Be Old and Sad: Understanding Depression in the Elderly.* Lexington, MA: Lexington Books, 1987.

Binstock, R. H., and L. K. George, eds. *Handbook of Aging and the Social Sciences.* 3d ed. San Diego: Academic Press, 1990.

Biracree, Tom, and Nancy Biracree. *Over Fifty: The Resource Book for the Better Half of Your Life.* New York: HarperCollins, 1991.

Bird, Carolina. *Second Careers. New Ways to Work After 50.* Boston, MA: Little, Brown & Co., 1992.

Birren, James E., and K. Warner Schaie, eds. *Handbook of the Psychology of Aging.* 3d ed. New York: Harcourt Brace, 1990.

Birren, James E., Bruce Sloane, and Gene D. Cohen. *Handbook of Aging and Mental Health.* 2d ed. New York: Academic Press, 1992.

Brody, Baruch. *Life and Death Decisionmaking.* New York: Oxford University Press, 1988.

Brody, E. *Women in the Middle: Their Parent-Care Years.* New York: Springer Publishing Co., 1990.

Brody, Howard. *The Healer's Power.* New Haven, CT: Yale University Press, 1992.

Brontë, Lydia. *The Longevity Factor.* New York: HarperCollins, 1993.

Brown, Arnold S. *The Social Processes of Aging and Old Age.* Englewood Cliffs, NJ: Prentice-Hall, 1990.

Brown, Judith N., and Christina Baldwin. *A Second Start: A Widow's Guide to Financial Survival at a Time of Emotional Crisis.* New York: Simon & Schuster, 1987.

Brubaker, Timothy H. *Family Relationships in Later Life.* Newbury Park, CA: Sage Publications, 1990.

Butler, R. N., and H. P. Gleason. *Productive Aging: Enhancing Vitality in Later Life.* New York: Springer Publishing Co., 1985.

Butler, Robert N., and Myrna L. Lewis. *Aging and Mental Health: Positive Psychosocial and Biomedical Approaches.* New York: Merrill, 1991.

————. *Love and Sex after 60.* New York: Harper & Row, 1988.

C

Callahan, D. *Setting Limits: Medical Goals in an Aging Society.* New York: Simon & Schuster, 1988.

Carlsen, M. Baird. *Creative Aging: A Meaning-Making Perspective.* New York: W.W. Norton, 1991.

Chambre, Susan. *Good Deeds in Old Age: Volunteering by the New Leisure Class.* Lexington, MA: Lexington Books, 1987.

Chapman, Elwood N. *Comfort Zones: A Practical Guide for Retirement Planning.* Los Altos, CA: Crisp Publications, 1987.

Cherlin, Andrew J., and Frank F. Furstenberg. *The New American Grandparent: A Place in the Family, A Life Apart.* New York: Basic Books, 1988.

Chinen, A. B. *In the Ever After: Fairy Tales and the Second Half of Life.* Wilmette, IL: Chiron Publications, 1989.

—————. *Once Upon a Midlife: Classic Stories and Mythic Tales to Illuminate the Middle Years.* Los Angeles: Jeremy P. Tarcher, 1992.

Christensen, Alice, and David Rankins. *Easy Does It Yoga for Older People.* San Francisco: Harper & Row, 1979.

Coberly, Lenore M., et al. *Writers Have No Age: Creative Writing with Older Adults.* Binghamton, NY: Haworth Press, 1985.

Cohen, Gene D. *The Brain in Human Aging.* New York: Springer Publishing Co., 1988.

Cole, T. R. *The Journey of Life.* New York: Cambridge University Press, 1992.

Cole, Thomas R., David D. Van Tassel, and Robert Kastenbaum, eds. *Handbook of the Humanities and Aging.* New York: Springer Publishing Co., 1992.

Coleman, B. *A Consumer Guide to Hospice Care.* Washington, DC: National Consumers League, 1990.

Collins, E. R., Jr., and D. Weber. *The Complete Guide to Living Wills.* New York: Bantam Books, 1992.

Commerce Clearing House, Inc. *Social Security Benefits.* Chicago: Commerce Clearing House, Inc. 1992.

Connor, J. Robert. *Cracking the Over-50 Job Market.* New York: Plume, 1992.

Cousins, Norman. *Anatomy of an Illness.* New York: W. W. Norton, 1979.

D

Day, Christine L. *What Older Americans Think: Interest Groups and Aging Policy.* Princeton, NJ: Princeton University Press, 1990.

Doress, Paula Brown, Diana L. Siegal, and the Midlife and Older Women Book Project. *Ourselves, Growing Older.* New York: Simon & Schuster, 1987.

Dychtwald, Ken. *Age Wave.* Los Angeles, CA: Jeremy P. Tarcher, 1989.

E

Edinberg, Mark A. *Talking with Your Aging Parents.* Boston, MA: Shambhala Publications, 1987.

Erikson, E. H. *The Life Cycle Completed: A Review.* New York: W.W. Norton, 1982.

Erikson, E. H., J. M. Erikson, and H. Q. Kivnick. *Vital Involvement in Old Age.* New York: W.W. Norton, 1987.

F

FannieMae Customer Education Group. *Money from Home: A Consumer's Guide to Home Equity Conversion Mortgages.* Washington, DC: Federal Publications, 1992.

Feltin, Marie. *A Woman's Guide to Good Health After Fifty.* Glenview, IL: AARP and Scott, Foresman, 1987.

Fischer, D. H. *Growing Old in America.* Expanded ed. New York: Oxford University Press, 1977.

Fischer, Kathleen. *Winter Grace: Spirituality for the Later Years.* New York: Paulist Press, 1985.

Fischer, Lucy Rose, and Kay Schaffer. *Older Volunteers: A Guide to Research and Practice.* Newbury Park, CA: Sage Publications, 1993.

Fischer, R. B., M. L. Blazey, and H. T. Lipman, eds. *Students of the Third Age—University/College Programs for Retired Adults.* New York: Macmillan, 1992.

Fowler, M., and P. McCutcheon, eds. *Songs of Experience.* New York: Ballantine, 1991.

Friedan, Betty. *The Fountain of Age.* New York: Simon & Schuster, 1993.

Fries, James. *Aging Well.* Menlo Park, CA: Addison-Wesley, 1989.

G

Gaudio, Peter, and Virginia Nicols. *Your Retirement Benefits.* New York: Wiley, 1992.

Gelfand, Donald E. *The Aging Network, Programs & Services.* 3d ed. New York: Springer Publishing Co., 1988.

Gillespie, Ann E., and Katrinka Smith Sloan. *Housing Options and Services for Older Adults.* Santa Barbara, CA: ABC-CLIO, 1990.

Goldman, Connie. "Late Bloomer" audio cassette. Available from Connie Goldman Productions, 926 Second Street, Suite 201, Santa Monica, CA 90403. (310) 393-6801.

Graebner, W. *A History of Retirement.* New Haven, CT: Yale University Press, 1980.

Gutmann, D. L. *Reclaimed Powers: Toward a New Psychology of Men and Women in Later Life.* New York: Basic Books, 1987.

H

Haber, C. *Beyond Sixty-Five.* New York: Cambridge University Press, 1983.

Hill, T. Patrick, and David Shirley. *A Good Death: Taking More Control at the End of Your Life.* New York: Addison-Wesley, 1992.

Horne, Jo. *Homesharing and Other Lifestyle Options.* Glenview, IL: AARP and Scott, Foresman, 1988.

I

Inlander, Charles B. *Medicare Made Easy (A People's Medical Society Book)* Reading, MA: Addison-Wesley, 1989.

—————. *Take This Book to the Hospital with You.* Allentown, PA: Peoples Medical Society, 1992.

J

Jacobs, Ruth. *Be An Outrageous Older Woman.* Manchester, CT: Knowledge, Ideas, and Trends, Inc.

Jones, Reginald L., ed. *Black Adult Development and Aging.* Berkeley, CA: Cobb & Henry, 1989.

K

Kaufman, S. R. *The Ageless Self.* New York: New American Library, 1986.

Kehoe, M. *Lesbians over Sixty Speak for Themselves.* New York: Harrington Park Press, 1989.

Kemper, D. W., M. Mettler, J. Giuffre, and B. Matzek. *Growing Wiser: The Older Person's Guide to Mental Wellness.* Boise, ID: Healthwise, 1986.

Kemper, Donald, and Molly Mettler. *Healthwise for Life: Medical Self-Care for Healthy Aging.* Boise, ID: Healthwise, 1992.

L

Laslett, Peter. *A Fresh Map of Life: The Emergence of the Third Age.* Cambridge, MA: Harvard University Press, 1991.

Lee, Alice, and Fred Lee. *A Field Guide to Retirement: Fourteen Lifestyle Options for a Successful Retirement.* New York: Doubleday, 1991.

Legal Counsel for the Elderly. *Organizing Your Future: A Guide to Decision-Making in Your Later Years.* Washington, DC: Legal Counsel for the Elderly, 1991.

M

Mace, Nancy L., and Peter V. Rabins. *The Thirty-six Hour Day: A Family Guide to Caring for Persons with Alzheimer's Disease, Related Dementing Illness, and Memory Loss in Later Life.* New York: Warner Books, 1989.

Maddox, George L., ed. *The Encyclopedia of Aging.* New York: Springer Publishing Co., 1987.

Markides, K. S., and C. Mindel. *Aging and Ethnicity.* Newbury Park, CA: Sage Publications, 1987.

Matthews, Joseph L. *Elder Care: Choosing and Financing Long-Term Care.* Berkeley, CA: Nolo Press, 1991.

————. *Social Security, Medicare and Pensions: A Sourcebook for Older Americans.* 3rd ed. Berkeley, CA: Nolo Press, 1990.

Mercer, William M. *1993 Guide to Social Security and Medicare.* Louisville, KY: William M. Mercer, Inc., 1992.

Mockenhaupt, Robin, and Kathleen Boyle. *Healthy Aging.* Santa Barbara, CA: ABC-CLIO, 1992.

Moody, Harry R. *Abundance of Life.* New York: Columbia University Press, 1988.

Morris, Robert, and Scott A. Bass, eds. *Retirement Reconsidered: Economic and Social Roles for Older People.* New York: Springer Publishing Co., 1988.

O

Olsen, Nancy. *Starting a Mini-Business: A Guide Book for Seniors.* Sunnyvale, CA: Fair Oaks, 1988.

P

Petras, Kathryn, and Ross Petras. *The Only Retirement Guide You'll Ever Need.* New York: Poseidon Press, 1991.

Pifer, A., and L. Brontë, eds. *Our Aging Society: Paradox and Promise.* New York: W. W. Norton, 1987.

Porcino, Jane. *Living Longer, Living Better: Adventures in Community Housing for Those in the Second Half of Life.* New York: Continuum Publishing, 1991.

Pynoos, J., and E. Cohen. *The Perfect Fit: Creative Ideas for a Safe and Liveable Home.* Washington, DC: AARP, 1992.

R

Regnier, Victor, and Jon Pynoos, eds. *Housing for the Elderly: Design Directives and Policy.* New York: Elsevier Science, 1987.

S

St. Claire, Allison. *Travel and Older Adults.* Santa Barbara, CA: ABC-CLIO, 1991.

Schneider, Edward L., and John W. Rowe, eds. *Handbook of the Biology of Aging.* 3d ed. New York: Harcourt Brace, 1989.

Schulz, James H. *The Economics of Aging.* 5th ed. Westport, CT: Auburn House, 1992.

Scott-Maxwell, Florida. *The Measure of My Days.* New York: Knopf, 1968.

Seeber, E. *Spiritual Maturity in the Later Years.* New York: Haworth Press, 1992.

Selden, Ina Lee. *Going into Business for Yourself: New Beginnings after 50.* Glenview, IL: Scott, Foresman, 1989.

Sennett, D., ed. *Full Measure: Modern Short Stories on Aging.* St. Paul, MN: Graywolf Press, 1988.

Sennett, D., and A. Czarniecki, eds. *Vital Signs: International Stories on Aging.* Saint Paul, MN: Graywolf Press, 1991.

Silverstone, Barbara, and Helen Kandel Hyman. *You and Your Aging Parent: A Family Guide to Emotional, Physical & Financial Problems.* 3d ed. New York: Pantheon, 1989.

Solomon, David H., Elyse Salend, Anna Nolen Rahman, and others. *A Consumer's Guide to Aging.* Baltimore, MD: Johns Hopkins University Press, 1992.

Strom, R. D., and S. K. Strom. *Becoming a Better Grandparent.* Newbury Park, CA: Sage Publications, 1991.

T

Torres-Gil, Fernando M. *The New Aging: Politics and Change in America.* New York: Auburn House, 1992.

H

I

OMB. *See* United States Office of
Management and Budget
(OMB)
Operation Able   391, 400-401
organic mental disorders   86
organizations   25-26, 371-372,
395, 399, 409-410, 419-420, 424,
429, 445, 448, 453, 460
Osler, William   133
osteoarthritis   184-185, 197
osteoporosis   79, 186, 188, 196,
202, 211-212
out-migration   36-37
Over the Hill Gang International
453
overload   251
overweight   189, 193, 197-198
ownership, home   171, 304, 310

P

paratransit   342-344
part-time work   143-146
pedestrians   336-337, 339
pension funds   316
pension plan(s)   25, 127, 155,
158-159, 164-165
perception   87, 92
performing arts   455
periodicals   455
personal care   119
personal support services   257
personality   97, 215, 227, 295-296,
408-409
Peterson, Esther   323
phased retirement   122
physical activity   79-80, 384
physical agility   338
physical aging   67-68, 75-77
physical appearance   82-83
physical changes   79, 102, 184, 274
physical coordination   80-82
physical energy   78
physical examinations   207
physical features   184

physical fitness   348, 373, 451
physical health, decline in   173
physical illness. *See* illness(es)
physical losses   216
physical responses, complex   81
physical wellness   183-184, 186-
187, 203
physician   207
Pierce, Franklin   19
pneumococcal vaccine   206
political parties   348
poor health   83, 85, 173, 198, 405
population aging   36, 42
poverty   25, 45, 61, 63-64, 163,
167, 302, 449
power of attorney   170
prayer   50, 435
pregnancy   1, 201, 242, 422
preretirement   159-160, 177, 379,
392, 437
presbycusis   212-213
prevention   203-205, 209, 211-213
problem solving   93-96
processes of aging   69
productive aging   122, 423
productivity   155-156
professional occupations   140
prostate cancer   208
psychoanalysis, traditional   232
psychological wellness   214-216,
220-221, 231
psychotherapy   232-234
public transit   333, 335
public welfare   382
pull factors   37
purchasing power   138

Q

quality of life   183-187

R

race   1-2, 51-53, 60-61, 252, 254,
276, 406

V

vacation choices   456
vaginal dryness   202
Ventura-Merkel, Catherine   366
veterans   19-20, 49, 447
violence   44
vision   68, 89-90, 212, 286, 336-337, 341, 442
visiting nurses   256
vitamin C   193, 196
vitamin supplementation   193
volunteer organizations   424-429
volunteer programs   395-399, 402-429
volunteer work   395-399, 402-429
volunteering   395-399, 402-429
volunteers   395-399, 402-429
voter(s)   105

W

walking   188-189, 192, 292, 310, 336, 345, 415, 453
water intake   196
weight   187-189, 192-193, 196-198, 411
weight loss   196, 198
well-being   448
wellness   183-203

white males   25
whites   1, 45, 47, 55, 118, 159, 252, 303, 449-450
widowhood   32-33, 54, 56, 58-59, 61, 118, 177, 238, 242, 245-246, 255, 258, 274-281, 303
widows   7, 9, 13-14, 16, 171, 198, 250, 258, 273, 277-281, 291
will(s)   170-171
Williams, T. Franklin   133
wisdom   8, 10, 12, 16, 71, 114, 225-228, 259, 351, 356, 435
The Women's Place Inc.   180
work   121-151, 441
work ethic   2, 172, 178, 432, 435
working with objects   399, 402
workplace education   389
writing   445
Wuthnow, Robert   410, 412

Y

youth, cultural bias toward   349
youth labor shortage   179

Z

zoning   316-319, 322, 326-327